Women and
Executive Office

Women & Executive Office

Pathways & Performance

edited by
Melody Rose

LYNNE
RIENNER
PUBLISHERS

BOULDER
LONDON

Published in the United States of America in 2013 by
Lynne Rienner Publishers, Inc.
1800 30th Street, Boulder, Colorado 80301
www.rienner.com

and in the United Kingdom by
Lynne Rienner Publishers, Inc.
3 Henrietta Street, Covent Garden, London WC2E 8LU

Library of Congress Cataloging-in-Publication Data
Women and executive office : pathways and performance / edited by Melody Rose.
   p. cm.
  Includes bibliographical references and index.
  ISBN 978-1-58826-851-8 (hc : alk. paper)
  1. Women government executives—United States. I. Rose, Melody.
  JK721.W36 2012
  352.230820973—dc23

                                            2012018805

British Cataloguing in Publication Data
A Cataloguing in Publication record for this book
is available from the British Library.

Printed and bound in the United States of America

 The paper used in this publication meets the requirements
of the American National Standard for Permanence of
Paper for Printed Library Materials Z39.48-1992.

5 4 3 2 1

For Simone, Madison, Cloe, and Bella

Contents

Tables and Figures

Tables

Figures

Women and
Executive Office

1

Women as Executive Political Leaders

Melody Rose

THE 2008 CANDIDACIES OF HILLARY CLINTON AND SARAH PALIN brought into sharp relief the fact that the United States is among a shrinking list of nations that has never elected a female chief executive. The rapid advancement of political women in both legislative and executive capacities across the globe has increasingly challenged US pride of place in the advancement of female politicians generally, but the obvious absence of a female US president is particularly noticeable. The United States ranks roughly 70th among nations in its inclusion of women in its national legislature, while it has become increasingly common across Latin America and Europe for nations to elect a female chief executive. Throughout the world, women have been advancing at record speed in the assumption of executive leadership positions in nations both democratic and autocratic, leaving the United States, the "land of the free," in the unenviable position of having to explain the inexplicable: why no female US president.

A generation of scholarship dedicated to the study of legislative women has advanced our understanding and placed special focus on the barriers, opportunities, and pathways for women who seek those positions (Burrell 1994; Dodson 2006; O'Connor 2001; Reingold 2008; C. S. Rosenthal 1998, 2002; Rosenthal and Peters 2010; Swers 2002; Thomas 1994). Aided by a larger "*n*" factor, scholars of women's legislative leadership have taken the lead in understanding advancement of US women in the political arena. It is time to bring the same descriptive focus and holistic assessment to the study of executive women. In this volume, we pay particular attention to women's paths toward executive political roles in the United States and the barriers they face en route.

1

But what does it mean to be an "executive" woman? In this book we deliberately take an inclusive approach to that definition, both by including subnational positions and by expanding the list of "executive" jobs in the national arena. Namely, we consider the *traditional* executive positions to be mayor, governor, and vice president/president. We augment that list with the *unconventional* executive roles of presidential administrative appointee and Speaker of the House. These roles have characteristics similar to those on the traditional list and have been added here in order to advance working knowledge of the range of challenges and opportunities of women in executive functions and the paths women take to executive office.

For the purposes of this volume, executive roles are defined as having five common features. First, these roles uniquely feature solitude. Executive leaders are very frequently an "only," in which individual action is often exercised and personal responsibility is paramount. In contrast, in a legislative role, individual officeholders have many—sometimes hundreds—of peers. That environment is often thought to be one that lends itself to collective action and collaboration, qualities routinely associated with typical female behavior.

The solitary quality of the executive role is related to the second common feature of executive positions: often, as the "only," a female executive falls under greater external scrutiny that is inherently gendered, and her gender may be incongruous with the public's expectations of the office. The singular image of the executive striking out alone (or the "great man" model of leadership; see Duerst-Lahti and Kelly 1995) may simply be incongruent with gender stereotypes (Huddy and Terkildsen 1993).

Third, an executive typically sits atop a broad organizational structure. "Political executives usually sit at the apex of some hierarchy and are looked at as the top official in charge of their respective organizations" (Duerst-Lahti and Kelly 1995, 307). Certainly this is true for House Speakers and cabinet-level appointees, who manage sizable and complex organizations. Along with this internal management requirement, the executive has an analogous external role, often functioning as a liaison to other branches of government. While the rank-and-file congressperson plays no such role, the Speaker of the House certainly does.

Fourth, these roles tend to be reactionary in nature: they frequently respond to policies developed within a legislative body, by either implementing, rejecting, or adjudicating their suitability. While the *traditional* executives may figuratively be agenda setters, they can rarely create policy through initiation. The *unconventional* executives chosen for study here fall into the same boat.

Finally, as opposed to legislative figures, executives are policy generalists, responding to a wide range of policy initiatives created elsewhere. For example, whereas the legislator or council member can drill down into the finer points of environmental policy, developing expertise in ports and waterways or nonvehicular transportation, the executive would find herself confronting all manner of environmental policy considerations.

These five characteristics are common across the studies offered here, and they begin to define for the reader our scope of inquiry and rationale. We also deliberately insist on subnational study in this work. Many women have served as mayor or governor, and their impact and roles are overdue for careful scholarship. However, the authors of this volume inherit certain methodological challenges that will become apparent to the reader. Namely, though the large number of individuals serving in mayoral positions in particular does provide ample and rich data, those data are not always easily accessed, as our authors explain in the chapters that follow. These methodological challenges have in the past made gender-focused mayoral explorations untenable areas of study, and our emphasis here on that office breaks new intellectual and methodological ground. It also elevates our understanding of female politicians to include these understudied roles and provides necessary and exciting findings about diversity and inclusion to the field of women and politics.

Of course prior efforts have been made to understand and interpret the role of women in or running for executive offices, but those efforts have been at times fractured and not as numerous as studies of legislative women. Due to the work of Borrelli (2002), Borrelli and Martin (1997), Clift and Brazaitis (2003), J. Dolan (2000, 2001a, 2001b, 2002, 2004), Falk (2010), K. Ferguson (1985), Han and Heldman (2007), Martin (2003), and Watson and Gordon (2003), we have begun to think about the nexus of executive leadership and the participation—or absence—of women within it. Still, the lion's share of this foundational literature is focused on national executive office and, even more specifically, the bureaucracy. One of the objectives of this volume is to lay bare the diversity of executive office itself and the varied roles women have played within different levels and types of executive service.

Beyond this foundational literature, efforts also have been made to examine particular barriers to executive office, such as media coverage (Bystrom et al. 2004). Given the disparity in coverage across executive offices, not surprisingly these studies, too, are focused largely on the national level. And given the small "n" problem of women running for the US presidency, these studies tend to focus on one (Carroll 2009; Heldman, Carroll, and Olson 2005; Lawrence and Rose 2010) or a few (Falk 2010) candidates.

Mayoral and gubernatorial studies rarely include a gender lens, and the larger "n" poses different methodological challenges. Few women have served as governor (34 at the time of this writing), and nearly half of the states have never elected a woman governor. The literature in this field is emergent, due to the growing and recent expansion of women into this statewide office; here, the field often focuses on the rhetoric of women governors (Marshall and Mayhead 2000) or case study analysis of specific female governors' experiences (Madsen 2009). A recent addition to this literature is the autobiography of former governor Barbara Roberts (D-OR), only the third female governor in US history to have penned her own story (after Madeleine Kunin [D-VT] and Sarah Palin [R-AK]) (Roberts 2011). A few other volumes offer analysis of a particular female governor (Ferguson and Paulissen 1995; Scheer 2005) but, due to limited cases, cannot generalize the nexus between gender and the office of governor.

Alternatively, due to the obvious plethora of opportunities, many more women have served as mayors. But few scholars have used gender analysis to study them. One early effort was by Grace Hall Saltzstein (1986), who measured the impact of female mayors in opening doors for women in city jobs. We build upon this early work and discover that female mayors have made inroads, and that women of color in particular are advancing through mayoral positions.

Intellectual Contributions

Beyond defining the realm of executive women as a distinct scope of research within women and politics, this volume represents a number of contributions to the field's methodology and theory. A wide variety of methods are represented here: ethnographic explorations of women's narratives, word cloud representation of keyword frequencies, elegant statistical analyses, and content analyses provide a snapshot of the sophistication and array of methods available in contemporary women and politics studies, and we hope that this field will continue to break new methodological ground.

A variety of substantive theoretical concepts are challenged in the course of this book, and I hope as editor of the volume that these challenges will be met with additional research and that a dialogue around women in executive roles will grow. For example, one critical challenge offered by several of the authors here is to the widely used concept of the political "pipeline" for women politicians. Women, we often argue, will advance to national executive leadership by flooding the path to advancement at the local level. Here, however, we are confronted with certain assumptions about women's interest in national office as well as the assumption that national office ascends naturally from local service. Pei-te Lien and Katie Swain, in Chapter 8, critique that assumption, however, arguing that women of color in particular may view local service as the ultimate achievement in political advancement; when we overlook this perspective, we may inadvertently essentialize female political leadership and fundamentally misunderstand female ambition. For instance, as Susan Carroll and Kira Sanbonmatsu point out, mayoral studies can allow us to embrace a far more holistic picture of women's leadership successes (see Chapter 7).

Additionally, this book considers in a variety of ways *how* women come to seek executive office: What is the role of financial viability, the political party, and personal networks? To what degree are pathways to executive service distinct from legislative office, and what do these various executive posts have in common? Understanding how women decide to run and appreciating all the factors that effectively enhance or prevent executive office seeking in the United States is critical to untangling the puzzle of "why no woman president." We must also consider why the dearth of women executives extends beyond the White House to other executive offices. Women are not faring much better in local executive office than in the nation's capital.

A number of our authors find that it requires advanced research and new thinking to learn how women come into their executive roles. Perhaps because voters in the United States generally don't associate women with the qualities of executive leadership (Duerst-Lahti and Kelly 1995; Heldman 2007), how women manage to assume these roles at all is of great concern. Implicit in the book is the argument that women will find diverse pathways to executive office and that a more advanced conceptualization of gender will be required for future studies. Because media continues to be a nuanced and critical source of difficulty (see Chapters 3 and 9), female candidates will likely approach running through a variety of different "models of adaptation" (see Chapters 2 and 4). Even considering campaign requirements as fundamental as finance and political party support, we discover that women candidates can be enormously resourceful and creative in establishing their viability, in ways that are often unexpected (see Chapters 6, 10, and 11).

One of the continuous themes of the book is the enduring importance of male influence in executive offices. Whether by inhibiting or encouraging their female partners' interest in leadership (see Chapter 8), or by maintaining an essential role in nominating and advancing women through the executive branch (see Chapter 5), men must be part of the study of women's advancement in political office. New to this line of inquiry is research regarding the role of the male partner and gender politics in national executive elections; a male partner presents a particular challenge for female presidential candidates in ways that had not been fully appreciated before the 2008 election (see Chapter 12).

Of course, no volume such as this can be exhaustive. While we have attempted here to survey the opportunities and challenges for women in a variety of executive posts, and in so doing have expanded the definition of "executive" pathways, we have necessarily left some stones unturned. Due to the limits of space and time, this volume does not address every state-level executive role; the job of attorney general, for instance, also falls within the scope of our executive definition but is not included here. Similarly, we are unable to accommodate consideration of heads of agencies, secretaries of labor or education, and other state- and local-level executive roles. Within our executive agencies chapter, we restrict our thinking to cabinet and White House staff (see Chapter 5), knowing that more can be said of career bureaucrats in future research. We hope that this volume will inspire scholars to think more holistically about women and executive office as a discrete area of study and that future scholarship will help fill the gaps left here.

Organization of the Book

The chapters in this book fall into three natural sections. Part 1, "The Federal Level," is dedicated to an examination of women in a variety of national, twenty-first-century executive positions; here our examination extends to both traditional and unconventional roles to include the presidency and vice presidency as well as the House speakership and presidential appointees. The purpose of this section is to investigate national executive pathways in the United States and to learn how women have or have not sought and served in those roles. Here we can explore some interoffice comparisons and contrasts and define some offices as executive that may not usually be considered. Part 1 begins with Regina G. Lawrence and Melody Rose, who examine the ways in which women candidates run for highly masculinized executive offices—in this case, the US presidency and vice presidency—and conclude that female candidates develop "modes of adaptation" for success and must employ a clear gender strategy (see Chapter 2). From here we consider the vice presidency more fully in Chapter 3 with Kim L. Fridkin, Jill Carle, and Gina Serignese Woodall's study of the media's coverage of 2008 vice presidential candidates Sarah Palin and Joe Biden. Given the significant role of media in national campaigns, candidate message and news media coverage develop a disconnect that harms women's efforts to reach national service, a trend investigated in this chapter. In Chapter 4, Cindy Simon Rosenthal and Ronald M. Peters Jr. broaden our understanding of executive office through an examination of the House speakership: using the earlier work of Mary Parker Follett, Rosenthal and Peters examine Nancy Pelosi's particular brand of leadership at the top of the legislative branch to argue that the position is rightly considered executive in function. Chapter 5 rounds out this first section of the book with Julie Dolan's analysis of the Obama administration's record of inclusion through the appointment process and the significance of women's leadership of the federal bureaucracy.

Part 2, "The State and Local Levels," explores the pathways for executive office holding at the subnational levels. Chapter 6 by Richard Herrera and Karen Shafer, a study of female governors and their policy agendas, sheds new light on the impact of women in statewide executive posts. Chapter 7 follows, with Susan J. Carroll and Kira Sanbonmatsu's careful study of women's decisions to run for mayoral offices and their pathways to getting there. Building upon these themes and examining some popular assumptions regarding women's ambition for national office, Pei-te Lien and Katie E. O. Swain underscore the consideration of female mayors in Chapter 8, adding to the work of Carroll and Sanbonmatsu through a deep exploration of the experiences of female mayors of color, explicitly challenging the field's affinity for "pipeline" theory.

Part 3, "Challenges for Women Executives," explores contemporary barriers facing women who seek executive office. Chapter 9, by Dianne Bystrom, Narren Brown, and Megan Fiddelke, finds that newspaper coverage of female mayors and governors is different in quantity but similar in quality of coverage when tested against men in the same jobs: quite the opposite of Fridkin, Carle, and Serignese Woodall's findings on vice presidential coverage back in Chapter 3, which reminds the reader that although executive offices have certain commonalities, their dissimilarities are also compelling. Denise L. Baer considers the role of recruitment by political parties in women's advancement to executive office in Chapter 10 and finds that in contrast to other work on candidate emergence, high-level political activism is not gendered but that gender recruitment is both polarized and gendered, particularly for executive office seekers. Victoria A. Farrar-Myers and Brent D. Boyea reflect on the financing of the 2008 presidential election in Chapter 11, demonstrating both the essential role that finance plays in American elections at all levels and the multiple pathways that women pursue to establish financial viability. Finally, Chapter 12, by Kelly Dittmar, focuses our attention on one of the most insidious and neglected barriers to women's advancement in executive roles: the role of the traditional female spouse and the powerful gender politics that subtly require the successful candidate to have the support of such a "helpmate."

These final chapters offer a complex understanding of the particular challenges faced by twenty-first-century women in pursuit and governance of executive offices and the ways in which the twenty-first-century United States retains some deeply embedded norms and practices that create a misalignment between executive roles and female gender expectations. Certainly there is no one set of challenges for women seeking executive offices, nor should we assume women will forge a single path to success. Rather, the cumulative lesson is that women pursuing executive positions will be creative and strategic in overcoming obstacles and in defining success. We also discover that some progress has been made against these obstacles, and we offer those updates to the larger field of women and politics. The book concludes in Chapter 13 with an outline of what future research in this field might address and where the opportunities lie for better understanding.

Future Research

As stated at the outset of this introduction, much has been accomplished in the study of particular aspects of executive office. Still, the field of political science is overdue for an examination of women in executive offices and their opportunities and challenges in the twenty-first century. Until recently, data challenges prevented such inquiry: with no woman elected to the presidency and few who have occupied the governor's mansion, and with numbers hard to track at local levels, certain women's leadership pathways and experiences have fallen out of the storyline. Today, with larger sets of numbers, better data collection methods, and a growing appreciation for the need to expand our definition of "executive," we can bring focus to this line of inquiry and provide a 360-degree assessment of women in executive contexts in the United States. Still, these advancements indicate that we are really just beginning to define a course of study. The primary objective of this book is to establish a "state of the field" assessment of methodological advancements, theoretical conundrums, and conceptual challenges—and to identify areas for further research opportunities. While this work cannot claim to be definitive, we do hope it provides a spark for further inquiry.

Part 1

The Federal Level

2

The Real '08 Fight: Clinton vs. Palin

Regina G. Lawrence and Melody Rose

THE YEAR 2008 WILL BE REMEMBERED AS THE FIRST YEAR A woman came close to securing a major party's presidential nomination, and the first time a Republican woman was nominated as vice president. In the pages that follow, we argue that though Senator Hillary Clinton and vice presidential candidate Sarah Palin faced a similarly masculinized terrain, they assumed two distinct modes of adaptation,[1] each fraught with its own unique pitfalls and opportunities. Political scientists and future female candidates alike can learn from the lessons of 2008 and possibly forge new pathways beyond the modes demonstrated by candidates Palin and Clinton.

In particular, we build upon the limited definitions of the notion of "running as a woman" provided in academic literature to offer a typology of the ways women might run for national executive office, focusing on how female candidates associate themselves (or not) with "women's issues" and how they make (or do not make) explicit gender-based appeals. We assess the messaging of Hillary Clinton and Sarah Palin in light of this typology, and we conclude that these candidates ran "as women" in different ways and to different degrees. To fully capture the differences between these candidates' modes of adaptation, however, we argue that it is also necessary to develop a more nuanced understanding of a third dimension of "running as a woman": to what degree and how female candidates adapt their personal affect to traditional heterosexual expectations of femininity. Indeed, the "real fight" of the 2008 election was arguably a contest between competing definitions of femininity and womanhood relative to national executive office. This chapter examines the ways in which women run for national executive office, shedding light on some key examples from 2008 and looking forward to what the nation might witness in 2012 and beyond.

Literature Review

The challenges in running for the presidency (and vice presidency) are many. Every candidate must face a complex electoral environment that, in the US context, includes reliance on the media, byzantine party nominating rules, and daunting fund-raising challenges. On the surface, these would appear to be sex-neutral challenges that any—and every—executive branch aspirant must face. But no woman has served as president or vice president—despite numerous efforts spanning three centuries (Falk 2007). This reality suggests that while the challenges of presidential politics are sex neutral on their face, their impact may not be.

Indeed, the gendered expectations and norms surrounding executive office provide the female candidate with a series of land mines and traps she must navigate. The very language used to characterize presidential elections revolves around the "great man" model of the presidency, which depends upon sporting and military metaphors (Duerst-Lahti 2006). On the military side, for example, the war hero is often held up as the perfect executive candidate.[2]

As a result of these and other gendered presidential terms and associations, the job of president (or vice president) is masculinized implicitly and insidiously. As a consequence, female candidates may face an uphill road to viability and credibility. Paul and Smith (2008) find, for instance, in polling data of likely Ohio voters in 2006, that when potential female candidates were placed on an experimental ballot alongside likely male competitors, respondents were more likely to remark that the women were unqualified, despite having remarkably similar credentials. Indeed, a long line of research in the so-called Goldberg paradigm, the tendency to evaluate men more positively than women in relation to stereotypically masculine jobs, has discovered stubborn attitudinal barriers (see Carroll 2009 for a review). Female candidates therefore must find ways of breaking through these barriers on the road to the White House.

What Does It Mean to Run "as a Woman"?

The notion that female candidates face special challenges and strategic choices is often acknowledged—if not always thoughtfully—in the real world of politics. As Witt, Paget, and Matthews (1994) explain, campaign consultants have long understood "running as a woman" as something to be avoided. Of course, they do not mean the mere biological fact of sex, since by the early 1990s obtaining office had become easier for female candidates. Rather, they suggest that political consultants have warned their clients against certain campaign tactics thought to be ill advised for female candidates, including emphasizing one's femininity through overtly sexualized or delicate images; campaigning explicitly on "women's issues," particularly reproductive rights; or making explicit appeals to women voters. This precautionary notion may be what a reporter had in mind when asking presidential hopeful Congresswoman Patricia Schroeder in 1987, "Are you running as a woman?"[3] Even in recent election cycles, women politicians have explicitly denied using gendered strategies, as evident in Congresswoman Nancy Pelosi's (D-CA) comments on her election as the first woman Speaker of the House: "I didn't run as a woman," Pelosi said. "I presented my credentials as an experienced legislator, skilled organizer, astute politician. I didn't want anyone to vote for me or against me because I was a woman." Interestingly, Pelosi added: "But the fact that I am a woman is a giant bonus" (PBS 2007).

As Pelosi's last comment suggests, some might argue for the electoral benefits of embracing feminine identity in pursuit of elected office. Yet in academic circles, the notion of "running as a woman" is evoked more often than it is defined. Indeed, the notion of women's special challenges in obtaining office within the masculinized context of electoral politics has arguably shaped the literature to such an extent that the tactics and strategic opportunities uniquely available to female candidates have been less thoroughly catalogued.

Because "presidential capacity is gendered to be masculine . . . women who dream of a presidency must negotiate masculinity, a feat much more difficult for them than for any man" (Duerst-Lahti 2006, 15). Women face a series of double binds, Jamieson (1995) tells us, and must negotiate each with care; in this context, "running as a woman" simply means how to negotiate these binds strategically. When attempting to negotiate the double binds of running as a woman for a man's job, Jamieson explains, women are faced with the seemingly impossible challenge of balancing their femininity against received definitions of competence that are generally associated with the masculine. One strategy suggested by Kahn is that women should anticipate and compensate for gender bias by "speak[ing] more extensively and persuasively about their policy concerns" (1996, 135). This strategy counsels the female candidate to suppress gender as a voting consideration by working strategically within the masculine framework. Dianne Bystrom, analyzing the campaigns of women running for nonpresidential office, offers rather different advice to the "bound" candidate: "It appears that women candidates may be most successful running a positive or mixed-message campaign emphasizing mostly feminine or a balance of feminine and masculine image traits" (Bystrom et al. 2004, 109). Based upon her careful review of women's media strategies, Bystrom (2003, 105) advises the candidate not to abandon the feminine while she straddles the femininity/competence double bind.

Beyond the counsel to avoid gender traps, relatively few scholars have employed the notion of "running as a woman" methodically, particularly in the context of the national executive. Indeed, the options for women adapting to a masculine office appear limited. Experimental work in the field of psychology demonstrates that the public associates the presidency in particular with foreign policy and the military, often thought to be strongholds of male policy competence. Smith, Paul, and Paul (2007) find, for instance, much less gender incongruence in experiments presenting women as US Senate candidates than in experiments putting forth female presidential candidates, despite the fact that increasing percentages of US voters report that they would elect a female presidential candidate.

Therefore, gender-office alignment would seem difficult to attain for the female presidential candidate unless she de-emphasizes her gender, employing a strict "equality/sameness" strategy in which she presents herself (as Pelosi claimed to do) in gender-neutral terms emphasizing her equal credentials for the job (Lawrence and Rose 2010). But the reality of double binds (that is, of competing public expectations for women in public life) means that there may also be electoral benefits to running more explicitly "as a woman," because much of the public still expects women to behave in particular ways and display particular attributes—and because women are an important constituency in many electoral settings. By the same token, there may also be electoral costs for failing to evoke at least some familiar markers of femininity.

Against the backdrop of the masculinized executive electoral environment, and with very little research demonstrating how women in the past have tried to adapt, we attempt here two innovations. First, we offer a fuller definition of the strategies that "running as a woman" comprises. While precise definition of the notion has often been lacking in the literature, one exception is the work of Herrnson, Lay, and Stokes, who define "running as a woman" as a twofold effort, which "stress[es] issues that voters associate favorably with female candidates and target[s] female voters" (2003, 244). We begin by building upon this definition, recognizing that a full typology must include tactics considered both well and ill advised, but tactics that are nonetheless available uniquely to female candidates. We then employ that framework to assess the campaign messaging of Hillary Clinton and Sarah Palin in the 2008 election. Our goal here is not to argue the advisability of running "as a woman" for national executive office, but rather to gauge the extent to which Clinton and Palin embraced distinct modes of adaptation in 2008.

Running on "Women's Issues"

The first element of female electoral strategy noted by Herrnson, Lay, and Stokes (2003) overlaps with an array of academic literature exploring how women candidates may gain office by associating themselves with issues that the public associates favorably with women. In the context of congressional and state legislative races, Hernnson, Lay, and Stokes argue that women benefit when they emphasize issues that voters positively associate with women and stress that female candidates should demonstrate "gender issue ownership." Much of the women and politics literature implicitly or explicitly counsels the female candidate to highlight her alignment with typically feminized policy strengths such as health care, education, and children's and women's needs as broadly understood—policies the public identifies as being within women's expertise (Iyengar et al. 1997; Kahn 1996; Kahn and Gordon 1997).

Therefore, one way that female candidates run "as women" is to embrace an issue agenda stereotypically associated with feminine attributes of nurturing and care—and in some contexts, the strategy works. For instance, Falk (2007) notes that media coverage of women's gubernatorial campaigns is more favorable to them than the coverage of women's campaigns for the US Senate, presumably because the public's understanding of the governor's position aligns with stereotypes of women: both are focused on "softer" issues of public policy, such as education, health, and child welfare. In some settings, therefore, where there is office-gender congruence, women can actually benefit from stereotyping at the ballot box.

The question, of course, is how viable this strategy is in the national executive context. To the degree that the public associates the presidency and vice presidency with national security rather than "care" issues, running on women's issues may not be effective. Yet this strategy arguably must be kept in the female presidential candidate's quiver, both because the public may expect a woman to speak credibly on these issues, and because, in some election years, foreign policy and national security may not be the most salient issues for voters. In such circumstances, some benefit may redound to the candidate whose gender the public associates with key care issues. Moreover, recognizing that campaign strategies are not dichotomous categories is important. Female candidates may emphasize women's issues to a greater or lesser degree in various contexts. The female executive candidate may align herself with women's issues primarily or only secondarily, for some audiences but not others, or modulate her messaging across the phases of her campaign.

Making Gender-Based Appeals

Hernnson, Lay, and Stokes's (2003) notion of "targeting female voters" as a key feminine campaign strategy overlaps to some degree with the real-world understanding of "running as a woman" noted by Witt, Paget, and Matthews (1994). Though political consultants may at times caution against it, targeting women voters is not necessarily a losing strategy in contests in which the voting public is predominantly female—such as the 2008 Democratic primary contests in key states in which women made up over 50% of the primary electorate. What may be more problematic is the *way* in which the female candidate targets women voters. A campaign may do so by employing the first strategy described above: by highlighting "care" issues, candidates are also likely to win over women voters who are typically concerned about those issues (Witt, Paget, and Matthews 1994).

But this notion of "targeting female voters" does not fully capture another way this strategy might be carried out: through deliberate appeals to women voters—as women—to support the candidate. The candidate who "runs as a woman" may do so by appealing to female voters on the basis of gender (theirs and hers). This strategy may be successful, based upon Kathleen Dolan's (1998, 2004) findings that within some electoral conditions, women are more likely to use gender-related issues to make their candidate selections. This kind of campaign might explicitly argue that, as a woman, the candidate brings special qualifications to public office—what we dub a "difference" strategy (Lawrence and Rose 2010)—or make explicit calls to group-based identity and solidarity. In the difference strategy the female candidate may choose to emphasize the qualities that distinguish her from her male counterparts or, if relevant, the historical achievement for women represented by her campaign. This approach is quite distinct from what we dub the "equality" strategy because it entails emphasizing, not downplaying, gender or sex difference. The difference strategy is what Speaker Pelosi seemingly denied doing in her campaign, and, the evidence suggests, Hillary Clinton also largely avoided in her 2008 presidential campaign (Lawrence and Rose 2010). Again, this strategy might be openly embraced by the female candidate, or employed only partially or haltingly.

Assessing the Clinton and Palin Campaigns

In order to tentatively assess the degree to which Hillary Clinton and Sarah Palin ran "as women" in the terms described above, we conducted qualitative analyses of a data set including some of the candidates' pivotal speeches, interviews, and advertisements. Because the length and type of their respective campaigns differed in critical ways, we attempted to find the most analogous speeches possible within the 2008 electoral context. In the case of Senator Clinton, the analysis below focuses on a major address she made in Iowa just weeks before that state's crucial Democratic caucus (December 16, 2007), remarks she offered at her alma mater, Wellesley College (November 1, 2008), and her June 7, 2008, speech in Washington, DC, in which she conceded the Democratic nomination to Barack Obama. In the case of Governor Palin, who ran a much shorter vice presidential campaign and therefore produced fewer speeches overall, we focus on the speech she made the day her candidacy was announced (August 29, 2008), her Republican convention speech accepting her nomination as John McCain's running mate (September 3, 2008), and her speech given for the campaign's weekly radio address on September 6, 2008. Thus, we analyze an "introductory" speech from early in each campaign (Clinton's Iowa speech and Palin's initial announcement speech), the major culminating speech of each campaign (Palin's speech at the Republican convention and Clinton's concession speech), and one speech offered primarily to a more specialized audience of friendly constituents (Clinton's Wellesley remarks and Palin's radio address).

In addition to these speeches, we analyze key television interviews with both candidates. Fortuitously, Katie Couric of CBS News and Charlie Gibson of ABC interviewed both Palin and Clinton during the 2008 campaign, allowing us to compare the content of interviews provided to the same journalists and within roughly the same context. Governor Palin's ABC News interview with Charlie Gibson aired September 11 and 12, 2008; her CBS News interview with Katie Couric aired September 24 and 25, 2008. Senator Clinton's interview with Charlie Gibson aired May 14, and her Couric interview aired in two parts on May 5 and 14.[4]

Finally, we examine several of each candidate's campaign ads, again choosing ads that are as comparable as possible given the differences in offices sought. We examine Clinton's first television ad from the 2008 campaign, which aired in August of 2007 in the key state of Iowa; her Christmas ad, also aired in Iowa in December of 2007; the "Dorothy" ad aired in Iowa in late 2007; and the "3:00 a.m." ad that aired prior to the Ohio and Texas primaries in 2008.

For the Sarah Palin ads, we were compelled by the very different dynamics of her brief campaign to select ads from a compressed time period. Palin quickly went from a virtual unknown on the national scene to nearly instantaneous political celebrity status to an equally rapid decline in public approval (Romano 2008). In light of her meteoric rise and fall in the public eye, we focus here on the first McCain campaign ad that featured Sarah Palin, "Alaska Maverick," aired early September in key markets, and two ads the McCain campaign then quickly aired in what it called "a forward-leaning effort to counter the shameless smears that have prevailed during Gov. Palin's introduction to the American voter" (Allen 2008).

We analyze these speeches, interviews, and ads looking for indicators of "running as a woman" as defined above. Specifically, we look for references to policies defined by Herrnson, Lay, and Stokes as "women's issues" (2003, 253): education/school finance, health care, social security, welfare reform, the plight of the working poor, elderly/senior issues, abortion rights/right to life, marriage, lesbian and gay rights, women and religion, and gun control. We also look for any explicit or implicit gender solidarity appeals by each candidate.

Despite our best efforts to compare the Clinton and Palin gender strategies as objectively and judiciously as possible, our approach encountered methodological limitations. Palin and Clinton are apples and oranges in many ways, not least because we are comparing one of the best-known women in the world with (at the time) a relative national newcomer. The speeches obviously differ in that for Clinton, these were not necessarily early "introductions" to the general public in the same way that Palin had to introduce herself. Also, of course, the speeches analyzed here were not given in the same time period: by the time Palin was on the national stage, Barack Obama had won the Democratic nomination, and Clinton had exited the race.

Two qualifiers should also be noted regarding the Clinton and Palin ads. First, as a vice presidential candidate, Palin may have had less control over her messaging during the campaign, particularly in the McCain campaign's television ads, than a presidential candidate would enjoy. Second, the Palin ads appeared in the context of an overall McCain general election ad campaign that was deemed highly negative by reputable researchers (Halloran 2008). While only one of the Clinton ads we include in this analysis was a comparison/attack ad challenging Barack Obama (specifically his readiness to be commander in chief), the McCain ads featuring Sarah Palin went directly negative against Barack Obama even before Palin addressed the Republican convention (Allen 2008).

Their electoral environments differed also in the sense that the two women ran for different offices with distinct campaign requirements. One candidate ran a two-year marathon bid for her party's nomination, while the other was chosen rather abruptly to join the McCain ticket and made a nine-week sprint in a general election. Finally, the two women represent different party, generational, and regional interests. For these reasons, we do not assume that our findings below are widely generalizable beyond these cases, nor would we predict that these two women would choose similar gender strategies.

The analysis below reveals that, according to the framework sketched here so far, neither Clinton nor Palin unabashedly ran "as a woman." In terms of the first, public policy dimension, we discover that Clinton embraced numerous positions defined by Herrnson, Lay, and Stokes (2003) as "women's issues." Palin did not. With respect to the second category of targeting women voters with gender-based appeals, we find that Palin made some overtures to women voters in her earliest appearance, and that Clinton did so sparingly—in these texts, only when addressing her all-women's alma mater, which presents a unique audience not generalizable to the wider electorate.

Hillary Clinton: Equality Feminist Candidate

In our previous work, we argue that Hillary Clinton positioned herself within a narrative of "equality" feminism (Lawrence and Rose 2010), and taken overall, hers was not a particularly feminine message. Equality feminism posits that men and women function similarly in public office; the equality feminist candidate presents herself as the equal of her male competitors in terms of intellect and policy competence and stakes her claim to power in largely gender-neutral terms.

The present analysis reveals a somewhat more nuanced picture. When analyzed in terms of Herrnson, Lay, and Stokes's (2003) list of "women's issues," Clinton appears to have run "as a woman." We find that Clinton evoked certain "women's issues" very frequently in her campaign, though she used them to bolster her claim to policy experience as much as to achieve gender-issue alignment. The two policy agendas most frequently cited in the Clinton texts were health care and education. Clinton made repeated calls within these texts to the imperative of improving education, from prekindergarten opportunities to increased affordability of college tuition. And she explicitly foregrounded children in making the case in her Iowa speech that she was the candidate with the "experience" to bring about "change" in these policy areas: "For 35 years I have been a change-maker," she said, recalling her work for the Children's Defense Fund.

Clinton's holiday ad, aired in Iowa in December 2007, crystallizes this policy-oriented focus on "care" issues. The ad, called "Presents,"[5] finds her alone by the Christmas tree, tying ribbons as she puts the finishing touches on her holiday policy gifts. The camera zooms in on the gift tags: "universal health care," "alternative energy," and the like are placed with care by the candidate. The focus is thus on domestic issues; the only gift tag hinting at the vexing area of foreign policy offers a reassuring, "caring" message: "Bring Troops Home." The ad concludes by emphasizing the public's associations between women, domestic "care" issues, and Hillary Clinton herself: "Where did I put universal pre-K?" the candidate asks herself, lighting up with a smile as she finds the final package.

Given the high-profile (and controversial) role she had played in her husband's administration's efforts at health-care reform, unsurprisingly Clinton offered multiple references to health policy in the texts we analyzed. Clinton could not have avoided these issues when campaigning for the presidency—nor should she have, since polling throughout the campaign showed voters believed Clinton was the "better" candidate to handle health care (see for example Hart/McInturff 2008). Her frequent discussions of health-care policy thus arguably served a dual purpose: they associated Clinton with "care" issues but also underscored her effort to run as the most qualified candidate on the dais. In fact, emphasizing health care arguably helped her to solidify an equality feminist claim: that she would bring equal policy experience to the job of the presidency.

One issue from the Herrnson, Lay, and Stokes's list—women's rights—shows up more selectively in Clinton's messaging, however. In these texts, Clinton sometimes spoke directly to the history of women's rights and her advocacy of women's rights globally. In her Wellesley remarks, Clinton detailed the ways that women are abused and denied equal rights around the world ("Women continue to be raped as a casualty of conflict, trafficked for commercial advantage, denied education and health care and family planning, not given access to credit, denied their rights as citizens"), and she framed her work on behalf of women's rights as self-evidently about promoting women's equality ("If we don't stand for women's rights, we will never stand for our best values. That has to be a part of American foreign policy"). In her Iowa speech, in contrast, Clinton did not detail the specific ways women are mistreated, and she framed her advocacy differently:

> Women's rights are human rights and human rights are women's rights. It's not only what we believe, here in our country, it's what we know is important for our national security. Countries that deny women their rights are often the countries that we have problems with, aren't they? . . . [W]hen I am president I will continue to make the changes on behalf of women that are good and right for women and smart for national security.

In other words, for the Iowa audience, Clinton subsumed her stand on "women's issues" under the framing of her credentials and toughness on national security—smart positioning for a woman trying to negotiate her feminine policy expertise within the masculinized context of presidential politics. Indeed, not since her husband ran for the office in 1992 has a modern presidential candidate been able to campaign for the presidency without a clear foreign policy platform. By defining women's rights as a matter of foreign policy, Clinton simultaneously ran as a woman and as "any other" presidential candidate.

Clinton's Appeal to Women Voters

It is not surprising that Senator Clinton's most overt appeals to women voters were made while speaking at Wellesley, where she acknowledged the particular challenge of women in public life by telling an anecdote about a senior law firm colleague who once told her she could not practice litigation because she "didn't have a wife" and therefore no one to make sure she had clean socks for trial; Clinton concluded the story by wryly observing that "I had always washed my own socks." She also told the story of how she chose Yale over Harvard because a senior male Harvard professor told her, "We don't need any more women." Clinton continued by telling the

Wellesley students, "In so many ways, this all women's college prepared me to compete on [sic] the all boys' club of presidential politics," and described the importance to little girls of watching her campaign for the presidency.

Clinton's references to the history of discrimination were not confined to this all-women's university. As early as December 2007, while speaking in Iowa, Clinton punctuated her remarks by enjoining the crowd, "Let's make history together," a subtle reference to the historic qualities of her candidacy. Clinton's ad campaign also reveals a pointed effort to target women voters in the months leading up to the Iowa and New Hampshire contests (see Lawrence and Rose 2010). This strategy was revealed most clearly in mid-December 2007, when the Clinton campaign aired a new television ad in Iowa, "Dorothy," named for Clinton's mother.[6] The ad begins with a black-and-white photo marked, "Dorothy and Hillary 1948," featuring a toddler Clinton in a bonnet, apparently taking her first baby steps. Dorothy Rodham's description of her daughter forms the audio track of the ad: "What I would like people to know about Hillary is what a good person she is. She never was envious of anybody. She was helpful. And she's continued that with her adult life, with helping other women." Rodham's voice continues, while the camera cuts to footage of her and her daughter: "She has empathy for other people's unfortunate circumstances." Clinton's mother concludes, "I think she ought to be elected even if she weren't my daughter."

The "Dorothy" ad thus hits many key feminine notes, highlighting the candidate's "empathy" with "other women." The Clinton campaign made no secret that Dorothy (both the ad and the person) was being deployed to mobilize female voters, particularly older women who, in the words of one reporter, "might feel an emotional bond with Mrs. Clinton—seeing her like a daughter or seeing something of themselves in her" (Healy 2007c).

But overall, beyond occasional references to women's rights, sex discrimination, "history," and her own ability to empathize with other women, Hillary Clinton demonstrated little effort to "run as a woman" by making gender-based appeals. She generally used gender-neutral language in her public statements, only occasionally making more overt gender-based arguments.[7] As she told Katie Couric and repeated often during the campaign when asked about the role of gender in the election, "Obviously, race and gender are part of it, because of who the candidates are." Beyond that, Clinton rarely raised gender as a salient consideration for voters—until she exited the race. In her concession speech she broadened her Wellesley remarks by talking about the importance of those "who lifted their little girls and little boys on their shoulders and whispered in their ears, 'See, you can be anything you want to be.'" Speaking poignantly of her challenges and aspirations as a female candidate, she famously declared that her campaign, while not shattering the ultimate glass ceiling, had "made 18 million cracks" in it.

Sarah Palin: Postfeminist Candidate

The Palin interviews and speeches reveal a mode of adaptation distinct from (though not always diametrically opposed to) Clinton's. While Clinton positioned herself within a traditional equality feminist narrative by only selectively acknowledging the sex discrimination she faced and presenting herself as more like her male competitors than different from them, Palin reached for a position that might be understood as postfeminist in its suggestion that we live in a postgender world where gender discrimination has become irrelevant. Compared with Clinton, she made virtually no policy remarks on "women's" issues, and she made fewer overt appeals to women as *voters,* though she frequently identified herself with mothers.

In the texts analyzed here, Palin never volunteered positions on "women's" issues. Only in the Gibson interview, where she was asked pointed questions about her views on abortion, gay rights, and stem cell research, did Palin remark on policies typically associated with female candidates. In fact, with only one exception, Palin did not speak to women's rights across any of the texts we analyze here. Nor did she outwardly identify with the feminist movement or its aims, and though she positioned herself as fighting against the "good ole boy" system in her home state of Alaska, she framed herself as an outsider fighting against what she called a culture of insider politics and "self-dealing" in politics, not explicitly as a woman battling entrenched male power.

In this respect, Palin cast herself as the gender-neutral equal of the men she competed against in political life, echoing Clinton's equality feminism strategy. This strategy was repeated in the McCain campaign's first ad introducing Governor Palin, "Alaska Maverick," which cast Palin in strictly gender-neutral terms as better able to bring about "reform" than Barack Obama. The 30-second spot mentioned only one policy area, claiming that Palin "took on the oil producers." No "care" issues were mentioned.

However, Palin did address gender inequality once during her interviews used in this study, and her words on the subject reveal a very different orientation to sex discrimination than that evinced by Hillary Clinton. In her ABC interview, Palin was asked, "Is it sexist for people to ask how can somebody manage a family of seven and the vice presidency?" Palin responded by claiming,

> I'm lucky to have been brought up in a family where gender has never been an issue. I'm a product of Title 9 [sic], also, where we had equality

in schools that was just being ushered in with sports and with equal opportunity for education, all of my life.

I'm part of that generation, where that question is kind of irrelevant, because it's accepted. Of course you can be the vice president and you can raise a family. . . .

I replied back then, as I would today, "I'll do it the same way the other governors have done it when they've either had [a] baby in office or raised a family." Granted, they're men, but do it the same way that they do it.

Palin's remarks on the role of Title IX in her life reveals much about her approach to public life as a woman. Title IX, a segment of the 1972 Education Act credited with bringing educational parity to women within sports but more broadly in the classroom, is a by-product of the mid-twentieth century women's rights movement. But its association with equal opportunity, specifically sporting and educational opportunity, allowed Palin to use Title IX to dismiss the question of whether she faced sex discrimination on the campaign trail. Title IX, she implied, made her life in competitive sports and politics possible while it also made feminism and sex discrimination obsolete. Significantly, the only women's rights policy Palin mentioned voluntarily in these texts is 37 years old, and she mentions it in order to dismiss the notion that women face particular challenges in public life.

Palin and Gender Appeals

Despite the gender-neutral appeals described above, Palin famously reached out to women voters when John McCain introduced her to the nation as his running mate. At the event in Dayton, Ohio, on August 29, Palin appeared to target Hillary Clinton's female supporters when she acknowledged Geraldine Ferraro's place on the 1984 Democratic ticket and Clinton's historic achievement: "It was rightly noted in Denver [at the Democratic National Convention] this week that Hillary left 18 million cracks in the highest, hardest glass ceiling in America. . . . [B]ut it turns out the women of America aren't finished yet and we can shatter that glass ceiling once and for all." Senator McCain echoed this gender appeal as he introduced his chosen running mate by calling Palin "a role model to women and reformers all over America."

Apart from these overt appeals to Clinton supporters to move over to the McCain-Palin ticket, our texts also suggest a clear effort to emphasize Palin's affiliations with traditional women's identity groups. Palin famously offered her identification with hockey moms at the Republican National Convention when she declared that the difference between a hockey mom and a pit bull is "lipstick." Across the texts we analyze here, she frequently mentioned her status as a military mom and consistently referenced her longtime volunteer role in her local Parent Teacher Association (PTA); significantly, at the Republican convention Palin also commented on her youngest child's special needs. Overall, Palin's appeals to women and her own bid for power were often couched in terms of motherhood. In this sense, Palin perhaps came closer than Clinton did to running "as a woman" but by employing distinctly postfeminist techniques.

The McCain-Palin campaign also evoked gender solidarity—along with a masculine sense of chivalry—in the two other ads we analyzed, titled "Disrespectful" and "Fact Check."[8] In the first of these ads aimed against the Obama campaign, a female announcer intones, "They dismissed her as 'good-looking.' That backfired. So they said she was 'doing what she was told.' Then, desperately, called Sarah Palin a liar. How *disrespectful*," the announcer concludes, drawing out the word with disdain. In the second ad, the visuals flash back and forth between black-and-white stills of Barack Obama and grainy footage of a pack of wolves prowling the woods. The female announcer claims that, according to the *Wall Street Journal,* Obama "air-dropped a mini army of 30 lawyers, investigators, and opposition researchers into Alaska to dig dirt on Governor Palin." The narrator continues, "As Obama drops in the polls, he'll try to destroy her." In both ads, the campaign subtly evokes traditional gender roles (and, some might argue, traditional racial stereotypes): Obama should be "respectful" of Sarah Palin, but instead, like the wolves pictured in the ad, he seeks to "destroy" her. But "Disrespectful" also draws from a postfeminist sensibility to disarm Palin's critics: Why, the ad implicitly asks, should Sarah Palin not be taken seriously just because she is an attractive woman?

Discussion: Two Modes of Adaptation

When confronted with the masculinized terrain of presidential politics, two women—seeking separate executive offices and representing different generations, constituencies, regions, and parties—largely avoided "running as women" in the ways most often described in scholarly literature. Each evoked "female" policy issues only selectively and limited her appeals to feminine solidarity. Yet we also find subtle but instructive differences in how they ran. For Clinton's part, we see a candidate who ran as an equality feminist: admitting (though not emphatically highlighting) the challenges presented to political women, she in many ways strove to be perceived as much "like the guys." Clinton most closely approximated running as a woman in her alignment with feminized policy areas—though she did so in service to an equality-based rather than a feminine "difference" strategy. Palin, alternatively, remained quite distant from these policy areas, assiduously avoiding them but for her response to a pointed interview question about sexism on the campaign trail. Meanwhile, Palin frequently invoked her status as a mother even as she framed herself as a "maverick," perhaps a way of appealing to women voters, particularly conservative women.

While analyzing these candidates on these two dimensions of issue positioning and gender appeals is revealing, it does not fully capture the palpable differences between them. We turn in this final section to an exploratory discussion of a third dimension of "running as a woman": the dimension of personal affect and feminine symbolism. On this personal affect valence it would seem, we find the greatest divide between the two candidates.

Displays of Femininity

As noted above, Witt, Paget, and Matthews (1994) briefly define the notion of "running as a woman" in cautionary terms and in terms of three dimensions, one of which is overtly feminized displays. Their discussion suggests that the female candidate should avoid appearing delicate or sexualized or otherwise presenting herself in ways that viscerally remind the audience of her gender. This caution is echoed by research on how female candidates typically present themselves in their advertisements and public appearances: generally, female candidates favor more formal business attire, for example, in order to shore up their credibility against gender stereotypes (Bystrom et al. 2004; Kahn 1996).

Yet it seems that one way in which a female candidate may "run as a woman" is by adapting her physical appearance and behaviors, such as her clothing and speaking style, to cultural expectations of femininity, demonstrating a personal affect that evokes traditional notions of femininity—a tactic that remains largely unacknowledged in the academic literature. Perhaps because that literature has focused on how hard women candidates must work to establish an image of competence, less recognition has been given to the concessions female politicians make every day to expectations of feminine style, and even less discussion has occurred regarding how a conventionally "attractive" appearance may be an electoral boon—an ironic fact, given that the literature has often rued the "hair and hemlines" focus of media coverage of female politicians (Aday and Devitt 2001; Heith 2003). Indeed, some female candidates might employ feminine displays as a proactive campaign strategy and not merely a grudging concession to cultural norms. Candidates might also display traditional femininity in the way they present their ambitions, their families, and their views on sex roles in society at large.

As an opening heuristic for exploring this unexplored terrain, this element of campaign strategy can be understood in terms of two competing prototypes. The highly "feminized" candidate would project traditional heterosexual femininity through visual cues in dress, body language, and appearance, and she would publicly embrace traditional sex roles in the family and express support for traditional sex roles in society at large, downplaying the challenge her candidacy might pose to those roles. The highly feminized candidate would also justify her office seeking through service to others in order to deflect claims of personal ambition. She would, in other words, display what in an earlier day might have been considered "true womanhood."[9] A highly "feminist" strategy, by contrast, would downplay the candidate's feminine appearance; acknowledge her own ambition; promote a progressive, equality-based vision of family relationships (or perhaps eschew traditional nuclear family relationships altogether); and emphasize the candidate's historical achievements in terms of the long fight for women's advancement. While these categories are unlikely to describe perfectly candidates in the real world, and while we are mindful of more androgynous possibilities outside of these prototypes, they offer a useful heuristic for thinking about how traditional notions of feminine identity might be evoked on the campaign trail.

This dimension of campaign strategy was raised pointedly during the 2008 campaign with the entrance of Sarah Palin onto the national stage. As the title of the *New York Times* article from which we draw this article's title suggests, the "real fight" in 2008 was between the competing images of womanhood evoked by the two very different women who had entered the national electoral arena. (Readers who doubt this argument may engage in a thought experiment, recalling the specific reactions of their female friends and colleagues to Governor Palin's candidacy. Our bet is that a fair proportion of reactions centered on Palin's manner of speaking, "beehive" hairdo, and other displays of traditional femininity.)

Indeed, these two candidates' competing modes of adaptation seem to reflect different ways of "doing gender." Duerst-Lahti notes that "much of the heat around gender performances, or the way individuals 'do gender,' derives from contests to make one version of gender the hegemonic form, the form that is recognized as right, just, proper, and good. It is the form most able to control all other forms, and therefore it becomes most 'normal'" (2006, 28). In this vein, we suggest that Sarah Palin's entrance onto the national stage did not simply usher another woman to within striking distance of the White House. Palin brought with her an almost utterly different "version of gender," one that perhaps signals a distinct mode of adaptation for the female executive candidate, particularly one appealing to conservative voters. While a complete comparison of their respective feminine displays is beyond the scope of this article, let us briefly consider the ways Governor Palin evoked traditional femininity in her quest for executive office.

Veiled Ambition. According to deep-seated American cultural norms, ambition to professional political advancement by women is unseemly—even unwomanly. As Witt, Paget, and Matthews (1994) explain, the term *public woman* in an earlier day was a reference to prostitution, and historically women were encouraged to stay out of the public sphere, including politics. Even today women in politics often feel compelled to create an "ambition narrative" to explain their motivations for public office, and those narratives generally center on serving vulnerable populations, particularly children (Lawrence and Rose 2010).

Sarah Palin adapted to that social prohibition by drawing a quite traditional feminine veil over her own ambitions. Clad in the (expensive)[10] trappings of feminine symbols—stiletto heels, silk skirts, lipstick, and pearls—Governor Palin also embraced that most traditionally feminine justification for power: motherhood. Indeed, her frequent references to herself as a "mom" arguably served the double purpose of creating a connection with women voters and establishing herself as a "true" woman who does not seek power for power's sake. In her speeches, she often led her introduction of herself with the phrase, "I never really set out to be involved in public affairs." She repeatedly described herself as having been an "average hockey mom" who went from the PTA to the governorship; though she would mention the string of offices she held on the way, she offered no narrative explaining what propelled her forward on this path of public office holding except vague references to a desire to "put the government . . . back on the side of the people" and to bring about "reform."

Another aspect of Sarah Palin's candidacy widely commented on in 2008 was how she showcased her large family, including her infant son, in her campaign appearances. Indeed, in her acceptance speech at the Republican convention, Palin spent nearly a third of her speaking time introducing her husband and children, implicitly underscoring her values as a conservative woman and symbolically embracing the traditional role of women in the family.

In fact, Palin's three major speeches affirm her embrace of traditional gender roles both inside and outside her family: she explicitly referred multiple times to running mate McCain and husband Todd Palin as special *men,* a subtle cue to careful ears that hers is a conservative view of gender roles. She referred to her marital mate as "still the man that I admire most in this world" and described her running mate as "the kind of man I want as our commander in chief." Palin thus sent subtle signals to conservative voters of the proper order of things, despite her historical place on the Republican ticket.

Of course, it bears mentioning that despite their very different affectations of feminine style, both Clinton and Palin also made rather explicit efforts to masculinize their images, reminding us that one method of adaptation is to "out-male" the male competition (Duerst-Lahti and Kelly 1995). Though the idea that "women may wear masculinist ideology, but they cannot embody it because masculinity is an exclusively male prerogative" may be true (Heldman 2007, 21), these two candidates certainly attempted to demonstrate their "toughness." The masculinization of Hillary Clinton's campaign, which became more pronounced as she fell behind in the delegate count (Lawrence and Rose 2010), was crystallized in her infamous "3:00 a.m." ad released in late February, prior to the Texas and Ohio primaries.[11] In stark contrast to the Dorothy ad described above, in this ad a gravelly male voice intoned: "It's 3 a.m. and your children are safe and asleep. But there's a phone in the White House and it's ringing. . . . Your vote will decide who answers that call, whether it's . . . someone tested and ready to lead in a dangerous world. . . . Who do you want answering the phone?" Clinton famously donned boxing gloves on the campaign trail and assumed a series of manly postures, including drinking shots with union workers in a local Indiana bar, while tough-as-nails male surrogates delivered a manly message on behalf of their candidate (United Steelworkers of America Local 6787 president Paul Gipson, for example, introduced Clinton at a campaign event as a leader with the requisite "testicular fortitude" to make difficult decisions [Pearson 2008]).

Meanwhile, Sarah Palin, dubbed "Sarah Barracuda" from her high school basketball days, deployed visual cues that were simultaneously hypermasculine (pictures circulated of her hunting, snowmobiling, and brandishing semiautomatic weapons) and defiantly feminized (red spike heels, formfitting skirts, and long hair, along with her trademark wink and air kisses). Going Clinton one better and perfectly capturing her own gender affect, Palin declared partway through the general election campaign that in her team's battle against the Democratic ticket, "The heels are on, the gloves are off" (Milbank 2008) As David Carr of the *New York Times* quipped, Palin is "a Rachael Ray with a 4x4, who can not only make a meal in under 30 minutes but hunt and kill the main course" (Carr 2008).

Thus, the female national executive candidates in 2008 ran not only as women but, in a sense, *as men*. Future research might further elucidate this phenomenon, exploring, for example, the connections between Clinton's and Palin's respective gender styles and Duerst-Lahti's (2006, 29) notion of the predominant forms of masculinity in presidential politics. Nevertheless, clearly a key component of "running as a woman" seems to be the most obvious component of all: how the female candidate deploys traditional gender affectations.

Conclusion

While Clinton ran on a narrative familiar to the "second wave" women's movement, focused on achieving equality with men by claiming equal expertise and competence, Palin's mode of adaptation was nearly postfeminist, defined by "a set of assumptions . . . having to do with the 'pastness' of feminism" and a tendency to overtly sexualized displays (Tasker and Negra 2007, 1). While Clinton ran as a feminist candidate who donned pantsuits and could hold her own with the guys, Palin ran as a feminized candidate for whom feminism is passé, all the while cloaked in the trappings of conventional femininity with occasional gender-bending twists. In subtle and not-so-subtle ways, each woman "did gender" quite differently—differences that were not lost on reporters and the public. One observer summed up the difference this way: "Senator Clinton is a politician who also happens to be a wife and mother. Ms. Palin is a wife and mother who also happens to be a politician" (Carr 2008). A Republican male voter noted that McCain's choice of Governor Palin had clinched his vote because "she is anti-abortion, anti-gay-marriage, anti-Big Oil, a lifetime member of the N.R.A., she hunts, she fishes—she is the perfect woman!" (D. Kirkpatrick 2008).

The differences seen in Clinton's and Palin's modes of adaptation reveal the complexities of women running for masculinized executive offices. Of course, as discussed above, campaign strategies are rarely neatly categorical; they are better imagined as falling along a continuum of strategic choices and along various dimensions of campaign strategy. The strategies a female candidate chooses and the success of those strategies may vary greatly depending upon the office she seeks, the candidate's own particular attributes, the partisan and ideological identity of her key constituencies, and the political context in which she competes.

Variables influencing gender strategies in executive races include, importantly, the particular office a woman seeks. In running for the vice presidency, Governor Palin was chosen by her running mate Senator McCain—not by voters, which would seem a profoundly different testing ground for gender strategy. And while a presidential contender is running from an undeniable foundation of ambition, a vice presidential running mate can frame her ambition in the context of service: Sarah Palin could argue that she did not seek power, but rather that she was called to it. No modern female presidential candidate can credibly make such a claim.

The role of party and ideology in gender strategy options clearly needs more research as well, since a candidate's sex "is not a simple, straightforward influence on the public's evaluations but instead can set off a fairly complex set of considerations" (K. Dolan 2004, 84). Falk and Kenski (2006) find that party identification plays a major role in voter affinity with women presidential contenders, and recent work by Schreiber (2002, 2008) reminds us that gender-based consciousness and calls for group identity are not the exclusive domain of liberal women. Indeed, conservative women may have distinctive modes of gender consciousness that could deeply shape the strategies of conservative female politicians like Palin.

While we have attempted here to refine the notion of "running as a woman" by adding a third, often-overlooked element of gender affect to the more familiar duo of women's issues and appeals to gender solidarity, the notion may well require further refinement. In particular, the question of what constitutes a "women's issue" deserves attention. While the Herrnson, Lay, and Stokes (2003) conceptualization is a touchstone, other scholars (e.g., K. Dolan 2008) refer to "compassion" issues that focus on *care,* most notably, such as education, health care, welfare, and children's issues. The categorization and labeling of other "women's" issues are more nebulous and open to debate. For example, K. Dolan (2008, 116), citing Bystrom (2006) and Witt, Paget, and Matthews (1994), implicitly charts a subgroup of issues that might be referred to as "female" issues that impact women exclusively or disproportionately, such as reproductive rights and family policies, though she doesn't give them a name. Others define the category of women's issues even more broadly, to include environmental issues and concerns of ethnic minorities (e.g., Herrnson, Lay, and Stokes 2003; Rosenwasser et al. 1987). One indicator that the category of "women's issues" deserves refinement is research on the legislative behavior of female lawmakers which reveals more pronounced action with regard to issues directly impacting women (e.g., abortion, sex discrimination, and family leave policies) compared with those less directly related to women in particular, such as health care and education (Barnello and Bratton 2007; Reingold 2000; Swers 1998). In short, while our efforts here to operationalize "running as a woman" suggest various modes of adaptation in female campaigns for national executive office, these results may ultimately also demonstrate the limits of our understanding of what it means to "run as a woman." Further consideration of this concept is warranted as scholars continue to make sense of the relationship between candidates, issues, and gender. The complex strategies employed by these two female executive candidates also perhaps confirm journalist Gail Sheehy's observation that, in 2008, "nobody knew how to run a woman as leader of the free world" (Sheehy 2008). Future campaigns will give scholars opportunities to tease out the ways in which party, office, and gender interact to produce a panoply of gender adaptations.

Notes

The title of this chapter is from a *New York Times* article title by Patrick Healy, analyzing the distinct messaging of these two female candidates. See Healy (2008).

1. Many thanks to Melody's friend and colleague Annette Jolin, who suggested the "modes of adaptation" framework.

2. Today only one woman wears four stars (Ann Dunwoody), and no woman to date has been elevated to the status of five-star general, a designation reserved for generals who preside over major wars.

3. Avoiding the trap by evoking biological fact, Schroeder responded with her usual aplomb, "Do I have an option?" (Dowd 1987).

4. The speeches and interviews analyzed in this article are available in their entirety at the American Presidency Project at the University of California, Santa Barbara, at www.presidency.ucsb.edu.

5. Hillary Clinton campaign ad, "Presents." http://www.youtube.com/watch? v=yzBvQ9EeF3k. Accessed June 27, 2012.

6. Kate Phillips. "Clinton Ad: Dorothy Speaks." New York Times, December 13, 2007. http://thecaucus.blogs.nytimes.com/2007/12/13/clinton-ad-dorothy-speaks/

7. Clinton did sometimes blame gender bias for the treatment she received at the hands of the media, particularly as the campaign wore on into the spring. And on one occasion in particular—in the aftermath of a disappointing debate performance in October of 2007 in which she was roundly attacked by her male competitors—Clinton was accused of "playing the gender card" by pointing out the all-male "piling on." See Lawrence and Rose (2010) for a discussion.

8. McCain-Palin campaign ads, "Disrespectful." http://www.youtube.com/ watch?v=b0pSXmT101. Accessed June 23, 2012; and "Fact Check." http://www .youtube.com/watch?v=LK4oWay1VbE. Accessed June 23, 2012.

9. As first defined by historian Barbara Welter in 1966, the concept of "true womanhood" originated in the mid-19th century in the United States and is defined as women's adherence to four "cardinal virtues": "piety, purity, submissiveness, and domesticity" (152).

10. Palin was roundly criticized, when, two weeks before Election Day the *New York Times* revealed the campaign had spent $150,000 for the vice presidential candidate's wardrobe. The expenditures came from high-end designer retailers, which appeared to undermine the candidate's "every woman" message (Healy and Luo 2008).

11. Hilary Clinton ad, "3:00 a.m." http://www.youtube.com/watch?v=7yr7od FUARg. Accessed June 23, 2012.

3

The Vice Presidency as the New Glass Ceiling: Media Coverage of Sarah Palin

Kim L. Fridkin, Jill Carle, and Gina Serignese Woodall

I found someone with an outstanding reputation for standing up to special interests and entrenched bureaucracies. . . .
  The person I'm about to introduce you to is . . . a concerned citizen who became a member of the PTA, then a city council member, and then a mayor, and now a governor.. . . And I am especially proud to say in the week we celebrate the anniversary of women's suffrage, a devoted wife and a mother of five.
  She's not—she's not from these parts and she's not from Washington. But when you get to know her, you're going to be as impressed as I am.
  —John McCain, introducing Sarah Palin
  as his running mate, August 29, 2008[1]

American political pundits, news reporters, and the general public have long speculated about the criteria that presidential nominees consider when choosing their vice presidential running mates (Hiller and Kriner 2008; Sigelman and Wahlbeck 1997). Nelson (1988) systematically examines vice presidential selection processes from the 19th century to the current era and identifies two different sets of criteria used to identify vice presidential finalists: (1) governance criteria and (2) election criteria.

Governance criteria include political and appointive experience (e.g., competence to become president) as well as loyalty to the president. Hiller and Kriner (2008), looking at elections from 1940 to 2004, also find that presidential nominees pay special attention to candidates with relevant experience in public service.

Election criteria, according to Nelson, includes assessments of the vice presidential finalist's ability to broaden the presidential candidate's appeal in the general election and the finalist's capacity to unite the party. Presidential candidates consider a variety of factors to "balance the ticket" including ideology, geography, religion, governing experience, and age (Adkison 1982; Hiller and Kriner 2008). For example, researchers have identified the size of vice presidential finalist's state as important (Dudley and Rapoport 1989; Sigelman and Wahlbeck 1997). Presumably, a vice presidential candidate is likely to carry his or her own state in the general election. If the state is larger, a vice presidential candidate from a larger state will help secure more electoral votes for the ticket. However, Hiller and Kriner's (2008) more recent study suggests that changes in the presidential nominating process have made candidates less focused on state size, relying more heavily on vice presidential candidates with considerable governing experience.

In 2008, Democratic presidential nominee Barack Obama may have used governance criteria when he picked Senator Joe Biden to be his vice presidential nominee. Senator Joe Biden's extensive foreign policy experience, including serving as chair of the Foreign Relations Committee, made him an attractive vice presidential nominee (Barone and Cohen 2007). Republican presidential nominee John McCain may have relied more heavily on election criteria when choosing Governor Sarah Palin of Alaska. Governor Palin's conservative credentials may have reassured conservative Republicans who were suspicious of Senator McCain. Furthermore, some have speculated that Senator McCain chose Governor Palin as a way of attracting former Hillary Clinton supporters who may have been disillusioned with Barack Obama as the Democratic nominee (Seelye 2008). Finally, the choice of Governor Palin, given her gender and age, may have been viewed as a way of balancing the Republican ticket (Corsaro 2008).

In this chapter, we will examine how the choice of Governor Sarah Palin as the Republican vice presidential nominee was covered by the news media. Examining how Sarah Palin was covered in the news is an important question because if Sarah Palin was treated differently—and more negatively—than her male counterpart, then news coverage may have hurt her electability. If women candidates are seen as a "drag" on the ticket, perhaps because of how they are treated in the press, then future presidential candidates may be less likely to choose a female running mate. If presidential candidates are discouraged from picking women as running mates, then women will be denied an important pipeline to the presidency.[2]

Additionally, we will compare Sarah Palin's press treatment to Senator Joe Biden's treatment in the press. We will also compare news coverage of Sarah Palin with the first female Democratic vice presidential nominee, Geraldine Ferraro in 1984. Between 1984 and 2008, the political and media environment changed radically. For instance, citizens have become much more open to the idea of a female president. In 1984, only 79% of the public said they would be willing to vote for a woman president candidate. However, by 2008, 92% of people said they would be willing to vote for a woman for president (CBS News 2006). In addition, the media landscape has been transformed over this period, with the rapid growth of cable news as well as the emergence of the Internet. By looking at media treatment of Sarah Palin, we will improve our understanding of how the news may alter women's electoral success at the dawn of the twenty-first century. We begin our exploration by offering hypotheses regarding expected coverage patterns of Sarah Palin given what we know about gender differences in press treatment of political candidates more generally.

Expectations Regarding Gender Differences in the News Media

During campaigns, people learn about political candidates mainly through the lens of the news media. While candidates try to present their messages unfiltered, via campaign speeches and political advertisements, the bulk of what citizens learn about candidates comes from news portrayals of their candidacies (Graber 2001; Leighley 2003).

However, vice presidential candidates may face different constraints than other candidates. While vice presidential candidates are rarely the focus of scholarship, a study by Graber (1976), examining the 1968 and 1972 presidential elections, suggests vice presidential candidates receive little news attention in general. In particular, less than 5% of the stories on the television news and in the top 20 US daily newspapers were mainly about the vice presidential candidates in the 1968 and 1972 elections. Moreover, vice presidential candidates receive significantly less photographic coverage when compared with their running mates (Moriarty and Popovich 1989).

Vice presidential candidates, because they are less newsworthy than their running mates, may have difficulty generating news coverage. Press attention may be reserved for these candidates if they do something especially novel, such as making a gaffe or lobbing particularly negative attacks at their opponent. Given these limitations, vice presidential candidates may have an especially difficult time generating coverage for their preferred message.

Will a female vice presidential candidate face different obstacles than a male candidate for vice president? Vice presidential candidates, because they are a "heartbeat" away from the presidency, may be evaluated in terms of their potential executive strengths. Georgia Duerst-Lahti explains that "executive political power is arguably the most manly of all areas" (1997, 11). The president is commander in chief of the military as well as manager of the economy, and women are seen by the public as less suited than men for each of these roles (Heldman, Carroll, and Olson 2005). Therefore, the office of vice president may be an especially difficult office for a woman to obtain.

On the other hand, the office of vice president does not have a great deal of independent power and the vice president may be seen as more of a "helper" to the president. If people are hesitant about granting a woman a great deal of executive power, they may be more willing to place a woman in a position with less power, which may complement a woman's perceived "communal" strengths (Heilman 2001).

How might the news media cover women candidates for vice president? Researchers have demonstrated that women candidates, in general, are often treated differently than male candidates. For example, studies conducted in the 1980s and 1990s suggest that women receive less coverage overall and less prominent coverage in specific than their male counterparts (e.g., Kahn 1996; K. Smith 1997). Furthermore, women candidates often receive more negative coverage, garnering more criticisms in the press than male candidates.

More recent research suggests that gender differences in the amount of coverage may be fading (e.g., Bystrom et al. 2004). However, coverage of women candidates continues to cater to a stereotype, focusing on women candidates' appearance, their spouses, and their children (e.g., Aday and Devitt 2001; Bystrom, Robertson, and Banwart 2001; Devitt 1999; Heldman, Oliver, and Conroy 2009). In addition, press coverage tends to emphasize women's stereotypical strengths regarding personality traits and policy domains, even when women candidates choose to emphasize alternative messages (Kahn 1996).

Lawrence and Rose (2010), in their book *Hillary Clinton's Race for the White House,* uncover evidence for both equitable and inequitable treatment among the news media. For example, they found that Hillary Clinton was not disadvantaged in terms of the quantity and prominence of media attention. Hillary Clinton did receive more negative press attention, especially when compared to her primary rival, Barack Obama, and especially early in the nomination campaign. However, much of the coverage accorded to Hillary Clinton was the result of the press's standard operating procedure (e.g., emphasis on the horserace, the reliance on the "game" frame) and not a reflection of a gender bias by the news media. Finally, while outright sexism was not absent from the mainstream media, it was not widespread. However, examples of sexist media treatment were more common among the "new media," especially from cable news commentators and commentators via the Internet.

Finally, Bystrom, Brown, and Fiddelke, in Chapter 9 of this collection, compare newspaper coverage of men and women candidates running for mayor and for governor. The authors find some gender differences in the quantity of coverage. For example, male candidates were the focus of twice as many stories as female candidates. In terms of issue coverage, men and women candidates were treated similarly. However, male candidates were more often linked with the "masculine" issues of budgets and crime, and female candidates were more likely to be associated with the "feminine" issues of education.

In this chapter, we will look at different content categories where coverage of Governor Sarah Palin and Senator Joe Biden may differ. First, we look at whether the amount of coverage differs for Governor Palin and Senator Biden. While some past research suggested that women candidates often received less coverage—and less prominent coverage—than comparable male candidates (e.g., Kahn and Goldenberg 1991, but also see Bystrom, Robertson, and Banwart 2001; Devitt 1999; K. Smith 1997), we expect these differences might have been muted or reversed in 2008. Since Sarah Palin, as the first woman Republican vice presidential candidate, was a "novelty," news organizations may have spent more time focusing on her candidacy, compared to Senator Biden (Flowers, Haynes, and Crespin 2003). Heldman, Oliver, and Conroy (2009), in an extensive analysis of coverage patterns in seven elections, finds Sarah Palin and Geraldine Ferraro received more coverage than their male counterparts.

In addition to differences in the quantity of coverage given to Sarah Palin and Joe Biden, the news media may have differed in "how" they covered the two vice presidential candidates. In particular, scholars studying media treatment of women candidates have found that the news media tend to focus on the physical appearance of female candidates more so than that of their male counterparts (Aday and Devitt 2001; Devitt 1999; Heith 2001; Heldman, Carroll, and Olson 2005; Heldman, Oliver, and Conroy 2009; Woodall and Fridkin 2007). News attention on nonsubstantive issues, such as appearance, may ultimately hurt the candidate's chances of election (Heflick and Goldenberg 2009). If potential voters learn little about the policy priorities or qualifications of women candidates, they may be less likely to support these candidates at the polls.

In this chapter, we also look at press attention to the candidates' appearance, children, and spouses. Prior work, focusing on the presidential bid of Elizabeth Dole, found the news media spent more time focusing on Dole's image and marital status, compared to her male counterparts (e.g., Devitt 1999, 2001; Heldman, Carroll, and Olson 2000). Similarly, Heldman, Oliver, and Conroy (2009) found that the news media's attention to the families of Geraldine Ferraro and Sarah Palin far outpaced the coverage given to the families of male vice presidential candidates.

Furthermore, we look at whether the news media differ in how often they aired criticisms of Sarah Palin and Joe Biden. Research on media coverage of women candidates suggests that women often receive more critical coverage than their male counterparts (e.g., Heldman, Oliver, and Conroy

2009; Kahn 1996). Because politics may still be viewed as a male domain, women who try to compete in this male sphere often receive more critical press treatment. Similarly, we examine whether the press relied more on personal criticisms than substantive criticisms when covering Governor Palin, compared to Senator Biden. Given the expected emphasis on "the personal" for Sarah Palin (e.g., appearance, family), more personal criticisms might have been aimed at Governor Palin, compared to Senator Biden (Aday and Devitt 2001).

Next, we look at coverage in the news focusing on stereotypes. In particular, people hold stereotypes about women's perceived personal strengths as well as their perceived strengths regarding policy areas (e.g., Huddy and Terkildsen 1993). For instance, people view women as being more compassionate, more honest, and better able to deal with social policy, like education and health care. On the other hand, men are more likely to be seen as strong and knowledgeable and excelling at defense and economic issues (e.g., Kahn 1996; Sapiro 1981/1982). We look at whether press coverage of Governor Palin and Senator Biden reinforces these stereotypes.

When looking at how the press cover the vice presidential candidates, we must compare what the candidates are talking about with what the news media is reporting. For instance, if Governor Palin is talking exclusively about "female" issues (e.g., issues corresponding to women's perceived strengths) and the news media is covering these issues, then the news media are doing an accurate job mirroring Governor Palin's messages. However, if the news media are focusing on "female" issues and Governor Palin is talking mostly about "male" issues, like the taxes and the budget deficit, then the news media is misrepresenting Governor Palin's message. In our analysis, we compare Governor Palin and Senator Biden's "controlled" messages (i.e., their speeches) with the news media's coverage to examine the possibility of gender differences in how the news covers these vice presidential candidates.[3] Prior research, examining candidates for governor and the US Senator, indicates the press does a much better job mirroring the messages of male candidates, compared to female candidates (Kahn 1996).

Finally, Sarah Palin and Joe Biden are just two candidates and coverage patterns may reflect some idiosyncrasy of their candidacies. To see whether gender differences in coverage patterns reflect a more general pattern, we compare coverage of the 2008 vice presidential candidates with that of Geraldine Ferraro and George H.W. Bush in 1984, the only other modern US campaign featuring a woman vice presidential candidate. We expect gender differences in coverage patterns to be consistent between 1984 and 2008. For example, the choice of Representative Ferraro was novel and therefore newsworthy. Hence, we expect her candidacy to generate more press attention than that of Republican George Bush. Similarly, we expect more attention to physical appearance for Geraldine Ferraro as well as more discussion of her husband and family. The tone of coverage may be more critical for Representative Ferraro, with more personal criticisms being leveled at her candidacy, compared to George Bush's. Finally, coverage of Geraldine Ferraro and George Bush is likely to reinforce common gender stereotypes, with the news media emphasizing "female" traits and issues in their coverage of Representative Ferraro.

Design

To examine gender differences in coverage of Sarah Palin and Joe Biden, we looked at three types of campaign content. First, we examined television news coverage of Governor Palin and Senator Biden to see how the major news sources represented their candidacies. Second, we content analyzed the campaign speeches of Governor Palin and Senator Biden to see what the candidates chose to emphasize in their own campaign communications. By comparing television news content with the candidates' controlled messages, we can see whether the news media distorted or represented the candidates' messages in their coverage. Finally, we conducted a content analysis of news coverage of front-page stories in the *New York Times* during the 2004 and 1984 general election campaigns, comparing Governor Palin and Senator Biden to coverage of Democrat Geraldine Ferraro and her opponent, Republican George H.W. Bush. With the *New York Times* analysis, we can see whether gender differences in news coverage were consistent across these two disparate campaigns.

In the content analysis of the television coverage of Sarah Palin and Joe Biden, we used LexisNexis to identify and collect every news transcript that aired on NBC, CBS, ABC, FOX, and CNN focusing on the candidates' respective campaigns.[4] Our sampling procedure produced 261 news transcripts total, with each story averaging 15 paragraphs.[5] In coding the news transcripts, we treated the paragraph as the unit of analysis within the transcript.[6]

We began our examination of coverage patterns on August 29, 2008, when John McCain announced Sarah Palin as his running mate and continued through Election Day, on November 4, 2008.[7] We looked at coverage from mainstream news shows, both in the morning and evening (e.g., the *Today* show, *NBC Nightly News with Brian Williams*), as well as more opinion-based news analysis shows (*Hannity & Colmes; No Bull, No Bias with Campbell Brown*).

We examined television news, as opposed to newspapers, Internet, or radio, due to the fact that the vast majority of citizens still obtain the bulk of their news information from TV.[8] Throughout the long campaign, nearly 80% of voters relied on television news programs for their election coverage, while just over 25% used the Internet for the same news (Pew Research

Center 2008). Additionally, according to Nielsen (2008), although the Internet played a pivotal role in the 2008 presidential campaign, the vast majority of citizens continued to receive their news *only* from the TV on Election Day (135 million), versus those who *only* got their news online (5.2 million).

In short, our goal was to capture the news coverage of the vice presidential candidates viewed by most citizens. By selecting the major news networks (ABC, CBS, and NBC) as well as the two most popular cable news programs (FOX and CNN), we could examine the bulk of both candidates' news coverage from late August to Election Day.

We coded several dimensions of television news content, including the attention devoted to candidates' families and appearance, as well as specific issue and trait coverage. In addition to our content analysis of news coverage, we coded the available 2008 campaign speeches for Sarah Palin and Joe Biden. Using the same period of time as the news coverage content analysis, August 29, 2008, to November 4, 2008, we coded speeches for Palin and Biden using all complete speeches available through LexisNexis.[9] The search yielded 32 speeches, with 22 for Governor Palin and 10 for Senator Biden.[10] As with our news coverage content analysis, the paragraph within the transcript was the unit of analysis.[11]

Our goal in content analyzing candidate speeches was to assess the candidates' own agenda, regarding policy and campaign matters. While we could not code every speech given by the candidates, many of the speeches were drawn from a small number of stump speeches that vary only marginally from one another. We coded the speeches for the same issues and traits examined in the content analysis of news coverage, using a modified codesheet.[12]

Finally, we compared newspaper coverage of the 2008 vice presidential candidates to that of the 1984 vice presidential candidates, Geraldine Ferraro and George H.W. Bush. In this content analysis, we used ProQuest to find all front-page *New York Times* articles discussing Geraldine Ferraro and George H.W. Bush from September 1, 1984, to Election Day, on November 6, 1984, and the *New York Times* online to find all front-page articles mentioning Sarah Palin and Joe Biden from September 1, 2008, to Election Day on November 4.[13] Our sampling procedure produced 177 *New York Times* articles total, with an average number of approximately eight paragraphs discussing the candidates per article. Again, we treated the paragraph as the unit of analysis.

In comparing newspaper coverage of the 2008 vice presidential candidates to the only other election with a female running for vice president, we hoped to see whether gender differences in press treatment were consistent across these two election years. While the specific issues of the day were quite different in these campaigns, gender differences in press treatment, such as more coverage of the female candidates' family and attire, may appear in both of these election years.

Results

In 2008, the nomination of Sarah Palin as the Republican vice presidential was a great deal more newsworthy than the nomination of Joe Biden as the Democratic running mate. And not surprisingly, more coverage was given to Governor Palin than Senator Biden. In the television news stories discussing the vice presidential contenders, Governor Palin received almost twice as much coverage as Senator Biden. More specifically, the stories about Sarah Palin were almost twice as long as the stories about Senator Biden, averaging about 19.2 paragraphs. Stories about Senator Biden, in contrast, averaged about 10.1 paragraphs.[14]

When we compare coverage of the 1984 and 2008 candidates, we see the same pattern. Looking first at 2008, 53 front-page stories focused on Sarah Palin's candidacy from September 1 through Election Day, while Joe Biden's candidacy received only 43 front-page stories. In 1984, the gender difference in media attention was more substantial. Three times as many front-page stories were published about Geraldine Ferraro's historic candidacy, compared to George H.W. Bush's candidacy, 61 stories to 20 stories.[15] We see the same gender differences in coverage when we look at the number of paragraphs mentioning the four candidates on the front page of the *New York Times*. Representative Ferraro received almost 10 paragraphs (9.95) per story, while only seven paragraphs per story focused on George Bush. More than 20 years later, we see the same thing. About seven and a half paragraphs per story discussed Sarah Palin, while only six and a half paragraphs focused on Joe Biden in the *New York Times* front-page stories.[16]

Sarah Palin and Geraldine Ferraro received more news attention than their male counterparts. However, what is the content of this coverage? We turn next to the news media's emphasis on the candidates' appearance. As an illustration, consider a *New York Times* article published on September 12: "Hillary Clinton struggled for years to achieve hair credibility. Now Ms. Palin's upsweep is being praised and derided across the Internet. Do her bun and bangs signal that Ms. Palin does not want to attract attention to her appearance—even as she wants to remain presentably attractive?" (Hoffman 2008).

In addition to focusing on appearance, the news media may also spend more time discussing the families of women candidates when compared to their male colleagues. Consider the following quote by CNN's John Roberts during an on-air story: "Children with Down's syndrome require an awful lot of attention. The role of vice president, it seems to me, would take up an awful lot of her time, and it raises the issue of how much time will she have to dedicate to her newborn child?" (quoted in Harris and Frerking 2008). Similarly, Sally Quinn, in a column for Washingtonpost.com said, "Her first priority has to be her children. . . . When the phone rings at 3 in the morning and one of her children is really sick what choice will she make?" (quoted in Harris and Frerking 2008).

We systematically examine the emphasis on the appearance and families for vice presidential candidates by first turning to our content analysis of television news coverage in 2008. As the data in Figure 3.1 indicate, Sarah Palin's appearance was mentioned in almost two-thirds of the stories airing on cable and broadcast news programs. In stark contrast, only a handful of stories (5%) airing about Joe Biden mentioned his appearance. Similarly, the coverage of Sarah Palin's children and spouse received significantly more news attention than Joe Biden's children, grandchildren, or spouse.

When we look at the *New York Times* coverage of the four candidates, we find the same pattern (see Figure 3.2). First, both women candidates received more attention to their appearance than did their male counterparts. However, Sarah Palin's clothes, hair, and accessories received more press scrutiny. The *New York Times* spent little time discussing the children of the running mates, but the women candidates did receive somewhat more news attention than their male counterparts. And spouses of the women candidates were more likely to receive press attention in the *New York Times,* especially the husband of Representative Ferraro, who became the subject of intense press scrutiny regarding his financial dealings. In fact, no campaign issue during the entire 1984 presidential campaign received more media attention than Ferraro and her husband's personal finances (Patterson and Dani 1985).

These findings suggest that Sarah Palin and Geraldine Ferraro were subject to coverage focusing more extensively on their family and their

Figure 3.1 Differences in Coverage of Appearance and Family

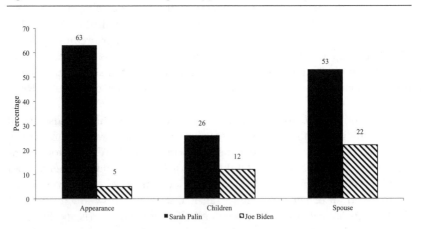

Note: The difference between Sarah Palin and Joe Biden are statistically significant at $p < .05$ for appearance and family coverage.

Figure 3.2 *New York Times* Coverage of Appearance and Family, 1984 and 2008

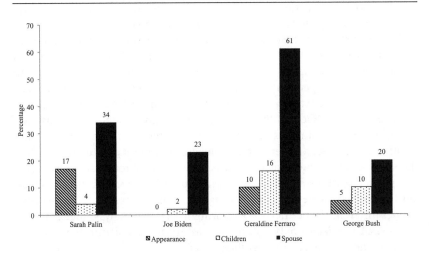

appearance. Such discussion may have trivialized their historic candidacies, focusing more on the personal than substantive aspects of their bid for the vice presidency. In the next section, we look at the tone of coverage given to candidates. We begin by examining the criticisms leveled at Governor Palin and Senator Biden during television coverage of the 2008 campaign. In our examination, we differentiate between personal criticisms (e.g., criticizing Sarah Palin's decision to run for vice president given the needs of her Down syndrome infant) and substantive criticisms (e.g., critiquing Sarah Palin's position on energy policy while governor of Alaska). Given the emphasis on family and appearance, we expect the news media to air more personal criticisms of Governor Palin, compared to Senator Biden. With regard to substantive criticisms, the gender differences may be less dramatic, but we continue to expect Palin's candidacy to generate more criticisms, given previous research showing that women candidates receive more negative coverage, compared to their male counterparts (e.g., Kahn 1996).

Sarah Palin does receive more criticisms than Joe Biden when we look at substantive and personal criticisms. Sarah Palin receives, on average, one personal criticism (i.e., 1.02) in each news story on television, while Joe Biden averages 0.14 mentions per story. Sarah Palin is also subject to more substantive criticisms than her male counterpart. More than two substantive criticisms (i.e., 2.09), on average, are leveled at Sarah Palin in each of the news stories about her, compared to less than one substantive criticisms (0.94) for Joe Biden. These differences are substantively as well as statistically significant ($p < .01$).

We also look to see whether the tendency to criticize Palin more than Biden is consistent across the different news programs. As the data in Figure 3.3 indicate, Palin receives more criticisms on network news programs and CNN, compared to Biden.[17] However, the magnitude of the differences is much greater on CNN than the networks.governor Palin is criticized on substantive matters more than four times per story on CNN, compared to less than one time per story for Senator Biden. Similarly, almost three personal criticisms per story are aimed at Sarah Palin on CNN, while personal criticisms of Joe Biden on the same news program are almost nonexistent.

While Sarah Palin was more likely to be subjected to personal and substantive criticisms, in general and on the network news programs and CNN, the story differs somewhat for Fox News. The differences in substantive and personal criticisms lobbed at Biden and Palin is not statistically different for Fox News. Perhaps the ideological slant of Fox News dampens the gender differences in criticisms appearing in the other news outlets. On Fox News, and Fox News only, Palin does not receive significantly more substantive and personal criticisms than Biden.

To see whether the negative coverage given to Sarah Palin is generalizable to the print media and across campaigns, we look at the number of criticisms published in the *New York Times* in their coverage of the 2008 and 1984 campaigns. For this analysis, we do not distinguish between substantive and personal criticisms because personal criticisms are exceedingly rare in the *New York Times* coverage. In particular, only 8% of the articles examined contained any reference to a personal criticism. When we compare criticisms for the four candidates, we find the women vice presidential

Figure 3.3 Differences in Personal and Substantive Criticisms of 2008 Vice Presidential Candidates by News Program

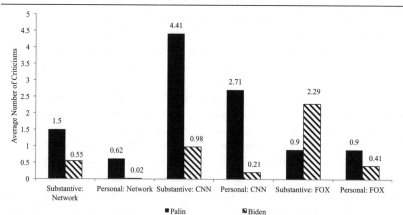

Note: Differences are statistically significant ($p < .05$) for all news programs except Fox News (substantive and personal).

candidates receive more criticisms in the newspaper than their male counterparts, but the differences do not reach statistical significance. In 2008, an average of 0.72 criticisms per article was published about Sarah Palin, while an average of about 0.35 criticisms was published about Joe Biden. In 1984, the differences were a bit more dramatic: Geraldine Ferraro was criticized an average of 1.38 times per article, while George Bush received, on average, 0.48 criticisms per article. These results reinforce the findings from the 2008 television news analysis, though the gender differences in the *New York Times* are more modest.

The news media, and especially television news coverage of the 2008 election campaign, tended to cover Governor Palin differently than Senator Biden, devoting more coverage to her appearance and her family and spending significantly more time criticizing her on personal dimensions. We find a similar, albeit less dramatic pattern, when we look at *New York Times* coverage of Sarah Palin and Geraldine Ferraro. We now turn our attention to coverage of the candidates' personality traits. While traits are a form of "personal" coverage, assessments of candidates' traits are an important criterion when citizens evaluate candidates for president and sub-presidential offices (Fenno 1996; Funk 1996; Markus 1982).

People adhere to gender stereotypes regarding personality characteristics, with people viewing women as possessing communal traits (e.g., honesty, compassion, empathy), while men are more likely to be seen as exemplifying agentic traits, like leadership and strength (Huddy and Terkildsen 1993; Lawless 2004; Rosenwasser and Dean 1989).

We looked at whether the television news coverage reinforced these trait stereotypes in their coverage of Sarah Palin and Joe Biden during the 2008 campaign. We classified traits, based on the political science and social psychology literature regarding gender stereotypes (e.g., Huddy and Terkildsen 1993; Kahn 1996; Sapiro 1981/1982; Woodall and Fridkin 2007).[18] Turning first to trait coverage on television, the data in Figure 3.4 show a dramatic divergence in how Senator Biden and Governor Palin were described by television news journalists. "Female" traits dominated coverage on Sarah Palin, accounting for 71% of her trait coverage, while more than three-quarters of Joe Biden's trait coverage focused on male traits, like "experience."

Not all of the traits used to describe Governor Palin and Senator Biden can be categorized as "male" or "female." For example, the most frequently mentioned positive trait for Governor Palin was "maverick," and the most frequently discussed negative trait for Senator Biden was "loose cannon."[19] However, when we look only at traits corresponding to women's perceived strengths or men's perceived weaknesses, we find stark gender differences in coverage.[20]

Turning to the discussion of issues, we can see if the television news coverage continues to emphasize the candidates' stereotypical strengths.[21]

Figure 3.4 Coverage of "Male" and "Female" Traits in Television News Coverage

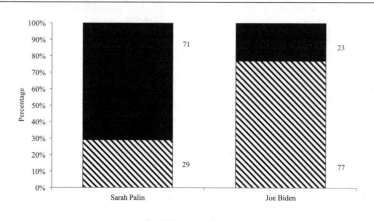

Note: Female traits include honest, moral, family-oriented, compassionate, and empathetic. Male traits include experienced, intelligent, knowledgeable, strong leader, competent, tenacious, assertive, and ambitious.

Just as people have stereotypes regarding men's and women's personality characteristics, people also have views based on stereotypes regarding men and women candidates' areas of policy expertise. Women are viewed as better able to deal with compassion issues, like education and health care, while men are seen as more adept at dealing with economic issues and foreign policy (e.g., Leeper 1991; Rosenwasser and Seale 1988; Sapiro 1981/1982). These stereotypes about what issues men and women candidates can deal with more effectively can influence voters' overall evaluations of the candidates as well as their eventual choice (Fridkin and Kenney 2009; Lawless 2004).

As the data in Table 3.1 indicate, the television news coverage of the 2008 campaign focused on "male" issues, over "female" issues. This emphasis is not surprising given the severe economic crisis facing the country as well as ongoing US wars in Iraq and Afghanistan. However, the focus on "male" issues is significantly higher for Joe Biden, compared to Sarah Palin. Almost 9 out of every 10 issue mentions is about "male" issues for Senator Biden. While the majority of Governor Palin's issue coverage is about "male" issues, "female issues" are twice as likely to be discussed for Governor Palin, compared to Senator Biden.

Even though coverage of "female" issues is greater for Governor Palin than Senator Biden, we do not know whether this difference represents the candidates' own choice of issues. If Sarah Palin is talking about "female" issues more than Senator Biden, then the television news media are representing

Table 3.1 Emphasis on "Male" and "Female" Issues in News Coverage and Speeches

	Television News Coverage[a, b]		Speeches[c]	
	Palin	Biden	Palin	Biden
"Male" issues (percentage)	67	89	92	69
"Female" issues (percentage)	23	11	8	31
N	656	403	450	297

	New York Times, 2008		*New York Times*, 1984	
	Palin	Biden	Ferraro	Bush
"Male" issues (percentage)	46	43	16	82
"Female" issues (percentage)	54	56	84	18
N	186	39	130	57

Notes: The paragraph is the unit of analysis.
a. Difference is statistically significant at $p < .01$ (Z score = 8.03).
b. Difference is statistically significant at $p < .01$ (Z score = 4.81).
c. Difference is statistically significant at $p < .05$ (Z score = 8.06).

these messages in their coverage. To examine the candidates' own messages, we content-analyzed the candidates' stump speeches during the campaign. As the data in Table 3.1 illustrate, Governor Palin actually talked about "male" issues significantly more often than Senator Biden, according to content of their speeches. In other words, Sarah Palin is focusing almost exclusively on "male" issues like the economy and energy in her speeches. However, the news media do not mirror Sarah Palin's emphasis on "male" issues in their coverage of the campaign.[22]

The greater emphasis on "female" issues for Sarah Palin runs counter to what we would hypothesize based on party expectations: Governor Palin being a Republican candidate and Senator Biden being a Democratic candidate. In particular, literature on issue ownership (Petrocik, Benoit, and Hansen 2003) indicates that Republicans are seen as having an advantage on economic issues and national defense, while Democrats are viewed as advantaged on social policy (e.g., social security, the environment, and health care). The differences in party ownership correspond to the stereotypical "male" and "female" issues. Therefore, based on purely partisan differences, we might expect "male" issue coverage to be greater for Sarah Palin, compared to Joe Biden.

When we look at the *New York Times* coverage, gender differences in coverage in 2008 disappear. In particular, about 40% of the issue coverage emphasized "male" issues for Palin and Biden (46% and 43%, respectively), while "female" issues received more attention (54% and 56%, respectively). While the *New York Times* discussed the same types of issues for both vice presidential candidates, the issue discussion did not follow the candidates' own emphasis. And again, the press did a better job representing Biden's message than Palin's message. More specifically, Governor Palin only talked about "female" issues in 8% of the issue mentions in her speeches, while the *New York Times* discussed "female" issues 46% of the time in their coverage of Sarah Palin. Senator Biden, in contrast, talked about "female" issues 31% of the time, while the *New York Times* discussed these issues 56% of the time.

The *New York Times* was less equitable in their coverage in 1984. The *New York Times* spent the vast majority of the time (i.e., 84%) discussing "female" issues for Geraldine Ferraro and spent about the same amount of time focusing on "male" issues for George Bush (i.e., 82%). The gender difference in coverage given to these two candidates is quite dramatic. However, we do know whether these differences mirrored the candidates' own emphases in their campaigns.

Overall, we see the news media—with the exception of the *New York Times* in 2008—spend more time discussing "female" issues for women candidates and emphasizing "male" issues in their coverage of male candidates. And in 2008, the television news emphasis on "female" issues for the woman candidate did not echo her own emphasis.

Conclusion

During the twentieth century and into the twenty-first century, the vice presidency has become predominately an executive post, while maintaining the constitutional role as "president of the Senate." Vice presidents in the modern era regularly attend cabinet meetings and receive executive assignments. Vice presidents have worked with leaders on Capitol Hill, served on the National Security Council, and acted as high-level representatives of the government to foreign heads of state (Hatfield 1997).

The office of vice president is something more than the largely ceremonial role of earlier eras. Therefore, when electing the president and vice president, the public needs to learn whether the candidates are qualified for their office. In 2008, the public's view of Sarah Palin was necessarily colored by the coverage she received in the news media. Our study suggests that the news media covered Sarah Palin differently than her male counterpart, Joe Biden. Sarah Palin received significantly more press attention about her family and her appearance. The tendency of the news to focus on these non-substantive topics is not something idiosyncratic to television news or to Sarah Palin. Indeed, we found the *New York Times* focused more heavily on these subjects in its coverage of Sarah Palin, compared to Joe Biden in 2008. And the *New York Times* was more likely to mention Geraldine Ferraro's appearance and family in its coverage, when compared to George H. W. Bush in 1984.

The attention to these types of nonsubstantive matters has been found by other scholars looking at other female candidates, both in contemporary elections and campaigns from earlier eras (e.g., Falk 2007; Heldman, Carroll, and Olson 2005; Lawrence and Rose 2010). For example, Falk (2007), in her book, *Women for President: Media Bias in Eight Campaigns,* studied the presidential campaigns of eight female presidential candidates (Victoria Woodhull, Belva Lockwood, Margaret Chase Smith, Shirley Chisholm, Patricia Schroeder, Lenora Fulani, Elizabeth Dole, and Carol Moseley Braun) and found that physical descriptions of women were given four times as often as those of the men who ran in the same election. The attention to nonsubstantive matters for women candidates means less space available to discuss the women candidates' issue positions, policy priorities, and relevant political experience. The focus on appearance and family may also signal to potential supporters that the woman candidate is not a serious contender.

In addition to focusing on appearance and family, news outlets, we found, were more likely to criticize Sarah Palin, compared to Joe Biden, in their coverage. Again, the greater critical coverage was found among television news programs *and* the *New York Times*. And like Sarah Palin, Geraldine Ferraro received more critical coverage than her counterpart, George H.W. Bush, in the *New York Times*. Furthermore, Sarah Palin received significantly more personal criticisms in television news coverage of her candidacy, compared to Joe Biden, reinforcing the focus on personal matters for the female candidate.

We also found that television coverage of Sarah Palin reinforced common gender stereotypes about women candidates. Sarah Palin was more likely to be described as possessing "female" traits, such as emotionality or maternalism, or lacking "male" traits, such as competence or experience. This pattern of coverage is problematic for women candidates because "male" traits correspond to "agentic" traits, viewed as necessary for political leadership (Huddy and Terkildsen 1993; Rosenwasser and Dean 1989).

Coverage of policy matters also reinforces gender stereotypes with Sarah Palin receiving more coverage of "female" issues, compared to Joe Biden. We also find a much greater emphasis on these "female" issues for Geraldine Ferraro, compared to George H. W. Bush in the *New York Times* coverage of the 1984 campaign. The greater emphasis on "female" issues for Sarah Palin is problematic for a number of reasons. First, "male" issues dominated the political landscape in 2008 (e.g., the economy, foreign policy, defense issues) and often top the policy agendas in presidential elections, more generally. Therefore, since the television news devoted less attention to these issues for Sarah Palin, coverage may have prevented potential supporters from learning about Palin's views on these important issues.

Second, Sarah Palin was actually discussing "male" issues more frequently than her male counterpart, Joe Biden. However, the television news coverage and the articles in the *New York Times* were not mirroring Governor Palin's emphasis on issues like the economy and energy. In other words, while Sarah Palin was talking about "male" issues, identifying these issues as salient and trying to demonstrate her competence for dealing with these issues, the news media did not reflect her message. Since Governor Palin was discussing "male" issues, her highly publicized run for the presidency may have been able to dispel common gender stereotypes about women's competence regarding these issues. However, since television coverage of her candidacy did not echo her own emphasis, revision of these damaging stereotypes was unlikely to take place.

The results of our study suggest that the news media may have been an impediment to Sarah Palin as she campaigned for the vice presidency. The news media focused on trivial matters, reinforced gender stereotypes, and published more criticisms of Sarah Palin, compared to Joe Biden. And Sarah Palin was not unique. Many of the gender differences found in the 2008 campaign were also evident in news coverage of the 1984 election. If the news media are an obstacle for women candidates for vice president, then presidential candidates may be less likely to nominate women candidates for the vice presidency, women candidates may be less likely to accept the nomination, and women will be denied an important pipeline to the presidency.

Notes

1. Transcript of John McCain from the *New York Times* online introducing Sarah Palin as his vice presidential running mate in Dayton, Ohio, on August 29, 2008. "McCain and Palin in Dayton, Ohio." http://www.nytimes.com/2008/08/29/us/politics/29text-palin.html?ref=politics.

2. Of the 47 vice presidents of the United States, nine (19%) have ascended to the presidency through the death or resignation of the president. In addition, in the last 50 years, vice presidents and former vice presidents have run for president six times. Of the 13 presidential elections since 1960, five (38%) have featured a sitting or former vice president (vicepresidents.com).

3. Differences in coverage of Governor Palin and Senator Biden may reflect party differences. In looking at candidates' campaign messages we can account for possible differences in the issues they discuss.

4. We collected data on the major networks (NBC, CBS, and ABC) because they are the major noncable networks that continue to have morning and evening newscasts. We added CNN and FOX to our sample, since, according to the Nielsen ratings, they were (and are) the two most watched cable news networks.

5. Intercoder reliability was calculated at 74%. The method we used was the average percent agreement across specific content categories. The transcripts were

coded by a trained graduate student and an undergraduate honors student. Reliability checks were done by an author of this paper.

6. We collected the transcripts, as opposed to viewing tapes, for efficiency reasons. Moreover, we collected data on *news* sources, as opposed to *nonnews* sources in which all the political candidates garnered some attention (e.g., *Saturday Night Live, The Daily Show with John Stewart*), (1) because we were interested in the tone and content of the material presented by the mainstream news outlets and (2) because, for news, most citizens rely on the big three networks and cable TV news shows (Pew Research Center 2008; Prior 2007).

7. While it is possible that we are missing some of Joe Biden's coverage by starting five days after he was announced as Barack Obama's running mate (August 23, 2008), an analysis by the Pew Research Center's Project for Excellence in Journalism suggested that "in just two days, Palin emerged as a bigger story overall for the week than her Democratic counterpart, Joe Biden. Even though her selection came late in the week, Palin was a significant or dominant factor in 12% of the campaign stories, according the Campaign Coverage Index. That compares with 8% for Biden, who spent much of last week in the limelight and gave his acceptance speech" (Jurkowitz 2008).

8. In a study by Pew, the proportion of people who say they got their news "yesterday" from TV, newspapers, or radio has declined since the early 1990s. However, the percentage in the last decade who say they have watched only TV news has been relatively stable, while those for TV *and* radio have fallen steadily (Pew Research Center 2008).

9. We began our examination of speeches on August 29, 2008, when John McCain announced Sarah Palin as his running mate and continued through Election Day, on November 4, 2008.

10. Although Palin and Biden gave considerably more speeches throughout the 2008 campaign than LexisNexis retrieved, their speeches were not available through alternative sources. After exhaustively searching the Internet as well as contacting the respective party organizations, we determined that a collection of campaign speeches did not exist and that the overall number of speeches given was unknown.

11. While many more speech excerpts were available only online, only complete speeches were coded in order to gain a better understanding of the issues the candidates focused on, by the candidate rather than the issues emphasized by the news media. Speeches were coded using transcripts for reasons of efficiency as well as the lack of availability of complete audio or video speech files. Available taped speeches were largely excerpts of longer speeches, selected for use by news outlets.

12. The content analysis codesheets are available upon request from the authors of this chapter.

13. While the *New York Times* online did not provide the traditional page breaks of the paper version of the *New York Times* found in the ProQuest database, microfiche copies of the *New York Times* were used to determine whether candidates in the 2008 campaign actually received front-page coverage or not.

14. This difference is statistically significant at $p < .10$, based on the one-way ANOVA (F = 23.20, d.f. = 1,259). While the stories about Sarah Palin were significantly longer than the stories about Joe Biden, about the same number of stories aired about both candidates (i.e., 131 stories for Sarah Palin and 130 stories for Joe Biden).

15. Geraldine Ferraro may have received more coverage than George H.W. Bush because Bush was the incumbent vice president in 1984, while Geraldine Ferraro was relatively new to the national political landscape.

16. While these gender differences in paragraphs of coverage are consistent across these two disparate election years, they do not reach conventional levels of statistical significance.

17. The differences across NBC, ABC, and CBS are not statistically different from one another, so we collapse the three news networks into one category: network news programs.

18. Female traits include being honest, moral, emotional, family oriented, maternal, compassionate, and empathetic. Male traits include being experienced, intelligent, knowledgeable, strong, competent, tenacious, assertive, and ambitious along with being a strong leader and a fighter.

19. The most frequently mentioned positive trait was "experience" for Biden (a "male" trait) and the most frequently mentioned negative trait for Palin was "inexperienced" (a "female" trait).

20. We didn't look at "male" and "female" trait coverage in the *New York Times* because such coverage was scant. For example, less than 30 "male" or "female" trait mentions were published during the 1984 campaign and a total of 46 "male" or "female" trait mentions were publish during the 2008 campaign. In comparison, almost 400 "male" or "female" trait mentions appeared in the television news coverage of the 2008 campaign.

21. Female issues include education, health care, family values, abortion, civil rights, human rights, environment, social security, women and politics, ethics, violence toward women, and government reform. Male issues include defense, economy, taxes, foreign affairs, business, terrorism, and war. Some issues are not classified as male or female (e.g., the issue of "media elites").

22. We did not find differences in the coverage of "male" and "female" traits and issues by news program (i.e., CNN, Fox News, network news programs).

4

Nancy Pelosi as Organizational Leader: In the Footsteps of Mary Parker Follett

*Cindy Simon Rosenthal
and Ronald M. Peters Jr.*

AS THE 111TH CONGRESS INCHED TOWARD ITS CONCLUSION IN 2010, House Speaker Nancy Pelosi was heralded as the most powerful Speaker since Joseph G. "Uncle Joe" Cannon, who ran the House with an iron fist in the first decade of the twentieth century. One hundred years later Speaker Pelosi's approach to governing the House was fundamentally different. Where Cannon ruled with an authoritarian style, Pelosi governed by an extensive organizational network and a collaborative approach that Cannon would not have recognized. Cannon also would not have recognized the extent of executive leadership tasks that a modern Speaker must perform.

A twenty-first-century House Speaker bears responsibility for functions that gradually were institutionalized and fostered the emergence of specialized House leadership careers (Polsby 1968). Polsby identifies the growth of internal complexity and resources as one measure of institutionalization, and he dates the "take off" to modernization near the turn of the twentieth century (168). The reform movement of the 1970s further increased the power of the Speaker over bill referral, floor management, and committee appointments. Today, the House Speaker presides over an expansive and fragmented array of policymaking committees and advocacy caucuses and administers a complex of specialized staff agencies (e.g., the Library of Congress, the Government Accountability Office, the Architect of the Capitol, and an extensive physical plant spilling across Capitol Hill requiring security and administration). In addition the twenty-first-century Speaker must be the master of around-the-clock communications efforts and a nonstop campaign of fund-raising, media, and political operations.

In this chapter, we explore Pelosi's approach to leadership in both historical and theoretical contexts. We take our inspiration for this analysis from pioneering female political scientist Mary Parker Follett, whose work analyzing organizations, power, and management was underappreciated during her lifetime. Though a scholar of the twentieth century, Follett's analysis presaged the executive leadership demands of the twenty-first century and feminist understandings of leadership style. She first subjected the American speakership to rigorous analysis (1904) and later posited a very modern understanding of the experience of power and creative leadership (1924). She understood the Speaker as a fundamentally political officer with an obligation to pursue partisan policy goals. In her work on organizational leadership, Follett argued that effective executive leaders depend less on formal authority and more on a successful balancing of talents, interests, and prerogatives of organizational members. Fittingly, Follett's insight and vision of strong party leadership and participatory style should be realized in the first woman to hold the office—Nancy Pelosi who held the speakership from 2007 to 2011.

How does Follett's general theory of organizational leadership apply to the political management of the House? Powerful Speakers at the close of the 19th century could rely upon the party machines of that day, which allowed for the exercise of hierarchical authority. Today, in an era of divided party government, Speakers confront a multitude of rivals from within their own caucuses, in the minority party, in the Senate, and of course from the White House and the executive agencies. The House of Representatives is populated by members who are elected via primary elections and thus have an independent foundation for their political careers. Thus, the task facing House Speakers now more than ever demands a creative approach for which Follett presciently offered a prescription. In the gendered language of the day, Follett wrote perceptively about the challenges applicable to a Speaker in the twenty-first century:

> What this officer does attempt to do is so to balance the various considerations so as to accomplish his own aims, please his party, satisfy individuals, meet the reasonable expectations of the minority, and appear respectable to the country—a laborious task greatly increased by the large number of new men and the importunity of members for particular places. (Follett 1904, 222)

In a recent book that we coauthored, we argue that Speaker Pelosi mastered the elements of the speakership in a way that other recent Speakers have not (Peters and Rosenthal 2010). She operated in a new American political landscape shaped by five factors: (1) sharply polarized partisan alignments, (2) increasing demographic diversity in the electorate and among elected officials, (3) new communications technology and a fragmented news environment, (4) a requirement for leadership campaign fund-raising prowess, and (5) the imperative for congressional leaders to deploy new organizational and operational strategies. In this new environment, Speaker Pelosi plied the craft of policymaking, political management, and executive leadership with considerable success.

In this chapter, we analyze Pelosi's executive role based on personal interviews, including with Speaker Pelosi, the public record, and original research. We first explore the contributions of Mary Parker Follett that inform our analysis; second, describe Speaker Pelosi's own circumstances and leadership style; third, analyze an example of Pelosi in action by examining the health-care debate; and fourth, suggest a few gender observations to be drawn from Speaker Pelosi as executive leader.

Congress as a Complex Organization

Why include a chapter on the speakership in a book on executive women? Certainly Nancy Pelosi's rise to become the first woman to lead the House of Representatives has historical significance. She is at the top of her game. More importantly, the speakership represents the executive center of the legislative branch of government in all its complexities. The Speaker is the only officer of the House of Representatives specifically mentioned in the US Constitution, standing second only to the vice president in the line of presidential succession. The Constitution also specifies a relationship of equality between the separate branches of government, and the Speaker must work as a policymaking partner with the president, though the political context will dictate whether that partnership is conflictual or cooperative. As Follett wrote, the Speaker is no "mere moderator" (304) and should be recognized as "uniting power and responsibility" (1904, 309).

Most considerations of the US House have focused on legislative policymaking, partisan theories of government, and interbranch relationships (e.g., Arnold 1990; Cox and McCubbin 1993; Fisher 2007; Green 2010; Krehbiel 1991; Rohde 1991; Sinclair 1995; Strahan 2007). But there can be little doubt that the House is a complicated institution by whatever measure—budget, staff, information processing, or environmental pressures. With an annual budget in excess of $1 billion, the House comprises 435 individual members, some 126 standing, select, or special committees and their various subcommittees, leadership offices, and hundreds of specialized caucuses; the House also employs close to 9,000 staff working on the Hill (Ornstein, Mann, and Malbin 2008). One obvious complexity is the tension between institutional needs and those of the individual representatives. Salisbury and Shepsle (1981) describe the Congress as a collection of member-centered enterprises whose staffs are more tied to individual members than to the institution. The House requires executive leadership, and atop this complex institution sits the Speaker (Cooper and Brady 1981). As Cooper and Brady (1981) write in their review of the congressional context and personal leadership style, the complexities of the House (particularly party strength) challenge the skills, integrative capacity, and ultimate effectiveness of House Speakers. In sum, the House is a complex institution with a history of institutional development that has led to an important executive role for the Speaker, with respect to parliamentary, institutional, and partisan functions. To assess Pelosi's executive leadership skills and style, we turn to three works of Follett. Her initial analysis of the speakership, *The Speaker of the House of Representatives* (1904), provides the historical backdrop for the modern manifestations and development of the office. Her second critically acclaimed work, *Creative Experience* (1924), presaged a contemporary style of participatory leadership. Participatory leadership has in turn been associated with twenty-first century women leaders in the public and private sectors. Third, in a series of lectures in 1926, Follett built on these two books to articulate a conception of leadership as "cumulative control and cumulative authority" located not in a single executive but reinvested in the entire enterprise (Tonn 2003, ch. 21). Follett's analysis was far ahead of its time. The office of the speakership today demands that Speakers engage in the process of "creative experience" in leading members to group consensus from the bottom up and gathering power to organize for the success of the enterprise. We see in Speaker Pelosi that kind of executive leadership.

Follett's Analysis of the Speakership

As a young Columbia University doctoral student, Mary Parker Follett undertook the first systematic study of the speakership of the US House of Representatives. *The Speaker of the House of Representatives* (1904) was the second major study of Congress to argue for a quasi-parliamentary form of administration. Where Woodrow Wilson's *Congressional Government* (1885) criticized the dominance of the committee rooms in the congressional system and argued for assertive leadership of Congress by the president, Follett believed that for congressional-presidential cooperation to occur, the Speaker must gain mastery over the House. Follett took as her model Speaker the Republican Thomas Brackett Reed. Reed had defeated obstructionism in the House by counting a quorum, ruling dilatory motions out of order, and creating the basis for strong party government in the House.

The early twentieth-century Speaker had considerable power, especially after the Reed Rules were finally accepted into the standing protocols of the House. The office, however, had been popularly understood to be that of a presiding officer—more an institutional parliamentarian than partisan politician. Follett argued that for the American governmental system to function effectively, power and responsibility had to be melded. Citing changes in the House rules empowering the Speaker, Follett hoped for a further centralization of power:

> The central, vital fault of our political system is its lack of leadership. There is no one man or body of men whose duty it is to bring forward public measures. The result of the division of legislative initiative is legislative inefficiency. The little unity and coherence we have in legislation is due chiefly to the control which has been assumed by the Speaker. (1904, 310)

Follett's faith in an empowered speakership did not anticipate the accumulation of power under Speaker Joe Cannon, who took the office in 1903, and the backlash to concentrated authority that quickly followed. Cannon brought to completion the project in party governance that Reed had articulated when he said that "the role of the minority is to make a quorum and draw their pay" (as quoted in Wolfensberger, 2010). While at the apex of his power, Cannon ruled with an iron fist, treating the Democratic minority and dissidents in his own conference with equal indifference, but his control was broken and his coalition was fractured in 1911 by the revolt of Republican progressives.

Follett's Theory of Organizational Leadership

From her pathbreaking study of the House, Follett turned her attention to the demands of leadership in the American democratic political system. Here again, her work was far ahead of its time. In 1924 she published *Creative Experience,* a study of the implications of expertise on the role of leadership in a democracy. During the Progressive movement, bureaucracy was emerging as a source of governmental capacity and expert public administrators. While some saw bureaucracy as a threat to government by the consent of the governed, Follett argued, the concept of government by consent no longer served to adequately define the democratic ideal because it functioned more often as "power over" rather than "power through" the people.

> Men study "the art of persuasion," the method of obtaining consent, but it is usually merely a method of obtaining "power-over," the pernicious aim of much of our activity. The case of expert and people should be wholly a case of "power-with." The validity of the "will of the people" depends on the distinction between power-over and power-with. In many of the methods used to "persuade," consent becomes hardly distinguishable from coercion. (1924, 199–200)

Follett believed that the dominant classes in American democracy functioned under the veneer of popular consent afforded by elections. "In a
power-society . . ." she wrote, "it is the desire of the dominant classes
which by the sorcery of consent becomes the will of the people" (1924,
209). The integration of popular desires, she thought, could not be done at
the ballot box but only through a modern style of management in which expert administrators stood in a participatory relationship to the public. The
"creative experience" with respect to public policy would require the participation of every member of the community or affected party. The goal is
to build consensus from the ground up (power-with) rather than to impose
it from above (power-over).

Within the concept of representation, the "power-over" and "power-
with" dichotomy stresses both representatives' obligations to pursue their
constituents' interests and representatives' duty as members of a legislative
body to integrate the perspectives that each member brings to the table. Follett described the relationship this way.

> There are two integrations a representative had to make: first, the integra-
> tion of the point of view he brings from his constituents with that brought
> by the other representatives from their constituents; secondly, the represen-
> tative should go back and persuade his constituents not that a better way
> than theirs has been found, but that they must try to unite their old point of
> view, or their present point of view as developed since his election or ap-
> pointment, with that formed in the representative group. (1924, 241)

Late in her career (1926–1928), Mary Parker Follett gave a series of
three lectures on behalf of the Bureau of Personnel Administration that
would solidify her reputation as a preeminent organization and management
thinker. She returned to ideas first articulated in *The Speaker of the House of
Representatives* and emphasized that leaders could create a genuine partnership with others, without abandoning their obligations to secure and use
power. In short, leaders could empower others to achieve progress and unity:

> The type of administrative leader demanded by present-day thinking is not
> the man who wishes to do all the leading himself, but one who wishes to
> develop leadership all along the line; one who does not wish to do peo-
> ple's thinking for them, but to train them to think for themselves. (quoted
> in Tonn 2003, 419)

Implications for Legislative Leadership Today

Follett's thinking maps well on the modern problems facing legislative
leaders. First, Follett claimed that the Speaker of the House must be its true
leader, the initiator of its policy agenda, and the force that drives that

agenda to fruition. Follett envisioned the Speaker as powerful and central to the institution. Second, she argued that the approach that should be taken is not "power over" members (as Cannon did) but rather "power with" members (as Pelosi does), presuming a more collaborative approach and a style of leadership that gathers power to the center and then shares responsibility for its exercise. In Follett's view, a leader must foster and participate in a process of creative experience in which consensus emerges through human interaction in groups. In public bureaucracies, we might call this bottom-up or participatory management; for legislative bodies, the emphasis is on governing by consensus.

Follett's view that the House would witness an inevitable tendency toward a centralization of power in the speakership was quickly proven wrong. The period of czar rule in the House was very short, extending from Reed's six years until Cannon's removal from the Rules Committee in 1910. For the next 60 years, the speakership shrank relative to the power of committees, which stood largely independent of party leadership control.

The Legislative Reorganization Act of 1970 reversed that balance of power and a new trend of empowering the Speaker began. The Democratic Caucus codified some changes in the early 1970s, and the Republicans accelerated the trend when they returned to power in 1995. By the twenty-first century, the speakership had been restored to something approaching the authority envisioned by Follett. Today, however, the authority of the Speaker must be gathered by creative leadership rather than supplied by the operation of local party machines.

We now observe in Pelosi a Speaker whose approach to party leadership Follett would recognize as engaging the process of "creative experience," leading from the bottom up and empowering members. That this process takes place almost exclusively within the majority party caucus is consistent with Follett's faith in party governance as a remedy to the ills of the American political system's diffusion of power.

Speaker Pelosi: Cumulative Power, Cumulative Authority

Nancy Pelosi was passionate about and took a strategic approach to organizational matters. Whether watching her organizing the House Democrats as a functioning team or managing the details of a huge policy initiative such as health-care reform, we saw the evidence that Pelosi fulfilled an approach to leadership that Follett prescribed over a century earlier. Speaker Pelosi dominated the speakership in a way that her predecessors did not or could not.[1] As leader she sought to accommodate factions within her caucus by emphasizing "power with" her colleagues, and she gathered to the speakership unprecedented power to use for policy ends. She was no mere moderator over parliamentary debates. By one account, nearly every key policy negotiation was hammered out at her conference table.[2] We trace her organizational approach by considering how she structured her leadership team and committee appointments, her integration of political operations and messaging, her outreach to various factions within the Democratic Caucus, and her approach to policymaking.

Leadership Team, Committees, and Intraparty Factions

The Pelosi style was evident in her initial decisions about her leadership team and committee appointments in the 110th Congress. In organizing and sharing power, she emphasized three principles: competency, loyalty, and diversity. She believed in putting people into positions suited for their talents but consistent with her vision of policy. She rewarded those who had been loyal to her. And she valued her party's diversity and wanted the party leadership to reflect it.

Balancing these principles was no simple matter. Upon becoming Speaker, she sought to reward Congressman Rahm Emanuel (D-IL), who had successfully led the Democratic Congressional Campaign Committee (DCCC). Emanuel had helped to reelect members from marginal districts, recruited many of the new Democratic members, and worked tirelessly on the 2006 campaigns. Emanuel considered a contest for Democratic whip. But Pelosi, balancing loyalty with the principle of diversity, convinced Emanuel not to challenge Congressman James Clyburn (D-SC), the incumbent chair of the Democratic Caucus seeking to move to whip and to remain the highest-ranking African American in the party's leadership. Instead, Pelosi promised Emanuel an enhanced portfolio in the role as caucus chair. Pelosi diffused a potential contest that might have divided the caucus.[3] To round out her leadership team, she named Congressman Xavier Becerra of California assistant to the Speaker, providing a voice at the leadership table for Hispanic and progressive members.

While adroitly handling the aspirations of Emanuel and juggling the third and fourth ranked leadership positions, Pelosi was roundly criticized for backing John Murtha in a challenge of Steny Hoyer for majority leader.[4] Murtha, who had been the party's voice in opposition to the Iraq War, had managed Pelosi's campaign for party whip between 1998 and 2001 against Hoyer, and Pelosi's desire to reward her loyal friend trumped her desire for competency in leadership. Murtha was an improbable candidate: a well-known deal maker and pork barrel specialist on the Appropriations Committee. Except for his opposition to the Iraq War, his skills as an effective spokesperson for the House Democrats paled beside the genteel, moderate, and savvy Hoyer.

Pelosi's support for Murtha was surprising but not unprecedented (Peters and Rosenthal 2010, ch. 3). Tip O'Neill (D-MA), Bob Michel (R-IL), and Newt Gingrich (R-GA) all took active roles in leadership contests, but more often, Speakers avoid taking sides in intramural fights. To publicly oppose a member with a strong caucus following risks the Speaker's own support. While the long race for whip left a residue of tension, Pelosi and Hoyer had worked together for three years. Nonetheless, Hoyer had been her adversary, and Murtha had been loyal. Hoyer defeated Murtha by a vote of 149 to 86. In the end, Pelosi emerged from the caucus vote with a triumphant Hoyer by her side and announced, "Let the healing begin!" Misstep behind her, it was time to move on.

In terms of the committee system, Speaker Pelosi became the first leader in over 100 years, Republican or Democrat, to take direct charge over committee appointments for her party, subject to the ratification of the Democratic Steering and Policy Committee (SPC) and the Democratic Caucus. Two of her closest allies Rosa DeLauro (D-CT) and George Miller (D-CA) cochaired the SPC. Most Speakers have resisted this power and the potential political fallout that might follow, but Pelosi embraced this power. For Pelosi, such authority gave her the opportunity to reward loyalty, foster competence, and ensure diversity in committee appointments.

Pelosi respected seniority in the 110th Congress in most instances except the removal of fellow Californian Jane Harman from the House Intelligence Committee.[5] House Democrats bid for subcommittee leadership slots based on a complex of House and party rules that value committee seniority or subcommittee seniority in the case of the Appropriations Committee. The committee assignments also require a deft balancing of the diversity of interests from progressives, the conservative Blue Dogs, women, African Americans, Hispanics, and equity across state delegations. In the end, Pelosi emerged from the committee appointment process without rebellion from her caucus. Without upsetting more senior members, Pelosi advanced the interests of junior members, who won assignments based on their district, reelection needs, interests, and expertise. A number of at-risk freshmen for example, Heath Shuler (D-NC), Jason Altmire (D-PA), John Hall (D-AZ), and Harry Mitchell (D-NY), ended up with subcommittee chairships. Women fared well with Speaker Pelosi. Between the 107th Congress (just before she became the Democratic leader) and the 110th (when she became Speaker), Pelosi promoted the careers of her female colleagues and doubled the number of female chairs and subcommittee chairs even while the women had less seniority overall (Peters and Rosenthal 2010, 218). Transfers for returning members were heavily influenced by seniority and the diversity of the caucus.

Again in the 111th Congress, Pelosi was challenged to appoint a diverse leadership team and to advance her own policy preferences. As she had done two years before, she sought to avoid intramural fights and to bring order to the leadership. With Majority Leader Hoyer and Whip Clyburn firmly in place, the key races were among younger members eager to move up the leadership ladder. With Emanuel moving to the White House to become President Obama's chief of staff, the position of caucus chair was up for grabs with Congressman Chris Van Hollen of Maryland, the chair of the DCCC, and longtime Pelosi loyalist John Larson of Connecticut, the incumbent caucus vice-chair, both contending.[6] Congressman Xavier Becerra of California, Debbie Wasserman Schultz of Florida, and moderate veteran Democrat Marcy Kaptur of Ohio all had their eyes on the caucus vice-chair post.[7] Congressman Joe Crowley of New York, a leader of the New Democrats, angled to become vice-chair of the DCCC, a position that Wasserman Schultz coveted after deciding against a race for caucus vice-chair.[8]

To resolve these competing ambitions, Pelosi used the kind of informal power that Follett so admired. Pelosi first persuaded Van Hollen to remain at DCCC but offered him simultaneously the position of assistant to the Speaker (Becerra's old job) and responsibility for protecting and reelecting incumbents (a task that had been assigned to Emanuel as the caucus chair in the 110th Congress).[9] Larson became caucus chair and Becerra, the caucus vice-chair. Pelosi split the position of DCCC vice-chair in two with Crowley named as vice-chair for fund-raising and Wasserman Schultz as vice-chair for incumbent protection.[10] Once again, Pelosi had satisfied the ambitions and talents of her members, avoided major fights, and ensured a loyal leadership team.

On the committee side, Pelosi also demonstrated her willingness to centralize power in the 111th Congress even while publicly asserting neutrality in a historic fight between two committee chairs. Henry Waxman of California, a Pelosi ally, challenged John Dingell of Michigan to chair the powerful Energy and Commerce Committee. Dingell, the dean of the House, had frustrated Pelosi's legislative priorities for tighter climate protection standards imposed upon the automobile industry. This unseating of a longtime committee chair represented a clash of titans. When the Democratic SPC met to make its committee chair nominations, Waxman earned the nod by a vote of 25–22, an indication of Pelosi's behind-the-scenes support for Waxman. On November 20, 2008, Waxman won full caucus support by a vote of 137–122. Media accounts attributed his margin of victory to a better-organized campaign, as well as to the support of Californians and members who had benefitted over the years from campaign contributions from Waxman. Dingell's support was drawn from among Rust Belt members, the Congressional Black Caucus, Blue Dog Democrats, and other moderates.[11]

The Waxman-Dingell contest was critical to the Pelosi speakership in several respects. First and foremost, Pelosi could not achieve her policy goals without the help of others—the essence of Follett's cumulative control and cumulative responsibility. Waxman had been a staunch advocate of energy conservation and climate protection policies during his 30-year congressional career; Dingell had been steadfast in support of Detroit automakers. Second, the contest served important institutional goals. The Democrats had accepted in 2006 the Republican policy of term-limiting committee chairs amidst considerable grumbling by senior members, but the attachment to seniority was strong and deep in the caucus, especially among the veteran black members. Interestingly, the House adopted new rules for the 111th Congress, eliminating term limits for committee chairs, but the message of the election of Waxman reinforced the power of the Speaker. While seniority is fundamental to the politics and norms of the House, Pelosi had shown that she could control a majority on the SPC, albeit narrowly.

While Pelosi avoided getting caught in the middle of this fight, she was surely pleased by the result. Dingell's ouster bolstered Pelosi's power and that of the California delegation. Pelosi got the best arrangement: Dingell gone without her appearing to have forced him out.[12] Moderate committee chairs now were on notice that they too might be challenged and thus might think twice about defying the Speaker. The Republican majority leadership had mishandled the committee chairs, bypassing seniority, interviewing candidates for the jobs, and imposing term limits. For Pelosi, another path was taken.

Internally, Pelosi and her leadership team developed an elaborate and regular system of consultations with the different factions of the Democratic Caucus. She met weekly with the freshman and sophomore classes of the caucus—a group she called her "majority makers." She also attended to the Blue Dogs, the most conservative members of her caucus. The net effect of these various communications efforts knit together the diverse interests within her caucus. Where the Republicans under Newt Gingrich and Dennis Hastert had sought to impose party discipline and adherence to party line votes, Pelosi sought to listen to her members and then allow them the opportunity to agree or disagree. She achieved liberal policy success while allowing moderate Democrats to vote their districts.

Politics and Message

Pelosi's integration of organizational units extended beyond the leadership team and committees to include the staff. The roots of her communication efforts dated back to the early 1990s when she established the "message board" within her party caucus. She had ties to loyal staffers in the DCCC, in other leadership offices, in the committees, and even with the White House. Policy, message, and campaign strategy are of a piece.

Pelosi also established a sophisticated, centralized system of communications directed both internally and externally (Peters and Rosenthal 2010). The Speaker's top staffers coordinated media contacts and an array of fact sheets, public events, press releases, one-minute floor speeches, member interviews, and press conferences. Pelosi centralized the communication operation in a way that previous Speakers did not. She also diversified that effort beyond the traditional mainstream media to include the blogosphere, cable television, specialized Internet-based publications, and social media. In a typical week, the staff booked interviews for more than 20 members on talk radio, nationally syndicated cable television shows, and local television broadcasts. Pelosi herself appeared frequently on the major television news programs and sat for extended interviews with journalists. Such appearances were rare for her predecessors, and in the early part of her speakership she generated two to four times the news coverage of any of her predecessors except Speaker Gingrich (Kedrowski and Gower 2009).

Making Policy

Pelosi is sometimes criticized for writing bills in the Rules Committee or in the leadership suite. She took charge with her initial "6 for '06" agenda in January of 2007 and the Obama administration's stimulus bill in January of 2009. But by and large, Pelosi preferred to work through the committee system rather than around it. Instead of running over the committee chairs, she cooperated closely with them, especially her allies, such as Henry Waxman at Energy and Commerce, George Miller at Education and Labor, and Charlie Rangel at Ways and Means. But she also worked closely with chairs with whom she was not philosophically aligned. For example, she worked with John Dingell, then chair of Energy and Commerce, on the 2007 energy bill and with Collin Peterson on the 2007 agriculture bill. Ultimately with the passage of health-care reform, Pelosi credited a wide circle of leaders, committee chairs, and Dean of the House Dingell, who was granted the symbolically important honor of closing the historic debate.

Pelosi sought to develop bills in committee for two reasons. First, she believed in the committee system and believed that "regular order" generally produces better legislation. She bypassed the committees only under the press of political necessity or national emergency. Second, she believed that the committees and subcommittees were the best venues for developing consensus and compromise within her fractious caucus and, on occasion, across party lines. By allowing issues to gestate in the committees, she avoided having to take a heavy-handed approach because many issues could be resolved before floor consideration required leadership intervention.

While Pelosi usually followed regular order, she and her leadership team were deeply invested in monitoring and on occasion massaging the committee process. The Speaker, majority leader, whip, and caucus chair all had policy staffs that worked closely with committee and subcommittee staffs. The Speaker nurtured her relationships with the chairs. When a chair faced an intractable issue within the committee, the Speaker often intervened to facilitate compromise. In fact, Pelosi preferred this method of coalition building. She was loathe to bargain for individual votes and did not typically use earmarks to whip votes, as her Republican predecessors had routinely done. Thus, the Democratic majority reduced the number and value of earmarks by two-thirds of those under the previous Republican leadership. Instead, she searched for policy compromises that could gain the support of blocs of like-minded members. Often, she made concessions to the moderates to the disgruntlement of the liberal Democrats, a classic example of Follett's conception of representatives' dual obligations to their constituents and to the collective caucus. In fact, a primary example would be Pelosi's willingness to yield on her signature priority—climate change—in the 2007 and 2009 energy bills to move health-care reform ahead of energy legislation in 2010. To illustrate her approach, we consider the health-care bill in more detail.

Health Care: Creative Experience in Action

Pelosi's approach to organizational leadership borrowed from techniques developed by her Democratic and Republican predecessors since the reforms of the early 1970s, but was nonetheless distinctive. She merged Follett's preference for strong party government and her faith in creative experience. Pelosi's leadership in pushing health-care reform through the House illustrates these distinctions.

President Obama, not Speaker Pelosi, made the initial decision to place health-care reform at the head of the agenda for the 111th Congress. Obama's approach to major legislation provided Pelosi with the room she needed to manage the Democrats' complex policy agenda. Instead of sending prepackaged bills to the Hill, Obama preferred to enunciate general principles and then ask Congress to develop the specific legislation. Speaker Pelosi turned to a bottom-up approach to draft the legislation.

Her approach was grounded in the committee system, to which she was much more deferential than had been her Republican predecessors. Thus, just as Obama deferred to the Congress while seeking to guide its deliberations, Pelosi worked with the chairs, recognizing a talented senior group of legislators empowered to guide committee policy deliberations. Her only caveat was that their work proceed within parameters acceptable to the leadership.

Pelosi referred the health-care legislation to three major House committees: Energy and Commerce, Ways and Means, and Education and Labor. Their chairs, Waxman at Energy and Commerce, Rangel at Ways and Means, and Miller at Education and Labor, were Pelosi allies who would reliably work toward the president's objectives. With a supermajority on Ways and

Means and a solid liberal contingent on Education and Labor, the Energy and Commerce Committee became the focal point of negotiations. Critical negotiations took place between Waxman and Blue Dog Democrats led by Mike Ross of Arkansas. The key issue was the structure of a public insurance plan to be offered in a legislatively created insurance exchange. Waxman spoke for liberal Democrats who favored setting up the public plan based on Medicare reimbursement rates to doctors and hospitals. This approach had two advantages: (1) saving money, though at the expense of underfunding service providers, and (2) putting the public option at a competitive advantage against private plans offered in the exchange. While the Blue Dogs generally favored deficit reduction, many were pressured by doctors and hospitals in their districts. Their preferred alternative would require the managers of the public plan to negotiate rates with service providers. Although Pelosi sided with the liberals on substance, she realized the necessity of moving the bill from committee. She intervened to accede to the Blue Dog demand for negotiated rates.

Once all three committees had cleared legislation for floor consideration, Pelosi assumed full control to merge the three bills into a single comprehensive bill. She included the public option based on negotiated rates. To solace liberals, she included a surtax on wealthy Americans to cover the cost. In the endgame, the legislation's treatment of abortion services became the critical issue. Around a dozen pro-life Democrats, led by Bart Stupak of Michigan, demanded language that would exclude abortion coverage by any public or private plan offered in the insurance exchange. The Speaker's proposal would have required insurance companies to sequester premiums so that only that portion paid by policyholders would cover abortions. At issue between Stupak and Pelosi was whose language preserved the principle of the Hyde Amendment: that no public funding would go to abortion services.

Pelosi sought a compromise with Stupak up to the last minute. Stupak agreed to the inclusion of his language on an annually renewable basis, but Pelosi could not sell this to prochoice Democrats. Stupak then demanded a vote on an amendment incorporating his language into the bill. Pelosi had no choice but to accede, and the Stupak amendment was adopted. The House then passed the bill on a near party line vote with only one Republican in support, 220–215.

After a contentious August recess during which the Tea Party movement reared up in opposition to the bill, President Obama relaunched health-care reform in a September address to a joint session of Congress. Negotiations on the Senate Finance Committee broke down, and Senate majority leader Harry Reid negotiated the final terms of the Senate bill, which passed 60–40 on a party line vote. As the House and Senate contemplated merging a bill in conference, Senator Scott Brown (R-MA) unexpectedly won the Massachusetts January 18 special election to fill the seat vacated by Edward Kennedy's death. Brown's victory meant the Democrats' loss of a filibuster-proof Senate majority and threw the bill's prospects into doubt. Brown's election was taken as an indication of public opposition to the health-care bill, and Democrats began to doubt the wisdom of proceeding.

At this critical juncture, Pelosi asserted extraordinary leadership. Facing sentiment that the Democrats should pare back their bill in order to secure its passage, Pelosi denounced this "eensy-weensy spider" approach, insisting that the Democrats not abandon their historic quest to fundamentally revamp the nation's health-care system.[13] She saw only one viable path to enact comprehensive reform. The House would have to approve the Senate bill as written. Since House liberals objected to aspects of the Senate bill, the Democrats would turn to the use of budget reconciliation to amend the legislation once it was signed into law. This strategy required Pelosi to corral a House majority from within Democratic ranks on the promise that the reconciliation package would also become law.

To gather Democratic votes, Pelosi engaged in an extraordinary exercise of leadership. Having convinced the White House and Senate leadership of the strategy, she now had the responsibility to convince her House colleagues to vote for the Senate bill. Her approach was at first indirect. She conducted a series of meetings with the Democratic Caucus and with various groups of Democratic members to listen to their advice and gauge their mood. According to one account,

> One of Pelosi's first moves was an appeal for calm. Take a breath, she told her members, and don't say anything publicly that might set off a stampede. In caucus meetings, she listened—and then, ever so slowly, she started to push. "After Massachusetts, there was a big Democratic caucus, everybody was trashing health care, and you left the room thinking, 'This is just never going to happen,'" one senior Democratic aide recalls. "And then, the next caucus, she's talking about how we're going to do it. . . . I thought there was no way in hell."[14]

Once the strategy of comprehensive reform was set, Pelosi's first and most critical task was to create a psychological environment in which her members could see a way forward. Brown's election had traumatized congressional Democrats. Politicians take election outcomes very seriously, as democracy presupposes they should. Here, the message from the voters seemed to be, "Stop!" Yet from a procedural point of view, Brown's election meant only that the Democrats did not have a filibuster-proof majority; they could still proceed under the reconciliation instructions of the budget process. What was required was faith and confidence.

Pelosi had to convince the liberals that they could trust the Senate. Too often, House Democrats had been asked to cast unpopular votes only to see House-passed bills die in the Senate. The cap and trade bill was a good example. They were now being asked to vote for a Senate bill, elements of which were strongly opposed by many House Democrats. Some of their most important objections could be addressed in the reconciliation "side-car" (i.e., enacting some modifications to the Senate bill in separate companion legislation) only if at least 50 Senate Democrats would be sure to vote for it.

Moderate Democrats had a different concern: their support for the bill might put their seats in jeopardy. It was among these members that the margin of victory would be found. Thus,

> when her whips brought her a list of 68 House Democrats whose votes they considered to be in play, Pelosi decided to personally lobby each of them. As a speaker who understood her individual members' districts and constituents, she had a good sense of which of her politically endangered colleagues were least likely to jeopardize their seats with a yes vote—enabling her to allow the most endangered ones to vote no.[15]

Herein lies the essence of Pelosi's leadership approach. Having engaged in the therapeutic work to convince the Democrats that they could win, she now had to reap the needed swing votes one at a time. She could draw upon her efforts over time to cultivate relationships with her members both as individuals and in groups. Her weekly meetings with freshmen during the 110th Congress and new freshmen Democrats in the 111th Congress were key. She had strong allies among the Blue Dog Democrats, progressives, and New Democrats, and she maintained a mental "favor file," that is, a crowded ledger of preferment and obligation to reward her supporters. Her political operation stood ready to provide members with the support they would need to win reelection. Not only did she know the members' districts politically and demographically, but she also was familiar with their key supporters. Pelosi drew on all these resources in calibrating the vote to ensure a minimum winning coalition. When a member agreed to support her, the member might expect to receive congratulatory calls from supporters back home.

Pelosi did not work alone. In addition to her leadership teams' extensive whip operation, she was supported by the Obama White House, external interest groups, and other House Democrats. The process was both strategic and political. To secure the support of the core liberal constituency for the bill, she negotiated a reconciliation package that "fixed" some of the most egregious provisions of the Senate bill (such as the "Cornhusker Kickback," a classic Washington backroom deal which gave an extra $100 million in Medicaid funds for Nebraska). These special provisions had cast a pall on the bill and were inconsistent with Pelosi's approach to coalition building. Instead of trading favors to win individual votes, she preferred to alter policy to secure blocs of votes. The best example was her effort to regain the support of the pro-life House Democrats. The Senate version of the bill that they were now asked to support was unsatisfactory to the Stupak bloc. To win their votes Pelosi sought a commitment from President Obama to sign an executive order ensuring that no federal funding under the legislation would go toward abortion services. In some cases Pelosi orchestrated political pressure. One example was her efforts to gain support from Congressman John Barrow of Georgia. Representing a rural Georgia district with a constituency 44% African American, Barrow was threatened with a Congressional Black Caucus–endorsed candidate in the Democratic primary.[16]

Health-Care Reform as Follett Might See It

Let us place this account of Pelosi's leadership on health-care reform in the context of Follett's notion of creative management. Follett argued that an effective organizational leader must engage the organization members in collaboration. The synergies that result will produce better policy and a committed organizational culture. The organizational leader in Follett's scheme of creative management is a professional public administrator, an expert, but she clearly recognized the Speaker as the leader on policy.

Follett's approach sought to avoid the pitfalls of "top-down" management inherent in hierarchical governmental bureaucracies. We have sought to ask, how might her theory apply in the context of the modern House speakership, especially given her early work in which she stressed the critical role of the Speaker as a party leader? To answer this question, we recognize that the House of Representatives is not a hierarchical institution. Indeed, it is an inherently flat organization in which each member has but a single vote, is placed there by the voters back home rather than the party leaders in Washington, and thus enjoys an autonomy unknown to government bureaucrats.

The challenge of the Speaker of the House is the converse of that of the public organizational leader in a bureaucratic setting. Where an administrative organizational leader has the power to impose his or her vision of organizational goals and mission, the political organizational leader (the Speaker of the House) is not in a position to simply command the votes of the members. That leader must find a way to enlist their support, in part by engaging them in the process. She or he must also draw on every resource at her or his disposal to leverage votes and to build a majority coalition from the bottom up rather than the top down. In Follett's day, the House of Representatives and its leaders whom she admired functioned in a top-down system because the political parties controlled the nominations of their local candidates. But with the advent of the direct primary in the early 20th century, the party machines began to wither.

While the health-care legislation victory was described by some as trench warfare with Pelosi and her lieutenants muscling the bill over the goal line, the actual triumph was secured through endless individual consultations, attention to the personal circumstances of each member, and carefully crafted policy and procedural nuances that secured the final House vote.[17] This is the essence of the creative experience.

The Woman as Speaker

Speaker Pelosi embraced a collaborative style of leadership with her Democrat members that was in keeping with Follett's conception of the creative experience. It also reflected the conclusions of scholars who have studied women's leadership (see, for example, Helgesen 1990; Jewell and Whicker 1994; C. Rosenthal 1998; Tolleson-Rinehart 2001). Many social scientists have come to recognize that leadership is a gendered phenomenon in which the paths to power as well as the practice of leaders are shaped by their formative experiences as boys and girls and as men and women (Acker 1992; Kenney 1996).

Speaker Pelosi first sought elected office in her own right as a middle-aged woman who had devoted much of her adult life to the raising of her five children and electing Democrats to office as a party activist. Her childhood was shaped by the powerful twin influences of her father, Thomas D'Alesandro, longtime Baltimore mayor and former congressman, and her mother, Annunciata, matriarch of the household and full partner in the day-to-day enterprise of tracking political favors and turning them into votes. All six children in the D'Alesandro home were put to work in the family business of politics, and Pelosi herself writes of the organization required to maintain her own household of five children born in the space of six years (Pelosi 2008). Pelosi's own conception of leadership combines tireless organizing, endless attention to personal details, and engagement in the process by everyone according to his or her talents. Reflecting on her investiture as Speaker in 2008 where she made history calling the House to order "for all of America's children," Pelosi writes: "I consider my involvement in politics as an extension of my role as a mom. More than anything else, I am a wife, mother, and grandmother. If I had never done anything in addition to being a mother of our five children, and not a grandmother, I would consider my life a happy success" (168). When writing about the health-care reform package for the Capitol Hill publication *Roll Call*, Pelosi referenced its importance to families and future generations no fewer than eight times.[18] (We document Pelosi's frequent references to families, children, and future generations in our book [see Peters and Rosenthal 2010, ch. 6].)

While Follett never married nor had children, she too honed her sensibilities on organizational leadership through the experience of serving families in the settlement house movement. Denied an academic career, she turned her attention to urban activism in Boston, enhancement of opportunities for poor immigrant neighborhoods, and education for young people in social centers (akin to today's after-school programs) about the values and skills of citizenship (Tonn 2003, ch. 10, along with Graham 1996).

The skills of collaborative leadership are not unique to women, nor are they totally new to the House of Representatives. Congressional leaders today build their successes on cultivating consensus, bridging factions, assuaging concerns, and rallying support. Speaker Jim Wright was fond of saying that leadership is merely a "license to persuade," and persuasion requires a commitment first to listening. Speaker Gingrich adopted the mantra of "Listen, learn, help, lead" while Democratic leader Dick Gephardt, sometimes nicknamed "Iron Ears," was recognized for his patience in hearing members out. Speaker Pelosi followed this path but placed new and heightened emphasis on running the Democratic Caucus as a "meet market" with heavy intraparty consultation and "therapy" or prayer sessions with her members.

What was distinctly gendered about her leadership were the roots of her premium on listening, consultation, and consensus building. She connected her executive leadership style to her gendered roles as mother, grandmother, and wife. She invoked rhetoric about congressional policymaking that resounded with references to children, families, women, and the welfare of future generations. We note, however, that her collaborative efforts stopped with the boundaries of her caucus and did not extend to her Republican colleagues in the House. She was a fierce partisan with a sharp tongue and intensely competitive campaign focus.

Pelosi acknowledged the fundamental philosophical differences between Democrats and Republicans and then turned her attention to building the creative experience within the confines of her caucus. She chose to ignore (and at time even to ridicule) the views of the GOP minority. Follett saw conflict not as a difference to be ignored but a challenge to be tackled. How she might have viewed this aspect of the Pelosi speakership is unknown, but for the most part the hyperpartisan environment of the contemporary Congress represents a new reality for any Speaker in the new American politics.

Conclusion

Nancy Pelosi led a very different House than did Thomas Reed or Joe Cannon. In the middle of the health-care struggle, she described the challenge of leadership in this way: "'You go through the gate,' she said. 'If the gate's closed you go over the fence. If the fence is too high, we'll pole-vault in. If that doesn't work, we'll parachute in. But we are going to get health care reform passed for the American people.'"[19]

Pelosi led the House with cumulative control and responsibility as Follett advocated.[20] No detail was too small to attend to in the Pelosi regime and coordination was the goal. One might even imagine that Follett was describing Speaker Pelosi when she stated: "You cannot always bring together the *results* of departmental activities and expect to coordinate them. You have to have an organization which will permit an interweaving all along the line. Strand should weave with strand, and then we shall not have the clumsy task of trying to patch together finished webs" (quoted in Tonn 2003, 417).

Notes

1. John Bresnehan, "Pelosi's Power Reigns Supreme," *Politico*, November 12, 2008; Glenn Thrush, "With the 111th, the Age of Pelosi Dawns," *Politico*, January 8, 2009; Jared Allen, "Armed with More Democrats, Pelosi Poised to Get Tougher," *The Hill*, November 5, 2008.

2. Paul Kane, "Pelosi Makes History, and Enemies, as an Effective House Speaker," *Washington Post*, May 2, 2010.

3. Jennifer Yachnin, "Pelosi, Emanuel Cut Deal," *Roll Call*, November 13, 2006.

4. Alan K. Ota, "Experience Counts in the House," *CQ Weekly*, November 13–17, 2006, p. 3128–3131.

5. The relationship between Pelosi and Harman had never been close. Published accounts suggested that Pelosi was unhappy about the prominent role Harman had taken in supporting the Bush administration's counterterrorism policies, appearing on national talk shows twice as often as Pelosi. Harman was also more conservative than Pelosi, who intended to continue the Democratic assault on Bush administration national security policies.

6. Tory Newmyer and Keith Koffler, "Emanuel Move Shakes Up Democrats," *Roll Call*, November 6, 2008.

7. Steven T. Dennis, "House Leadership Races Immediately Underway," *Roll Call*, November 5, 2008; Jared Allen, "Dems Back Off Leadership Challenges," *The Hill*, November 10, 2008; Steven T. Dennis and Tory Newmyer, "House Leaders' Races Lack Zest," *Roll Call*, November 17, 2008.

8. Victoria McGrane and Ryan Grim, "Crowley, Wasserman Schultz in Leadership Battle," *Politico*, December 3, 2008; Patrick O'Connor and Ryan Grim, "Why Becerra Rebuffed Obama," *Politico*, December 17, 2008; Steven T. Dennis, "Becerra's Snub of Trade Job Ices Others' Ambitions," *Roll Call*, December 17, 2008.

9. John Bresnehan, "Pelosi Recruits Van Hollen for New Role," *Politico*, December 9, 2008.

10. McGrane and Grim, "Crowley, Wasserman Schultz in Leadership Battle."

11. Mike Soraghan, "Reps. Dingell, Waxman, Trade Salvos in Battle," *The Hill*, November 11, 2008; John M. Broder and Carl Hulse, "Behind House Struggle, Long and Tangled Roots," *New York Times*, November 23, 2008; Mike Soraghan

and Jared Allen, "Waxman Gains Edge from Steering Committee," *The Hill,* November 19, 2008; Alexander Bolton, "Panel Fight Reaches Up to Leaders," *The Hill,* November 17, 2008.

12. Tory Newmyer, "Waxman's Coup Worries Moderates," *Roll Call,* November 10, 2008; Jonathan Allen, "Dingell's Defeat Part of a Pattern of Growing California Clout," *CQ Today Online News,* November 20, 2008.

13. Harold Myerson, "Nancy Pelosi—It's Her House," *Los Angeles Times,* March 26, 2010.

14. Jonathan Cohn, "How They Did It," part 5, *The New Republic Online,* May 26, 2010 .

15. Myerson, "Nancy Pelosi—It's Her House."

16. Tory Newmeyer and Steven T. Dennis, "No Vote Came Easy for Pelosi," *Roll Call,* March 23, 2010.

17. Ibid.

18. Nancy Pelosi, "Health Law Crowns Democrats' Achievements," *Roll Call,* May 27, 2010.

19. Renee Lauth, "The Power of Pelosi," *Boston Globe,* March 26, 2010.

20. While the triumph of health-care reform may have ultimately sown the seeds of the Democrats defeat at the polls in November 2010, we do not consider the political rout a sign of a failure of organizational leadership by Pelosi. Even skilled organizational leaders can be overtaken by events and circumstances such as economic crises.

5

Women in the Obama Administration: Insiders, or Outsiders Looking In?

Julie Dolan

SHE HAS BEEN DESCRIBED AS "THE ULTIMATE INSIDER," PRESI-
dent Obama's "proxy-in-chief," and "the world's most influential right-
hand woman" (Malveaux 2009; Cottle 2009). Even so, very few Americans
have ever heard of Valerie Jarrett, a top senior adviser to President Barack
Obama. A longtime friend of both Barack and Michelle Obama, Jarrett's
appointment was announced less than two weeks after Obama was elected
president, making it one of the first appointments filled by the president-
elect (Parsons 2008). Although Jarrett receives little press attention and remains relatively invisible to the American public, her role as one of the
president's closest and most influential advisers gives her an extraordinary
opportunity to shape policy inside the White House. In the history of the
United States, very few other women have held such prestigious positions
in the executive branch.[1]

Shortly after he was elected in November 2008, President Obama appointed a number of additional women to serve in his cabinet. He selected
onetime campaign rival Hillary Clinton as his secretary of state, sitting Arizona governor Janet Napolitano as secretary of homeland security, sitting
Kansas governor Kathleen Sebelius as secretary of health and human services, and Congresswoman Hilda Solis as his secretary of labor. Having a
seat at the table certainly provides these women with powerful positions
and access to the president, but scholars have questioned whether or not
women in executive positions in government have the same access to power
as their male colleagues (Borrelli 2002; Duerst-Lahti 1997; Duerst-Lahti
and Kelly 1995; Stivers 1993). In particular, MaryAnne Borrelli (2002) contends that even while women have made substantial progress into presidential cabinets over the last 50 years, most of them are quite unlike Valerie

Jarrett—they remain on the outside looking in, placed in positions that provide relatively few opportunities to shape presidential and departmental agendas.

Are Obama's female appointees outsiders looking in, or has he charted a new path by appointing women to real positions of power in his administration? Drawing on presidential appointee data from the last 12 presidential administrations,[2] I examine Obama's cabinet-level appointees[3] to determine how well positioned his female appointees are to exercise influence and shape public policy from their executive branch posts. To do so, I first provide a descriptive overview of Obama's appointees, comparing his record on female appointees with the records of previous presidential administrations. After that, I draw on a typology of cabinet types first suggested by Nelson Polsby (1968) and employed by Borrelli (2002) in her own analysis of women in the cabinet to estimate these women's opportunities for influence.

The rest of the chapter unfolds as follows: I first explain why the executive branch is a worthy site for study. As many scholars concur, the executive branch provides ample opportunities for political appointees and career administrators to exercise political and policy influence. But because much of their work is obscured from public view and not obvious to most, I spend some time explaining the nature of administrative discretion to illustrate the ways in which these administrative positions provide opportunities for influence. Second, I discuss the gendered nature of the bureaucracy. Here I draw on leading scholars in the area who theorize that gender greatly influences access to power in the executive branch, resulting in fewer opportunities for executive women to exert influence and exercise leadership. Finally, I use data on the top tier of presidential appointees to estimate women's potential for influence in the Obama administration. Doing so suggests that women are making real strides in the Obama administration, and that their capacity to influence presidential priorities, initiatives, and policymaking is quite strong.

Discretion and Influence in the Executive Branch

Why study female appointees and bureaucrats? This entire volume examines women across different types of executive positions, and presidential appointees and bureaucrats are probably the least well known of these individuals to the public. Even so, the executive branch has long been recognized as a significant player in governance (Borrelli and Martin 1997; Long 1952; Meier 1993; Rourke 1984). The president selects about 7,000 individuals through the appointment process to help him make sure laws are successfully implemented, government services delivered, and budgets accounted for. Yet high-ranking appointees constitute only a tiny fraction of the total number of the individuals working in the federal executive branch (Pfiffner 1996). Ready to join them in carrying out the president's objectives are thousands more administrators who serve in the ranks of the career bureaucracy. Like their appointee counterparts, these individuals are spread across the multitude of government departments, agencies, and bureaus. Collectively, these individuals are often referred to as the "fourth branch of government" (Long 1952; Meier 1993). They toil away in relative anonymity, but their actions are absolutely essential to the smooth functioning of government.

Sixty years ago, Norton E. Long proclaimed "the bureaucracy is in policy, and major policy, to stay," not only because it serves as an instrument to carry out congressional and presidential directives, but also because it is an excellent mechanism for "registering the diverse wills that make up the people's will and for transmuting them into responsible proposals for public policy" (1952, 809). Not only does the bureaucracy have a statutory role to play in implementing law, but it also serves a representative role, giving voice to interests that may have been neglected throughout the legislative process by Congress, the president, or both. Since Long wrote, many additional scholars have investigated the ways in which the bureaucracy implements policy, gathers information and advises other policymakers, uses discretion in carrying out its roles and responsibilities, and serves a representational role for various groups in the populace (Downs 1967; Golden 2000; Meier 1993; Ripley and Franklin 1991; Rourke 1984).

A primary difference between individuals in the executive and legislative branches is the nature of their role in public policy making and implementation. While the legislative branch fashions and passes laws that ultimately govern the country, congressional members take a decidedly more hands-off role when it comes to putting these laws into effect. This responsibility falls to the members of the executive branch, who often are required to develop rules, regulations, and guidelines to clarify how the laws will be implemented and enforced.

Further, executive branch officials often must exercise discretion in carrying out their administrative duties. An example with obvious gender implications helps to illustrate the nature of this discretion. The National Institutes of Health (NIH) was established as part of the Department of Health and Human Services as an agency charged with conducting and supporting research to improve the health of the nation (NIH 2010). As part of its mission, NIH funds clinical research studies to assess the efficacy of medical treatments on various conditions. For years, however, women were summarily excluded from these studies. In one study of the effects of aspirin in reducing heart attacks, 20,000 men participated while no women were included (Baird 1999). Other studies on aging examined only men, despite the fact that women's life expectancies are longer than men's and have been for many years. For many years, middle-aged men were considered the "normal" patient and research findings were extrapolated to women, even though men and women are biologically and physiologically different and sometimes respond differently to the same treatment (Glazer 1994).

To address the deficit in knowledge about women's health and the efficacy of various medical treatments, Congress passed the NIH Revitalization Act in 1993. The law authorized greater funding for studying women's health conditions such as breast and ovarian cancer and osteoporosis (Baird 1999). In addition, the law made clear that any research studies funded by NIH were now *required* to include women as research subjects and gave the NIH director responsibility for ensuring compliance with the law.

While Congress dictated that women would need to be included in future clinical trials, NIH were left to figure out how to ensure such outcomes were achieved. NIH proceeded by issuing guidelines for prospective scholars and grant applicants that specify what must be included in the research plans and proposals they submit for funding. The actual law specifies that "the Director of NIH shall . . . ensure that . . . women are included as subjects" in clinical research projects and makes clear that cost of including women cannot be used as a reason to bar women from studies,[4] but says little about how NIH staff should proceed to enforce compliance. In its published guidelines, NIH requires that virtually all research proposals describe how they will conduct research to detect any differences between the sexes. If funded, investigators must include analysis of sex differences in their annual progress reports and in their final research report to NIH (NIH 2001). Thus, administrators at NIH are essential for clarifying what the law requires and for making policy to enforce existing law. The use of this power provides them with much policymaking authority.

As this example illustrates, the use of administrative discretion provides public servants in the executive branch with the power and ability to influence policy outcomes with significant consequences for women and men in the United States. Yet scholars have suggested that women and men are not always equally well positioned to wield this influence. The next section discusses this literature in some detail before moving on to an analysis of Obama's appointees and their opportunities for influence.

The Gendered Bureaucracy

Representative bureaucracy theory suggests that having more women in the ranks of the executive branch will shape policy outputs to more accurately reflect the substantive preferences of women in the population (for an overview, see Dolan and Rosenbloom 2003). However, feminist scholars argue that gender greatly influences access to power in the executive branch, resulting in fewer opportunities for executive women to exert influence and exercise leadership (Borrelli 2002; Duerst-Lahti 1997; Duerst-Lahti and Kelly 1995; Stivers 1993). Over the next few pages, I discuss each theory in more detail, highlighting its relevance for assessing Obama's appointees.

The essence of representative bureaucracy theory is the belief that a bureaucracy that is demographically representative of the population, or one that provides *passive* representation to the larger population, will produce policy outputs that are consistent with the diverse perspectives and preferences of the populace (*active* representation) (Mosher 1968). Thus, the expectation is that when the bureaucracy is a microcosm of the population in terms of salient political characteristics such as gender, race, and class, it will produce policy outputs that reflect the diverse preferences of these different groups in society.

Many scholars examine the passive representation of women, or the extent to which women are placed in various administrative positions, to gauge how likely it is that any particular bureaucracy will represent the substantive interests of women in the population. The expectation is that having women in presidential cabinets and in other administrative positions is a necessary, but not sufficient condition, for producing policy that reflects the diverse wills of the citizenry, as Long (1952) suggested many years ago. On this score, the picture is encouraging. Women have greatly increased their share of executive positions as both political appointees and career administrators in the last few decades. As Figure 5.1 shows, women's progression into presidential cabinet posts has continued to inch upwards, with most presidents appointing greater numbers of women to cabinet-level positions than have their predecessors. The same pattern appears in the uppermost ranks of the career bureaucracy, the Senior Executive Service (SES). These individuals work closely with presidential appointees to implement government policy but have permanent positions that are not subject to change when presidential administrations change. When the SES was established during President Jimmy Carter's administration, women held 3% of these positions. Today, 31% of SES members are women (Office of Personnel Management 2010).

Yet despite the fact that women continue to make numerical gains, feminist scholars have identified barriers that make it difficult for female administrators to exercise influence even when they arrive in these positions. In particular, they argue that the masculinized nature of leadership and governance in the United States works against women, making them outsiders or tokenized "others" in the bureaucracy (Borrelli 2002; Duerst-Lahti 1997; Duerst-Lahti and Kelly 1995; Stivers 1993). For example, Camilla Stivers (1993) argues that female administrators are fundamentally disadvantaged because public organizations have been created by men, for

Figure 5.1 Proportion of Women Serving in Presidential Cabinets over Time

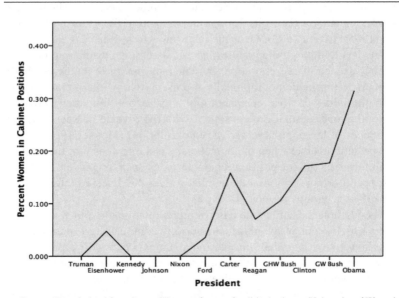

Source: Data derived from James King, professor of political science, University of Wyoming, and James Riddlesperger, professor of political science, Texas Christian University, data set on presidential appointees, with permission of the authors.

men. As she explains, women's organizational realities are quite different from men's because they are essentially outsiders who historically have not been expected to participate in the public sphere. Because women were largely absent from governance for well over 100 years, they did not have the same opportunities to shape organizational cultures or to influence professional norms. In their absence, a gendered bureaucracy evolved that today places incompatible demands on women when they attempt to assume leadership roles.

As Stivers (1993) maintains, the effect is that executive leadership has become nearly synonymous with masculinity. We expect leaders to demonstrate qualities such as aggressiveness, dominance, assertiveness, and competitiveness (masculine traits) so that women who aspire to be leaders embrace these values at the risk of being perceived as unfeminine. She concludes that our "ideals of leadership conflict with expectations about women's behavior" (8) so that women must be able to manage the tension between being feminine and being a leader. In fact, she argues that women must figure out how to manage their femaleness while men face no comparable challenges. For men, gender is not an issue in public organizations—they have long been and continue to be the norm.

Georgia Duerst-Lathi and Rita Mae Kelly similarly argue that governance and leadership are infused with masculinity and that "those who are masculine or who perform masculinity well have advantages in gaining and holding leadership positions in governance" (1995, 19). Drawing on the work of political theorist Wendy Brown, who argues that politics is the most masculine of endeavors, Duerst-Lahti (1997) takes the criticism a step further by arguing that the executive branch is the most masculine branch of government. As she explains, "masculinism is particularly important [in the executive branch], as it places men at the center of executing the form of public power that carries the most discretion" (15). As was discussed above, administrators wield discretion in carrying out their jobs, and such discretion provides power.

Most central to this chapter, MaryAnne Borrelli (2002) draws on the work of these feminist scholars and argues that female cabinet appointees are essentially outsiders looking in, token females who are selected by presidents to showcase their gender rather than provide substantive representation to women in the population. While presidential administrations continue to appoint women to their cabinets, often improving upon the record of their immediate predecessor in the White House, she argues that presidents do so in order to showcase a commitment to women and gender equality rather than to welcome women to the table or share the levers of power with them.

Borrelli (2002) argues that women have had relatively less influence in presidential cabinets for a variety of reasons. First, they have served disproportionately in positions distant from the president's agenda, most often in the outer cabinet. Yet real power resides in a handful of positions located in the inner cabinet: the heads of the Departments of Defense, Justice, State, and Treasury. Three of these departments (all but Justice) were established by an act of Congress in 1789 shortly after the ratification of the US Constitution, and they continue to exert disproportionate influence within the cabinet and upon the president. Yet it took more than 200 years before a woman was tapped for an inner cabinet position. When Borrelli wrote in 2002, Janet Reno was the sole woman to have served in the inner cabinet. She was appointed to her position as attorney general (head of the Justice Department) by Bill Clinton in 1993. The vast majority of women have served in outer cabinet positions that are more distant from the president's agenda.

Second, Borrelli notes that female appointees often arrive in their positions with less Washington experience, fewer political connections, and less policy expertise relevant to their job compared to their male colleagues, rendering them less powerful in their own right. She draws this conclusion by drawing on a three-part typology developed by Nelson Polsby (1978) to categorize cabinet members as policy generalists, policy specialists, or liaisons.

Policy specialists are experts in their prospective department's issue area and are relatively rare in presidential cabinets. Only about 5% of all male and female cabinet members have been characterized as policy specialists. Generalists are defined as individuals who are "chosen from the [president's] campaign leadership and from . . . the president's closest friends" (Borrelli 2002, 45). Historically, the vast majority of female appointees (84%) have been policy generalists. Valerie Jarrett, profiled at the beginning of this chapter, surely would fit the bill, as would Karen Hughes, who served from a powerful White House post in George W. Bush's first administration. Both of these women had long-standing relationships with their bosses and played key roles on their presidential campaigns (Fletcher 2009; Hughes 2004). To be sure, a great number of male appointees also arrive with generalist backgrounds. But the majority of male appointees (52%) can be categorized as liaisons: individuals who have "long-standing relationships with their prospective department's clients or issue networks and with the legislative branch" (Borrelli 2002, 45). With such established Washington connections, Borrelli argues that policy liaisons can behave more autonomously than policy generalists, who are typically more reliant on the president for policy initiatives and support. Policy generalists, and thus most women who serve in the cabinet, operate from positions as less powerful administrative actors.

Third, Borrelli (2002) distinguishes between insiders and outsiders and notes that insiders are more likely to wield influence than outsiders. She defines these individuals as those who were serving in the cabinet or subcabinet when nominated or who have otherwise spent the majority of their careers in the national government. Historically, Borrelli notes that about 47% of male and female cabinet secretaries have come to their positions as insiders.

Thus, while representative bureaucracy theory leads us to believe that having more women in administrative positions will lead to better policy outcomes for American women, feminist scholars caution us that the picture is more complex. To estimate women's access to influence in the Obama administration, I use both representative bureaucracy and Borrelli's framework to investigate Obama's appointees.

Methods

I first examine the extent of passive representation for women in the Obama administration. How has the Obama administration fared in terms of appointing women to administrative positions? What do Obama's appointments tell us about passive representation in the federal executive? Second, I follow Borrelli's lead in looking more closely at the types of positions held by women. Drawing on Polsby's typology, as utilized by Borrelli, I examine what percentage of Obama's top appointees are in the inner versus outer cabinet, can be categorized as generalists, liaisons, or specialists, or have insider or outsider status. If Obama is charting a new course with his female appointees, we should expect to see more women serving in those positions that afford greater opportunities to influence policy.

My analysis draws from three different sources. First, I draw on James King and James Riddlesperger's comprehensive database of all cabinet members appointed from the Truman through Obama administrations. The database includes details about each appointee, such as basic demographic data (race, gender, age when appointed), previous occupational history, and placement in the cabinet. To get a sense of the percentages of women serving in lower-level executive branch positions,[5] I use the White House database of "Nominations & Appointments," made publicly available through the White House web page.[6] Because gender is not specified in this database, I rely on first names to identify likely gender of the appointee. For gender-neutral names, I examine presidential statements or other press coverage to determine if the appointee is male or female. Finally, I draw on biographies of each cabinet secretary to gain additional information about previous policy expertise gained at the state or local level.

Findings

Looking specifically at Obama's cabinet-level appointments, we see encouraging evidence that suggests women are continuing to make gains, that the bureaucracy is becoming more passively representative of gender than ever before. President Obama has improved upon the record of his predecessors by appointing more women to official cabinet posts than did any other president during his first term. Four women serve in Obama's cabinet out of 15 official cabinet posts, one more than was appointed by either Bill Clinton or George W. Bush after assuming office (Center for American Women and Politics 2010). When I include additional posts that Obama designated as cabinet rank, half of which are filled by women, women constitute exactly one-third (33.3%) of the more broadly defined cabinet. Bush appointed women to just over a quarter of these type of positions (26.3%) in both his first and second term (Kamen 2009).

Beyond the cabinet, President Obama has also appointed slightly more women to additional positions in the executive branch than did any of his predecessors. As of this writing, Obama has appointed women to slightly less than one-third (30.1%) of the available positions (White House Database 2010). President George W. Bush selected women for 26% of positions requiring Senate confirmation while President Clinton appointed slightly more women (28.2%) during his first term (Garcia 1997; Kamen 2009). Thus, the Obama cabinet and administration is now more passively representative than any cabinet and administration have ever been before, suggesting women are better positioned than ever before to provide substantive representation to women in the population.

Turning to their opportunities for influence, how do these women compare to their male colleagues? On the whole, there is evidence that Obama's female appointees are a relatively powerful group, serving in influential posts central to President Obama's agenda. Hillary Clinton's appointment as secretary of state means that women continue to have a seat in the inner cabinet. Janet Napolitano also commands a fairly influential cabinet post as head of the Department of Homeland Security (DHS). Obama made history by appointing Napolitano as the first woman to head DHS, a department created in the aftermath of the terrorist attacks on September 11, 2001. While she is not part of the inner cabinet, the DHS's role in combating terrorism ensures that she will enjoy great access to the president. Obama also made history by appointing the first Hispanic woman to a cabinet post when he selected former congresswoman Hilda Solis as his secretary of labor (Greenhouse 2009) and made additional history by appointing Lisa Jackson as the first African American to serve as Environmental Protection Agency (EPA) administrator (EPA 2009).

Additional evidence confirms that women are serving in positions central to Obama's agenda. In national opinion polls leading up to the 2008 election, Americans identified the economy, energy, health care, and foreign policy as their top four priorities, and Obama made these issues central during his campaign (Saad 2008). Looking at the corresponding cabinet positions, we see that Obama appointed women to half of them: Kathleen Sebelius at Health and Human Services and Hillary Clinton as secretary of state. In addition, Obama appointed other high-ranking women to cabinet-rank positions dealing with each of these policy areas. For health-care policy, Obama appointed Nancy-Ann DeParle to head up his White House Office of Health Care Reform (Serafini 2009). Ambassador to the United Nations Susan Rice joins Hillary Clinton on Obama's foreign policy team. For his economic policy team, Obama appointed Timothy Geithner as secretary of treasury. But he also appointed Christina Romer as head of the Council of Economic Advisers, a position considered cabinet level by most presidential administrations. Filling out the economic policy team are Peter Orszag at the Office of Management and Budget and Larry Summers as head of the National Economic Council. For energy policy, Obama appointed Nobel Prize–winning physicist Steven Chu, one of three Asian American men to serve in the cabinet (Gary Locke and Eric Shinseki are the other two).

How do women fare when it comes to their status as insiders or outsiders? Here I use a slightly more broad definition of insiders than does

Borrelli, who counts only those serving in the cabinet or subcabinet at the time they were nominated or who otherwise spent the majority of their career in the national government. In addition to these individuals, I also include all of those whose position upon nomination was elsewhere in the federal government or in Congress. Because President Obama came to office after eight years of Republican rule, I expect to see fewer individuals drawn from the previous administration and more individuals plucked from the career ranks of the bureaucracy or Congress. Applying this definition to earlier administrations, I get virtually identical numbers of insiders as did Borrelli: 48% of women and men have been insiders in previous presidential cabinets by my measure, 47% by her measure. Yet in Obama's cabinet, women have the edge: 36% of the men and 50% of the women are insiders. Hillary Clinton and Hilda Solis are both insiders, coming directly to their posts from seats in Congress. The cabinet includes two additional men who served immediately prior in Congress: Ray LaHood and Kenneth Salazar. In addition, Secretary of Defense Robert Gates was a holdover from the Bush administration and Timothy Geithner was serving as the director of the Federal Reserve in New York when appointed by Obama (Department of Treasury 2010).

What types of skills do these women bring with them? Are they policy generalists, specialists, or liaisons? The most basic definition of a policy generalist is someone who worked on the presidential campaign or is a close friend of the president. Looking solely at those in the official cabinet, more men than women could be correctly categorized as generalists (27% men, 0% women). But when I include all positions designated as cabinet rank as well as the White House staff (such as Jarrett), greater proportions of women are drawn from the ranks of close associates of the president (57% women and 39% men). The overall picture that emerges is that Obama placed more of his female confidantes in positions close to him in the White House and placed more of his male confidantes in official cabinet positions.

Differentiating between policy specialists and liaisons is a bit more tricky. The majority of the cabinet members in Obama's administration have policy expertise that is relevant to their departments: Eric Holder served as the deputy attorney general in the Clinton administration, Secretary of Education Arne Duncan has spent the vast majority of his career working in educational policy, and Janet Napolitano was recognized as a national leader on issues central to the jurisdiction of DHS such as border security and immigration (DHS 2010). One measure of relevant policy expertise is whether or not individuals had any experience in their departments before being appointed as secretary. Here, men in the Obama cabinet appear to have much greater policy expertise. Thirty-six percent of the men had served previously in the departments that they were appointed to lead while none of the women had such experience. But this statistic omits policy expertise that could be developed in state and local governments. For example, Secretary of Education Arne Duncan had spent the vast majority of his career working on educational policy: as the chief executive officer of the Chicago Public Schools and as the director of a nonprofit educational foundation. Thus, to make sure I was not omitting policy expertise gained at other levels of government, I read through the biographies of all of the cabinet secretaries in order to identify relevant policy expertise that might not be captured in King and Riddlesperger's data. Doing so, I found nearly two-thirds (64%) of Obama's male cabinet picks qualify as policy specialists and 25% of the women secretaries do (Janet Napolitano). Only one woman and one man qualify as liaisons: Hillary Clinton as secretary of state and former Iowa governor Thomas Vilsack as secretary of agriculture.

Conclusion

What do these findings reveal about the nature of executive leadership in the Obama administration? Are women still outsiders looking in, or have they made real gains in this presidential cabinet? As the book goes to press in late 2012, the picture is very encouraging. Women serve in historically high numbers in both the cabinet and the subcabinet, they continue to exert influence through positions in the inner cabinet and in departments and offices central to the administration's agenda, and they bring a wealth of insider experience. The only area in which women lag behind men in the cabinet is in their role as policy specialists, but they continue to make progress on this front, too. Whether or not women will continue to serve in such important positions in future presidential administrations is an open question. But since presidents usually do not want to appear to be underperforming their predecessors, I am optimistic that women will continue making inroads into presidential cabinets and contribute their executive leadership skills to the benefit of the American population.

Notes

1. Karen Hughes served in a similar capacity for President George W. Bush during his first administration and was then described by some as "the most powerful female staffer in White House history" (Walsh 2001).
2. I would like to thank James King and James Riddlesperger for sharing these data with me.
3. Because the focus of this chapter is on women in the bureaucracy more broadly, my analysis examines cabinet members as well as other high-ranking administrators such as cabinet-level appointees and White House staff. Cabinet and

subcabinet appointees have received the most attention in the literature (Borrelli 2002; Borrelli and Martin 1997; Martin 1989, 1991), perhaps because their numbers provide the strongest clues about presidential priorities. I expand my analysis to include White House staff because they, too, can be powerful players in their own right and have the ability to shape policymaking from the executive. Further, with the exception of Kathryn Tenpas's (1997) work, there is very little systematic research on women serving as White House advisers.

4. National Institutes of Health Revitalization Act of 1993. Pub. L. No. 103-43.

5. As the earlier discussion of administrative discretion made clear, not only cabinet-level appointees are capable of influencing policy. While presidents receive far more press attention for cabinet appointments than they do for lower-level positions, I include lower-level appointments to gauge the administration's record on passive representation of women more broadly.

6. See http://www.whitehouse.gov/briefing-room/nominations-and-appointments.

Part 2

The State and Local Levels

6

Women in the Governor's Mansion: How Party and Gender Affect Policy Agendas

Richard Herrera and Karen Shafer

IN THE 2010 GUBERNATORIAL ELECTIONS, ONE OUTCOME WAS certain: a woman would be elected governor of Oklahoma and New Mexico. What was uncertain was which party would hold the office since both major party candidates in each race were female. A bit further West, Arizona became the first state to elect three different women consecutively as their state's top elected official. The governor in Arizona has not been a "he" since 1997. The 2010 election demonstrates that female governors are no longer atypical. Yet little systematic research has been done on female governors.

The purpose of this chapter is to take the first step in analyzing quantitatively how female governors govern. We set the stage for that analysis by providing the historical context of female governors. We discuss their career paths to the gubernatorial mansion and find that while many female governors previously held state offices, more recent governors have taken a different path. We then consider the role of the governors and the literature on female political executives and legislators. Using their State of the State addresses, we derive the policy agendas of female governors highlighting the areas they emphasize. Finally, we turn our analysis to how party interacts with gender and the partisan differences between female governors.

As governors, women assume the leading policymaking position in state government. Though obtaining this high office is itself significant, these electoral gains by women at the state level may portend gains elsewhere.[1] Governors are well positioned to ascend a political career ladder and be seriously considered for national offices. Presidents Jimmy Carter, Ronald Reagan, Bill Clinton, and George W. Bush, for example, all served as their states' top executives prior to becoming president. Most recently, several of the potential 2008 vice presidential candidates for both Barack Obama and John McCain were women governors with Sarah Palin ultimately chosen as a presidential running mate. President Obama's cabinet includes four former governors, two of whom are female. We can hail the increase in women governors on many dimensions such as enhanced representativeness of women, successful climbing of political career ladders, and role-modeling for other women aspiring to elected office, but does their ascendancy matter for policy in their states?

Of the 37 gubernatorial races in 2010, 10 women competed for governor in 8 states.[2] Including primary elections for governor, 24 women competed. Women are running for the top state-level office in high numbers, yet analysis of those women who become governor is sparse. Though scholarship on US governors has increased (e.g., J. Cohen 2006; DiLeo 1997; Herzik and Brown 1991; Jacoby and Schneider 2001), there remains little research on female political executives. A little over a decade ago, much of that scarcity was accurately ascribed to the lack of subjects (Weir 1996). Simply, too few females sought and gained governorships. For that reason, the early studies of women governors tended to be historical and descriptive (Weir 1996). Revealing to be sure, but they do not provide the analytical tools necessary to address whether female governors "reshape the political agenda" (Carroll 2001, 2003; Dodson and Carroll 1991; Durning 1987). Though true in 1996, the number of women elected governors over the past 15 years allows for the statistical analysis of their activities and behaviors (see Table 6.1). Of the 34 female governors who have ever held the highest state executive office in the United States, over half of them served since 2000.

Women Governors and Career Ladders

A full understanding of how these women governors impact state policy agendas begins with tracking their previous political experience. This understanding also contributes to the discussion of how women, when they choose to, move up the political ladder. For our purposes, examining their political background also provides us with a set of expectations regarding how they approach the office of governor. While the governorship has long been considered a stepping-stone to national office, it is also a sought-after prize in its own right. Reaching the pinnacle of state government is a tremendous feat and speaks not only to ambition but to talent and perseverance, and, of course, some degree of luck and timing. An emerging literature on women's ambition and career choices is pursued by some scholars of women and politics with an implicit purpose of determining what is preventing women from seeking higher offices (e.g., Carroll 1985a, 1985b; Fox and

Table 6.1 All Female Governors, Their Terms, and Their Paths to the Governor's Mansion

Female Governors	Years in Office	Appointed	Elected from Statewide Office	Other Office	Legislative Experience
Nellie Ross (D-WY)	1925–1927	*			
Miriam "Ma" Ferguson (D-TX)	1925–1927, 1933–1935	*			
Lurleen Burns Wallace (D-AL)	1967–1968	*			
Ella Grasso (D-CT)	1975–1980		*		*
Dixy Lee Ray (D-WA)	1977–1981			**	
Vesta Roy (R-NH)	1983	*			*
Martha Layne Collins (D-KY)	1984–1987		*		
Madeleine Kunin (D-VT)	1985–1991		*		*
Kay Orr (R-NE)	1987–1991		*		
Rose Mofford (D-AZ)	1988–1991	++			
Joan Finney (D-KS)	1991–1995		*		
Ann Richards (D-TX)	1991–1995		*		
Barbara Roberts (D-OR)	1991–1995		*		*
Christine Todd Whitman (R-NJ)	1994–2001		*		
Jeanne Shaheen (D-NH)	1997–2003		+		*
Jane Hull (R-AZ)	1997–2003	++			*
Nancy Hollister (R-OH)	1998–1999	++			
Jane Swift (R-MA)	2001–2003	++			*
Judy Martz (R-MT)	2001–2005		*		
Olene Walker (R-UT)	2003–2005	++			*
Ruth Ann Minner (D-DE)	2001–2009		*		*
Linda Lingle (R-HI)	2002–2010			*	
Kathleen Sebelius (D-KS)	2003–2009		*		*
Janet Napolitano (D-AZ)	2003–2009		*		
Jennifer Granholm (D-MI)	2003–2011		*		
Kathleen Blanco (D-LA)	2004–2007		*		*
M. Jodi Rell (R-CT)	2004–2010	++			*
Christine Gregoire (D-WA)	2005–present		*		
Sarah Palin (R-AK)	2007–2009			#	
Jan Brewer (R-AZ)	2009–present	++			*
Beverly Perdue (D-NC)	2009–present		*		*
Mary Fallin (R-OK)	2011–present		*		*
Nikki Haley (R-SC)	2011–present			*	*
Susana Martinez (R-NM)	2011–present		*		

Source: "History of Women Governors Fact Sheet" from Rutgers University's Center for American Women and Politics (2010a).
Notes: ++ Serving in a statewide elected office at the time of appointment.
** Held an executive appointed position.
# Ran unsuccessfully for Republican nomination for lieutenant governor.
+ Served in the US Senate.

Feeley 2001; Fox and Lawless 2003, 2004, 2005; Lawless and Fox 2005). The discussion of women's ambition is taken up in this volume as well by Lien and Swain in their chapter on women mayors (see Chapter 8). We do not intend to take up the discussion in this chapter at the depth of our cocollaborators. The discussion in their chapter does, however, beg the question of what path women governors follow to the top political executive in their states.

We found that female governors follow one of three paths to the governor's mansion: (1) appointed from a statewide office, (2) elected from a statewide office, or (3) elected from another elected office.[3] Embedded in the first two categories is the importance of holding a statewide office that is proximate to the governor's office. We also found a common and significant political experience that led to those positions, specifically in the statehouse.

In Table 6.1, we show the 34 women governors and their paths to the governorship. This table is an expansion of Dolan, Deckman, and Swers's (2007, 275–284) work charting female governors from Nellie Ross through Christine Gregoire. We update the list through 2011 and indicate the governors' previously held positions. We also highlight information regarding the overlap of political experience and categorize the types of experience prior to becoming governor. The list demonstrates and supports the conclusion of Dolan, Deckman, and Swers (2007) that holding a statewide office is the dominant path followed by women to the governorship. Almost 60% (18) of the 31 women governors held such an office preceding their election to office. Moreover, of the eight who took office as a result of an appointment to fill a vacancy in the governorship, seven had held a statewide office. In all, 80% of women governors were elected to a statewide office prior to ascending to the top executive position in their state.[4] And as others have found, the lieutenant governor (or its equivalent, such as Arizona's secretary of state) is the most likely stepping-stone office for all women who became governor.[5]

Updating and categorizing Dolan, Deckman, and Swers's (2007) work by adding the six women governors to the list confirms their conclusions about the dominant route to the governor's mansion and also suggests an alternative. Three of the six most recent women governors did not hold a statewide office (Sarah Palin, Nikki Haley, and Susana Martinez). Indeed, they all followed different tracks. Palin was a former mayor, Haley, a state representative, and Martinez, a district attorney. Of course, it is too early to tell whether their paths prove pathbreaking, but they do represent a departure from the usual course followed by women seekers of the top state office.

Women governors with state legislative experience are indicated in the last column of the table. While most women who became governor had previous state-level executive experience (and two, Palin and Lingle, at the local level as former mayors), 16 also had legislative experience. In the universe of women governors, almost half served in their states' legislatures. In the sample we use to analyze state-of-the-state speeches, from 2000–2010, 10 of the women served in the statehouse. That represents over half of our sample and is instructive to our expectations regarding women governors' policy agendas. Insofar as their past experience with the policymaking process is important to predicting their future approach as governor, that experience is significant. A woman whose only previous experience formulating policy is as an executive might approach the statewide process with a wide-ranging view. Those women whose experience also includes a legislative career may also draw on specialized expertise in particular policy areas. This look at career paths suggests that women governors in the United States have many experiences making policy on which to base their agenda-setting approaches, enriching our expectations for our study.

The Role of Governors

Among the prominent roles that governors play in state government are those of agenda setters and chief policymakers, an increasingly important role with the devolution of responsibilities back to the states (Gross 1989; Herzik and Wiggins 1989; A. Rosenthal 1990; Vinovskis 2008). At least since the Reagan years, state governments have shouldered more of the programmatic imperatives of government. As this type of federalism continues to unfold, scholars have focused more intently on the policymaking process at the state level (e.g., J. Cohen 2006; DiLeo 1997; Herzik and Brown 1991; Jacoby and Schneider 2001). That governors play a substantial role in shaping policy agendas is evident through their power of initiation. In state policy making, as Herzik reminds us, "governors are the most central and visible individual actors influencing state policy" (1991, 27) and hold a significant advantage over state legislatures in setting the policy agenda (Jewell and Morehouse 2001).

This key role governors play in shaping policy led to increased attention in the scholarly literature (e.g., Bratton and Haynie 1999; Coffey 2005; DiLeo 1997; M. Ferguson 2003; Hall 2002; Herzik 1991; Morehouse 1998; Van Assendelft 1997). Much of this research, however, is limited for a number of reasons. Some of the research on state policy agendas uses a limited sample of governors for analysis (DiLeo 1997; Morehouse 1998; Van Assendelft 1997) or examines other inputs into the policymaking process such as public opinion (J. Cohen 2006). Other research focuses on a single policy area (Rigby 2008; Vinovskis 2008) or the personalities of governors (Barth and Ferguson 2002). Very little systematic and longitudinal analysis is available of the policy agendas of governors or on the distinct role female governors play in shaping that agenda (Herrera and Shafer 2008; Shafer and Herrera 2009, 2010).

Women as Executive Office Holders

Although evidence is limited and episodic, it indicates that female governors do impact the state's executive branch. Female governors appoint more women to office than their male counterparts (Riccucci and Saidel 2001), and those women hire more women in their departments and agencies (Carroll 1987; Carroll and Geiger-Parker 1983). Women governors also appear to be more sensitive to women's issues in the content of executive orders (Dolan, Deckman, and Swers 2007). However, whether these distinctions translate into female governors pursuing a specific policy agenda is unknown.

At the gubernatorial level, studies on gender do not address the policy priorities of sitting officeholders.[6] Much of the research is about candidates. Some studies addressed how women compete in elections (K. Dolan 2005; Kahn 1994, 1996) as well as how voters receive their candidacies (e.g., Fox and Oxley 2003; Oxley and Fox 2004; Lawless 2004; Sanbonmatsu 2002b). Other researchers examined the personalities of women in leadership positions and found that women who run for governorships hold a personality distinct from their male counterparts (e.g., Barth and Ferguson 2002; Winter 1987). In her study of candidates, Kahn (1996) found that women gubernatorial candidates are comparatively more likely to emphasize "male" policy issues and less likely to emphasize "female" policy than women Senate candidates. Those male policy issues include economics and business, central parts of state policy pursued by governors (Herzik 1991). This difference suggests that women governors may focus on the general business of being governor, which is to deal with all of the issues facing the states, especially economic ones.

Governors must deal with an all-encompassing set of issues as part of their job. They are generalists by definition. Neither gender nor party should affect significantly the types of policy categories governors address in their policy agenda. Therefore, little systematic difference should appear in the overall policy agendas of governors. Against this backdrop, gender should not be expected to have a strong mitigating effect on the major sets of policy priorities female governors present to the state legislatures and to citizens of their states.

Women in the Statehouse

While scant scholarship on female governors exists, a wealth of scholarship has been done on women in legislatures. In state legislatures, women are considered change agents who reshape policy agendas (Thomas 1991). Scholarship is clear that female state legislators have distinct policy priorities (Bratton and Haynie 1999; Carroll 2001, 2003; Dodson and Carroll 1991; Swers 2002; Thomas 1991, 1997; Thomas and Welch 1991). Women legislators tend to introduce bills related to health, welfare, and education (Bratton and Haynie 1999; Dodson and Carroll 1991; Reingold 2000; Thomas 1991, 1994; Thomas and Welch 1991) and give less priority to business issues (Thomas 1991; Thomas and Welch 1991). Among their legislative priorities, women emphasize policies related to women's rights, health, families, and children (Carroll 2001). Finally, women legislators are likely to sit on committees related to health and welfare and are less likely to sit on business or economic committees (Thomas and Welch 1991). This research suggests that female governors will likely hold an interest in policies related to health, social welfare, women's issues, and education. Recall also that Table 6.1 shows that many women governors not only held statewide elective office prior to becoming governor but also had legislative experience. Potentially, in addition to addressing the statewide issues that any governor must consider, women governors may find a prominent place in the agendas they present in their State of the State speeches for their specialized interests.

We do not anticipate female governors will emphasize these policy areas as extensively as female legislators because the legislative and executive branches are inherently different. When legislators pursue their policy agendas, specialization in a few policy areas is necessary both for the institution to function and for legislators to accomplish their priorities (Fenno 1973). The committee structure provides legislators with the opportunity to specialize in issues that are their priorities, and these priorities, at times, differ by gender. Female political executives, on the other hand, must present a comprehensive outline of their policy agendas in a way that individual state legislators may not. Governors must address a wide array of state policies without the freedom to specialize. This requirement suggests fewer gender-specific policy agendas at the executive level compared to the legislative level.

Gender and Party Effects in the Governor's Mansion

We know from previous research at the legislative level and from scholarship on how voters perceive and react to the gender of candidates, that party interacts with gender differently for Republicans and Democrats. Gender effects may also vary within the Democratic and Republican parties (Carroll 2003; Fulton 2011; Koch 2000, 2002; McDermott 1997; Sanbonmatsu and Dolan 2009; Swers 2002). For example, between 1988 and 2001 Republican women legislators moved to the right, which decreased the ideological gap within that party and increased the gap between Republican and Democratic female legislators (Carroll 2003). In her study on Congress, Swers (2002) found the behavior of Republican women changed in regard to women's issues when that party became the majority party; no such accommodation to party control occurred for Democratic women.

In addition, the electoral process may result in different standards for Republican versus Democratic women candidates. Although party is a strong cue, stereotypes of women do impact voter behavior (Fulton 2011; Koch 2000, 2002; McDermott 1997; Sanbonmatsu and Dolan 2009). Voters evaluate women differently depending on their party. Voters may infer that Democratic women are more liberal and Republican women are more moderate than they are (Koch 2000, 2002; McDermott 1997; Sanbonmatsu and Dolan 2009). Given voters' perceptions, female Republican governors may avoid emphasizing certain issues or address them in particular ways so they are not perceived as too liberal and possibly alienate their base. Female Democrats do not have to balance such concerns.

This research suggests that the party of the women governors may affect the way in which policies are presented. For example, Republican and Democratic female governors may devote the same amount of attention to policy areas but do so in a manner that reflects their party affiliation. We suspect the language used to discuss each policy area differs by party rather than being united by gender. This difference is reasonable to expect. Governor Palin (R-AK), for example, is likely to discuss educational reforms in her address differently than Christine Gregoire (D-WA).

In summary, we expect that female governors will be generalists when constructing and presenting their policy agendas because they hold a generalist office. We do not expect gender to have a strong mitigating effect on their agendas. While we do not anticipate that party differences will be found in the policy agendas of female governors in terms of the volume of the speeches devoted to each area, we do expect party differences to be prominent in policy alternatives. To test our expectations regarding gender and party we content-analyzed over 500 state-of-the-state speeches delivered from 2000 through 2010.

State of the State Addresses

At the beginning of each legislative session, typically early in the year, governors outline their policy agendas for the upcoming session in their State of the State address. The timing of these speeches as well as the specific policy and budget proposals included means that "they best approximate the governor's actual policy agenda" (Herzik 1991, 30).[7] In addition, the State of the State address is likely the most visible speech given by the governor in any given year and has two targeted audiences—the public and the legislature. The media are also an intended audience of the governor. Most of the public will rely on media reports and summaries of the governor's speech rather than the actual speech so communicating clearly to the press is a necessary step for governors to reach voters. The purpose of these speeches is to influence the legislative process either directly by setting the governor's agenda for the legislative session or indirectly by gaining public support for this agenda, or both. On a more practical level, governors deliver this type of speech consistently throughout all of the states and the texts are public records.

The data for this analysis are the US governors' State of the State addresses from 2000 through 2010. The total number of speeches in the analysis is 518 and includes all the speeches given during the decade.[8] Of those speeches, Democrats gave 48%, Republicans delivered 51%, and the rest were given by independents. The 17 female governors who served in the 2000s gave 14% of the total number of State of the State speeches delivered (see Table 6.2). Democratic women delivered 62% of these speeches while Republican women gave 38%.

Method and Policy Dictionary

When executing a content analysis of speeches—or any documents—the researcher is faced with the question of what method of analysis to use. Traditionally, content analysis is done manually with a group of trained individuals who code the documents. Using this method, usually the sentence or the paragraph is the coded unit. Increasingly, researchers use computer-aided methods to content-analyze texts. Because the computer has to be "trained" to recognize word patterns, the coding unit in these types of analyses is often the words themselves or short phrases. Both methods of

Table 6.2 Female Governors Who Served from 2000 to 2010

Female Governor	State	Party	Number of Speeches Given, 2000–2010
Christine Todd Whitman	NJ	R	2
Jane Hull	AZ	R	3
Jeanne Shaheen	NH	D	3
Judy Martz	MT	R	2
Jane Swift	MA	R	1
Olene Walker	UT	R	1
Ruth Ann Minner	DE	D	8
Jennifer Granholm	MI	D	8
Linda Lingle	HI	R	8
Janet Napolitano	AZ	D	7
Kathleen Sebelius	KS	D	7
Kathleen Blanco	LA	D	4
M. Jodi Rell	CT	R	6
Christine Gregoire	WA	D	6
Sarah Palin	AK	R	3
Beverly Perdue	NC	D	1
Jan Brewer	AZ	R	1

Source: "History of Women Governors Fact Sheet" from the Rutgers University's Center for American Women and Politics (2010a).

content analysis have their benefits and drawbacks. The computer-aided techniques are more cost effective and quicker as coders are not needed and the reliability rate is near 100%. Manual coding, assuming that the coders are well trained, has higher validity rates since words may have different meanings in different contexts.

Faced with these trade-offs, we decided to use a computer-aided technique for our content analysis to efficiently and reliability code more than 500 speeches. The first step in this process was to develop a data dictionary with a high validity rate for our five policy areas under investigation—health, social welfare, education, macroeconomics and commerce, and women's issues. Then we calculated the frequency with which the words in our data dictionary appear in each of the speeches as a proportion to the total words spoken. The resulting number provides a measure of the different policy priorities emphasized by each governor.

We relied on several sources to develop a data dictionary for each policy area. First, we included the policy labels used by researchers who have categorized legislation or committee assignments in their analysis of gender differences among state legislators (Bratton and Haynie 1999; Thomas 1991). To supplement that list, we included keywords used by the Policy Agendas Project (Policy Agendas Project 2006) to describe each policy area, and also the policy words used in Coffey's (2005) analysis of State of the State speeches. Finally, to avoid overlooking any keywords, we performed a detailed manual content analysis of 10 speeches. The resulting list of words became the initial dictionary.

Consistent with other significance testing, we sought a 90% confidence level that the words used in each policy area accurately measured the underlying concept. To test the validity of the initial dictionary, we randomly selected 25 speeches and determined the number of times a word in the initial dictionary accurately represented the policy area being addressed. Dictionary words that reflected a different policy area or had no policy content were stripped from our data dictionary to minimize Type I errors.[9] Words in the data dictionary must be "disambiguous," that is, they should fall within one policy area or another but not both. Those words that were not disambiguous were also removed from our dictionary. Finally, we also eliminated words that appeared less than five times in the set of 25 test speeches because we did not have sufficient data to conclude they accurately measured the underlying concept.[10] The final data dictionary appears in Table 6.3, and the dictionary correctly identifies speech associated with each policy area between 90% and 100% of the time.[11] Because of the care we have taken in developing our data dictionary we can replicate the validity rates typically found in manual content analysis while still benefiting from the advantages of computer-aided techniques.

Table 6.3 Data Dictionary (Stemmed) by Policy Areas

Health	Social Welfare	Education	Macroeconomics and Commerce	Women's Issues
Biomed	Elder	Academ	Busi	Abort
Coverag	Foster	Charter	Compani	Discrimin
Disabl	Suffic	Class	Corpor	Domest
Diseas	Welfar	Colleg	Econom	Gender
Health		Educ	Entrepreneur	Infant
Hospit		Elementari	Export	Newborn
Medicaid		Kindergarten	Farm	Pregnanc
Mental		Math	Foreclos	Rape
Nurs		Principl	Global	Sexual
Prescript		Read	Incom	
Uninsur		Scholarship	Industri	
		School	Inflat	
		Secondari	Infrastructur	
		Standard	Job	
		Student	Manufactur	
		Teach	Regul	
		Tenur	Research	
		Univers	Tax	
			Tourism	
			Train	
			Unemploy	
			Wage	

A Note on the Women's Issues Category

Creating the women's issues category, central to a study of gender and the policy priorities of governors, was more challenging than creating the other policy categories. We know from the research at the legislative level that women legislators introduce more bills related to women, children, and family issues (Bratton and Haynie 1999; Thomas 1991), so we developed a dictionary for women's issues separate and distinct from health, social welfare, or education. We employed the same method as for the other policy areas. The initial dictionary included the language used to discuss issues such as reproductive services, child care, discrimination, and domestic violence.

When executing the validity testing to ensure the data dictionary accurately identified words associated with each policy area, it became immediately clear that some words often associated with women's issues would not accurately capture this policy area. For example we initially included *child* in the women's issue dictionary. During the validity testing, the word *child* (the most frequently appearing women's issue word) was not correctly capturing women's issues but rather other issue areas under investigation— most often health or education. The word *child* infrequently captured the idea of child care for working mothers, as we expected. As noted earlier, words in the data dictionary must be disambiguous, and the word *child* failed this requirement and did not accurately capture the women's policy issues frequently enough, so we struck it from our data dictionary.

As with the other categories, the women's issues policy area dictionary had to meet the threshold of correctly identifying a women's issue over 90% of the time. We also encountered the problem of using words that appeared infrequently but were important for defining the issue area. We made an exception to our rule of dropping words that appeared five or fewer times in the women's issues category. Given the centrality of these policy areas to gender, we retained the words *gender, infant,* and *newborn.* These words—like the others in the women's issues dictionary—correctly captured a women's issue 100% of the time so we are confident with their inclusion.

Policy Agendas in the State of the State Speeches

To apply the data dictionary to the 500-plus speeches we used Lowe's (2011) JFreq (v.0.2.3) program to create a matrix of all of the words that appear in all of the speeches. We then aggregated the policy-specific words by category. State of the State addresses vary in length, so we took the totals by policy areas and divided that figure by the total number of words in the document excluding stop words.[12] As a result we have a measure of the volume of each speech devoted to a specific policy area.

The average State of the State address is just about 4,400 words long, and once stop words are removed, the typical speech contains about 2,145 words with some sort of contextual meaning. Virtually no partisan difference exists in speech length.

Examining overall gubernatorial priorities, the average-length speech includes macroeconomic and commerce policy words the most at 68 times per speech. Education is the second most discussed topic with 45 words, health is mentioned 14 times, and social welfare and women's issues words appear at the same frequency with approximately one occurrence on average per speech (see Figure 6.1). Since our unit of analysis is words rather than sentences or paragraphs, they are proxy measures for the actual volume of the speech devoted to each area. For example, Jennifer Granholm's 2004 State of the State speech had the highest number of mentions in the area of macroeconomic and commerce policy for a female governor with 197 of the 3,875 words in her speech appearing in the data dictionary. To suggest, however, that only 5% of her speech was dedicated to macroeconomic and commerce policy would be inaccurate. Of her 106-paragraph speech, 43 paragraphs address this policy area, and her emphasis on this area is summed up in her first content-specific paragraph: "The state of the

Figure 6.1 Average Mentions of Each Policy Area in 2000–2010 State of the State Addresses by All Governors, Democrats, and Republicans

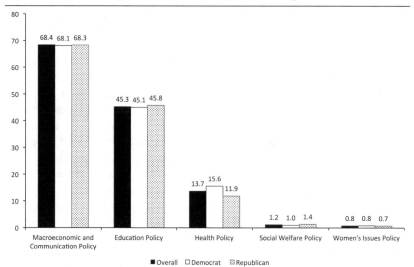

Note: The partisan differences in the proportion of words devoted to health policy is significant at $p < .001$, the partisan difference for social welfare is significant at $p < .01$, and, the partisan difference for education policy is significant at $p < .10$. There is no significant partisan difference in the area of education and women's issues.

state tonight is one of total determination: Michigan will attract and keep good jobs." The number of times a data dictionary word appears in a speech—and the percent of words in each area—does, therefore, provide an efficient way to compare the relative priorities of each governor and allows for analysis of the differences in policy agendas among governors.

Proportionately, governors devote more of their speeches to macroeconomics and commerce and education policies. This finding is not surprising since these two issues usually dominate those faced by the states, especially in the first decade of the 2000s, and is consistent with prior research on the central agendas pursued by governors (Herzik 1991). After the September 11, 2001, attacks, the US economy sank into a small recession. The decade ended with states trying to react to the 2008 recession, the worst states have faced since World War II (Fehr 2010). In January 2000 the national unemployment rate was 4%, but by December 2010 it was more than double at 9.4% (Bureau of Labor Statistics 2011). Throughout the decade the economic outlook for both states and their citizens worsened considerably and grabbed the lion's share of the governors' attention.

Education, too, played a dominant role during this and many decades. Education has always been one of the most fundamental responsibilities assumed by the states under federalism. More recently, with the National Governors Association's role in the 1990s in the formulation of the Goals 2000 legislation to the adoption of the No Child Left Behind Act in 2001, states have been at the forefront of education reform efforts. The increased focus on measuring school success coupled with the priority of education policy and the struggle to deliver it made this policy area a focus of governors.

Health policy words appeared with the third-highest frequency, well behind macroeconomic and commerce and education issues but substantially more often than social welfare policy and women's issues. In the late 1990s the Children's Health Insurance Program (CHIP) expanded healthcare coverage to children of lower-income families, expanding states' Medicaid programs and increasing the states' costs due to the increased number of children served. Moreover, the rise in unemployment added approximately 6 million individuals to the Medicaid program between 2003 and 2009 with the cost of this program being the second-largest expense for most states behind education (Kaiser Family Foundation 2010). Both social welfare policies and women's issues did not play a prominent role in governors' speeches. Given the economic situation in the decade and the need to address education and health care as major policy responsibilities of states, governors may have chosen not to address these areas as heavily as they might otherwise.

Partisan and Gender Differences in the Policy Agendas of Governors

Turning to overall partisan differences, we found significant divergence between the emphases Democrat and Republican governors' placed on health policy and social welfare policy, while we found no differences in the areas of macroeconomic and commerce policy, education policy, and women's issues policy (see Table 6.4 and Figure 6.1). Democratic governors were

Table 6.4 Mean Proportion of Dictionary Words Used in Each Policy Area by Party

Policy Area	Democrat	Republican	Difference	Significance
Macroeconomic and commerce policy	.0317	.0318	.0000	n.s.
Education policy	.0210	.0214	.0003	n.s.
Health policy	.0073	.0055	.0017	$(p < .001)$
Social welfare policy	.0005	.0006	.0002	$(p < .01)$
Women's issues policy	.0004	.0003	.0000	n.s.
N	248	265		

significantly more likely than their Republican counterparts to address health policy in their State of the State speeches. Democrats used health-related words approximately 25% more often than Republicans. This difference in health policy was the most substantive between the parties. Republicans were more likely to emphasize social welfare policy, using such words a third more often than Democrats. However, since neither party emphasized this area, the substantive difference was small.

Considering only the female governors, the same partisan differences emerge. As with the overall population, no significant difference appeared in macroeconomic and commerce policy, education, or women's issues (see Table 6.5). However, more substantive gaps emerge in the areas of health and social welfare (see Figure 6.2).

Of the five policy areas under consideration, Democrat and Republican female governors are more divergent in their emphasis on health policy issues. Democrats used health-related policy words 40% more frequently on average compared to their Republican counterparts. Moreover, female Democrats discussed health policy more frequently than all other governors. These findings suggest that female Democrat governors specialize in the area of health care, carrying over an area emphasized by female state legislators.

The opposite situation occurred with regard to social welfare policy. Female Republican governors devoted more than twice the emphasis to this area compared to their Democrat counterparts. In other words, this policy area appeared more than twice as frequently in a speech by a female Republican governor than by a female Democrat. In addition, female Republican governors emphasized this policy area more than all other governors. This finding suggests that female Republican governors specialized in social welfare policy, another policy area that female state legislators tend to emphasize.

Gender and party differences played a distinct and separate role in setting the policy agendas of governors. Female Democrats specialized in

Table 6.5 Mean Proportion of Dictionary Words Used in Each Policy Area by Party Female Governors

Policy Area	Democrat	Republican	Difference	Significance
Macroeconomic and commerce policy	.0336	.0310	.0026	n.s.
Education policy	.0210	.0173	.0036	n.s.
Health policy	.0074	.0044	.0030	$(p < .01)$
Social welfare policy	.0003	.0007	.0004	$(p < .05)$
Women's issues policy	.0004	.0003	.0002	n.s.
N	44	27		

**Figure 6.2 Average Mentions of Each Policy Area in 2000–2010
State of the State Addresses by All Governors, Female Democrats,
and Female Republicans**

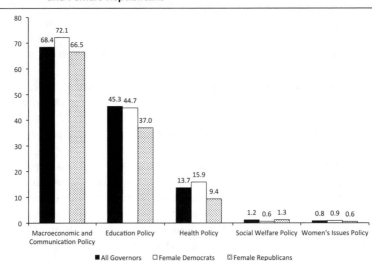

Note: Regarding only female governors, the partisan differences in the proportion of words devoted to health policy is significant at $p < .01$, and the partisan difference for social welfare is significant at $p < .05$. There is no significant partisan difference in the areas of education, macroeconomics and commerce, and women's issues.

health policy while their Republican sisters emphasized social welfare. This emphasis may have been a result of a personal interest governors had in these policy areas. Also, this specialization may have been shaped during their time in the state legislature.

How They Say It: Partisan and Gender Differences in the Presentation of Policy Agendas

As shown above no significant differences were found in the amount of attention Democrat and Republican female governors placed on three of the five policy areas under consideration: macroeconomics and commerce, education, and women's issues. Yet because of the ideological differences between the parties, there are reasons to expect that female governors confronted those issues differently based on party differences. Additionally, we have demonstrated that female Democrats spent more time addressing health policy than all other governors, while Republicans focused more on social welfare than Democrats. These differences likely expanded beyond just the volume of speech dedicated to each area, but also to how the governors talked about these issues. The results from our computer-aided content analysis provide the first insight into differences in how female Democrat and Republican governors present their policy agendas.

This analysis uses words as data points making possible the performing of statistical tests on the frequencies in which those words appear in the speeches adjusted for speech length. Table 6.6 summarizes the words used significantly more often by female governors of one of the parties. In each policy area, certain words are used significantly more by women of one party, indicating that both gender and party shape the policy agendas of female governors.

We have already shown that female Democrats emphasized health policy issues more in their State of the State addresses than their Republican counterparts. They also discussed the issue differently by being significantly more likely to talk about disease, health, Medicaid, and prescriptions. These topics played a much smaller role in the speeches of Republican governors. Another way to look at how women from each party emphasized issues is illustrated in the word clouds in Figures 6.3 and 6.4. These word clouds include all of the data dictionary words in the health policy area and use font size to show which words appear more frequently.[13] Democrats focused on

Table 6.6 Partisan Language Differences: Words Used Significantly More by Democrat or Republican Female Governors

Words by Policy Area	Emphasized More By . . .	Significance Level
Macroeconomics and commerce		
Busi	Democrats	$(p < .05)$
Entrepreneur	Democrats	$(p < .05)$
Incom	Republicans	$(p < .001)$
Manufactur	Democrats	$(p < .05)$
Research	Democrats	$(p < .10)$
Tax	Republicans	$(p < .05)$
Education		
Charter	Republicans	$(p < .05)$
Colleg	Democrats	$(p < .001)$
Kindergarten	Democrats	$(p < .001)$
Math	Democrats	$(p < .05)$
Scholarship	Democrats	$(p < .05)$
Tenur	Republicans	$(p < .10)$
Health		
Diseas	Democrats	$(p < .10)$
Health	Democrats	$(p < .001)$
Medicaid	Democrats	$(p < .001)$
Prescript	Democrats	$(p < .001)$
Social Welfare		
Welfar	Republicans	$(p < .05)$
Women's Issues		
Discrim	Democrats	$(p < .05)$
Infant	Democrats	$(p < .05)$

Figure 6.3 Word Cloud for Health Policy Area, Female Democratic Governors, 2000–2010

Figure 6.4 Word Cloud for Health Policy Area, Female Republican Governors, 2000–2010

uninsur
prescript
coverag
hospit
mental
medicaid
nurs
diseas
disabl

subtopics such as *prescription, nurses, Medicaid, coverage,* and *hospitals* while Republicans addressed *coverage, hospitals,* and *mental* more frequently than other words in this area. These differences suggest that not only was health policy a priority for female Democrats but their approach differed from Republican women governors.

Moving to social welfare policy, an area more central for female Republican governors than any other, the difference was primarily in the emphasis on the word *welfare*. Republican women used this term significantly more frequently in their speeches (see Table 6.6) while Democrats rarely mentioned it.

While we found no significant partisan differences in the volume of the speeches dedicated to macroeconomics and commerce, education, and women's issues, how the Democrat and Republican female governors addressed the policies was different. As shown in Table 6.6 significant partisan differences occurred in the manner in which the governors addressed these issues. In the macroeconomic and commerce policy area, Republicans focused more on tax policy signified by the use of the terms *income* and *tax*. This greater emphasis suggests income tax reform or changes played a much more substantive role for Republicans than Democrats. Democrats, on the other hand, spoke more about the business environment, using words such as *entrepreneur, manufacturing, research,* and *business*. These words suggest female Democrats concentrated more on increasing business within the state rather than tax reform. The word clouds for this policy area also highlight the different words emphasized by each party (see Figures 6.5 and 6.6).

Substantive differences are also seen in education between the two parties even though the amount of the speech devoted to the policy area was the same. In this area the ideological differences between the two parties are readily observable. Republicans were significantly more likely to mention charter schools in their State of the State addresses as well as teacher tenure (see Table 6.6). Democrats were much more likely to place attention on college, kindergarten, math, and scholarship in their discussion of education policy.

Finally, in regards to women's issues, Democratic women were significantly more likely to discuss discrimination and infants than Republicans. What is particularly striking is that neither of these terms is used at all by Republican governors. The predominant issue for Republicans is related to domestic violence.

Conclusion

Overall our analysis has demonstrated some important differences in how party shapes the policy priorities of female governors. While women of

Figure 6.6 Word Cloud for Macroeconomic and Commerce Policy Area, Female Republican Governors, 2000–2010

both parties were focused on the predominant issues of economics and education that all governors must address, Democrats systematically concentrated more on health policy areas while Republicans emphasized social welfare. These findings suggest that some of the policy specialization that occurs among female state legislators carries over into the governor's mansion. However, that carryover is limited. We conducted tests between those women with and without legislative experience and found that those without legislative experience were more likely to emphasize education and social welfare. Among the other three types of policy areas, we found no statistical differences in the areas emphasized between the two groups. Experience as a legislator appears to have a complex impact on future female governors. A more detailed type of analysis that includes tracking the bill sponsorship patterns and committee memberships among those with legislative experience might further our understanding of whether a legislative agenda is carried over into a gubernatorial one and the extent of any carryover effect of legislative experience for female governors. We found that the role of executive as well as party affiliation exerts a much stronger influence than legislative experience on female governors' policy agendas.

Our analysis demonstrates the role of party in shaping the policy agendas of female governors. While in some policy areas the relative emphasis was the same for all female governors, party effects were strong as one party emphasized certain themes over others, suggesting that party and gender played an interactive role in setting the governor's agenda.

Notes

1. Women hold positions in many other statewide offices such as attorney general, secretary of state, and lieutenant governor. For a listing of those positions and the women who occupy them, see "Statewide Elective Executive Women Fact Sheet" (2011) from the Rutgers University's Center for American Women and Politics (2011).

2. Arizona, California, Florida, Maine, New Mexico, Oklahoma, South Carolina, and Wyoming (Center for American Women and Politics 2010b).

3. We exclude from this discussion the first three women who served as governors because of the unusual circumstances of their service. All three, Nellie Tayloe Ross, Miriam "Ma" Ferguson, and Lurleen Burns Wallace either succeeded or ran in place of their husbands. The only other exception is Dixy Lee Ray, who was elected as governor of Washington with no previous electoral experience. We, therefore, refer to 31 female governors rather than the 34 total.

4. While Sarah Palin's (R-AK) previous electoral position was of mayor of Wasilla, she had run unsuccessfully for the Republican nomination for lieutenant governor, suggesting that she was seeking a strong stepping-stone office.

5. The previous experience of women as lieutenant governors (or an equivalent office) prior to assuming the governorship following a resignation from office of a sitting governor is noted in Dolan, Deckman, and Swers (2007, 295; see especially

footnote 15). Regardless of the state-dependent steps to becoming first in the line of succession, the process of succeeding a departing governor prior to the end of a term is the same.

6. We do know that there are no gender differences in the use of the veto power (Klamer and Karch 2008).

7. State of the State addresses have typically been used to measure the policy agenda of governors (e.g., Coffey 2005; DiLeo 1997; Herzik 1991; Van Assendelft 1997).

8. In some states budget or inaugural addresses are given in lieu of State of the State addresses, and we have used those speeches instead. In addition, some states with a legislature that meets only once every two years do not have annual State of the State addresses.

9. For example, our original dictionary included the word *test* as an education policy word. However, this term often was used in a nonpolicy way. For example, in Jodi Rell's (R-CT) 2005 speech she stated, "Yes, it has been a difficult year for Connecticut, in so many ways. We have been tested and we have been tried, but we have prevailed." The original dictionary also included *insurance* as a health policy word but it often referred to auto, house, or worker's compensation insurance. These words and words that performed similarly were not included in our final dictionary.

10. The only exception to this rule was in developing the women's issues dictionary. See the following discussion for additional information.

11. The words in the data dictionary are stemmed so that the analysis includes all versions of the word (e.g., singular and plural).

12. Stop words are words such as *a, the,* and *what* that are devoid of any specific meaning. We have excluded them for our analysis to focus on words that should substantively contribute to the overall intent of the speech.

13. In both Figures 6.3 and 6.4 the word *health* is excluded from the analysis because it appears substantively more often than the other words and dominates both diagrams.

7

Entering the Mayor's Office: Women's Decisions to Run for Municipal Positions

Susan J. Carroll and Kira Sanbonmatsu

SURPRISINGLY LITTLE RESEARCH HAS FOCUSED ON WOMEN SER-
ving in local elective offices in the United States (for reviews, see Flammang 1997; MacManus and Bullock 1993). Even less research has investigated elected women serving in executive positions at this level of
government. Moreover, much of what we know about women elected officials at the local level is based on studies conducted in the 1970s and 1980s
(e.g., Carroll and Strimling 1983; Johnson and Carroll 1978; Karnig and
Walter 1976; Karnig and Welch 1979; MacManus 1981; Merritt 1977;
Saltzstein 1986; Stewart 1980; Welch and Karnig 1979). Recent research is
relatively scarce (although see Deckman 2006, 2007; Smith, Reingold, and
Owens 2009; Weikart et al. 2006).

Several possible explanations can be given for the paucity of research
on women elected officials at the local level. First, in recent years as more
women have entered Congress and even sought the presidency, scholars of
women and politics have increasingly shifted their focus away from state
and local politics, where traditionally more women officials could be found,
to the seemingly more glamorous arena of national politics.

Second, studying women in local politics has proven to be very difficult, especially given the vast number of municipalities and localities in the
United States and the strong disciplinary preference for research based on
representative samples with findings that are generalizable beyond the
boundaries of the specific cities studied. Despite the potential for large Ns
suitable for statistical analysis, research design issues have proven to be
particularly complex. For example, with more than 35,000 municipal and
township governments across the United States holding elections in different months and years (US Census Bureau 2002), nothing approaching a

115

comprehensive national list of municipal officials exists, much less a list of all women serving in municipal offices. Consequently, the problems involved in trying to draw a representative sample of women municipal officials that will produce findings generalizable for the country as a whole are daunting.

Third, an assumption seems widespread that women are better represented in local politics than in state and national politics and consequently that the major barriers to increasing women's representation exist primarily at higher levels of office. Because the United States has so many municipalities and thus thousands of local council and mayoral positions nationwide, it is true, as Julie Dolan, Melissa Deckman, and Michele L. Swers suggest, that "today, women are more likely to serve at the local level of government than at the state or national level" (2007, 187). There are many more officeholding opportunities and thus undoubtedly many more women serving in elective office at local than state and national levels. In addition, gender differences on a variety of indicators tend to be smaller when the focus is on local politics, suggesting greater parity between women and men at this level. For example, although public opinion surveys typically reveal a gender gap in interest in national politics with women less interested than men, women citizens are as interested as men in local politics (Burns, Schlozman, and Verba 2001, 102). Moreover, while an ambition gap exists among citizens with women less interested in officeholding than men (including mayoral office), women express more interest than men in serving on school boards, and they express the same level of interest as men in serving in local office (Lawless and Fox 2005, 49). Lawless and Fox (2005, 41) also found women citizens were more likely than men to have sought local office.

Women might have more interest in serving in office at local than at state and national levels for a number of reasons. Local offices are often nonpartisan, and personal contact with voters is often more important than large sums of money in influencing election outcomes. These aspects of local politics may be particularly attractive to women who are just starting out in politics. Also, women might be more likely to get involved at the local level because the political issues that arise in women's daily lives (e.g., the quality of their children's education, the safety of their families, the conditions of the streets in front of their houses) frequently fall within the domain of local government. Finally, serving in an office that is much closer to home than most state or national capitals might seem more manageable for women with family responsibilities.

Yet despite the many reasons to expect that women might be well represented in local politics, it is not clear that women fare better proportionately at the local level than at other levels of officeholding. While comprehensive, recent data are lacking, the existing evidence is mixed at best. In

2001, the most recent year for which data are available, women were 25% of elected county commissioners and 39% of elected and appointed school board members (MacManus et al. 2005, 121), meaning that the proportions of school board members and county commissioners who were women in that year was greater than the 22.4% of state legislators and 13.6% of members of Congress who were women (Center for American Women and Politics [CAWP] 2011b). However, women, who constituted 22.3% of elected city council members in 2001, were no better represented on city councils that year than they were in state legislatures (K. Nelson 2002). Moreover, in 2011 women are only 16.7% of mayors of cities with populations of 30,000 and above, compared with 23.5% of all state legislators and 16.4% of all members of Congress (CAWP 2011b). Thus, women currently constitute a notably smaller share of big-city mayors than of state legislators and are only marginally better represented among big-city mayors than they are among members of Congress.

Not only do the existing data suggest that women are not uniformly better represented at the local level, but also that, at least among big-city mayors where data are available, the proportion of women decreases as city size increases. While 16.7% of cities with populations over 30,000 had women mayors as of January 2011, women were mayors of only 11.7% of the 256 cities with populations over 100,000 and 8.0% of the 100 largest cities (CAWP 2011b).

Moreover, the proportion of women mayors of large cities has not grown over the past two decades (see Figure 7.1). Proportionately, women hold the same percentage of positions as mayors of cities with populations over 30,000 in 2011 than they did in 1990, and today fewer women are mayors of these cities than in the late 1990s and early 2000s. Similar trends are also evident in larger cities. For example, in 2000 more women served as mayors of cities with populations over 100,000 (17.5%) and as mayors of the 100 largest cities (12.0%) than serve in these positions in 2011 (CAWP 2000). These statistics suggest that more research is needed to help us understand why women remain so poorly represented among mayors of big cities.

Very few of the past studies of women in local elective offices have focused on the factors that affect women's decisions to run for these offices. Researchers have more frequently studied the relationship between the representation of women in local office (especially local council) and various aggregate indicators such as electoral arrangements (e.g., at-large versus district elections), council size, region, and community characteristics (e.g., Alozie and Manganaro 1993; Bullock and MacManus 1990; Fleischmann and Stein 1987; Karnig and Walter 1976; Smith, Reingold, and Owens 2009; Trounstine and Valdini 2008; Welch and Karnig 1979). Similarly, several studies have focused on the impact of women local elected officials

Figure 7.1 Women Mayors of Large Cities

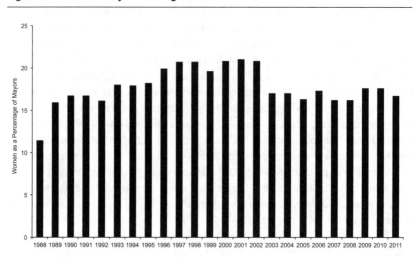

Source: CAWP (2011) and additional data provided by CAWP based on data collected from the US Conference of Mayors' website, www.usmayors.org.

on public policy, public attitudes, or political opportunities for other women (Beck 2001; Flammang 1985; MacManus 1981; Saltzstein 1986; Tolleson-Rinehart 2001; Weikart et al. 2006). In contrast, the recruitment of women to run for local elective offices and the factors that facilitate and impede their entry into local office have received less research attention, especially in recent years (although see Carroll and Strimling 1983; Darcy, Welch, and Clark 1994; Deckman 2007; Johnson and Carroll 1978; Knowles 2008; MacManus 1992).

In this chapter we use data from the 2008 CAWP Mayoral Recruitment Study to help address the gap in our knowledge about the recruitment of women who serve as local elected officials, comparing the factors that affect the entry of women into local office with what we know from previous research about the recruitment of women for political office more generally. We examine the women who are the chief executives of their local governments in cities with populations 30,000 and above, focusing on their backgrounds and their decisions to run for local office. The position of mayor is the key executive position in local politics, and the women who are executives of these sizable cities may constitute an important pool of experienced potential recruits for executive positions at other levels of government. By analyzing the factors that contributed to their decisions to run, we can better understand why, despite the factors that would seem to make local office particularly attractive, women continue to be underrepresented in local politics.

Methodology

We analyze data from the 2008 CAWP Mayoral Recruitment Study conducted by the Center for American Women and Politics (CAWP) about the factors that affect mayors' entry into office. This study was funded in large part by the Barbara Lee Family Foundation with matching funds from the Susie Tompkins Buell Foundation, Wendy McKenzie, and other donors.

The 2008 CAWP Mayoral Recruitment Study, based on a survey of the mayors of big cities (populations 30,000 and above), examines those women who have been successful officeholders in order to understand how women make the initial decision to seek municipal office and how they reach the mayor's office. Data were gathered through a survey instrument that consisted primarily of questions concerning the decision to seek office, previous political experience, and personal background.[1]

We sent the survey to the universe of women mayors (N = 189) and a random sample of an equal number of male mayors (N = 189) serving in early 2008.[2] A total of 182 mayors completed the survey for an overall response rate of 48.2%.[3] A majority of respondents completed the mail version of the survey although respondents also had the option of filling out the survey online. Since we surveyed the universe of women and more than half of them responded, we are confident that our women respondents are reflective of the population of women mayors. However, because we drew a random sample of male mayors, our response rate is somewhat lower for the men, and our resulting N is not large, we are more cautious in drawing inferences about male mayors.[4] We include data on male mayors for comparison purposes but we primarily focus our attention on women mayors. The small size of our samples means that it is unlikely that we will find statistically significant gender gaps. Therefore, unless we indicate otherwise, gender differences among mayors are not statistically significant.

Who Are Women Mayors?

We begin our analysis with a little background on women mayors. As noted above, there is an inverse relationship between proportion of women mayors and city size (beyond 30,000), and corresponding to this relationship, the women mayors who responded to our survey represent smaller cities than do the male respondents. The average population size for women mayors is 80,000 compared with 98,000 for men mayors.

Most mayors, both women and men, became mayor through direct popular election (64.3% of women and 68.7% of men). A large majority of these popularly elected mayors were selected through nonpartisan elections (85.5% of women and 79.0% of men). Fewer mayors, but more women than men (26.5% compared with 13.3%), became mayor after being elected to the council and then selected to serve as mayor by the other council members.[5] Some mayors were popularly elected to council and became mayor automatically because they were the top vote getter (5.1% of women compared with 9.6% of men).[6] A handful of mayors reached the office through appointment to fill a vacancy (1% of women and 6% of men).[7]

Most of the mayors in our study are non-Hispanic whites (86.7% of women and 91.5% of men) with African Americans constituting 8.2% of women and 2.4% of men.[8] The remaining 5.1% of women and 6.1% of men identify as Latino, Asian or Pacific Islander, American Indian, or mixed race.

Scholars have typically found gender differences in family situations among elected officials with women less likely than men to be married and to have young children (e.g., Carroll 1989; Carroll and Strimling 1983; Johnson and Carroll 1978). Consistent with previous research, the women mayors in our study were less likely than men mayors to be married or living as married (73.5% of women compared with 92.7% of men) and more likely to be divorced/separated (12.2% of women and 4.9% of men) or widowed (9.2% of women and 1.2% of men).[9] Women mayors also were slightly less likely to have one or more children under the age of 18 (20.6% of women compared with 24.4% of men), including a child under the age of six (3.1% of women mayors compared with 6.1% of men).[10]

Previous research has found that women public officials, compared with their male counterparts, tend to come more often from female-dominated professions and less often from male-dominated professions. This research also has found that women officeholders tend to be well educated although they are less likely than their male colleagues to have law degrees (e.g., Carroll and Strimling 1983; MacManus and Bullock 1995). We find similar patterns in the occupational and educational backgrounds of the mayors in our study (see Table 7.1). Slightly fewer women than men are lawyers (7.4%

Table 7.1 Mayors' Backgrounds: Selected Occupations (percentage)

	Women	Men
Elementary or secondary school teacher	21.1	6.4**
Lawyer	7.4	12.8
Real estate or insurance sales worker	6.3	9.0
Self-employed/small business owner	7.4	10.3
Other business	7.4	11.5
N	95	78

Notes: Columns do not sum to 100% because only the most common occupations are listed.
**$p < .01$.

of women compared with 12.8% of men). Women are significantly more likely than men to be teachers (21.1% of women compared with 6.4% of men), but less likely to hail from business-related occupations. Both the women and men are highly educated, with about four-fifths of respondents reporting at least a college degree (78.1% of women and 80.3% of men). Similarly, women are as likely as the men to hold master's degrees (26.4% of women and 24.7% of men). However, consistent with previous research and the fact that women mayors are less likely than men mayors to be attorneys, women are slightly less likely than men to have a law degree (8.8% compared to 12.4%).

Just as women mayors bring strong occupational and educational backgrounds to their mayoral positions, so too do they bring civic involvement and political experience. Undoubtedly, their civic and political activity provided both credentials and networks that were helpful in their pursuit of office.

As previous research has found for women officials at various levels of government (e.g., Carroll and Strimling 1983; Johnson and Carroll 1978), women mayors are joiners. Table 7.2 makes clear that ties between women mayors and women's organizations not only are quite common, but also generally predate women's election to office. Prior to seeking a municipal office, about a third of women mayors were members of the League of Women Voters (LWV), and half belonged to a women's civic organization other than LWV (Table 7.2). More than one-third were members of a women's business

Table 7.2 Women Mayors' Membership in Women's Organizations (percentage)

	Member Before Running for Office	Member After Running for Office
League of Women Voters	34.7	14.7
Other women's civic organization	50.5	4.3
A business or professional women's organization	38.3	3.2
A feminist group (e.g., National Organization for Women, Women's Political Caucus)	22.3	6.4
A sorority	21.7	0.0
A women's PAC (e.g., EMILY's List, WISH List, Susan B. Anthony List)	14.9	8.5
An organization of women public officials	9.7	35.5
A conservative women's organization (e.g., Concerned Women for America, Eagle Forum)	0.0	1.1
N	92 to 95[a]	

Notes: The survey question was as follows: "Have you ever been a member of the following organizations? If yes, please indicate whether you were a member before you ran for municipal office the first time or whether you joined later."

a. Depending on the number of respondents, the *N* for each cell ranges from 92 to 95.

or professional group, and more than one-fifth had joined a feminist organization. Notable proportions also belonged to a sorority or a women's political action committee (PAC). Interestingly, not a single woman mayor reported that she was a member of a conservative women's political organization before running for office. The women's organization women most commonly joined after running for office was, not surprisingly, an organization of women public officials, but a notable number also joined the LWV after running the first time.

Women mayors' preofficeholding involvement was not limited to women's organizations. Rather, mayors were active in a wide range of civic organizations before they sought elective municipal office the first time (see Table 7.3). Many women mayors—about one-fourth—not only joined women's organizations but also reported they were "very active" in those organizations. Among women mayors, the most common nonwomen's organization in which respondents were "very active" was a church-related or other religious group, with almost one-third of women mayors reporting active involvement in such a group. About one-quarter of women mayors were very active in a children's or youth organization, a service organization such as the Rotary Club, or a business or professional group. Gender differences in organizational involvement are apparent. Compared with men mayors, women were much more likely to have been active not only in women's organizations, but also in religious organizations and organizations focused on children and youth.

In addition to their involvement in civic organizations, some women mayors were also involved in partisan politics before seeking municipal office the first time. A clear majority of women mayors identified as Democrats

Table 7.3 Mayors' Activity in Civic Organizations Prior to Seeking Municipal Office (percentage)

	Women	Men
A church-related or other religious group	31.3	14.5**
Children or youth organization	29.3	20.5
Service club (e.g., Rotary)	28.3	25.3
Women's organization	25.3	3.6**
Business or professional group	23.2	24.1
Civil rights or race/ethnic group	8.1	2.4
Teachers' organization	5.1	3.6
Labor organization	1.0	3.6
N	99	83

Notes: The survey question was as follows: "Prior to becoming a candidate for the first time, how active were you in any of the following organizations?" This table reports percentage "very active" prior to running.
**$p < .01$.

(59.0%) compared with about half of the men (49.4%). Conversely, fewer women (30.5%) than men (39.5%) were Republicans.[11] Among mayors who identified with one of the two major parties, about one-quarter were members of their local party committee prior to running for municipal office the first time (29.4% of women and 25.0% of men), with some mayors also reporting committee positions and experience as a delegate to a party convention (see Table 7.4).

More common than party activity or civic activity was campaign activity prior to seeking municipal office. A majority of mayors had campaign experience, with more women than men reporting that they had worked on a campaign (62.6% of women and 57.8% of men). Some mayors had previously worked on the staff of a public official, though this particular experience was not common. Fewer female mayors than male mayors had worked on the staff of a public official (14.1% of women and 18.1% of men).

Most women and men mayors held at least one elective or appointive position prior to serving as mayor, with women somewhat more likely than men to have done so (86.3% of women and 72.0% of men).[12] Some modest differences were found in the types of offices that served as the starting point in the political careers of women and men. Among those who had served in a public position prior to serving as mayor, fewer women—about two-fifths—than men—about one-half—reported that their first office had been a seat on the city council (see Table 7.5). While women were slightly less likely to have served on council, they were somewhat more likely than men to have served on a local or county board or commission (35.4% of women compared to 27.8% of men) as their first office.

Consistent with the findings of other research on women elected officials at various levels of office (e.g., Carroll and Strimling 1983; Merritt 1977; Sanbonmatsu, Carroll, and Walsh 2009), the women in this study thus appear on almost every measure of civic and political involvement to have had as much or more experience than their male counterparts before becoming mayors. The only exception is for working on the staff of an elected

Table 7.4 Mayors' Party Activity Prior to Seeking Municipal Office (percentage)

	Women	Men
Member of local party committee	29.4	25.0
Delegate to local/state/national convention	20.0	15.3
Chair of local party committee	7.1	6.9
Member or chair of state/national committee	4.7	4.2
N	85	72

Note: The survey question was as follows: "Before you ran the very first time for municipal office, had you held any of the following party positions?"

Table 7.5 First Office Held by Mayors (percentage)

	Women	Men
Municipal council	40.5	53.7
Board or commission (local or county)	35.4	27.8
School board (local or county)	11.4	5.6
State representative	7.6	5.6
Local executive (e.g., city attorney)	3.8	3.7
Other	1.3	3.7
N	79	54

Notes: This table is limited to those mayors with previous officeholding experience. The data in this table are the first elective or appointive office held.

official—an experience women were slightly less likely to have had. But women were just as likely or more likely than men to have been active in civic organizations and political parties before seeking municipal office and to have held a previous elective or appointive position before becoming mayor. And women mayors were much more likely than men mayors to have worked on political campaigns before running for municipal office themselves.

The Initial Decision to Run:
Sources of Encouragement and Discouragement

We focus our analysis in this section and the next on mayors' decisions to run for municipal office the first time, rather than specifically on their decisions to seek the position of mayor. Not all mayors were popularly elected to the mayoralty, and many mayors had run for council or other local offices such as school board before being selected either by the public or their fellow council members as mayor. Because we were most interested in how people decide to run for office in the first place, we chose to focus the bulk of our survey questions on the mayors' first serious foray into electoral politics at the municipal level. For most of the mayors in our study—and for more of the women than men (74.5% compared to 65.1%)—the very first office they sought was a municipal council position. Nevertheless, a minority (19.4% of women and 26.5% of men) ran for mayor as their first office.

Recent research has found that women candidates frequently need encouragement before running for office (Moncrief, Squire, and Jewell 2001), but that potential female candidates may be less likely than potential male candidates to receive such encouragement (Lawless and Fox 2010a; Sanbonmatsu 2006). Following on the work of Moncrief, Squire, and Jewell (2001) about state legislative candidates' decisions to run, we asked mayors whether the decision to seek municipal office the first time was entirely their idea, whether they had not seriously thought about becoming a candidate until someone else suggested it, or whether it was a combination of their thinking and the suggestion of someone else.

We call those who ran because of encouragement "pure recruits": they had not seriously thought about becoming a candidate until someone else suggested it. The "pure recruit" response was the most common response among women; 43.3% of women mayors were pure recruits (see Table 7.6). One-third of women mayors were self-starters who decided to seek municipal office entirely on their own, and 23.7% of women mayors reported that their decision was a combination of their thinking and the influence of someone else.

Men were about evenly divided across these three response categories, with about one-third of men mayors falling into the pure recruit category, one-third into the self-starter category, and one-third into the mixed category (see Table 7.6).

Interestingly, our findings about women mayors depart to some extent from findings we have reported elsewhere for women state legislators. We found that women state legislators who ran for the legislature as their first elective office were more likely to be recruited to run rather than deciding to do so on their own. By more than a two-to-one margin, women legislators were pure recruits rather than self-starters (Carroll and Sanbonmatsu 2009). Thus, fewer women mayors than legislators ran because they were recruited (43.3% of mayors compared with 56.5% of legislators). And more women mayors than legislators were self-starters (33.0% of mayors and 21.8% of legislators).

We asked those mayors who ran at least in part because they received encouragement about the person who was most influential in encouraging them. The largest proportion of mayors of both genders were recruited by a friend, coworker, or acquaintance (32.3% of women compared with 44.4%

Table 7.6 Mayors' Initial Decision to Seek Municipal Office (percentage)

	Women	Men
It was entirely my idea to run.	33.0	33.7
I had already thought seriously about running when someone else suggested it.	23.7	33.7
I had not seriously thought about running until someone else suggested it.	43.3	32.5
N	97	83

Note: The survey question was as follows: "In thinking about your initial decision to seek municipal office the very first time, which of the following statements most accurately describes your decision?"

of men) (see Table 7.7). The next largest proportion of both women and men were recruited by an elected or appointed official (29.0% of women and 24.1% of men), followed by a spouse or partner (19.4% of women and 11.1% of men). Party officials and organizations—including women's organizations—were less frequently mentioned. Thus, personal sources—friends, coworkers, and spouses—and not formal actors appear to have been most important in encouraging women's candidacies.[13]

Although very few women mayors identified a women's organization as the most influential source of encouragement, women's organizations do play a role in women's candidacies. In response to a separate question, nearly one-fifth of women mayors (19.4%) said that a women's organization actively encouraged them the first time they ran for municipal office.

Potential candidates often confront a range of hurdles in their decision-making about candidacy. One of those hurdles is overcoming any attempts by others to discourage their candidacy. Scholarship on recruitment to public office has generally overlooked what could be called "negative recruitment" (but see Niven 2006). However, we find the officeholders in our study frequently ran despite efforts to dissuade them from doing so. A substantial proportion of mayors of large cities—40.2% of women mayors and 39.0% of men mayors—reported that someone tried to discourage them when they were making the decision to seek elective office the very first time.

Interestingly, however, the sources of discouragement were more often personal than political. Among those who encountered efforts to discourage

Table 7.7 Most Influential Source of Encouragement to Run for Municipal Office (percentage)

	Women	Men
Personal		
A friend, coworker, or acquaintance	32.3	44.4
My spouse or partner	19.4	11.1
A family member (other than spouse)	3.2	9.3
Political		
An elected or appointed officeholder	29.0	24.1
A party official and/or legislative leader		
from my party	1.6	3.7
Organizational		
A member of a women's organization	3.2	0.0
A member of another organization or		
association	9.7	7.4
Other	1.6	0.0
N	62	54

Notes: The survey question was as follows: "Who was the most influential person in encouraging you to run?" Data are presented for those legislators who ran because they were encouraged or recruited (not those who were self-starters).

their candidacies, a friend, coworker, or acquaintance was the most common source of discouragement (44.7% of women and 53.1% of men; see Table 7.8). Women and men were about equally likely to encounter discouragement from a spouse/partner (7.9% of women and 9.4% of men), but women mayors were more likely than men to face resistance from other family members (18.4% of women compared with 3.1% of men). Although attempts by political sources to dissuade mayors from running for municipal office the first time were somewhat less common than attempts by personal sources, nevertheless notable proportions of mayors were discouraged from running for office the first time by an elected or appointed official (26.3% of women and 37.5% of men). Women were less likely than men to encounter negative recruitment efforts by parties (7.9% of women compared with 18.8% of men), while women and men were equally likely to have been discouraged by a member of an organization (18.4% of women compared with 18.8% of men).

Because most mayoral contests are nonpartisan, political parties do not emerge in our study as particularly important in understanding the pathway to the mayor's office. Only 20.2% of women mayors and 15.8% of men mayors said that party leaders actively sought them out and encouraged them to run for municipal office the first time. Only about one-quarter of

Table 7.8 Sources of Efforts to Discourage Candidacy (percentage)

	Women	Men
Personal		
A friend, coworker, or acquaintance	44.7	53.1
My spouse or partner	7.9	9.4
A family member (other than spouse)	18.4	3.1*
Political		
An elected or appointed officeholder	26.3	37.5
A party official and/or legislative leader		
from my party	7.9	18.8
Organizational		
A member of a women's organization	2.6	0.0
A member of another organization or		
association	18.4	18.8
Other	5.3	0.0
N	38	32

Notes: The survey question was as follows: "When you were making your initial decision to seek municipal office the very first time, did anyone try to discourage you from running?" If respondent answered yes, he or she was asked to answer the following: "Who tried to discourage you?" Columns may sum to more than 100% because respondents could check more than one actor. Data are presented for those legislators who experienced efforts to discourage their candidacies.
*$p < .05$.

women and men mayors rated the party as very or somewhat active in recruiting municipal candidates in their area.

More than one-third of women and men (about 37%) reported that party leaders generally supported their candidacy the first time they sought municipal office, with almost no respondents reporting opposition. Nearly one-fifth of women (19.1%) and 14.5% of men said that they faced neutral or divided party leaders in that first race. Meanwhile, nearly half of women and men mayors reported that because they ran in a nonpartisan election, the question of party leader support was not applicable to how they reached their decision to seek municipal office the first time (42.7% of women and 46.1% of men).

The Initial Decision to Run:
An Assessment of Important Influences

To develop an overall assessment of the factors most important in influencing the initial decision to run for office, we asked mayors to rate 13 items as very important, somewhat important, not important, or not applicable to their decisions to run for municipal office the first time. The proportions of women and men evaluating each factor as "very important" to their initial decisions to seek municipal office are presented in Table 7.9.

Two observations are immediately apparent. First, family and personal considerations (as opposed to political considerations) emerge as the factors that are important for the largest proportions of both women and men. Second, women and men mayors are for the most part quite similar in how they evaluate the majority of the factors. Nevertheless, a few interesting gender differences are apparent.

Two of the three top factors for women are the approval of their spouse or partner and the fact that their children were old enough that they felt comfortable not being home as much. About three-fourths of women rated spousal support and almost three-fifths rated having older children as very important to their decisions to run. The only other factor ranked very important by a majority of the women mayors was the realization that they were just as capable of holding office as most officeholders (see Table 7.9).

Even more men mayors than women mayors (84.3% compared to 72.2%) rated spousal approval as very important. However, this gender difference is due to the fact that men were notably more likely than women to be married. Among those women and men who were married at the time of our survey, almost all said that spousal support was very important.

Women were more likely than men to rate "my children being old enough for me to feel comfortable not being home as much" as very important to their decisions to run although almost half the men did so. As noted

Table 7.9   Factors Rated Very Important in Mayors' Decisions to Seek
Municipal Office (percentage)

	Women	Men
Approval of my spouse or partner	72.2	84.3*
Realization that I was just as capable	71.4	56.6*
My children being old enough	57.7	45.8
Occupation with flexibility	46.4	53.0
My concern about public policy issues	44.3	32.5
My assessment that I could handle public scrutiny I might face	36.1	43.4
Financial resources for campaign	34.7	34.9
Sufficient prior political experience	21.7	6.0**
My longstanding desire to run	8.3	16.9
Having the support of my party	5.2	9.6
Participation in candidate training program or workshop	4.1	0.0
Contacts to enhance my career	3.1	4.8
Stepping-stone toward higher office	0.0	0.0

Notes: The survey question was as follows: "Below are various factors that have been suggested to be important in influencing decisions to run for office. Please indicate how important each factor was in affecting your decision to run for municipal office the first time." *N* ranges from 83 to 98. Cell entries represent percentage of respondents identifying the factor as "very important." Columns can sum to more than 100% because mayors rated the importance of each factor.
*$p \leq .05$, **$p < .01$.

earlier, men mayors were more likely than women mayors to have young children, and taken together, these two findings suggest that young children pose more of a constraint for women than for men. This pattern is consistent with the findings of earlier research on women officeholders (e.g., Carroll 1989; Strimling and Carroll 1983) and suggests that even at the local level where officials do not have to relocate or live apart from their families as state and federal office holders sometimes do, the responsibilities of parenting may more often deter women than men from seeking office—at least until their children are older and their parenting responsibilities have diminished.

Almost three-fourths of women mayors rated the realization that they were just as capable of holding office as most officeholders very important to their decisions to run (see Table 7.9). Although a majority of men also rated this factor very important, a significant gender gap nevertheless is evident on this factor, suggesting that having sufficient self-confidence was critical to more women than men.

Another gender difference apparent in Table 7.9 is consistent with this finding that self-confidence is particularly critical to women's decisions to run. Although less than a quarter of all women rated it as "very important," women were much more likely than men to say that having sufficient prior political experience was a key factor in their decision to run. Obtaining more political experience might well be one way women bolstered their confidence before running for municipal office. Not only were women more likely to rate prior political experience as important, but also as reported earlier in this chapter, women actually acquired more political experience than men before seeking municipal office for the first time.

Support for the conclusion that bolstering self-confidence is more important for women than men is also provided by another finding from our study—that more women than men (49% of women compared with 33.3% of men) reported attending a campaign training or workshop.[14] Although very few women and no men rated their participation in such training as "very important" to their decisions to run (see Table 7.9), nevertheless campaign training sessions and workshops may help build women's political confidence.

Several other factors were mentioned by sizable proportions of mayors as very important to their decisions to seek municipal office the first time. About half of both women and men rated as very important having an occupation that would allow them sufficient time and flexibility to hold office, and about two-fifths said that being able to handle public scrutiny was critical to their decisions. Men more often gave weight to both of these factors, but gender differences were small.

Gender differences were slightly larger on an item asking about concern over one or two particular public policy issues, with women more often than men (44.3% compared to 32.5%) rating this as very important to their decisions to run for municipal office the first time. In contrast, women less often than men pointed to a long-standing desire to be involved in politics as the reason they sought their current office. As Table 7.9 shows, while relatively few women or men rated a long-standing desire to run for office a very important consideration in their decision to run for municipal office the first time, women were less likely to do so than men. Thus, public policy concerns seem a more important factor, and long-term desire to run a less important factor, in motivating the candidacies of women than men.

A final factor that was critical for sizable proportions of both women and men was "having sufficient financial resources to conduct a viable campaign." No gender differences appeared on this item with about one-third of mayors of both genders rating money as very important in their decision to run for municipal office for the first time (see Table 7.9).

Although women were not more likely than men to view having sufficient financial resources as critical to their initial decision to run, they were more likely to think that raising money is harder for women than for men (see Figure 7.2). A majority of women mayors (52%) agreed that women have more difficulty than men raising funds, compared with only 21.7% of the men. In contrast, only 48% of the women responded that women and

Figure 7.2 Mayors' Beliefs About Gender and Fund-Raising

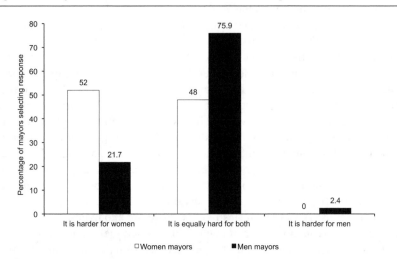

Notes: Survey question worded as follows: "Which of the following statements best reflects your view? It is harder for female candidates to raise money than male candidates; it is harder for male candidates to raise money than female candidates; or is it equally hard for both?" The relationship between gender and perceptions is statistically significant ($p < .01$).

men have an equally hard time raising money, compared with an over-whelming majority (75.9%) of the men. Thus, even though having sufficient financial resources does not appear to weigh more heavily in women's than men's decisions to run for local office, nevertheless a majority of women mayors do not perceive an equal playing field when it comes to money. When we asked those women who said women candidates have more difficulty raising funds about the most important reason why, 36% said that women are less comfortable asking for money for themselves, 30% reported that women do not have the same networks, and 18% replied that women raise money in smaller denominations.

The Decision to Seek the Mayor's Office

So far our analysis has focused on mayors' decisions to run for their very first office at the municipal level regardless of what that office might have been. However, consistent with this volume's focus on women in executive office, we also wanted to learn more about what motivated these mayors specifically to seek the position of mayor. Consequently, we asked mayors to choose from a closed-ended list of responses to the question, "Other than your desire to serve the public, what was the single most important reason that you decided to seek the municipal office you now hold?" Their responses are presented in Table 7.10.

Women's anecdotal stories about how and why they ran for local office often focus on their desire to bring about a change in public policy. For example, Barbara Mikulski (D-MD), currently the most senior woman in the US Senate, was first compelled to run for city council because of her opposition to the construction of a 16-lane highway in ethnic neighborhoods in Baltimore. US congresswoman Betty McCollum (D-MN) first decided to run for her first office, a city council position, when her daughter was injured on a poorly maintained park slide and the local government failed to repair the playground equipment. Former congresswoman Karen Thurman (D-FL) was a schoolteacher who decided to run for the city council after she organized her students to protest the council's proposal to close a public beach (Office of History and Preservation 2006, 737, 872, 876).

Our data suggest that stories like these are not anomalies. As we found in the previous section, women mayors often rated their concern over specific policy issues as very important in their decision to seek their very first municipal office and were more likely than men to do so. The data in Table 7.10 suggest that public policy considerations also played a critical role in motivating many women to seek mayoral office. Both women and men chose "my concern about one or more specific public policy issues" more frequently than any other response when asked to specify their most important reason for seeking their current office. However, this response was much more common for women than men (41.2% of women compared with 26.8% of men). Thus, many women mayors were motivated by a desire to change public policy, and public policy played a much larger role in women's than men's decisions to seek office.

Table 7.10 Top Reasons for Seeking Mayoral Office (percentage)

	Women	Men
My concern about one or more specific public policy issues	41.2	26.8*
My desire to change the way government works	20.6	20.7
Dissatisfaction with the incumbent	11.3	15.9
My long-standing desire to be involved in politics	9.3	19.5*
A party leader or an elected official asked me to run or serve	6.2	6.1
It seemed like a winnable race	1.0	1.2
Other	10.3	9.8
N	97	82

Notes: The survey question was as follows: "Other than your desire to serve the public, what was the *single most important reason* that you decided to seek the municipal office you now hold?"
*$p < .05$.

Meanwhile, women mayors were much less likely than men mayors to choose "my longstanding desire to be involved in politics" (9.3% of women compared with 19.5% of men) as the major reason they sought their current office. This finding also parallels the gender difference we found when we asked mayors to rate the importance of this factor in their decisions to seek their very first municipal-level office.

Notable proportions of women and men also reported that they sought their current office primarily because of a "desire to change the way government works" and "dissatisfaction with the incumbent." However, the proportions of women and men specifying these reasons were very similar. Few women or men (only about 6% of each) said that they sought the office of mayor primarily because a party leader or elected official recruited them.

Conclusion

Recent scholarship on women in politics has returned to the theme of the obstacles that remain for women candidates. In this chapter we have documented the pathways that women take to one office—the mayor's office—in order to assess the factors that facilitate and inhibit the movement of women into executive positions at the local level and shed light on the situation of women in municipal office more generally. While we often assume that women are better represented at the local level than they are in state-level positions, we have seen that it remains unusual for women to serve as mayors of large cities. Indeed, fewer women serve in such positions today than in the 1990s. The paucity of big-city women mayors has implications not only for municipal politics, but also for the political pipeline. Increasing the numbers of women mayors of large cities would increase the pool of political women with strong administrative experience—experience that could help position them to be strong potential candidates for executive positions at state and national levels.

Using survey data from the 2008 CAWP Mayoral Recruitment Study, we have shown that the path to the mayor's office is somewhat different for women compared with men. Women mayors lead cities that are smaller than the cities led by men. Women are less likely to have sought the mayor's office as their first municipal office. And women are less likely than men to become mayor through popular election and more likely to have achieved their positions through selection by their colleagues on the city council. These gender differences among mayors may reflect challenges that women face in achieving executive positions compared with legislative positions. Public officials, voters, and interest groups may be less accustomed to women serving in executive roles. With our data, we cannot determine if the dearth of women mayors stems more from a lack of support for women mayoral candidates or a decision of women to focus their efforts on seeking other public positions.

Our data do, however, speak to the considerations and backgrounds that lead to the mayor's office. Our findings on the backgrounds of mayors are very consistent with the findings of past research on women officeholders at various levels of government. Women mayors were highly educated but less likely than men mayors to be attorneys and have law degrees. Before running for municipal office the first time, women mayors were very active in both women's and other civic organizations. On most measures women had as much or more political experience than men mayors, with most having worked on campaigns for other candidates and having held at least one elective or appointive position prior to serving as mayor.

Consistent with the findings of research on state legislators, women in our study were more likely than men to be "pure recruits"—candidates who had not seriously thought about running for their first municipal office until someone else suggested it. About two-fifths of the women mayors were pure recruits. However, in a departure from research on state legislators that found that women were less likely than men to be self-starters, we found women mayors just as likely as men mayors to have decided on their own without outside encouragement to run for their first municipal office. About one-third of women were self-starters—fewer than the number who were pure recruits, but a sizable number nevertheless.

Two findings stand out in our analysis of the various factors that affect women's decisions to run for local office. First, actors in their personal lives are clearly more critical in affecting women's decisions to run at this level than are political actors and considerations. Friends, coworkers, spouses, and other family members were important sources of encouragement and discouragement for women's candidacies. Similarly two of the top three factors affecting women's decisions to seek municipal office were the approval of their spouse and the fact that their children were old enough that they felt comfortable not being home as much. Political considerations—such as public scrutiny, financial resources, political experience, and party support—were rated as important by notably smaller proportions of women mayors.

In some respects personal actors were as important for men as for women, suggesting that their importance may not be simply about gender per se. However, a couple of interesting differences appeared that suggest gender may be at work. First, we found that women were more likely than men to face resistance to their candidacies from family members other than spouses. Second, notably larger proportions of women than men were likely to rate the factor of their children being older as a key consideration in their decisions to run. Consequently, the importance of actors in their personal lives in affecting women's decisions about candidacy seems to reflect the influence of gender.

The other finding that stands out in our analysis of the various factors that affect women's decisions to run for local office seems clearly gender related. In both their decision to run for municipal office the first time and their decision to seek the mayoralty, women more often than men were motivated by their concern over one or two particular public policy issues and less often motivated by a long-standing desire to run for public office. For these mayors of large cities, policy considerations clearly played a more important role in women's decisions to run for office than in men's.

Notes

We are grateful to the Barbara Lee Family Foundation, the Susie Tompkins Buell Foundation, Wendy McKenzie, and the other donors whose generous support made this study possible. We also thank our co–principal investigator Debbie Walsh for her help in designing this research; Melody Rose and Tracy Osborn for useful comments; and Kelly Dittmar, Janna Ferguson, Susan MacManus, and Gilda Morales for valuable assistance.

1. The 2008 CAWP Mayoral Recruitment Study was administered by the research firm Abt SRBI Inc. Data collection for mayors began in late February 2008 and continued through early September 2008. Respondents received an initial letter on Eagleton Institute of Politics letterhead informing them of the study and inviting them to complete the survey online. This letter was also sent electronically to those respondents with publicly available e-mail addresses. Respondents who did not complete the Web survey after this initial invitation were sent a paper copy of the survey instrument with a postage-paid, self-addressed return envelope. Nonrespondents were subsequently recontacted with reminder messages and additional copies of the survey instrument. Towards the end of the data collection period, remaining nonrespondents received phone call reminder messages as well as invitations to complete the survey by phone. A majority of respondents (61%) completed the paper version of the survey although nearly one-third of respondents completed the Web version (32.4%) and some completed the phone version (6.6%). Respondents were promised confidentiality. At the same time that we conducted the survey of mayors, we conducted a parallel survey of state legislators (Sanbonmatsu, Carroll, and Walsh 2009).

2. We obtained the mayors' names and contact information from the US Conference of Mayors.

3. The response rate was higher among women mayors (52.4%) than among men mayors (43.9%).

4. A total of 955 male mayors of cities with populations 30,000 and above served at the time of our study. We randomly selected 20% of the men to survey (N = 189).

5. This difference is statistically significant at $p < .05$.

6. To describe their selection as mayor, 3.1% of women mayors and 2.4% of men listed "other."

7. This difference approaches statistical significance ($p < .10$).

8. The difference in percentage African American approaches significance ($p < .10$).

9. These differences are statistically significant at $p < .05$.

10. This difference does not appear to be a result of age differences. The women and men mayors in our study were similar in age (with an average age of 57 for women and 59 for men).

11. About 11% of both women and men mayors reported their party affiliation as independent or other.

12. This difference is statistically significant ($p < .05$).

13. In contrast, formal political actors such as party leaders and elected officials are much more likely to be the most influential sources of recruitment of state legislators to their first elective office (Sanbonmatsu, Carroll, and Walsh 2009).

14. This difference is statistically significant ($p < .05$).

8

Local Executive Leaders: At the Intersection of Race and Gender

Pei-te Lien and Katie E. O. Swain

THE STUDY OF LOCAL POLITICAL LEADERSHIP HAS LONG BEEN integral to the study of political science.[1] Nevertheless, in a review of paradigm shifts in urban political studies since the 1950s, Stone and Whelan note the need to "discard some past assumptions, rethink the nature of political change, and give more attention to politically marginal segments of the urban population" (2009, 98). With the rapid growth and diversification of the nation's population from Asian and Latin American immigration since the late 1960s, the faulty assumptions of classic pluralism and its negligence of the origins and persistence of racial inequality have been made ever more apparent. Meanwhile, in their chapter on women mayors (see Chapter 7 in this volume), Carroll and Sanbonmatsu lament that little has been written on local political women in the United States, and the silence is louder when it comes to women in local executive offices. Moreover, we observe that much of the research conducted on local political women in the second half of the twentieth century is implicitly a study of white women (Ostrander and Lien 2010). US political women of color in general, but executive leaders in particular, are therefore among the least known and often overlooked group of political women in any level of government. Their relative anonymity and marginalization in scholarly inquiries of leadership research has come about not just because of their relatively low levels of representation in leadership positions nationwide. Their invisibility is also due to the conventional, one-dimensional practice in political science research on women and minorities that tends to focus on the experiences of either women (who are mostly white) or racial minorities (who are mostly male).

The main goal of this chapter is to help advance understandings of the diversity within US women executive leaders, especially those elected officials who serve at the local level of government as mayors.[2] By diversity, we mean group-based differences marked by one's ethnoracial *and* gender identities. The meanings of diversity can and should include other dimensions of social identity such as sexuality and ability. However, due to data limitations and other considerations, we restrict our attention to racial and gender-based differences and commonalities in this study. Situated at the intersection of race and gender, US women of color are a special subset of women whose political experiences cannot be defined either by their racial or gender identity alone but by the fusing of the two. We address this deficit in extant research by adopting the intersectionality framework that considers the confluence of race and gender in understanding the experiences of women of color executive leaders (e.g., Crenshaw 1989, 1991; Dill and Zambrana 2009; Hancock 2007; Junn and Brown 2008).

Another goal of this study is to confront a prevailing bias in extant political and executive leadership research that pays most of the attention to national and statewide offices. This disparity in emphasis gives the impression that these offices are theoretically more important and interesting for leadership research than local-level offices. In addition, it assumes that women who serve in local-level offices treat these offices as secondary and as stepping-stones to higher offices. By extension, it also assumes that women who continue to serve exclusively as local executive leaders are somehow deficient in political ambition or other traditional leadership qualities such as aggression, decisiveness, and abilities to get things done. In order to debunk these myths, we study the electoral experiences of a small but steadily growing group of nonwhite political women executive leaders serving at the local level of government as mayors.

Trounstine (2009) maintains that studying politics at the local level ought to be integral to the study of political science, in part because local decisions may shape political outcomes at state and national levels and many nonlocal topics cannot be adequately studied without attention to local politics first. Studying local politics also helps illuminate the importance of sociodemographic and political contexts in structuring political behavior as well as the factors that shape the contexts themselves. The trend of devolution, meanwhile, is providing these municipalities with increased discretionary authority over a host of policy issues. In addition, the bulk of the nation's elected officials, including women of color executive leaders, are found at the local level. The sheer number of these offices makes them a dominant force among women of color executive leaders. In the United States, nonwhite women can be found to serve mainly in two types of municipal government with the mayor afforded more power in a mayor-council form than a council-manager form (Kemp 2007; Morgan, England, and Pelissero 2007). This variation in the institutional setup of the mayoral office along with the opportunity it provides for researchers to test empirically the relationship between institution and behavior are other benefits of studying local political phenomena offered by Trounstine. Yet with important exceptions, few studies have been conducted on minority mayors. Moreover, a recent review of black mayoralties finds that virtually all the studies are on big-city races or of particular, well-publicized black regimes (Marschall and Ruhil 2006). Our study helps fill the void in knowledge on the majority of the nation's black and other nonwhite mayors who are from small places.

Adopting an intersectionality framework that considers simultaneously the influence of race and gender in understanding the experiences of the growing presence of women of color executive leaders at the local level addresses a multifaceted deficit in extant research and helps move our understanding of women in politics squarely into the twenty-first century. To more clearly understand those experiences, and to highlight the unique political status and context women of color executive leaders are operating under in comparison to their male counterparts, we also include relevant information on men. What we find is a story that is as much about difference as it is about commonality. These women of color mayors vary not only amongst one another in their political experiences and backgrounds, but also in comparison to their male counterparts. That such differences abound cautions us against the use of monolithic terms like *black mayors* or *women mayors* that threaten to conceal more than they reveal. Yet commonality can be found amongst difference. The majority of these women of color mayors demonstrates a deep commitment to their communities rooted in civic involvement, and in staying local to bring positive change to their neighborhoods and communities, women of color mayors are challenging conventional notions of ambition. Only by using an intersectionality framework can we tell the story of the uniqueness and sameness of our women of color mayors.

Who are the women of color mayors situated at the intersection of race and gender in the United States in the twenty-first century? We begin to answer this research question by deconstructing the meanings of being women of color for those of African (or black), Hispanic (or Latina), Asian (including Pacific Islander) descent in the United States.[3] We review the historical rise of these nonwhite women elected officials in subnational offices and discuss the remarkable growth of the black women in the post-1965 era and reasons associated with the phenomenon. Utilizing a one-of-a-kind database and a telephone survey associated with the Gender and Multicultural Leadership (GMCL) project,[4] we take a snapshot of the parameters of women of color political leaders nationwide by examining the institutional and demographic contexts of their office. Zooming in on women of color (and their male counterparts) in mayoral positions, we further explore in this chapter their socialization experiences, social networks, trajectories to office, and style of leadership through their responses to a 2006–2007 telephone survey of a sample of minority elected officials associated with the GMCL database.

The Rise of Women of Color
in Subnational Elective Offices

Although Hispanic, Asian, and Native American women were elected to a number of state level offices as early as 1923 and 1924,[5] the first African American woman did not enter the state legislature until 1938 when Crystal Bird Fauset was elected into the Pennsylvania House. Despite their belated entry into the US electoral scene, black women have since dominated the small but steadily growing consortium of women of color elected officials nationwide. Based on analysis of data collected by the Joint Center for Political and Economic Studies that started to track the number of black elected officials (BEOs) on an annual basis in 1970, Chambliss (1992) finds that, between 1970 and 1989, the number of black county officials grew the fastest at the rate of 657% followed by that of black mayors (523%). She notes that the share of women among BEOs increased from 15% in 1970 to 25% in 1989 and that black women's rate of growth surpassed the growth rate of black men in the 19-year period. Although all regions have shown growth, the rate in the South is found to be most remarkable (759%). She attributes the dramatic growth to factors such as black access to the ballot made possible by the Voting Rights Act of 1965, the role of African American political organizations in registering blacks to vote, the switch from at-large to district or ward elections in the 1970s and 1980s, and the political environment that mobilized turnout through both negative and positive campaign messages.

The spectacular growth in the number of female BEOs in public office continued into the 1990s. According to Williams, between 1975 and 1993, the number of female black mayors rose from 12 to 95 or a growth rate of 692% (L. Williams 2001). In addition, she notes that black women are doing better than white women in terms of their proportion among mayors, state legislators, and representatives in the US House within their racial group nationwide. For instance, in 1993, 22% of black mayors were women, while only 16% among white mayors were women. By 1996, 31.5% of all BEOs were found to be women. Williams attributes the political success of black women to the civil rights–black power movement, especially the higher voter turnout of black women than black men and the higher support of black men than white men for women holding public offices. Another reason for the relative success of black women in public office holding, such as in the example of state legislators examined by Williams, is the higher socioeconomic profile of black females than their counterparts in the black community who are males or in the white community who are either males or females. Last but not least, black women may have a higher level of political consciousness than white women because of the perceived confluence of race, gender, and class oppression against black women (Gay and Tate 1998; Simien and Clawson 2004).

From the perspective of descriptive representation, locally elected black (and other nonwhite) women are scarce in number regardless of the offices they hold. However, relative to those serving in legislative functions, nonwhite women local executive leaders such as mayors are even fewer in number, and they arrive late onto the political scene. Among the political firsts of black women serving as local chief executives was Doris A. Davis, who became the first African American woman mayor of a major satellite city (Compton, CA) in 1973. Not until 2001 did a black woman become mayor of a major southern city, when Shirley Franklin became the chief executive of Atlanta, Georgia. Despite the ascendance in prominence of office, black women mayors are most often found to preside over smaller, poorer towns in southern states (Jennings 1991). They tend to hone their skills in churches, civil rights organizations, and classrooms as volunteers and teachers, differ from their white male and female counterparts in the experiences of racial discrimination, socialization, and economic status, and generally believe that they have a greater responsibility than whites to solve problems of the racially and economically disadvantaged.

Garcia and her coauthors (2008), writing on the stories of first Latinas as mayors, lament that the most challenging aspect of their endeavor is the lack of documentation and consistency among the few records found. Out of the approximately 75 Latina mayors in Texas, they identify Olivia Serna of Crystal City, Texas, as the first Latina mayor. Serna was elected to the city council and then appointed as mayor in 1979. In 1998, Betty Flores became the first Mexican American mayor to head a major city along the US-Mexico border. Looking at the national total figures of Latinos in elective offices between 1996 and 2009, one sees a 51% increase—from 3,743 in 1996 to 5,670 in 2009 (National Association of Latino Elected and Appointed Officials 2009; Sierra 2010). About 3 in 10 Latinos served at the municipal level in 2009, and 28% were women. Similar to blacks, the number of female Latina elected officials grew faster than the number of male Latino officials—the number of Latinas increased from 907 to 1,814 or by 100%, compared to an increase of 36% for Latino men. As a result, the female share of all Latino elected officials grew from 24% in 1996 to 32% in 2009, a number that is comparable to the figure for BEOs reported above.

Similar reasons that explain the female advantage among blacks may be used to explain the Latina rise in US politics. A study on Latina elected officials in California finds that 61% claim community activism as contributing to their election and 70% served as board members of a local organization (Takash 1993). Hardy-Fanta's (1993) research on Latina women in Boston suggests that their involvement in church and other community organizations may provide a training ground for participation in political campaign activities. Her study finds Latina women define politics as "promoting change. . . . That's political, that's what I mean by politics, that's what politics means to me" (Hardy-Fanta 1997a, 30). Their male counterparts focused, on the other hand, on gaining positions in government. The gender difference among Latinos may stem from the fact that Latina women seek office to address specific issues affecting their communities (Montoya, Hardy-Fanta, and Garcia 2000). Specifically, they are found to enter mainstream politics with a unique vision and set of resources; they bring with them experiences from grassroots politics and from their cultural networks and skills in order to address community-oriented issues (Garcia and Marquez 2001).

On the Asian American side, Carol Kawanami in Villa Park of Orange County became the first Asian and Japanese American woman mayor in 1980 (Chu 1989). In 1983, Lily Lee Chen of Monterey Park, California, became the first Chinese American woman to head a satellite city in the contiguous United States. Chu notes that there were four Asian women who held public office in 1970, none at the local level. The number went up to 40 in 1985, with 11 on city or county councils. Still, Chu finds Asian American women to be glaringly underrepresented in elective politics. The obstacles she identifies are many—from the prolonged immigration ban to difficulties in networking, fund-raising, and public relations—and they reflect cultural, racial, and sexual impediments for Asian women in the US political process. Her study shows that Asian women in local offices often do not have career plans to enter politics, but they have supportive families and an extensive experience of involvement in community affairs. Like other women, many do not run for office until after their children are out of high school, and despite the activity of groups supporting the candidacies of Asian Americans like the pan-Asian 80-20 Initiative, they still have difficulty receiving endorsements from political parties or other major organizations and community groups. Unlike other nonwhite women, they often cannot count on the support of a large ethnic constituency. Their electoral success is often attributed to their individual tenacity, personal contacts, and uniqueness in physical appearance, along with the positive stereotype of being a competent, capable, honest, and nonthreatening Asian woman. Other research on Asian American elected officials identifies issues of racial resistance against Asian candidates, male dominance in officeholding, and the need for both men and women to appeal to and address broader concerns than what is expected from their own racial/ethnic community (Geron and Lai 2001; Lai et al. 2001; Lien 2002; Takeda 2001).

To conclude, we find that the experiences of US women of color political leadership at the subnational level can be characterized by a mixture of both dramatic progress in descriptive representation by race and gender and the relative advantage of black women in the chance of occupying an elective office. Moreover, we observe that black, Latina, and Asian American women elected officials, including local executive leaders, share many common experiences but also important interracial differences. Black women are distinguished in their participation in the 1950s–1960s civil rights struggles and the benefits received from the creation of the majority-minority districts through the Voting Rights Acts of 1965 and subsequent amendments. Reaping from the same fruits of black success in voting rights, politically active Latinas have been keen on addressing issues affecting their local ethnic communities, and like black women, they are scoring more political gains in recent years than their male counterparts. Asian women's progress is hampered by the group's dotted immigration history, relative absence in the early history of minority rights and women's movements, stereotypes by race and gender, relatively small size, and lack of political infrastructure and leadership support networks. Yet these women of color all share a political root in community activism and a commitment to help improve their communities.

Below, we examine the contours and experiences of local-level women of color executive leaders in the examples of black, Latina, and Asian American women mayors who were in office in 2006–2007. We analyze the meanings of local executive leadership at the intersection of race and gender in terms of five sets of factors that may influence the emergence and the exercising of leadership: institutional structure, demographic context, socialization, trajectories to office, and style of leadership. The discussions concerning institutions, demographics, and socialization highlight important differences between women of color and their male counterparts. In order to expose these differences we compare women of color's presence and experiences to their male counterparts (in the GMCL database and survey) as well as to their male and female colleagues serving in municipal councils (in the database). The examination of trajectories to office and leadership styles that follows centers more squarely on women of color in order to shift the conversation from one about uniqueness to a conversation about sameness.

Institutional Structure of Local Women of Color Executive Leadership

Data from the GMCL project confirms the continuing scarcity of women of color executive leaders at the dawn of the twenty-first century. In 2006–2007,

148 women of black, Hispanic, and Asian descent nationwide were mayors. Women constituted 21% of the population of nonwhite mayors. Political women of color who served in mayoral positions constituted 10% of the 1,463 women of color municipal elected officials nationwide found in the GMCL database. The latter made up of 45% of the 3,237 political women of color elected at the subnational level.

Compared to women of color elected officials serving in other state and local offices, the percent female for the mayoral office is only slightly higher than the percent of those serving at the county level (18%), an institution that is considered hostile to the election of women (DeSantis and Rennar 1992; Lublin and Brewer 2003; MacManus 1996). The body that appears to be most accessible for women of color seeking election is the school board, of which officials are 39% female, followed by state legislature with 34% female. Nearly three-fourths or 109 of the 148 nonwhite women mayors are black, a quarter or 31 are Latina, and only 2 are Asian. Up to a quarter of black mayors are women, which is significantly higher than the 15% female among Latino and 10% female among Asian mayors. The highest share of women in every nonwhite group is found at the school board level, while the lowest share of women for both Latinos and Asians is found not at the county but at the mayoral level.

Past research found that women are less likely to occupy the mayor's office when that office is allotted more policymaking power (Smith, Reingold, and Owen 2012). Following this desirability thesis, we expect the majority of the nation's nonwhite women and men, especially women of color, to be elected from cities that are small in size and from systems that are relatively weak in power. To understand the relationship between race, gender, and form of municipal government, we linked up data associated with each nonwhite municipal elected official in the GMCL database to the municipalities that responded to the International City/County Management Association (ICMA) 2006 Form of Government Survey.[6] A total of 1,366 or 28% of the 4,864 nonwhite municipal elected officials are from municipalities that participated in the ICMA 2006 survey. Among these officials, 39% are from the mayor-council system, while 55% are from the council-manager system where the mayor's office is generally weaker in power. This distribution is comparable to the 34% and 55% breakdown of the total number of municipalities that returned the mail-in survey. However, a much higher percentage of blacks are in the mayor-council system (49%) than Latinos (29%) or Asians (17%). Conversely, a much higher percentage of Asians are in the council-manager system than Latinos or blacks. Men and women in each race are similar in this distribution pattern. Because the unreformed, mayor-council system is typically associated with group politics, this finding of the black advantage in this system may not be surprising.

Only 194 out of the total of 705 nonwhite mayors are from municipalities that participated in the ICMA survey. Of the 46 women of color mayors in municipalities that participated in the ICMA survey, a quarter are in the mayor-council system and nearly two-thirds are in the council-manager system. Both Asian women mayors are from the council-manager system, and the percentage breakdown for black and Latina women is about the same. The gender ratio in the form of government is less stark among males. Of the 148 male mayors of color from municipalities that participated in the ICMA survey, over one-third are in the mayor-council system, while three in five are in the council-manager system. As in the case of municipal officials as a whole, black males are most likely to be associated with the mayor-council system (48%) and Asian males are most likely to be associated with the council-manager system (83%).

Demographic Context of Local Women of Color Executive Leadership

In studying the demographic context of the leadership position of nonwhite mayors, we look at the geographic distribution, population size, and racial makeup of the cities where these mayors preside. Grofman and Handley's (1989) discussion of black representation across different levels of government suggests that the South has higher levels of black representation because the South has a far higher proportion of units of local governance coupled with a large black population. Jennings's (1991) study of black women mayors confirms their southern dominance. Marschall and Ruhil (2006) studied 309 cities in 40 states over a 30-year period in an effort to explain why some cities elect black mayors, while others do not. Using a pooled-probit model, the authors find that the South continues to depress the rise of black mayoralties, everything else equal. The authors find the racial context of the city to be the most crucial determinant of a black mayoral candidate's success. Persons (2007) likewise finds that there generally continues to be a disproportionate reliance on the black vote to elect a black mayor. In both 1990 and 2000, more than half of cities with a black mayor also had a black population of at least 40%.

Nearly all prior research paid attention only to big- or mid-size city mayors, providing little guidance on the majority of the nation's nonwhite mayors. As shown in Table 8.1, every two in three black women mayors are from cities with fewer than 5,000 in population in the 2000 census. Close to half of Latina mayors also fall into that category. The shares of small-city mayors are slightly lower for black and Latino male mayors, which are still much higher than those for Asian male mayors. Eight in 10 cities with Asian male mayors are larger than 5,000 in population; both cities with female Asian mayors (Davis and Duarte, CA) are in this category as well. The size of the 109 cities with black women mayors ranges from a mere 102 (Rentiesville, OK) to as large as 416,474 (Atlanta, GA) in population.

Whereas 11 of these cities are larger than 50,000, half of the cities with black women mayors are smaller than 2,208 in population. The size of the 37 cities with Latina mayors ranges from a tiny 32 (Los Ybanez, TX) to 185,401 (San Bernardino, CA) in population. Whereas six of these cities have a population that is larger than 50,000, half of the cities with Latina mayors are smaller than 5,731 in population.

Table 8.1 also shows that the average size of the city's population for female mayors of color is significantly smaller than that for their male counterparts in each of the racial groups. In addition, the average size of cities with black women mayors is significantly smaller than those with Latina mayors. The average size of cities with black male mayors is larger than those with Latino mayors, but not by much. Cities with Asian American mayors, male or female, appear to have the highest average population size, possibly due to the group's higher concentration in urban/suburban areas.

On the racial distribution of the city's population, data in the table show a picture of racial segregation for black and Latina/o empowerment at the city level, especially for Latina/os. Whereas the average percent black for cities with black female mayors is 62%, which is slightly higher than that for black male mayors, it is smaller than the average percent Latino for cities with Latina and Latino mayors. This means the majority of black and Latino mayors, especially women, rely on their own race to get into the chief municipal executive offices. In particular, we observe that up to 81% of Latina mayors and 77% of Latino mayors are from cities that are majority Latino. The percentage for black females from cities that are majority black is significantly smaller, but it is even smaller for black males. The case for Asian American mayors is quite different, for only 21% of males can claim to have a city's population that is majority Asian, while these officials have on average a much higher share of non-Hispanic whites than Asians in their cities' population. These findings reflect earlier work, which found that the majority of minority municipal officials come from places that are majority-minority with some significant differences by race/ethnicity and gender. While both black and Latino municipal elected officials come from places with large black and Latino populations respectively, Asian American municipal officials come from places where just about one-quarter of the population is Asian (Hardy-Fanta et al. 2006).

We find the geographic region of concentration of the nation's female local executive leaders also varies significantly by race and gender. Eight in 10 black women mayors are found to preside over cities in the South. Seven in 10 Latina mayors are found to be in charge of cities in the West—40% are in the mountain, 30% in the Pacific, and 27% in the southwest part of the region. Both Asian American women mayors are from California. By comparison, male mayors of color have a less skewed regional pattern of representation. For example, only 51% of Latino male mayors are found in

Table 8.1 Distribution of Racial Composition for Cities with Nonwhite Mayors (in percentage)

	Black		Latino		Asian		All Nonwhite Mayors	
	F	M	F	M	F	M	F	M
N	109	334	37	204	2	19	148	557
Within each race	25	75	15	85	10	90	21	79
City population < 5,000	68	63	46	43	0	21	62	54
Average city population	17,252	42,292	23,843	41,481	40,897	71,800	19,219	43,001
Black in city	62	58	3	4	7	5	46	37
Latino in city	4	6	70	68	26	12	21	29
Asian in city	1	1	2	2	17	25	2	2
Non-Latino white in city	32	34	22	26	49	57	30	32
Majority-[race] in city[a]	69	66	81	77	0	21	n.a.	n.a.

Source: GMCL database, 2006–2007.
Note: a. Refers to the percentage of cities with at least 50.01% of residents sharing the same racial identity as the mayor.

the West. Among Asian male mayors, 74% are still in the western region, but only 63% are from California. The southern region also dominates the population of black male mayors (77%). Yet not a single state has a higher share of BEOs than the 15% found in Mississippi of the population of black female mayors (and 12% among black male mayors). In contrast, up to 4 in 10 Latino male mayors are found in the state of Texas, while that state's share of Latina mayors is 27%, which is the same figure for California.

Socialization of Local Women of Color Executive Leadership

To help us better understand who among political nonwhite women serve as mayors, we first look at their socialization by examining whether they were born and educated in the United States and asking whether they grew up in a political family. We rely on the GMCL survey to help us understand these individual level factors. Among the 36 women of color mayors who participated in the GMCL telephone survey, 27 or 75% are black, 7 or 19% are Latina, and 2 or 6% are Asian. In contrast, of the 76 male mayors of color in the GMCL survey, only 34 or 45% are black, 35 or 46% are Latino, and 7 or 9% are Asian. Among the 112 mayors in the survey, 32% are women. The percent female is higher among blacks (44%) than among Latinos (17%) or Asians (22%).

Immigration Generation and Place of Education

The three groups of women mayors differ significantly in terms of their immigration status. Both Asian women were born in Asia. All the 27 black women belong to the fourth or more generation in the United States. The immigration generation status of Latinas is spread out more evenly across immigration generations. There are also major gender differences among Asians and Latinos in that only 43% of Asian men are foreign born while none of the Latinos are foreign born. A higher percentage of both Asian and Latino men are found in the second or higher generation than their female counterparts. All of the Asian men were educated mainly outside of the United States. Two of the six Latinas, two black men, and one Asian woman also indicated their having non-US-based education.

Political Family

Growing up in a political family has been found to be one of the strong predictors of political participation among US political women. For example, a comparison of political ambition among black and white women finds that both sets of women report unconventional sex role education in their backgrounds (Perkins 1986). In the GMCL survey, as high as half of black women and both Asian women were raised in a political family, but only one-third of Latinas claim to have this socialization background. A study of locally elected Latinas suggests a possible reason: for these women, becoming political was a process of social awakening, and the Latinos in the study had relatively little to say on the matter of developing a political self (Hardy-Fanta 1997b, 225). The data presented here also highlights the divergent experiences between men and women as a much higher percentage of Latino (46%) than black (16%) or Asian (14%) men were raised in a political family.

Trajectories to Office of Local Women of Color Executive Leadership

While the previous sections seek to highlight differences between women of varying ethnoracial backgrounds, the patterns that emerge from the discussion in the following two sections highlight experiences that women of color share with one another. In this section, relying again on the GMCL survey, we explore women of color's trajectories to office and then, in the final section, round off the conversation with a consideration of women of color's leadership styles. The question asked presently is how do women of color mayors get into that leadership position? To answer that question we examine women of color's motivation to run for office and their degree of civic engagement and prior officeholding as well as their campaign experiences. In keeping with prior research, the following examination suggests that, rather than abiding by traditional pipeline approaches, women's officeholding is often a culmination of years of community activism (Chu 1989; Fox and Schuhmann 1999; Rosser-Mims 2005).

Initial Political Motivation

Respondents in the GMCL survey were asked to indicate the most important reason influencing their decision to run for public office the very first time. Among the 36 women of color mayors in the survey, the most commonly mentioned primary reason is the desire to serve the community (64%). The mayor of Port Gibson, Mississippi, states, "I wanted to serve my community and I wanted to bridge the community together according to the racial mix up." In the Midwest, the mayor of Arcadia, Oklahoma, sees the need for leadership in her community and out west in Duarte, California, the mayor has similar concerns expressed in her belief that she can make things better in her community.

The desire to address an issue was the second most frequently cited motivator (44%) among the women of color respondents. The mayor of San Luis, Arizona, cites concerns over the quality of water in her community as motivating her to run for office and in Sunflower, Mississippi, the mayor's call to action came in the issues of poverty, schools, and the lack of proper roads. Other reasons such as a desire to make a difference/promote change, a desire to provide better representation, and personal ambition or qualification are mentioned by about a quarter of the respondents. Only one in six women mentions being encouraged or recruited to run, and they are all black.

Degree of Prior Involvement in Civic Organizations

Data in Table 8.2 demonstrate that black, Latina, and Asian women express high degrees of community activism as part of their politicization. In a scale from 0 to 10, the scores range from 7.4 for black females, to 8.3 for Latinas, and 9.0 for Asian females. Involvement in Parent Teacher Associations (PTAs) or Parent Teacher Organizations (PTOs) receives the second-highest scores among black females and Latinas. For Asian females, their highest score is with election campaign organizations. Civil rights organizations receive the next highest score among black women, but it is not among the top-ranked organizations for other racial and gender groups. Instead, political party organization is the third most popular type of civic organization that involved our Latina mayors. Women's organizations attracted participation but only by women. Taken as a whole, the last row of Table 8.2 shows that women of color mayors in each race report on average higher levels of prior civic organizational engagement than their male counterparts.

Prior Officeholding

Civic organizations can be a particularly important source of politicization for women of color given that nearly 4 in 10 nonwhite women mayors in the survey are in public office for the first time. Among those who served before, 52% among blacks and 43% among Latinas are found to have held their first elective office on the city council (or the equivalent municipal positions). This finding confirms past observations that women mayoral candidates emerge from the ranks of city council members (MacManus and Bullock 1999; Smith, Reingold, and Owen 2012). Scarcely any women of color mayors began their elective service on the school board or at the county level. Over half of the women of color mayors held appointed positions before. A higher percentage of Latinas (71%) than blacks (52%) did so. However, a higher percentage of blacks (24%) than Latinas (14%) report holding three or more appointed positions before. Only three women, all black, served on the staff of an elected official prior to their first bid for office.

Table 8.2 Degree of Prior Involvement in Civic Institutions Among Nonwhite Mayors (mean)

	Black		Latino		Asian		All Nonwhite Mayors	
	F	M	F	M	F	M	F	M
Neighborhood/community org.	7.4	7.5	8.3	6.3	9.0	7.4	7.7	6.9
PTA/PTO	7.4	6.6	6.6	4.9	8.0	4.0	7.3	5.6
Civil rights organization	6.7	6.0	4.3	3.1	5.0	3.4	6.1	4.4
Political party organization	6.0	6.1	6.3	5.5	5.0	3.9	6.0	5.6
Women's organization	6.2	2.2	4.0	1.8	8.5	2.4	5.9	2.0
Election campaign	5.2	6.2	6.3	5.7	10.0	4.7	5.7	5.8
Faith-based organization	5.7	6.0	5.0	3.7	5.5	3.6	5.6	4.7
Business group	5.1	5.2	5.1	5.3	6.5	4.0	5.2	5.1
Labor union	2.7	2.1	1.1	2.9	3.0	1.3	2.4	2.4
Index of prior involvement	5.8	5.3	5.2	4.3	6.7	3.8	5.8	4.7

Source: GMCL survey, 2006–2007.

Campaign Status and Competitiveness

Experiences in civic organizations and with prior officeholding, often on the city council, coupled with a desire to help the community may encourage these political women to set out on the campaign trail. In their most recent run for the current office, over half of black women and both Asian women, but only two in seven Latinas, ran as incumbents. The majority of Latinas ran in open-seat elections (57%), which is significantly higher than the 31% among black women. Incumbency characterizes the campaign status of the majority of every group of nonwhite men, with Latinos having the highest share at 66%. In their most recent general election campaigns, just over half of black and Latina women mayors indicate that their margin of victory over their closest opponent was greater than 10%. About 1 in 10 in each group ran unopposed. Compared to their female counterparts, males enjoyed a wider margin of victory over their closest opponent: 86% among Asians, 73% among blacks, and 77% among Latinos. About one in nine ran unopposed. The findings suggest that, as a group, women of color face greater electoral uncertainty than their male counterparts given the drag of incumbency and women of color's smaller margins of victory.

Style of Leadership by Local Executive Women of Color

Once in office, one might wonder if women of color mayors have a distinctive style of leadership from their male counterparts. One might also wonder about how women of color mayors conceive of their leadership role. In this empirical exploration of the last set of factors of local executive leadership, we studied their survey responses to a question probing for their concept of the representational role: in a situation when the views of constituents conflict with the elected official, whether it is more important that a mayor's vote reflect the views of constituents or the official's own informed judgment of what is best for the constituency. We also studied whether racial and gender differences occur in the patterns of their perception of gender differences in the style of governance and career ambitions. What we found is that the women of color surveyed consider themselves as trustees and consensus builders committed to serving their communities.

Concept of Representational Role

When given a scenario when the elected official's personal view is in conflict with his or her own perception of constituent opinion in a voting decision, over three in five respondents (63%) who hold mayoral offices believe that it is more important that the vote reflect the official's informed judgment and trust that constituents will support the decision (the trustee role). Only a quarter believe that it is more important that the vote reflect the views of constituents (the delegate role). Among women of color mayors, a higher percentage of Latinas (71%) than blacks (63%) identify with the trustee role. The popularity of the trustee concept of representation is also observed among women state legislators who may wish to avoid the negative connotations of "passiveness, subservience, weak leadership, and indecisiveness" associated with the delegate role (Reingold 2008b, 134).

Perceived Gendered Style of Governance

When asked to assess (from a list of prepared statements) the possible differences in the style of governance between women and men who serve in elective office, women of color mayors in the survey were found to be significantly more likely than male mayors of color to agree or strongly agree with the statements that women elected officials are better able to achieve consensus and to work harder than their male counterparts. Black men and women alike, but a higher percentage of Latinas than Latinos, would agree or strongly agree with the statements that female elected officials are more persuasive and are less interested in being in the limelight than in getting the job done. Conversely, a higher percentage of Latino than Latina mayors (31% vs. 14%) would agree or strongly agree to the statement that female elected officials are more likely to conduct policymaking behind closed doors than their male counterparts. Intriguingly, on this last statement, a slightly higher percentage of black females than males (26% vs. 20%) and as high as 43% among Asian men would also show support for this negative perception of women leaders.

Career Ambition

The received wisdom in the prevailing literature suggests that (predominantly white) women who serve in national or state-level offices usually get there as a result of moving up the career ladder. For example, Dolan, Deckman, and Swers (2007) highlight the case of former San Francisco mayor now US senator Dianne Feinstein. However, data in Figure 8.1 suggest that local women of color executive leaders do not treat their job as a springboard to a higher office. In a scale from 0 to 10 with 10 indicating the highest likelihood of running for a higher office, the average score for these women is less than 3, with Latinas having lower and Asians having higher scores than blacks. Not surprisingly, each group of men has a higher average score than its female counterpart. Women's relatively lower progressive ambition may be tied to the high interest and commitment to serving the local community. This idea is supported by stories on Latina mayors in a

Figure 8.1 Ambition for Higher Office Among Nonwhite Mayors (mean)

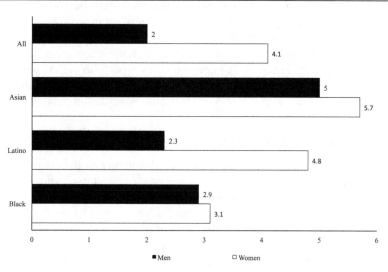

Source: GMCL survey, 2006–2007.

recent study of Latina officeholders in Texas (Garcia et al. 2008). These mayors did not see the office of mayor as a stepping-stone as did Dianne Feinstein. Rather, their goal, or the direction of their ambition, was to improve quality of life in their communities.

Conclusion

The study presented here aimed to accomplish two primary goals. The first was to advance our understanding of the diversity within US executive leaders by examining oft-overlooked executives who sit at the intersection of race and gender. The second goal was to confront a long-standing bias in the literature that treats federal and state-level office as somehow more important, more theoretically interesting, or both by debunking myths based on that framework. Examining women of color mayors along the dimensions of institutional structure, demographic context, socialization and social networks, trajectories to office, and styles of leadership has not only furthered our understanding of these pioneers in the rough and tumble world of local politics but also pointed to how we may begin deconstructing myths promulgated by insufficient scholarly attention to local politics and intersectionality.

The snapshot offered here reveals several conclusions we may draw with respect to the experiences of women of color mayors. To begin, women of color are most often found in executive leadership positions that are comparatively weak in political power, highlighting the challenges faced by those at the intersection of race and gender. The mayoral positions these women often hold are council-manager positions, which deny them veto powers. Moreover, they often preside over cities that are small in population and far from the national limelight. These women often hone their political skills in civic organizations before making their bid for office and, likely resulting from that engagement, cite service to the community as their primary motivation for office. Once in office, they report governing as trustees and project their efforts outwards into the community rather than treating their office as a stepping-stone for higher political office.

That women of color mayors do not see their office as a stepping-stone has implications for traditional theories of political ambition that have been developed from the utilitarian perspective of rational *men* and from *male* career patterns (Burt-Way and Kelly 1992: Fowlkes 1984). For example, Lawless and Fox (2010b) find that the gender gap between male and female officeholders increases with the stature of the level of office. The authors point to the burdens that traditional family roles place on women, a masculine ethos of politics that lessens the likelihood of their recruitment, and a belief among women that they must be extraqualified to win office as explanations for the gender gap in elected office. However, the authors take the career ladder approach to ambition as normative and neutral rather than treating it as a gendered standard of ambition. If we allow for the career ladder standard of ambition to be an inherently male standard of ambition, then Lawless and Fox may instead be explaining why female ambition does not map the pattern of male ambition rather than explaining why women lack ambition.

Not only have conceptions of ambition been developed from a primarily male perspective. Scholarly inattention to the ambitions of activists at the local level, particularly along racial lines, may lead to erroneous conclusions for people's motivations for engaging in politics (R. Moore 2005). Political women of color who "fail" to use the office of mayor as a stepping-stone are derided as lacking ambition by a framework rooted in white male experiences of political advancement. That political women of color focus their energies outward into the community rather than upwards into higher office suggests that ambition may not be unidimensional and instead points to the need for new articulations of ambition that account for these women's experiences. Further examination of local political women of color is essential if we are to deconstruct taken-for-granted myths like political ambition.

However, while these political women of color share some similar experiences on the road to executive leadership, treating women of color in the same monolithic fashion that scholars have treated political women generally will only further obstruct our view of the opportunities and obstacles they confront on the way to office. For example, Latina mayors are found primarily in the West, black women mayors in the South, and the two Asian female mayors in California. This regional differentiation means that these women confront very different political cultures in their bids for office. Asian women cannot rely on the votes of their ethnic group in the way that their black and Latina counterparts are, raising implications for electoral strategies. Other dissimilarities abound. These dissimilarities afford us great opportunities to further our understanding of executive leadership, an understanding that is likely to challenge conventional wisdom on, and lead to new articulations of, political leaders.

Notes

1. We appreciate an anonymous reviewer for pointing us to this fact.

2. Individuals who hold positions as mayors, vice-mayors, mayors pro tem, deputy mayors, or council mayors are collectively referred to in the chapter as mayors. We appreciate comments made by colleagues Christine Sierra, Dianne Pinderhughes, Carol Hardy-Fanta, and the book editor to improve an earlier draft.

3. Although we fully understand the need to include Native American or American Indian women in the discussion, and we will do our best whenever relevant, our ability to do so is hampered by the lack of both extant literature and empirical data on this group of women elected officials in executive positions. The research challenge may be directly linked to the group's settlement on reservations or in urban areas that are not necessarily in communities of large numbers.

4. The 2006–2007 GMCL survey is a systematic telephone survey of a sample of elected officials of color holding four levels of subnational offices across the 50 states of America who were identified in the GMCL database. It is the first multicultural, multioffice, nationwide survey of women and men of color elected officials serving at state, county, municipal, and school board levels of office in the United States. For information on the database, see Hardy-Fanta and colleagues (2007). For more details of the survey methodology, see Appendix A in Pinderhughes and colleagues (2009).

5. Soledad Chacon (NM) was the first woman and Latina to be elected into a statewide office in 1923. In 1924, Cora Belle Reynolds Anderson (MI) became the first Native American woman, and Rosalie Keliinoi (Territory of Hawaii) became the first Asian Pacific Islander American woman elected to the lower house of a state legislature. For more information, see Ong (2003).

6. The Form of Government Survey has been conducted by the ICMA for more than 30 years. This survey gathers the most comprehensive information available on form of government, election systems, provisions for referendum/recall, and term limits. In addition, it collects information on characteristics of the local governing body. In the 2006 survey, 3,864 of the 8,278 municipalities responded to the survey, resulting in a response rate of 46.7%.

Part 3

Challenges for Women Executives

9

Barriers Bent but Not Broken: Newspaper Coverage of Local and State Elections

Dianne Bystrom, Narren Brown, and Megan Fiddelke

Previous research shows differences in how the media covers female and male candidates running for political office, especially in the way they are framed and the images and issues with which they are associated. Most studies to date examine women and men running for legislative office, usually the US Senate. Some studies have looked at the media coverage of women and men running for executive office, primarily for governor and, more recently, US president. These studies suggest that the media coverage of legislative candidates as well as women running for state executive office has become less gendered over time, whereas the coverage of women running for president continues to reveal sex stereotypes and biases.

This study breaks new ground by focusing on the media coverage of women running for local and state executive office in 2008. Whereas most gender research on the 2008 campaign has focused on Hillary Clinton's presidential and Sarah Palin's vice presidential campaigns, we are interested in how newspapers covered women running for mayor and governor that year. Did the women running for local and state executive office in 2008 receive gendered coverage comparable to Clinton and Palin? Or was their coverage more equitable and gender neutral in keeping with the findings of recent research on female versus male mayoral and gubernatorial races?

Through a content analysis of state and local newspapers, we examine the coverage of the four women who ran for governor in 2008 (two winners and two losers) and their male opponents and a sample of six women who ran for mayor of cities of 100,000 or more in 2008 (three winners and three losers) and their male opponents. Little research exists on women mayor candidates, especially their media coverage.

Our analysis compares and contrasts female versus male media coverage for gubernatorial and mayoral races, especially the images and issues with which they are associated and the way in which they are framed. We also compare the coverage of women gubernatorial candidates to women mayoral candidates to see if they are covered similarly—or differently—by the media, particularly as scholars have speculated that governors deal with a mix of "feminine" issues (such as education and health care) and "masculine" issues (such as crime, taxes, and the economy) whereas mayors are responsible for more "masculine" issues (such as crime, construction, and law enforcement) and, thus, may receive media coverage congruent with these gendered associations.

Following our examination of the results of our content analysis, we discuss what obstacles and opportunities the media presents for women running for local and state executive office. First, we begin with a review of previous research on the media coverage of women political candidates.

Media Coverage of Women Political Candidates

Extensive studies by Kim Fridkin Kahn examining the newspaper coverage of women candidates running for election in the 1980s—which are summarized in her 1996 book, *The Political Consequences of Being a Woman*—found that this medium not only stereotyped female candidates by emphasizing "feminine" traits and issues, but also accorded them less coverage that often questioned their viability as candidates. However, Kahn also has noted that gender-stereotyped newspaper coverage can sometimes be used to a woman candidate's advantage—for example, by emphasizing her warmth and honesty or expertise on such issues as education or health care—in some electoral environments. Depending on the context of the election, Kahn argues, both women and men candidates can structure their campaign appeals to either capitalize on or dispel gendered beliefs.

Since Kahn's pioneering work, researchers have begun to find more equitable media treatment of female and male candidates running for state and federal office in the mid- to late 1990s and, especially, in the twenty-first century. For example, Kevin Smith (1997) found that female and male candidates running for governor or the US Senate in 1994 received about the same quantity and quality of coverage, except in open races. And in his study of 1998 gubernatorial races, James Devitt (1999) found that female and male candidates received about the same amount of coverage, but that women received less issue-related coverage than men did.

Studies of the newspaper coverage of female and male candidates running against each other in gubernatorial and US Senate races in 2000 and 2002 found even more parity, both in terms of the quantity and quality of coverage. In their book, *Gender and Campaign Communication: VideoStyle, WebStyle, and NewsStyle* (2004), Dianne Bystrom and coauthors found that women political candidates running in both primary and general election races for governor and the US Senate in 2000 received more coverage than men, and the quality of their coverage—the slant of the story and discussion of their viability, appearance, and personality—was mostly equitable. Still, these women candidates were much more likely to be discussed in terms of their sex, marital status, and children, which can affect their viability with voters.

Similarly, the coverage of female and male candidates running against each other for the US Senate and governor in 2002 was about even in terms of quantity, with 35% of the articles focusing on men and 34% on women. However, sex stereotypes were found in the quality of their coverage. For example, male candidates were linked significantly more often with the "masculine" issue of taxes whereas female candidates were associated more often with "women's issues" and discussed more often in terms of their marital status (Bystrom et al. 2004).

A study that focused on the newspaper coverage of a 2003 gubernatorial race between a Caucasian woman and Indian American man found that both sex and race were portrayed as positive candidate attributes (Major and Coleman 2008). Kathleen Blanco received far more coverage about her sex than opponent Bobby Jindal when they ran for governor. However, the gendered coverage—which was overwhelmingly positive—was used by the candidate's staff to Blanco's advantage, portraying her as the "older, experienced grandmother." Similar to the findings of other studies, Blanco was associated with "feminine" issues and Jindal with "masculine" ones, despite her expertise on the economy and his on health and education. According to the authors, this finding confirms the media's reliance on sex stereotypes to frame the coverage of female and male candidates.

Very few researchers have studied the media coverage of women mayoral candidates. A study of the newspaper coverage of six mayoral races— three male versus male and three female versus male—held between 2000 and 2003 found few gender differences (Atkeson and Krebs 2008). The three women mayoral candidates did receive less coverage of their qualifications as compared to men. However, women candidates did not receive more attention on feminine issues and less attention on masculine issues within the context of their races. Masculine issues received more media attention in all-male races, but the presence of a female candidate changed the scope of the issues covered in mixed-gender mayoral races. For example, education and social welfare received greater coverage in female versus male than male versus male mayoral races.

These female mayoral candidates, all three of whom won their elections, did not receive more coverage of personal issues than their male competitors but did receive more coverage of family and appearance than the eventual male winners in the male versus male races. Their hypothesis that male candidates would receive more masculine trait coverage and female candidates more feminine trait coverage was not supported, although the all-male races produced significantly more discussion of masculine traits than the female versus male races. The authors concluded that little evidence of gender bias existed in the press coverage of mayoral campaigns within the race context on issues, traits, appearance, and electability (Atkeson and Krebs 2008).

Although recent studies show that female and male candidates running for the US Senate, governor, and mayor are receiving more equitable media coverage—especially in terms of quantity and discussions of their viability, appearance, and personality—women candidates for president continue to receive more stereotyped coverage. For example, in her 2010 book, *Women for President: Media Bias in Nine Campaigns,* Erika Falk found that women presidential candidates in eight of the nine races studied received less newspaper coverage than the most comparable man, even if he had less experience, performed more poorly in the polls, or was less interesting. In terms of image attributes, women were more likely to have their attire and sex mentioned whereas men were more likely to have their age and appearance noted. The women presidential candidates also received less issue coverage than equivalent men running in the same race and were more likely to be portrayed as representing a special gendered interest.

Studies assessing the media coverage of recent women presidential candidates—Republican Elizabeth Dole and Democrat Hillary Rodham Clinton—as well as Republican vice presidential candidate Sarah Palin reinforce many of Falk's findings. For example, studies of Dole's campaign for the Republican nomination for president in 1999 found that she received less equitable coverage in terms of quality and, especially, quantity as compared to her male opponents (Aday and Devitt 2001; Bystrom 2006; Heldman, Carroll, and Olson 2005). Although she received less issue coverage than her male opponents, it was balanced between such stereotypical "masculine" issues as taxes, foreign policy, and the economy and such stereotypical "feminine" issues as education, drugs, and gun control. Dole also received more personal coverage than her male opponents, including references to her appearance and, especially, personality.

Studies also show that Clinton's bid for the 2008 Democratic nomination for president and Palin's campaign as vice president on the Republican ticket were covered by the media in a stereotypical and often sexist way. Although most studies show that Clinton received a great deal of media coverage—often more than her male opponents—she was more often framed negatively in terms of campaign strategies rather than issues.

In their 2010 book, *Hillary Clinton's Race for the White House: Gender Politics and the Media on the Campaign Trail,* Regina Lawrence and

Melody Rose document findings of their content analysis of Clinton's newspaper and television coverage. Not only were negative comments more frequently directed at Clinton, but the media's overwhelming "game-framed" coverage of the presidential primaries also highlighted her campaign as a struggling one, even when she was the decisive front-runner.

Other studies of Clinton's newspaper coverage also found that she was more likely to be "game-framed" in terms of her campaign strategies rather than her issue positions. For example, a study of newspapers in Iowa and New Hampshire, the first two presidential preference states, found that 27% of the stories focusing on Clinton were written in the strategy frame—including information on who's ahead or behind, opinion polls, fund-raising efforts, or predictions of outcomes—compared to 17% of the stories on eventual Democratic presidential nominee Barack Obama (Bystrom 2008). Only 8% of the stories focusing on Clinton emphasized issues compared to 24% of the stories about Obama. Similarly, a study that examined Clinton's media framing in the *New York Times* and *USA Today* found that 88% of the stories about Clinton employed a game frame whereas only 12% used an issue frame (Dimitrova and Geske 2009).

In another study of the 2008 presidential campaign, Diana Carlin and Kelly Winfrey (2009) examined examples from print media, television, and social networking to show how Palin was portrayed as a sex object while Clinton was attacked for her lack of femininity (e.g., overly ambitious, cold, calculating, scary, or intimidating). In Chapter 3 of this volume, Kim L. Fridkin, Jill Carle, and Gina Serignese Woodall compared Palin's media coverage to that received by Democratic vice presidential candidate Joe Biden in 2008 and Democratic vice presidential candidate Geraldine Ferraro in 1984. They found that Palin's media coverage, especially on television, focused more extensively on her appearance and family; was more critical on personal as well as substantive issues; and reinforced gender stereotypes by focusing on feminine traits and issues, even though she emphasized masculine issues in her speeches. Palin's coverage in 2008 mirrored the treatment of Ferraro as the first woman to run for vice president on a major party ticket.

In summary, recent analyses of the media coverage of female versus male political candidates have found that women running for legislative and local and state executive office often receive mostly equitable treatment—except that some women have been found to receive less issue coverage overall; more gendered issue coverage; more coverage of their marital status, sex, and children; and more questions about their qualifications for office. Women running for president and vice president continue to receive coverage that is more negative, questions their viability, focuses on campaign strategies rather than issues, and employs sex stereotypes.

Through our study of newspaper coverage of women running for local and state executive office in 2008, we are interested in learning if they received gendered coverage comparable to Clinton and Palin or more equitable and gender-neutral coverage in keeping with the findings of recent research.

Similar to most research conducted to date, we focused on the newspaper coverage of these female and male executive office candidates and did not take into consideration the communication strategies that may have contributed to their mediated portrayals. Some have suggested that one of the biggest problems faced by researchers examining the media coverage of female candidates is determining whether the differences found are due to media bias or the presentations by the candidates themselves (Fowler and Lawless 2009). Studies that have included controls to combat this difficulty have found, however, that media coverage does not echo the emphasis on issues female candidates seek to place on themselves (see for example Fridkin, Carle, and Woodall in Chapter 3 of this volume).

Based on recent research on the media coverage of female versus male political candidates, we seek to answer the following research questions:

1. Did female or male local and state executive candidates receive similar or different media coverage of their image traits in 2008?
2. Were female and male local and state executive candidates associated with "feminine" or "masculine" issues, respectively, in their media coverage in 2008?
3. Were female or male local and state executive candidates framed in similar or different ways by the media in 2008?

Method

For this analysis of the media coverage of female versus male political candidates, we focused on women and men running against each other for two executive levels of office—governor and mayor—in 2008. We included all four mixed-gender races for governor that took place in November 2008 in Indiana, North Carolina, Vermont, and Washington. All female gubernatorial candidates in the 2008 general election were Democrats with male Republican opponents. The North Carolina candidates ran in an open race, in which the Democratic woman won, whereas challengers ran against incumbents in Indiana, Vermont, and Washington, with all the incumbents (one female Democrat and two male Republicans) winning.

We further identified six mayoral elections that featured women running against men in cities with populations of 100,000 or more in fall 2008. Unlike gubernatorial elections, which are conducted on the first Tuesday of November, mayoral races in 2008 occurred throughout the year. To keep the time frame of our content analysis consistent, we chose mayoral races that occurred in November 2008 rather than on other dates of the calendar year. In choosing the mayoral races, we also considered the competiveness of the race to help ensure the expectation of similar media coverage. Thus, we chose mayoral races that took place in Eugene, Oregon; Fresno, California; Sacramento, California; Scottsdale, Arizona; Stockton, California; and Virginia Beach, Virginia.

Also, although the mayoral races were nonpartisan, the political allegiance of the candidates was well known. Our mayoral candidates included one Republican woman, five Democratic women, four Republican men (one who ran as an independent), and two Democratic men. Two races featured a female Democratic incumbent and a male Republican challenger. One race featured a female Democratic incumbent against a male associated with the Republican Party but running for mayor as an independent. One race featured a male Democratic challenger running against the female Democratic incumbent. The two open races featured a Democratic female running against a Republican male and a Republican female against a Democratic male. Three women—two who ran in open races and one who ran as an incumbent—won their races. Three men—all challengers—won their races.

Thus, we identified 10 races—4 gubernatorial and 6 mayoral—and 20 candidates—10 women and 10 men—for a content analysis of their newspaper coverage (see Table 9.1). We chose the largest newspapers in the states of the four gubernatorial races and the local city newspapers of the six mayoral races. First, we identified the total number of articles available from each newspaper through a search using the candidates' names from the time period from Labor Day through Election Day 2008, excluding letters to the editor from our universe. We identified a total of 583 articles, from which we chose 209 articles using a random sampling method from the 10 different newspapers covering these races from September 1 through November 4, 2008.

Following a training session with the coding instrument, two undergraduate students coded for the variables on a subsample of 21 articles, or 10% of the stratified sample, to establish intercoder reliability. The 21 articles were chosen at random and represented all newspapers covering the 10 races of interest to our study.

Intercoder reliability was assessed using Cohen's *kappa:*

$$\text{Cohen's } kappa = \frac{\% \text{ observed agreement} - \% \text{ expected agreement}}{(\# \text{ of objects coded}) \text{ x } (\# \text{ of coders}) - \% \text{ expected agreement}}$$

Only variables with a reliability coefficient equal to or greater than 0.6 are included in the analysis presented.

Following the coding of the entire sample, 6 of the 209 articles initially identified were excluded from our analysis as they were coded as neither

Table 9.1 Candidates and Newspapers Analyzed in 2008

Male Candidate/ Party/Status	Female Candidate/ Party/Status	Level of Office	Newspaper Analyzed	Election Outcome
Mitch Daniels Republican Incumbent	Jill Long Thompson Democrat Challenger	Governor Indiana	Indianapolis (IN) Star	Daniels won with 58%
Pat McCrory Republican/Open Race	Beverly Perdue Democrat/Open Race	Governor North Carolina	Charlotte (NC) Observer	Perdue won with 50.27%
Jim Douglas Republican Incumbent	Gaye Symington Democrat Challenger	Governor Vermont	Burlington (VT) Free Press	Douglas won with 55%
Dino Rossi Republican Challenger	Christine Gregoire Democrat Incumbent	Governor Washington	Seattle (WA) Times	Gregoire won with 53%
Jim Lane Republican Challenger	Mary Manross Democrat Incumbent	Mayor Scottsdale, AZ	Arizona Republic	Lane won with 50.22%
Henry T. Perea Democrat/Open Race	Ashley Swearengin Republican/Open Race	Mayor Fresno, CA	Fresno (CA) Bee	Swearengin won with 54%
Kevin Johnson Democrat Challenger	Heather Fargo Democrat Incumbent	Mayor Sacramento, CA	Sacramento (CA) Bee	Johnson won with 57%
Clem Lee Republican/Open Race	Ann Johnston Democrat/Open Race	Mayor Stockton, CA	Stockton (CA) Record	Johnston won with 56%
Jim Torrey Independent Challenger	Kitty Piercy Democrat Incumbent	Mayor Eugene, OR	Eugene (OR) Register-Guard	Piercy won with 51%
Will Sessoms Republican Challenger	Meyera Oberndorf Democrat Incumbent	Mayor Virginia Beach, VA	Virginian-Pilot	Sessoms won with 42%[a]

Note: a. Will Sessoms won the four-candidate race with 42% of the vote. Meyera Oberndorf received 38% of the vote and conceded the race. The other two candidates—Scott Taylor, who received 11% of the votes, and John Moss, who received 9% of the votes—were not included in the content analysis as the media coverage focused on the top two candidates.

mentioning nor focusing on a particular gubernatorial or mayoral candidate (e.g., several of these articles focused on the 2008 presidential race and merely mentioned one of the candidates of interest to this study). Thus, 203 articles were included in our analysis.

A statistical analysis computer program (STATA) was used to obtain descriptive statistics for all research questions posed in this chapter. Cross-tabulations were conducted and analyses with a significance level of $p < .05$ for the Pearson χ^2 tests are noted in the results presented.

Our coding instrument allowed us to conduct statistical tests for differences in two ways. First, the dyadic nature of the instrument allowed us to perform "side-by-side" or direct comparisons of female versus male coverage on the categories of image attributes and issues. Second, by using a variable that asked our coders whether or not the article was focused on a singular candidate, we were able to extract female-focused and male-focused articles from our sample of 203 stories. We used the gender focus variable to compare female verus male media coverage on such variables as story style (news, feature, or opinion); frame (issue, strategy, or candidate); and gender of the author.

Our coding instrument and statistical analysis controlled for such variables as incumbency and level of race. Tables presented within this chapter are all based on the results of two-by-two contingency tables with the level of race and gender built into the chi-square estimates. Further, because chi-square analysis subtracts the expected value from the observed value and then divides that number by the expected value, it mitigates if not negates any beneficial effects (at least where content analysis of media mentions are concerned) that an incumbent may experience.

In an effort to fully understand the manner in which journalists mediate political candidates in state and local executive races through their newspaper coverage, we looked at several different grouping schemes. First, we compare the newspaper coverage of female candidates to that of male candidates in the overall sample of gubernatorial and mayoral races. Next, we compare the newspaper coverage of female to male candidates within each level of race. Finally, we also compare the newspaper coverage of female candidates running for governor to coverage of those women running for mayor and then coverage of male candidates for governor to male candidates for mayor.

Results

Of the 203 articles analyzed, 112 (55%) were about gubernatorial races and 91 (45%) were about mayoral races. Articles about the three open races (53) comprised 26% of the sample with the majority of stories analyzed (150,

74%) on the seven incumbent versus challenger races. Of the articles sampled, 163 (80%) had a news story style, 29 (14%) were editorials/opinion articles, eight (4%) were features, and three (2%) were ad watches.

As for dominant story frame, nearly half (99, 49%) of the 203 articles analyzed were written in the strategy frame with the other articles split between the issue (55, 27%) and candidate (45, 22%) frames. (Our coders were not able to determine the dominant frame on four stories, or 2% of the sample.)

Of the 203 articles in our sample, the majority (113, 56%) focused on a singular candidate seeking office and 90 (44%) gave equal focus to both candidates. Table 9.2 summarizes the composition of the 113 candidate-focused articles by sex and level of race, political party, status, and outcome of the election.

In the subsample of 113 candidate-focused articles, 64 (57%) were about gubernatorial contenders and the remaining 49 (43%) were about mayoral candidates. Of the 64 articles that focused on only one gubernatorial candidate, 21 (33%) were focused on female candidates and 43 (67%) were focused on male candidates. Of the 49 articles that focused on only one mayoral candidate, 21 (43%) were focused on female candidates and 28 (57%) were focused on males. Thus, 42 of the 113 articles (37%) focused on female candidates and the remaining 71 (63%) focused on male candidates.

Table 9.2 Composition of Candidate-Focused Newspaper Articles Analyzed in 2008

	Total		Female		Male	
	Number	Percentage	Number	Percentage	Number	Percentage
Office candidate is seeking						
Governor	64	56.64	21	32.81	43	67.19
Mayor	49	43.36	21	42.86	28	57.14
Status of candidate seeking office						
Challenger	51	45.13	9	17.65	42	82.35
Incumbent	37	32.74	20	54.05	17	45.95
Open Race	25	22.12	13	52.00	12	48.00
Political party of candidate seeking office						
Democrat	57	50.44	39	68.42	18	31.58
Republican	56	49.56	3	5.36	53	94.64
Candidates election outcome						
Lost	52	46.02	23	44.23	29	55.77
Won	61	53.98	19	31.15	42	68.85
N	113	100	42	37.17	71	62.83

The 113 articles that focused on one of the two candidates running for office were almost evenly divided between Democratic (57, 50%) and Republican candidates (56, 50%). However, 68% (39) of the Democratic-focused articles were about female candidates and 95% (53) of the Republican-focused articles were about male candidates. As for candidate status, 45% (51) of the 113 candidate-focused articles were about challengers, 37 (33%) were about incumbents, and 25 (22%) were written about open-race candidates. Of the challenger-focused stories, 82% (42) were about male candidates and 18% (9) about female candidates. Incumbent-focused stories were split between female candidates (20, 54%) and male candidates (17, 46%). Stories focused on open-race candidates were split between females (13, 52%) and males (12, 48%).

Of the 113 candidate-focused articles, 54% (61) were written about the eventual winner (42, 69% men and 19, 31% women) and 46% (52) about the eventual loser (29, 56% men and 23, 44% women).

Next, we summarize our findings by candidate gender and level of executive office, reporting not only the significant differences but also the similarities in female versus male media coverage.

Female Versus Male Coverage Overall

Our analysis of the newspaper coverage of female versus male executive candidates in 2008 reveals that they were covered equitably in terms of image and story frame, with some differences in issue associations. As Table 9.3 shows, our side-by-side analysis of image and issue mentions in the sample of 203 articles shows that newspapers covering these races were significantly more likely to mention both candidates when discussing their personalities or issue emphasis than just the female or male contender. For

Table 9.3 Significant Differences in Female vs. Male Candidate Media Coverage, 2008

Variable	Female		Male		Both		Chi-Square	Significance
Candidate image								
Personality	31	(15%)	31	(15%)	42	(21%)	25.22	.001
Candidate issue								
City or state budget	4	(2%)	16	(8%)	42	(21%)	118.82	.001
Major industries	4	(2%)	1	(.5%)	12	(6%)	140.52	.001
Government infrastructure	5	(2%)	12	(6%)	19	(9%)	88.83	.001
K–12 education	15	(7%)	12	(6%)	22	(11%)	61.57	.001
Crime/violence	8	(4%)	16	(8%)	29	(14%)	85.99	.001
City or state growth	5	(2%)	7	(3%)	22	(11%)	118.89	.001
Gay marriage	3	(1%)	1	(.5%)	8	(4%)	131.91	.001
Govt. reform/ethics/								
corruption/welfare	2	(1%)	5	(2%)	13	(6%)	125.09	.001
City or state services	4	(2%)	7	(3%)	30	(15%)	138.65	.001

Note: N = 203.

example, 104 of the 203 stories (51%) mentioned the personality of the female, male, or both candidates. Of these stories, 31 commented on the female candidate's personality only, 31 mentioned the male candidate's personality only, and 42 mentioned both the female and male candidates' personalities.

When covering the issues, newspapers also were significantly more likely to mention both the female candidate and male candidate than one candidate or the other, although some gendered trends emerged. For example, the top issues discussed were city or state budget (62 stories, 31% of sample), crime/violence (53, 26%), education (49, 24%), city and state services (41, 20%), government infrastructure (36, 18%), and city or state growth (34, 17%). In all instances, the newspapers were significantly more likely to discuss both candidates in relation to these issues rather than just the female or male candidate.

However, some gendered trends do emerge in the issue coverage of female and male candidates. For example, male candidates were more likely to be singularly linked with the "masculine" issues of budget and crime/violence than female candidates. Female candidates were singularly linked slightly more often with the "feminine" issue of education.

Furthermore, our analysis of female-focused versus male-focused newspaper articles reveals only similarities in their coverage. As Table 9.4 shows, around three-fourths of the articles written about female and male candidates were news stories with women mentioned slightly more often in opinion or editorial pieces. Most stories written about both female and male candidates were in the strategy frame, with female candidates more likely than male candidates to be discussed in the strategy and, especially, the issue frames, and male candidates more likely to be mentioned in the candidate frame.

Table 9.4 Similarities in Female vs. Male Candidate Media Coverage by Article Focus, 2008

Variable	Total (N =113)		Female (N = 42)		Male (N = 71)		Chi-Square	Significance
Story style								
News	86	(76%)	30	(72%)	56	(79%)	0.80	n.s.
Feature	7	(6%)	3	(7%)	4	(6%)	0.10	n.s.
Op-ed	18	(16%)	8	(19%)	10	(14%)	0.49	n.s.
Ad watch	2	(2%)	1	(2%)	1	(1%)	0.14	n.s.
Dominant story frame								
Candidate frame	32	(28%)	8	(19%)	24	(34%)	2.83	n.s.
Strategy frame	49	(43%)	20	(48%)	29	(41%)	0.49	n.s.
Issue frame	30	(26%)	14	(33%)	16	(23%)	1.58	n.s.
Author's gender								
Female	34	(30%)	17	(40%)	17	(24%)	2.33	n.s.
Male	59	(52%)	20	(48%)	39	(59%)	2.33	n.s.

More than half of the candidate-focused articles were written by male reporters. Female candidates were covered almost evenly by male and female reporters whereas male candidates were covered by male reporters more than twice as often as female reporters.

Female Versus Male Gubernatorial Candidates

Again, our analysis of the media coverage of female versus male gubernatorial candidates in 2008 shows more similarities than differences. For example, the 112 articles that covered the gubernatorial races in our sample were significantly more likely to mention both candidates when discussing their personalities or issue emphasis than just the female or male contender. As Table 9.5 shows, 56 of the 112 stories (50%) on gubernatorial races mentioned the personality of the female, male, or both candidates. Of these stories, 16 (14%) commented on the female candidate's personality only, 18 (16%) mentioned the male candidate's personality only, and 22 (20%) discussed both the female and male candidates' personalities in the same article.

When covering the issues, newspapers again were significantly more likely to mention both the female candidate and male gubernatorial candidate than one candidate or the other, although some gendered trends emerged. For example, the top three issues discussed were budget (36, 32%), crime/violence (36, 32%), and education (35, 31%). Within these issues, the male gubernatorial candidates were more often linked with the "masculine" issues of the budget and crime/violence than the female gubernatorial candidates, who were slightly more often linked with the "feminine" issue of education.

Furthermore, our analysis of female-focused versus male-focused newspaper articles covering gubernatorial races reveals only similarities in their

Table 9.5 Significant Differences in Female vs. Male Gubernatorial Candidate Media Coverage

Variable	Female		Male		Both		Chi-Square	Significance
Candidate image								
Personality	16	(14%)	18	(16%)	22	(20%)	13.02	.001
Candidate issue								
City or state budget	3	(2%)	11	(8%)	22	(20%)	54.29	.001
Major industries	0	(0%)	1	(1%)	5	(4%)	94.12	.001
Public maintenance	3	(3%)	10	(9%)	12	(11%)	61.57	.001
K–12 education	9	(8%)	7	(6%)	19	(17%)	42.79	.001
Crime/violence	5	(4%)	11	(8%)	20	(18%)	45.10	.001
Goverment reform/ethics/ corruption/welfare	0	(0%)	2	(2%)	8	(7%)	89.48	.001
City or state services	1	(1%)	5	(4%)	7	(6%)	54.13	.001

Note: $N = 112$.

coverage. As Table 9.6 shows, most stories written about both female and male gubernatorial candidates were in the strategy frame, with female candidates discussed in the strategy and issue frames more often, and male candidates mentioned in the candidate frame more often. More than two-thirds of the candidate-focused articles about governors' races were written by male reporters.

Female Versus Male Mayoral Candidates

Again, our analysis shows that the 91 articles that covered the mayoral races in our sample were significantly more likely to mention both candidates when discussing their personalities or issue emphasis than just the female or male contender. As Table 9.7 shows, 47 of the 91 stories (52%) on mayoral races mentioned the personality of the female, male, or both candidates. Of these stories, 14 (15%) commented on the female candidate's personality only, 13 (14%) mentioned the male candidate's personality only, and 20 (22%) discussed both the female and male candidates' personalities in the same article.

The top three issues discussed by mayoral candidates in the subsample of mayoral candidate-focused stories were city services (28, 31%), budget (26, 29%), and city growth (24, 26%). Around 80% of the articles that mentioned these issues included both the female and male mayoral candidate, with men having a slight edge in stories written about the budget.

Our analysis of female-focused versus male-focused newspaper articles covering mayoral races reveals the same similarities in story frame that were found in the entire sample and stories focused on gubernatorial candidates. However, significant differences appeared as to the sex of the journalist covering the mayoral candidates.

As Table 9.8 shows, 78% of the articles written about both female and

Table 9.6 Similarities in Female vs. Male Gubernatorial Candidate Media Coverage by Article Focus, 2008

Variable	Total (N = 64)		Female (N = 21)		Male (N = 43)		Chi-Square	Significance
Story style								
News	48	(75%)	15	(71%)	33	(76%)	.21	n.s.
Feature	6	(9%)	3	(14%)	3	(7%)	.88	n.s.
Op-ed	8	(13%)	2	(10%)	6	(14%)	.25	n.s.
Ad watch	2	(3%)	1	(5%)	1	(2%)	.28	n.s.
Dominant story frame								
Candidate frame	19	(30%)	5	(24%)	14	(33%)	.52	n.s.
Strategy frame	25	(40%)	9	(43%)	16	(37%)	.49	n.s.
Issue frame	18	(28%)	7	(33%)	11	(25%)	.42	n.s.
Author's gender								
Female	15	(23%)	5	(24%)	10	(14%)	.01	n.s.
Male	40	(63%)	14	(67%)	26	(60%)	.01	n.s.

male mayoral candidates were news stories, with men more often covered in news stories and women more often featured in opinion pieces. Similar to our findings for the entire sample and subsample of gubernatorial candidate-focused stories, around half of the articles on mayoral candidates were written in the strategy frame, with female candidates more often discussed in the strategy and issue frames, and male candidates more often mentioned in the candidate frame.

Interestingly, female and male reporters were equally likely to cover mayoral races overall, with female reporters significantly more likely to cover the women mayoral candidates and male reporters to cover the male candidates for mayor.

Table 9.7 Significant Differences in Female vs. Male Mayoral Candidate Media Coverage, 2008

Variable	Female		Male		Both		Chi-Square	Significance
Candidate image								
Personality	14	(15%)	13	(14%)	20	(22%)	11.55	.001
Candidate issue								
City or state budget	1	(1%)	5	(5%)	20	(22%)	62.14	.001
Major industries	4	(4%)	0	(0%)	7	(8%)	54.51	.001
Public maintenance	2	(2%)	2	(2%)	7	(8%)	51.04	.001
K–12 education	6	(7%)	5	(5%)	3	(3%)	7.38	.007
Taxes	3	(3%)	5	(5%)	9	(10%)	37.25	.001
City or state growth	2	(2%)	3	(3%)	19	(21%)	64.67	.000
Gay marriage	2	(2%)	0	(0%)	6	(7%)	65.89	.001
Government reform/ethics/								
corruption/welfare	2	(2%)	3	(3%)	5	(5%)	36.66	.001
City or state services	3	(3%)	2	(2%)	23	(25%)	67.11	.001

Note: N = 91.

Table 9.8 Significant Differences and Similarities in Female vs. Male Mayoral Candidate Media Coverage by Article Focus, 2008

Variable	Total ($N = 49$)		Female ($N = 21$)		Male ($N = 28$)		Chi-Square	Significance
Story style								
News	38	(78%)	15	(71%)	23	(82%)	.79	n.s.
Feature	1	(2%)	0	(0%)	1	(4%)	.77	n.s.
Op-ed	10	(20%)	6	(29%)	4	(14%)	1.50	n.s.
Ad watch	0	(0%)	0	(0%)	0	(0%)	.00	n.s.
Dominant story frame								
Candidate frame	13	(27%)	3	(14%)	10	(36%)	2.83	n.s.
Strategy frame	24	(49%)	11	(52%)	13	(46%)	.17	n.s.
Issue frame	12	(24%)	7	(33%)	5	(18%)	1.55	n.s.
Author's gender								
Female	19	(39%)	12	(57%)	7	(25%)	3.80	.05
Male	19	(39%)	6	(29%)	13	(46%)	3.80	.05

Next we compare female candidates and male candidates by the level of executive office sought.

Female Gubernatorial Versus Mayoral Candidates

Significant differences and similarities emerged in our comparison of female gubernatorial candidates and female mayoral candidates (see Table 9.9). As for image attributes, both female gubernatorial and female mayoral candidates were infrequently discussed in terms of their appearance or children. They were almost equally discussed in terms of their personality.

In terms of issues, the budget was the top concern discussed by female candidates in 23% of the stories overall. Female gubernatorial and female mayoral candidates were just as likely to be linked with this issue. Education and taxes were each discussed by women candidates in 18% of the articles, with female gubernatorial candidates significantly more likely to be linked with education as compared to female mayoral candidates. Female gubernatorial candidates were also more likely to be linked with taxes, but not significantly so. City or state services were mentioned by women candidates in 17% of the articles, with female mayoral candidates significantly more likely to be linked with this issue.

Female gubernatorial candidates were also significantly more likely than female mayoral candidates to be linked with job loss. Female mayoral candidates were significantly more likely than female gubernatorial candidates to be linked with the issues of growth, crime, major industries, and gay marriage.

Table 9.9 Significant Differences and Similarities in Female Gubernatorial vs. Female Mayoral Candidate Media Coverage, 2008

Variable	Total (*N* = 203)		Governor (*N* = 113)		Mayor (*N* = 90)		Chi-Square	Significance
Candidate image								
Appearance	6	(3%)	5	(4%)	1	(1%)	1.91	n.s.
Children mentioned	3	(2%)	2	(1%)	1	(1%)	.15	n.s.
Personality	72	(35%)	38	(34%)	34	(38%)	.38	n.s.
Candidate issues								
City or state budget	46	(23%)	25	(22%)	21	(23%)	.04	n.s.
Job loss	9	(4%)	8	(7%)	1	(1%)	4.21	.04
Major industries	16	(8%)	5	(4%)	11	(12%)	4.19	.04
Public maintenance	24	(12%)	15	(13%)	9	(10%)	.51	n.s.
K–12 education	37	(18%)	28	(25%)	9	(10%)	7.34	.007
Crime/violence	17	(8%)	5	(4%)	12	(13%)	5.18	.02
Taxes	37	(18%)	25	(22%)	12	(13%)	2.60	n.s.
City or state growth	27	(13%)	6	(5%)	21	(23%)	14.11	.001
Gay marriage	11	(5%)	3	(3%)	8	(9%)	3.90	.05
Government reform	15	(7%)	8	(7%)	7	(8%)	.04	n.s.
City or state services	34	(17%)	8	(7%)	26	(29%)	17.10	.001

Male Gubernatorial Versus Mayoral Candidates

Significant differences and similarities also emerged in our comparison of male gubernatorial candidates and male mayoral candidates (see Table 9.10). In terms of candidate image, both male gubernatorial and male mayoral candidates were discussed almost equally in terms of their personality.

In terms of issues, the budget again was the top issue discussed by male candidates in 29% of the stories overall. Male gubernatorial and male mayoral candidates were just as likely to be linked with this issue. Other popular issues with male candidates were taxes (22%), services (18%), and the economy and education (both 17%). Male gubernatorial candidates were more likely to be linked with taxes and the economy, but not significantly so. Male gubernatorial candidates were significantly more likely to be linked with education. Male mayoral candidates were significantly more likely to be linked with services and growth.

Discussion

Our content analysis shows that women candidates for local and state executive office in 2008 were treated mostly similarly to their male opponents in the *quality* of media coverage (e.g., image attributes, issues, and story frames). However, the *quantity* of their coverage—as measured by candidate-focused articles—was less for female versus male candidates in these races.

Table 9.10 Significant Differences and Similarities in Male Gubernatorial vs. Male Mayoral Candidate Media Coverage, 2008

Variable	Total (N = 203)		Governor (N = 113)		Mayor (N = 90)		Chi-Square	Significance
Candidate image								
Personality	73	(36%)	40	(35%)	33	(37%)	.17	n.s.
Candidate issues								
Economy	35	(17%)	23	(20%)	12	(13%)	1.38	n.s.
City or state budget	58	(29%)	33	(29%)	25	(28%)	.00	n.s.
Job growth	15	(7%)	6	(5%)	9	(10%)	1.84	n.s.
Major industries	13	(6%)	6	(5%)	7	(8%)	.63	n.s.
Land use	8	(4%)	4	(4%)	4	(4%)	.15	n.s.
Energy issues	11	(5%)	7	(6%)	4	(4%)	.23	n.s.
Government infrastructure	8	(4%)	4	(4%)	4	(4%)	.15	n.s.
Public maintenance	31	(15%)	22	(19%)	9	(10%)	3.01	n.s.
K–12 education	34	(17%)	28	(25%)	8	(9%)	6.45	.011
Taxes	45	(22%)	31	(27%)	14	(16%)	3.46	n.s.
City or state growth	29	(14%)	3	(3%)	6	(7%)	14.58	.001
Gay marriage	9	(4%)	3	(3%)	6	(7%)	2.10	n.s.
Government reform	18	(9%)	10	(9%)	8	(9%)	.01	n.s.
City or state services	37	(18%)	12	(11%)	25	(28%)	10.82	.001

In terms of the quality of media coverage, these findings add support to recent studies that have documented mostly gender equitable coverage and do not reflect the stereotyped media coverage that presidential candidate Clinton and vice presidential candidate Palin received in 2008. However, our finding that these female candidates were the focus of fewer stories than their male opponents contradicts recent research that shows women garnering the same, or even more, media coverage than men.

As far as the quantity of their coverage, we note male candidates were the focus of twice as many stories as female candidates in the overall sample and gubernatorial race subsample. Female mayoral candidates were the focus of more stories (43%) than female gubernatorial candidates (33%), but still fewer than their male opponents (57%). Female and male candidates received almost equal coverage in the three open races (52% to 48%). Male challengers outnumbered female challengers by a multiple of 2.5 (5 to 2) but received 4.5 times (82% to 18%) more candidate-focused coverage. Perhaps most troubling is that the two male incumbents (both running for governor) received almost as many candidate-focused stories (46%) as the five female incumbents (54%), one of whom ran for governor and the other four for mayor.

As for the quality of their coverage, the only image variable that emerged for analysis in the female versus male candidate comparisons was personality. Newspapers were significantly more likely to mention both candidates when discussing their personalities than just the female or male contender. These female and male candidates—overall and by each level of race—were just as likely to be discussed in terms of their personalities—both positively and negatively. The following examples of personality coverage of female and male candidates illustrate these similarities.

In the open mayoral race between Republican Ashley Swearengin, the eventual winner, and Democrat Henry T. Perea, the *Fresno Bee* commented on the female candidate's sense of humor: "Though serious in her efforts to become the next mayor, Swearengin also is the practical joker in the campaign" (Boyles 2008, A1). In its coverage of the gubernatorial race between Republican governor Mitch Daniels of Indiana, who won his challenge from Democrat Jill Long Thompson, the *Indianapolis Star* wrote: "Daniels lacks the natural charisma that many successful candidates offer voters. . . . But the governor does have another side" (Pulliam 2008, A10). And "Long Thompson has earned a reputation as a tough campaigner . . . [but] the other Jill Long Thompson [is] someone who is studious and quiet, traits not often associated with politicians" (Ruthhart 2008).

In terms of issue coverage, we did find mostly similarities but some gendered trends. Budget, crime/violence, and education were the top three issues discussed in the overall sample of candidates and subsample of gubernatorial candidates. Female and male candidates overall were both linked in

68% of the stories that mentioned budget, 55% that discussed crime/violence, and 45% that mentioned education. Female and male gubernatorial candidates were both linked in 61% of the stories that discussed the budget, 56% that mentioned crime, and 54% on education.

However, a comparison of male versus female singular issue mentions—for both the overall sample and subsample of gubernatorial candidates—found men to be linked more often with the "masculine" issues of budget and crime. Also, female candidates overall and for governor were slightly more likely than male candidates to be linked with the "feminine" issue of education.

Not surprisingly, the top issues discussed in stories about female and male mayoral candidates were a bit different. They included city services (28 stories), budget (26), city growth (24), taxes (17), and crime (17). Around 80% of the stories on these issues mentioned both the female and male mayoral candidates. Again, when looking at stories that linked either the male or female candidate with the issue of budget, the men held a slight advantage.

Our examination of story frame—strategy, candidate, and issue—revealed no significant differences between female and male candidates, but several interesting observations. First, in keeping with the findings of research by Lawrence and Rose (2010) and Dimitrova and Geske (2009) on Clinton's newspaper coverage as a candidate for the Democratic nomination for president, the strategy (also known as the game) frame was the dominant story frame overall (43%) and in stories focusing on female (48%) and male (41%) candidates, female gubernatorial (43%) and male gubernatorial (37%) candidates, and female mayoral (52%) and male mayoral (46%) candidates.

However, unlike Clinton, female candidates for local and state executive office in 2008 were more likely to be covered in the issue frame than their male opponents. Women candidates were covered in the issue frame in 33% of the overall sample of candidate-focused stories, 33% of the gubernatorial stories, and 33% of the mayoral stories. On the other hand, men were more likely than women to be covered in the candidate frame in 34% of the stories overall, 33% of the gubernatorial stories, and 36% of the mayoral stories.

Although the sample of articles was three-fourths news stories, an examination of the 18 candidate-focused editorial and opinion pieces revealed some interesting observations. Female candidates were the focus of 45% of the opinion pieces overall, 60% of the editorials on mayoral races, and 25% of the editorials on gubernatorial races. When we examined these editorials, we found that the newspapers endorsed two female candidates for mayor (one a Democratic incumbent who lost her race and one a Republican in an open race) and six male candidates (a Democratic male and two Republican males, all challenging a Democratic female incumbent, in mayoral races, and Republican males in three gubernatorial races, including an incumbent, a challenger, and an open-race contender).

We also looked at the sex of the reporter covering these female and male executive office candidates. Of the articles that focused on either a female or male candidate, 52% were written by a male reporter and 30% by a female reporter (with the author of the remaining 18% of the stories either not listed or undetermined due to a gender-neutral first name). The stories focusing on gubernatorial candidates revealed even more of a gender gap in the sex of the reporter, with 63% of the stories written by male reporters and 23% of the stories written by female reporters. Interestingly, male and female reporters were equally likely (at 39% each) to write stories focused on mayoral candidates, which shows that local city newspapers employed female and male reporters equally to cover mayoral races whereas the states' largest newspapers were more likely to assign male rather than female reporters to cover the governors' races.

Also, it is interesting to note that female reporters were more likely to cover female candidates compared to male candidates in the overall sample of candidate-focused stories. Similarly, male reporters were more likely to cover male candidates than female candidates in the overall sample. In the subsample of stories focusing on the mayoral candidates the results were statistically significant, with female reporters more likely to cover women candidates and male reporters more likely to cover the men.

Finally, our comparison of women running for mayor and governor as well as men running for these executive offices revealed some significant differences. For example, female gubernatorial candidates and male gubernatorial candidates were significantly more likely than female and male mayoral candidates to be linked with the "feminine" issue of education. Female gubernatorial candidates were also more likely than female mayoral candidates to be linked with the issue of job loss.

Female and male mayoral candidates were significantly more likely to be linked to the issues of city services and city growth than female and male gubernatorial candidates. Female mayoral candidates were also significantly more likely than female gubernatorial candidates to be linked to the issues of crime, industry, and gay marriage.

Our comparisons of female to male gubernatorial candidates, female to male mayoral candidates, female gubernatorial to female mayoral candidates, and male gubernatorial to male mayoral candidates do not add support to the "congruency" notion that women may enjoy better coverage than men in races that emphasize "feminine" versus "masculine" issues. At the gubernatorial level, male candidates received almost equal coverage to female candidates on the "feminine" issue of education. At the mayoral level, female and male candidates received almost equal coverage on all issues, most of which could be considered "masculine."

Overall, our analysis provides mostly good news for female candidates interested in running for local and state executive office. Based on our findings, they can expect mostly equitable media coverage in terms of image and story frames. However, female candidates should be aware that the media is increasingly likely to discuss their personalities as part of the campaign coverage and to employ a strategy, or game, frame. Maintaining good relationships with reporters may help ensure that such coverage is fair and balanced.

Female candidates also can expect to be associated with a full range of important campaign issues including the budget, crime, and education at the gubernatorial level and city services, budget, growth, taxes, and crime at the mayoral level. Still, especially on the issues of budget and crime, female candidates for mayor and governor will need to emphasize their expertise as the media more often associates male candidates with these "masculine" issues. And female candidates, especially for governor, should continue to emphasize their expertise on the "feminine" issue of education as male candidates are closing the gender gap on this issue in their media coverage.

Based on our findings, female candidates for governor and mayor—especially incumbents—also need to be concerned about the amount of their coverage. Again, cultivating and maintaining good relationships with reporters and employing campaign strategies that maximize media coverage may help ensure more equitable coverage in terms of quantity.

10

Welcome to the Party? Leadership, Ambition, and Support Among Elites

Denise L. Baer

NEARLY A CENTURY AFTER AMERICAN WOMEN WERE GRANTED universal suffrage in 1920, and nearly half a century since the National Women's Political Caucus initiated party reform in 1968–1972, women's gains in legislative and executive office holding remain disappointing. If we were to create a gender index for women's rates of officeholding based upon population figures (in 2010, women were 51.7% of the population aged 18 and older), then state legislative office holding indices would range from maybe a low of 0.10 to a high of 0.40 depending on the state (with less than 0.25 overall); less than 0.17 for Congress and mayors of cities over 30,000; only about 0.20 for statewide executives; and at the executive levels a low of less than 0.12 for governors and 0.08 for mayors of large cities over 100,000 population.[1]

In particular, executive office holding especially among governors and mayors of larger cities remains a fraction of legislative rates. Are recruitment routes for executive office different from those for legislative offices? From the perspective of political parties whose function is to identify, recruit, and provide apprenticeship opportunities for leadership, executive office holding is widely considered qualitatively different from legislative office holding and attracts different types of individuals. Most important, being an effective executive requires different skills from legislating (Kunin 2008, 146–148). Depending on the level of office, executives usually must be policy generalists, whereas legislators can specialize. Executives must possess political skills in working with other branches of government as well as in direct management of their own office, agency, or branch of government. Elected executives must also be able to campaign effectively and present their agendas to the public in compelling ways, as well as work collaboratively with competing groups and businesses in the private sector. Second, executives must be strategic in their ambitions. Some executives may keep their office for a long period of time (e.g., a mayor who may remain in office for 10 or 20 years compared to a term-limited governor), but most view their office as a short-term platform from which they must plan for a career afterwards—whether through progressive ambition for a higher office or for a career in the private sector. While in office, executive officers are singular and any signs of weakness or errors in judgment can attract substantial competitors within their own party as well as in the opposing party that can foil the most strategic ambitions. Finally, executives are personally accountable for their decisions in ways that legislators whose vote is one among many are not. This level of responsibility can be grueling on a personal life. Legislators may work long hours, but they do have periods in recess, whereas the responsibilities of an executive position can be 24-7.

Leadership Recruitment or Candidate Emergence?

While women have made legislative gains, executive office—where one proffers a personal claim to leadership and becomes an elite among elites—has been more elusive. Jennifer Lawless (2012) and Jennifer Lawless and Richard Fox (2005, 2010b) have challenged us, rather than simply looking at barriers, to examine the candidate emergence process and how this process impacts ambition. This chapter examines leadership and ambition among women who are already leaders—women party elites. Research on leadership describes it as a relational set of skills and activities that can be learned (Harari 2002). Leadership is as diverse and differing among women as among men based on values, goals, and personal style (DeHart-Davis, Marlowe, and Pandey 2006; Fox and Schuhmann 1999; Jewell and Whicker 1993; J. Kirkpatrick 1974; C. Rosenthal 1998). If one rejects the claim that women have less of what it takes to be political rulers and leaders,[2] then we must ask if the political parties have been less than welcoming? Women, however, are active in both parties. While women have been active in third-party efforts, women have never organized a third party in the United States. Yet a growing party polarization between Republicans and Democrats provides differential opportunities for women. In an era where the women's movement is in decline,[3] understanding how political parties support or fail to support women becomes even more critical. This chapter examines how the chicken-and-egg problem of parties and leadership in a democratic society impacts women as potential leaders and provides an overview of the party pipeline for women, using a survey of Democratic and Republican national convention delegates to address the question of how well the parties have welcomed them as leaders.

Parties and Leadership: A Methodological and Theoretical Chicken-and-Egg Problem

A myth has become widespread that parties have weakened as political institutions (Baer 1993a; Baer and Bositis 1988) and that, therefore, parties are less important in recruitment (Cohen et al. 2008). This myth has encouraged scholars to turn blind eye toward how parties function with respect to women (Baer 1993b) and to not develop an understanding about the internal processes of party-centered candidate recruitment. Recent research has found a persistent gender gap in ambition among professional and activist women—a group of potential eligibles (Lawless and Fox 2005, 2010b). We also have a growing body of research on what Kira Sanbonmatsu (2002a, 792) calls the two halves of the story—women who run or have been elected and women who do not choose to run for office. But what we lack is information on party women—perhaps the most significant population for resolving the growing debate over competing explanations for women's disparate officeholding because these activist and potentially eligible women have also already entered the parties.

We do know that, until recently, the parties have been barriers and negative gatekeepers (Carroll, 1994; Sanbonmatsu 2002a, 2006). Historically, parties tended to support women candidates in more adverse circumstances to fill a candidate slot where their party had little change of winning (sacrificial lamb races) or steered women toward women's seats where the previous or current incumbent was a woman. How do we know when parties support or fail to support women candidates? Unfortunately, we lack good data here. Surveys of successful candidates fail to tell us how women might have been discouraged from even considering a race or how a failed candidate might have succeeded if she had received party support. We have many anecdotal stories from women who say they lacked critical party support, and we have surveys of potential candidate pools. All these data and stories fail to address whether these candidates or potential candidates were credible, strategic candidates (Cox and Katz 2002; Jacobson and Kernell 1983; Schlesinger 1966, 1991).

Party Recruitment: Inside Versus Outside Methods

The challenge for women and politics researchers is how to integrate women's status as social movement outsiders into regular party recruitment processes —each of which has changed over time (e.g., social movements are episodic) and in their use by women leaders (e.g., running as an outsider versus running as part of a party's recruitment program for women). Political parties are gendered institutions (Baer 1993a; Kenney 1996), and political recruitment routes can now be divided into three main types: typically male, typically female, and traditional party (see Table 10.1). Recruitment routes and styles are commonly understood as being solidified in the first political success, but they can also be useful in examining political transitions into new leadership arenas as well as reentry recruitment. The typology proposed here reflects the growing diversity of routes to political office for women, as well as the two-directional basis of power in the institutionalized party era.

Traditional party methods. Traditional party methods include institutional and sponsored recruitment, both of which may be used by male or female aspirants. Examples of the institutional route include previously holding state legislature office—the elective route (e.g., Senators Kay Bailey Hutchison and Debbie Stabenow, along with Lottie Shackelford, Democratic National Committee [DNC] vice-chair, and Jo Ann Davidson, Republican National Committee [RNC] cochairperson), holding a substantial role as a party contributor (e.g., Susan Turnbull, former DNC vice-chair), holding a

Table 10.1 Typology of Party Leadership Recruitment

Traditional Party

Institutional recruitment: generally self-selects and is chosen based on merit rising through normal channels.

Sponsored recruitment: can occur in one of two ways: The mentee is promoted by a high-profile mentor and rises though loyalty to existing leadership; similar to dynasties in that there is a party faction but differs in the lack of a family link. The ticket balancer rarely has any pre-existing tie to existing leaders and is chosen primarily for strategic electoral reasons (i.e., to neutralize a primary or general election opponent's electoral appeal or to strengthen the top of the ticket's appeal to a valued constituency).

Typically Male

Outside lateral leader entry: has alternative credentials established in another field; involves charismatic public persona or self-funding of the campaign.

Typically Female

Widow's accession: acts as a placeholder by taking on mantle of dead male kin/husband and is appointed or recruited to elective office ostensibly to continue the same policies.

Proxy: acts on behalf of living male relative and serves in office as a placeholder or surrogate.

Women's movement: is recruited to political party and elected office through women's movement and women's funding networks; usually does not determine election.

Dynastic succession: comes from independent individual accomplishment combined with the "male" power of a spouse who is the first-generation politician; reflects shared political networks and influence reflecting the rise of political "professional pairs" as well as family linkages to enhance political power.

leadership role in a major party faction (e.g., Linda Chavez-Thompson, DNC vice-chair), or holding a position as a Hill staffer in Congress (e.g., Representative Rosa DeLauro) or for a state legislator. Historically, women can also rise through the party hierarchy through work in women's clubs. In the past, this approach has been a recruitment route for Republican women to the vice-chair position in the RNC.

Those who are sponsored hold real, substantive positions and can display genuine political talent, but they rise primarily through their tie to an existing leader. One type of sponsored recruitment is the mentee (e.g., former secretary of state Condoleezza Rice under George W. Bush, who got her start as a staffer under the senior president Bush and has been discussed as a potential presidential candidate). Mentee recruitment can occur in both parties but has been more typical in the Republican Party culture (Freeman 1986, 198). Another type of sponsored recruitment is the ticket balancer. Relatively more common at the gubernatorial rather than the presidential levels, this recruitment method can suddenly raise the public stature of the individual chosen. For example, John McCain's elevation of Sarah Palin from an obscure Republican occupying a part-time Alaskan governor post to the Republican vice presidential nominee in 2008 catapulted her into the ranks of 2012 Republican presidential potentials. However, more typical is the selection of relatively unknown House member Geraldine Ferraro as the Democratic vice presidential nominee by Walter Mondale in 1984, whose candidacy failed to create presidential "buzz" in 1988.

Typically male. Typically male recruitment includes outside lateral leader entry. This method typically involves a charismatic public persona established through fame in another field or self-funding of the campaign. Classic male examples include John Glenn (astronaut), Sonny Bono and Fred Thompson (entertainment), and Wesley Clark (military). Another option is self-funding of a campaign—a female example might be Representative Ellen Tauscher (D-CA). Women are growing in stature in Hollywood and in other fields, but interestingly, these outside women leaders seem to be less willing to risk their stature by turning to politics.

Typically female. Typically female methods include a variety of recruitment mechanisms that span the entire range of dependent to independent political power. The *widow's accession,* for example, is historically a route to office for women in the prereform era. Of the 235 women who have served in the House, 39 filled vacancies caused by the death of their husbands. Nine of the 39 women serving in the US Senate as of 2011 filled their husband's vacancy. While the dominant route for women into politics until the 1970s (Kincaid 1978) and often serving as an interim appointment intended to maintain existing political alignments, the widow's accession remains significant as some women launch a successful political career. More recent House examples include Jo Ann Emerson (R-MO), Mary Bono Mack (R-CA), Lois Capps (D-CA), and Doris Matsui (D-CA), and former senator Jean Carnahan (D-MO), who was appointed to her husband's seat in 2001 but was defeated in the subsequent special election.

A proxy method is similar to the widow's accession but exists where there is a living male relative. It provides little personal influence for women while the spouse is living and is the typical role of a first lady or a congressional spouse. Eleanor Roosevelt developed an independent career later in life after the death of her spouse out of this type of role. This role is more common in other countries and is not a likely stepping-stone to later political office. In the United States, proxy recruitment is commonly used to boost the numbers of women without expanding the scope of women's power. As Goetz (2005) notes, when women are a proxy for male power, the purpose is to accentuate traditional male power as well as established class and ethnic power bases rather than to expand representation of women.

Proxy power is perhaps most obvious in the informal recruitment processes used in Democratic and Republican party conventions. Consistent with the Republican political culture (Freeman 1986), proxy power is more prevalent among Republican conventions. For example, in 2004, despite the campaign rhetoric playing off of the shorthand reference to George W. Bush as "W" to imply that the initial really stood for women, there were so many "delegate wives" that some observers concluded that *W* stood more often for *wife* than it did for *women* (Baer 2005; Ferguson and Marso 2007). Typically, the proportion of women rises more in incumbent-dominated conventions in the Republican Party than in contested conventions. In the 2004 convention, the proportion reached the highest levels ever, with as many as 25–40% of the women in many state delegations receiving their delegate slot as a "delegate-spouse."

The other two typically female methods of recruitment—women's movement and dynastic succession—are relatively new recruitment methods for women. The women's movement—except for the first generation of women's leaders such as former representatives Bella Abzug (D-NY) or Patsy Mink (D-HI)—rarely serves as the determinative factor for women's election to office. Dynastic succession is similar to the advent in many fields of professional pairs—couples who work professionally in the same field. While there are growing numbers of professional pairs where either both (the Clintons and the Doles) or only one (e.g., Representative John and his wife lobbyist Debbie Dingell; Senator Mitch McConnell and his wife, former labor secretary Elaine Chao) have held elective office, among women involved in politics, it remains unusual for the woman to turn their "pair" clout into elective office. In dynastic succession, the clout comes from the combined political careers and influence networks. Each partner gets access to influence networks pioneered by the other. The advantage of a dynastic succession is the ability to rise above negative gender stereotypes. Two examples of dynastic succession include former senators Elizabeth Dole (Republican from North Carolina and former secretary of labor) and Hillary Clinton (D-NY). These two methods of recruitment provide very different links to the women's movement. For those recruited through the women's movement, ties to the women's community are organic, while for those reliant on dynastic succession, these ties are optional and not developed as part of the politicization process.

As this review of the diverse recruitment channels used by men and women indicates, substantive representation of women's issues is much more likely with a movement-based recruitment channel (Baer and Bositis 1988, 1993; Cotter and Hennessy 1964; Goetz 2007; Mansbridge 1999). Leaders do reflect the groups who help to produce their first political victory. Thus, a focus on quotas alone provides only numerical representation, not genuine representation of women's issues. Based on gendered elite theory, as the opportunity structure for women changes, so will the type of women leaders.

Resources Available to Individual Leaders

Much of the focus on women's empowerment has focused on electing women to office. Once elected, women find holding a political office provides official power. Official leadership resources are essentially individual in nature. They include official executive or legislative powers and individual office resources, such as staff, electoral tenure, and the size of constituencies (e.g., Senators typically have larger constituencies than do Representatives). Once elected, reelection and extended tenure in office can allow leaders to expand their power base. Party and leadership offices among elected officials depend upon prestige among peer leaders. In addition to substantive policy expertise, party leadership portfolios based in part upon party factional strength have emerged in the current era. For example, membership and leadership of formal and informal party groups of elected officials can provide a new power base. Such group ties may have benefitted Nancy Pelosi's (Democrat representative from California and former chair of the Progressive Caucus) election as House Democratic Party whip over Steny Hoyer (D-MD) in 2002, and Newt Gingrich's (Republican representative from Georgia and founder of GOPAC) election as House Republican Party whip in 1989; however, it did not benefit Representative Michele Bachmann (Republican from Minnesota and founder of the House Tea Party Caucus) who was passed over in 2010 in her bid to serve as the House Republican policy chair.

A perceptual aspect also exists for individual power bases. Some leaders, for example, may also benefit from the status of being "on deck" For example, a relatively small group of individuals are viewed as "on deck" as a potential presidential candidate (Cronin and Genovese 1998). Being viewed as "on deck" is in part an elite view based upon insider/partisan conceptions, in party leaders' assessments of resources (e.g., fund-raising and endorsements), and in part a media assessment of leadership that reflects plebiscitary skills and gendered media frames that have treated many women candidates as less serious (i.e., providing less substantive news attention with a focus on novelty, the horse race, and appearance) (Falk 2010; Kahn 1996; Lawrence and Rose 2010).

While office resources are gender neutral, the perceptual aspects of being viewed as on deck are not. Women have received less media and insider attention as serious contenders for higher office—whether for senator (e.g., Barbara Mikulski's historic 1986 Senate victory in Maryland) or for president (Margaret Chase Smith in 1964, Shirley Chisholm in 1972, Pat Schroeder in 1988, Elizabeth Dole in 2000, and Carol Moseley Braun in 2004) (Falk 2010; Kahn 1996; Lawrence and Rose 2010). While in part based upon office seniority (tenure) and the perceptions of viability, these on-deck perceptions also impact women's ability to fund-raise for higher office (Farrar-Myers 2003). At this level, all women leaders must at some level acknowledge the potential of their base in women's issues.[4]

Thus a twofold chicken-and-egg problem has developed regarding women and executive leadership. First, do parties recruit women less—or have women been relatively less active in political parties? The second chicken-and-egg problem stems from the fact that executives at all levels (mayors, governors, presidents) are expected to lead their respective party unit. Once elected to executive office, an executive can remake the local party organization in his—or her—own image. Thus, are women recruited less for executive offices because they historically have not controlled executive office (and thus the top party leadership posts)? Answering this question requires understanding how party leadership functions. I now turn to an empirical examination of the informal barriers to executive recruitment within political parties.

Examining the Informal Barriers Within Parties: The Party Elite Data

How do the political parties structure the recruitment of women for executive office holding and candidate emergence? Ideally, as our theoretical model of party-based recruitment specifies, good data that directly answer this question would include qualitative studies of career-length recruitment channels and barriers for the two halves of the story (successful and failed candidates) as well as population data on factors associated with candidate emergence. Here, I can only examine the latter, but I do so with a new population group—party women. I explore this population through an analysis of the Party Elite Study (Baer and Bositis 1988), a series of quadrennial surveys of Democratic and Republican nominating convention delegates. Each presidential election year since 1976, an official list of the national convention delegates has been obtained from the two national parties and a questionnaire has been mailed immediately after each national convention to a systematic random sample of the delegates. The initial mailing has usually included approximately 1,000 to 1,100 delegate names, and the questionnaires have been mailed to their homes. Each year the return rate has been somewhere between 40% and 50% after one or two follow-up waves of questionnaires, a rate that compares favorably with other mailed questionnaires to political elites. In 1980 and 1984, this study also surveyed national committee members and state and county chairs in addition to convention delegates. The Party Elite Study provides a unique window into the thought patterns, experiences, and office ambitions of Democratic and Republican party activists and leaders—a group which includes large numbers of politically active men and women.

The analysis will focus primarily on the 1988 wave that to date is the only one that included an extended bank of questions focused on types of officeholding as well as aspects of party recruitment. While this data set is older, it is a singular data set for examining in depth the recruitment and socialization of political party men and women. If women's campaigns were highlighted by the 1980s, and women candidates were mainstreamed by the parties in the 1990s (Burrell 1992), these 1988 recruitment data should give a good picture of how women were welcomed by the parties. No other data set explicitly examines recruitment in such depth. Further, there is no reason to expect that internal party cultures structuring recruitment have changed markedly since 1988. The 1988 wave is solidly within the post-party-reform era, and the recruitment channels identified are highly likely to reflect patterns consistent from the 1980s to the present. Where possible and appropriate, pertinent changes over time will be noted.

Officeholding Among Party Leaders over Time

First I turn to an analysis over time of public office holding and ambitions for officeholding over time from 1980 to 2008 (see Table 10.2). The percent of men and women party activists and leaders who have held an elective or appointive public office varies considerably from convention year to convention year, and between men and women. Overall, anywhere from about a fifth to nearly half of men and women have held a public office. By contrast, anywhere from 80% to 90% of those surveyed had held a political party office (results not shown).[5] This finding demonstrates that the Party

Table 10.2 Comparisons of Officeholding and Ambitions for Future Office by Gender and Party, Within-Party Gender Differences, 1980–2008

	2008[a]		2004[a]		2000[a]		1996[a]		1992[a]		1988[a]		1984[b]		1980[b]	
	Men	Women	Men	Women	Men	Women	Men	Women	Men	Women	Men	Women	Men	Women	Men	Women
Democrats																
Percentage (n) of party leaders who																
Are a public office holder	**43.9***** (301)	**32.8***** (299)	**24.4**** (246)	**33.7**** (246)	**42.0**** (231)	**31.6**** (237)	33.5 (242)	28.6 (280)	**43.7***** (197)	**28.2***** (294)	**29.5*** (373)	**22.7*** (242)	**44.3***** (706)	**26.3***** (487)	**43.2***** (696)	**25.0***** (456)
Have ambitions for future office	**57.5**** (287)	**48.4**** (285)	58.7 (235)	53.2 (233)	59.1 (215)	53.1 (224)	52.8 (231)	47.9 (267)	**60.4*** (197)	**53.1*** (290)	48.8 (363)	50.0 (228)	—[c]		—	
Republicans																
Percentage (n) of party leaders who																
Are a public office holder	**40.1***** (411)	**23.8***** (189)	**47.7***** (277)	**30.3***** (218)	**46.8***** (263)	**27.1***** (166)	**46.2**** (279)	**33.9**** (168)	41.8 (94)	37.2 (164)	**37.0**** (395)	**24.3**** (144)	**44.0***** (686)	**26.0***** (415)	**42.5***** (837)	**22.8***** (298)
Have ambitions for future office	**53.1***** (392)	**40.4***** (176)	**59.2**** (272)	**49.5**** (206)	**61.6***** (255)	**43.3***** (157)	**57.5**** (273)	**41.2**** (165)	**55.9***** (195)	**38.9***** (162)	**48.9**** (376)	**37.2**** (137)	—		—	

Notes: Statistically significant differences are shown in **bold**: *p < .10, **p < .05, ***p < .001
a. Convention delegate sample only.
b. Four strata sampled within each party: national committee members, state chairs, county chairs, and convention delegates.
c. — indicates question not asked.

Elite data provide a good base for examining the relationship between parties and general public office holding.

There are persistent gender gaps in public office holding in both parties (see Figures 10.1 and 10.2). These gaps, however, are not explicable primarily through a lack of ambition. In both parties, a higher proportion of women have office ambitions than actually hold office. Among Republicans, the trend is for Republican party men to hold public office at higher rates in each of the eight conventions, and the results are statistically significant in seven of the eight conventions (excluding 1992). The trend of lower female officeholding is similar for Democrats with the exception of 2004, where Democratic women are statistically significantly *more* like to hold office than Democratic men, and in 1996 when the differences were not significantly different. The 2004 aberration seems to be due to a relatively lower proportion of Democratic men holding office rather than a change in officeholding among Democratic women.

When women activists are compared across party, Democratic and Republican women have similar officeholding levels. This trend is true for every year since 1980 except for 1992,[6] when Republican women are significantly more likely to have held a public office (results not shown). The officeholding gap between men and women is equal or larger among Republicans for each year considered except for 1992. In 1992, 37% of Republican

Figure 10.1 Democratic Party Leaders' Officeholding and Ambitions for Future Office, 1980–2008 (percentage)

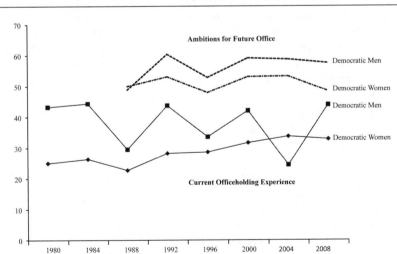

Note: Percentage for ambitions for future public office measured starting in 1988 and percentage holding public office currently measured starting in 1980.

Figure 10.2 Republican Party Leaders' Officeholding and Ambitions for Future Office, 1980–2008 (percentage)

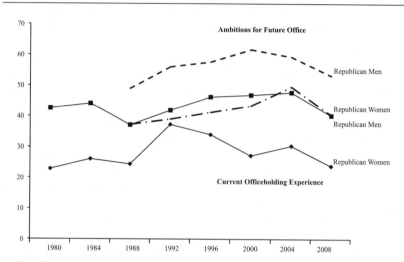

Note: Percentage for ambitions for future public office measured starting in 1988 and percentage holding public office currently measured starting in 1980.

women and 42% of Republican men had held a public office (a small gap of 5%) compared to only 28% of Democratic women and 44% of Democratic men (a larger gap of 16%).

A strong party difference, however, can be seen in terms of political ambition. Democratic women are nearly equally as ambitious for public office as are Democratic men. Only in 1992 and 2008 are there slightly lower ambition levels among Democratic Party women that are statistically significant. Republican women, in contrast, are significantly and systematically less ambitious for public office in all eight convention years compared to Republican men. In fact, Republican women's level of ambition is for the most part *less* than current officeholding levels among Republican men—which underscores the Republican ambition chasm for women. Among women activists, Democratic women are significantly more ambitious for public office generally compared to Republican women in 1988, 1992, 2000, and 2008 (results not shown). The fact that nationally active Democratic and Republican women have similar levels of officeholding despite the higher levels of ambition among Democratic women supports the argument that different party cultures can structure different recruitment paths and opportunities among Democrats and Republicans (Baer and Jackson 2009; Freeman 1986). This also suggests that contrary to the Lawless and Fox (2005, 2010) findings, ambition alone is not enough to make a candidate. I now turn to an in-depth analysis of recruitment using the 1988 wave of the Party Elite Study.

Type of Office-Seeking Activity

Party delegates and leaders were asked specific questions in the 1988 wave about whether they had run for nomination, won the nomination, run in the general election, or been elected to six different legislative bodies (school board, city council, county commission, state legislature, US House, and US Senate) and seven different executive positions (governor/lieutenant governor, statewide cabinet, state prosecutor, state judge, county or local prosecutor, county sheriff, and mayor). In addition, they were asked if they had sought any other offices, which could include minor elective offices (e.g., library board). Office seeking is important because it goes beyond envisioning running to taking active, concrete, and public steps to holding public office. These office-seeking behaviors were aggregated as part of a single summary typology and compared by party and gender (see Tables 10.3 and 10.4).

Only about a third to two-fifths of these party leaders and delegates had any office-seeking behavior, and Republicans had a significantly higher level of office-seeking activity. Interestingly, office seeking in general,

Table 10.3 **1988 Democratic and Republican Delegates' Type of Office-Seeking Activity by Party (percentage)**

Office-Seeking Activity	Democrat	Republican
None	**65.1****	**59.2****
Other and minor activity	**4.7****	**8.7****
Major legislative activity	**23.8****	**25.3****
Major executive activity	**6.4****	**6.9****
N	642	566
Major executive office seekers who also have major legislative office-seeking activity (percentage [*n*])	70.7 (41)	62.2 (37)

Note: Statistically significant differences are shown in **bold:** **p < .05.

Table 10.4 **1988 Democratic and Republican Delegates' Type of Office-Seeking Activity by Party and Gender (percentage)**

	Democrat		Republican	
Office-Seeking Activity	Male	Female	Male	Female
None	**61.8*****	**71.0*****	**55.8****	**67.6****
Legislative or other activity	**28.9*****	**26.9*****	**36.0****	**29.7****
Executive activity	**9.2*****	**2.0*****	**8.2****	**2.8****
N	380	245	403	145

Note: Statistically significant differences are shown in **bold:** **p < .05, ***p < .001.

while common, is still a minority activity even among party leaders and activists. Executive office seeking is relatively rare: only about 6%–7% in both parties had engaged in any office-seeking activity. In contrast, four times as many and about a fourth overall had engaged in legislative office seeking activity. What is noteworthy is that about 6 to 7 out of 10 of those engaged in executive office seeking had also engaged in legislative office seeking. For most—but not all—executive office seekers, executive office seeking is not a singular activity occurring in isolation from legislative activity. Women in both parties tended to have slightly, but significantly, lower levels of legislative and executive office seeking activities at all levels when compared to men in their own party. In both parties, much larger gaps can be found in executive office seeking behaviors (about a 3 to 1 ratio for Democrats and a larger 4 to 1 ratio for Republicans) than are found in overall or legislative office seeking behaviors. Clearly, these results underscore previous findings that ambition as an attitude is only one factor in successful officeholding, and that there are larger gender gaps for executive office seeking behaviors.

Recruitment Route for First Public Office Held

I next examined how legislative and executive office seekers differ in terms of their initial recruitment route into officeholding (see Tables 10.5 and 10.6).

Because of the relative rarity of executive office holding even among party elites, our focus here is less upon the characteristics of executive office holders than upon comparing differences in recruitment. Across parties, the majority of those seeking legislative and minor offices were recruited, while the majority of executive office seekers had sought their first elective office on their own. Legislative bodies typically have either formal partisan campaign committees or informal processes to help with recruitment and retention of a majority, and understandably, recruitment is common among office seekers of this type. However, the question focuses on the first public office. Given that most executive office seekers also have legislative

Table 10.5 1988 Democratic and Republican Delegates' Recruitment Route for First Public Office by Office-Seeking Type (percentage)

Recruitment Route for First Public Office	Legislative or Other Office Seeking Activity	Executive Office Seeking Activity
Recruited	**53.7****	**39.1****
Sought position on own	**46.3****	**60.9****
N	285	69

Note: Statistically significant differences are shown in **bold**: **p < .05.

Table 10.6 1988 Democratic and Republican Delegates' Recruitment Rate for First Public Office Among Office Seekers by Type of Office Seeking, Party, and Gender (in percentage)

First Public Office	Percentage
Legislative or other office-seeking activity	
Republican men	68.0
Republican women	54.8
Democratic women	46.8
Democratic men	35.1
Executive office-seeking activity	
Republican men	53.6
Democratic women	33.3
Democratic men	29.0
Republican women	25.0

experience, the fact that 6 out of 10 sought their first public office on their own underscores the singular importance of measuring ambition for office as a behavior as well as an attitude among public executives. Recruiting for public office varies by party and gender. The Republican Party is significantly more likely to have recruited legislative office seekers—55% and 68% respectively of Republican women and men say they were recruited. Among executive office seekers, more than twice as many Republican men (54%) say they were recruited compared to Republican women (25%). In the Democratic Party, by contrast, only a minority were recruited, and women have a slight edge over men in terms of recruitment for both legislative (47% to 35%) and executive (33% to 29%) office seeking. Among executive office seekers, a strong gender bias exists in the Republican Party with two men recruited for their first office compared to every Republican woman.

Party Office Versus Public Office Recruitment

Almost all (anywhere from 80% to 90%) of the party leaders and delegates held a current party office. Years of party service are significantly and positively associated with any type of office-seeking activity. Among Democrats, office seekers average 24 years and Republicans average 21 years of party service compared to 18 years for non–office seekers in both parties. But the positive relationship between length of party service and office-seeking does not explain the gap in gendered office-seeking activities. Women typically have the same or more years of service. Republican women (21 years) average significantly more years of experience compared to Republican men (19 years). And while Democratic women (19 years) have less experience on average than Democratic men (21 years), this difference is not large (data not shown).

To compare party mechanisms of recruitment, I examined party versus office recruitment (see Tables 10.7 and 10.8). When survey participants were asked about being recruited to their first political party office, I found no significant gender differences. And to the extent that there is a trend, women report being recruited to party office at slightly higher rates than do men in both parties. But if women start out on an equal playing field, their status as a party recruit does not benefit them as much as it does men. In both parties, men who are recruited for a party office are significantly more likely to be recruited for a public office. Of course, it is important to remember that these public offices can include appointive offices as well as elective offices. However, since a prestigious appointive office can be a stepping-stone to elective office, this overall gendered difference in recruitment does make the party less welcoming to women.

Demographic Characteristics and the Chinese Box Puzzle

The "Chinese box puzzle" model of leader recruitment separates different levels of recruitment (Prewitt 1970). Elective leadership, as the data have shown, is rare even among party men and women. At increasingly selective

Table 10.7 1988 Democratic and Republican Convention Delegates' Party and Office Recruitment (percentage)

	Democrat		Republican	
	Male	Female	Male	Female
Recruited	52.0	56.5	69.6	75.4
Sought position	48.0	43.5	30.4	24.6
N	331	186	368	145

Table 10.8 Recruitment for First Public Office by Party Recruitment for Party Office by Party and Gender (percentage)

	Democrat				Republican			
	Male		Female		Male		Female	
	Recruited	Sought Position	Recruited	Sought Position	Recruited	Sought Position	Recruited	Sought Position
Recruited	**44.0****	**17.8****	51.9	46.2	**71.9****	**48.7****	43.5	70.0
Sought office	**56.0****	**82.2****	48.1	53.8	**28.1****	**51.3****	56.6	30.0
N	50	45	27	13	96	39	23	10

Note: Statistically significant differences are shown in *bold:* **p < .05.

leadership selection levels ranging from social to community to politically mobilized, women may be able to use certain characteristics (e.g., education and occupation) as additional valuable resources in their office seeking. While women at the mass public level are less likely to have the known characteristics of the social strata of leaders (married, married to a high-status individual, employed full-time, high professional employment or business ownership, majority group [white] status, and education beyond the bachelor's degree), the next step is to consider how these factors impact officeholding within the parties (see Table 10.9).

While party men and women do demonstrate high social status compared to the general public, a comparison of the type of officeholding among male and female party elites shows some interesting patterns. Party women are less likely to be married than similar party men. More striking is the fact that party men in both parties are nearly all married—an asset for male leaders. Among those married, a quarter to half of party men volunteer that their spouse is a homemaker. Party men benefit from both bookends (either a spouse who is a homemaker or a spouse with a high-level professional or business occupation or both), while women only benefit from having a spouse with a prestigious occupation. Some intriguing party differences also appear that vary according to the office sought. Significantly, the proportion of married Democratic men who say that their employed spouse has a high-level professional or business occupation includes half of Democratic male non–office seekers, less than a third of legislative office seekers, and more than three-fifths of executive officer seekers. While at each level of office seeking, Republican women are about half again as likely to be employed than comparable Republican men, and among those employed, Republican women are significantly more likely to have a high-level professional or business occupation. As discussed earlier, party cultural distinctions differentially impede Republican women who are less educated, less often employed, and more often a self-identified homemaker. And both Democratic and Republican women suffer from structural disadvantages (i.e., party women tend not have a "house husband") to the extent that executive office holding is a two-person career.

Political Recruitment Characteristics and Gender

Research and theory discussed previously have shown that individuals are recruited into office through a variety of means. How do these recruitment factors impact the type of officeholding behavior (see Table 10.10)? This table includes traditional measures of ambition (getting ahead) to other recruitment factors such as family.

Overall, I find that party men and party women have similar patterns of political mobilization into politics both within and across parties. This discovery is heartening as political recruitment and mobilization is not gendered

Table 10.9 1988 Democratic and Republican Delegates' Demographic Characteristics by Officeholding Activity, Party, and Gender (percentage)

| | Democrat | | | | | | Republican | | | | | |
| | Male | | | Female | | | Male | | | Female | | |
	None	Legislative	Executive	None	Legislative	Executive	None	Legislative	Executive	None	Legislative	Executive
Married	75.0	80.7	85.7	59.3	59.7	80.0	85.5	87.8	100.0	79.4	90.7	50.0
Currently employed full-time	87.6	78.9	88.6	65.9	68.7	40.0	83.6	80.5	71.9	**42.3****	**35.0****	**100.0****
High-level professional or business occupation (if employed)	**47.5****	**62.0****	**71.9****	42.9	61.4	25.0	35.4	45.0	50.0	**41.5***	**69.2***	**100.0***
Self-described homemaker occupation (volunteered)	0.0	0.0	0.0	7.9	4.5	20.0	0.0	0.0	0.0	31.6	23.1	0.0
Spouse with a high-level professional or business occupation (among those married)	**49.6****	**28.8****	**62.5****	51.8	42.3	75.0	38.1	42.9	56.2	**33.9***	**63.0***	**100.0***
Spouse is a homemaker (among those married)	28.0	24.7	39.3	**0.0***	**5.0***	**0.0***	38.1	42.9	56.2	**0.0***	**2.7***	**0.0**
Nonwhite	8.3	11.0	8.6	12.8	9.0	20.0	1.4	4.0	3.0	2.0	2.3	0.0
Education beyond a B.A.	53.6	50.0	65.6	40.8	40.4	40.0	42.1	39.7	53.1	25.0	27.0	33.3
N	232	109	39	172	67	5	221	147	33	97	43	4

Note: Statistically significant differences are shown in **bold**: *p < .10, **p < .05.

Table 10.10 1988 Democratic and Republican Delegates' Political Recruitment Characteristics by Officeholding Activity, Party, and Gender (percentage)

| | Democrat | | | | | | Republican | | | | | |
| | Male | | | Female | | | Male | | | Female | | |
	None	Legislative	Executive	None	Legislative	Executive	None	Legislative	Executive	None	Legislative	Executive
First active through political campaigns	44.6	48.6	48.6	45.3	50.7	40.0	41.3	40.3	42.4	45.4	47.6	25.0
First active through desire to get ahead	5.6	7.3	5.7	**2.4****	**6.0****	**20.0****	1.8	4.7	3.0	**1.0***	**2.4***	**25.0***
First active through recruitment	10.3	11.0	5.7	**10.0****	**17.9****	**60.0****	15.1	18.9	21.2	18.6	16.7	0.0
At least one parent at least somewhat active in public affairs	65.5	68.2	80.0	73.4	73.1	80.0	66.5	69.8	66.7	63.3	76.7	0.0
First active through influence of family or friends	26.2	34.9	31.4	32.4	35.8	0.0	20.6	22.3	24.2	28.9	23.8	0.0
First active through ideological or interest group	22.7	29.4	28.6	30.0	28.4	20.0	30.7	25.7	15.2	22.7	38.1	50.0
First active through work for an interest or professional group	10.3	7.3	5.7	14.7	7.5	0.0	2.3	2.7	3.0	1.0	0	0
Would miss personal associations most if dropped out of politics	34.0	28.0	25.8	46.2	52.4	100.0	44.2	51.9	56.2	54.3	54.8	100.0
N	232	109	39	172	67	5	221	147	33	97	43	4

Note: Statistically significant differences are shown in **bold**: *p < .10, **p < .05.

in terms of access to opportunities to gain political skills among these party elites. The most common reason cited for political engagement was work in a political campaign—cited by anywhere from a quarter to a half of office-seeking groups of male and female party leaders. Nearly all come from politically active families. Except for Republican female executive office seekers, nearly two-thirds to four-fifths of the office-seeking groups of male and female party leaders had at least one parent who was active in political or community affairs. With the exception of Democratic and Republican women executive office seekers, about a quarter to more than a third of these office-seeking groups say that family or friends encouraged their political engagement. Recruitment generally for first political involvement (not a party or public office) is significantly more important as a factor for Democratic women executive office seekers.

Party women are interestingly similar to party men in what they enjoy in their political work. Citing personal associations as the most important thing that would be missed if they dropped out of politics is common regardless of the level of office seeking. However, ambition emerges as an important factor for women's public office seeking. While ambition as an attitude is a relatively rare reason for first involvement in politics, an underlying "desire to get ahead" is a significant and increasingly important factor for those Democratic and Republican women who are legislative and executive office seekers. Apparently, ambition is a complex phenomenon.

Party Factional Characteristics and Gendered Office Seeking

Political parties are not monolithic. Party elites are active in and responsive to different factional groups within their parties. I next examine whether this difference is related to office seeking behavior (see Table 10.11).

The results were quite variable within each party, within each gender, and between legislative and executive office seeking behavior. One can probably best interpret these findings as indicative of significant factors that differ among non–office seekers and between legislative and executive office seekers. Women are significantly more likely to represent a group in their party work than men, and Democrats are more likely to do so than Republicans. Generally, non-office-seeking party leaders of all types tend to be more sensitive and responsive to the views of interests within their party.

Among Democratic men, these significant variable factors included political party leaders, feminist leaders, family members, friends, and religious leaders. For Democratic women, these significant variable factors included feminist and religious leaders. Among Republicans, Republican men at different office-seeking levels had variable influences from family members and union, business, and minority and ethnic leaders. For Republican women, these variable factors included traditional women's groups, feminist

Table 10.11 1988 Democratic and Republican Delegates' Officeholding Behavior Characteristics by Officeholding Activity, Party, and Gender (percentage)

	Democrat						Republican					
	Male			Female			Male			Female		
	None	Legislative	Executive	None	Legislative	Executive	None	Legislative	Executive	None	Legislative	Executive
Represent a group in party politics	36.6	27.8	22.9	55.0	49.3	40.0	**17.0****	**23.6****	**6.1****	**20.6***	**34.9***	**75.0***
Party leaders have very much influence on opinion	**24.1***	**23.1***	**28.6***	25.3	28.8	20.0	19.1	27.7	27.3	29.9	25.6	25.0
Women's groups leaders have very much influence on opinion	7.4	11.0	5.7	21.1	28.8	40.0	1.8	4.8	3.0	**6.2****	**9.5****	**50.0****
Feminist leaders have very much influence on opinion	**6.1****	**10.1****	**0****	**11.7****	**26.3****	**40.0****	0.9	0.7	0	**2.1****	**9.5****	**25.0****
Family members have very much influence on opinion	**30.7****	**47.7****	**34.3****	25.1	28.8	40.0	**38.6***	**43.9***	**33.3***	32.0	39.5	25.0
Friends have very much influence on opinion	**23.4****	**35.8****	**22.9****	22.2	27.3	20.0	25.9	35.1	42.4	**20.6****	**21.4****	**25.0****
Religious leaders have very much influence on opinion	**7.4***	**11.9***	**11.4***	**2.9***	**10.6***	**20.0***	10.9	10.8	6.1	**5.2***	**9.3***	**0***
Union leaders have very much influence on opinion	12.7	17.4	17.1	17.8	18.2	0.0	**0.0****	**0.7****	**6.1****	**1.0****	**2.4****	**25.0****
Business leaders have very much influence on opinion	11.0	8.3	8.6	4.1	7.6	20.0	**15.5***	**20.3***	**21.2***	10.6	14.6	25.0
Minority/ethnic leaders have very much influence on opinion	15.4	17.4	14.3	16.9	19.7	20.0	**6.8****	**6.1****	**12.1****	8.2	4.8	25.0
N	232	109	39	172	67	5	221	147	33	97	43	4

Note: Statistically significant differences are shown in **bold:** $*p < .10$, $**p < .05$, $***p < .001$.

leaders, friends, religious leaders, and union leaders. These findings support the conclusion that the parties are not monolithic, and even within parties, other party groupings have different relationships with men and women and differential impacts on their recruitment.

Future Plans for Officeholding

I also examined ambitions for elective and appointive office by gender and party (see Table 10.12).

Even among those who have never engaged in any office seeking, about a third of Democratic men and women and Republican men all plan to run for elective office. A much smaller proportion of Republican women (17%) who have never engaged in office seeking aspire to run for office. But for Democratic men and women, and for Republican women, legislative and executive office holding activity is significantly and increasingly associated with plans to seek future elective office. While not significant, the trend is the same for Republican men. No significant differences were found for appointive office. This finding demonstrates that public office seekers are ambitious for future office—a positive finding for democracy. This also demonstrates that ambition is a learned process that reflects that old idea that one learns by doing—legislative and executive office seeking breeds more office seeking.

Conclusion

This chapter has reviewed the literature on the role of political parties and leadership and provided a gendered model of inside and outside methods of party recruitment. It has been argued here that research on officeholding in a democracy is at base an analysis of a two-way bidirectional process of leadership recruitment, not just simply candidate emergence. Women, while not new to the parties (Freeman 2000), really only gained significant traction in the post-reform-party era since the 1970s through the women's movement (Baer 2011; Baer and Bositis 1988). Women act on the parties as well as being formed by the parties. As activism in the women's movement is declining, recruitment of women and women's power base *as women* is becoming more institutional and less movement based. Political parties and the groups allied with them (including the women's movement) have emerged as central gatekeepers in providing resources and opportunities for leadership replacement.

The data here focused on initial recruitment factors that impact women's running for office, with an especial emphasis on executive office holding in a unique population where individuals are already mobilized as part of a

Table 10.12 1988 and 2008 Democratic and Republican Delegates' Future Plans for Office by Officeholding Activity, Party, and Gender (percentage)

1988

| | Democrat | | | | | | Republican | | | | | |
| | Male | | | Female | | | Male | | | Female | | |
	None	Legislative	Executive	None	Legislative	Executive	None	Legislative	Executive	None	Legislative	Executive
Plans to seek future elective office	**33.9****	**52.3****	**54.5****	**33.3*****	**60.0*****	**75.0*****	36.5	45.4	43.3	**17.4*****	**50.0*****	**75.0*****
Plans to seek future appointive office	17.9	25.2	24.2	20.8	24.6	25.0	18.6	17.9	16.7	12.0	15.0	25.0
N	232	109	39	172	67	5	221	147	33	97	43	4

2008

| | Democrat | | | | Republican | | | |
| | Male | | Female | | Male | | Female | |
	None	One or More	None	One or More	None	One or More	None	One or More
Plans to seek future elective office	**30.2*****	**57.9*****	**20.6*****	**54.9*****	**25.2*****	**59.7*****	**16.5*****	**54.5*****
Plans to seek future appointive office	**19.1*****	**9.5*****	**17.0*****	**15.4*****	**14.7*****	**13.6*****	**15.8*****	**11.9*****
N	82	126	194	91	143	154	133	42

Note: Statistically significant differences are shown in **bold**: **$p < .05$, ***$p < .001$.

network of political leaders. The analysis did not examine individual leadership resources, individual career paths, or leadership metaresources, but the results do provide a deeper understanding of whether women and women executive office seekers have been welcomed to the party using the only data set that allows us to examine in depth the populations of party men and women leaders. While the in-depth analysis uses data from 1988, the comparisons over time from 1980 to 2008 on within-party similarities and cross-party differences provide confidence that the 1988 results provide useful benchmarks for understanding how parties structure recruitment in the postreform era.

For political party women and men, important similarities demonstrate that high-level political activism is not gendered—men and women similarly get their start in politics by working on a political campaign or coming from a politically active family and say personal associations are the thing that they would most miss if they dropped out.

The data demonstrate that executive office seeking is rare for both men and women, even among political party elites, and it is here that we find a large gender "gulf" rather than just a gap. Some significant handicaps may specifically impact executive office seeking. Party women have similar demographic profiles to those of party men, but they do typically possess only one of the two bookends of party men—a spouse with a high-profile occupation and spouse who stays at home—which erects a structural barrier for women candidates. And most executive office seekers in this study sought their office on their own—a singular fact for those studying recruitment. But the parties do recruit, and contrary to many who argue that the parties do not recruit, recruitment is a very significant factor in both parties both for party office and for public office. Further, executive office seekers tend to also have legislative office seeking experience, and this experience might also serve as an early recruitment factor. Nonetheless, the gender gap in executive office seeking is really more of a gulf—a multiplicative factor ranging from 3 or 4 to 1 rather than a spread of a few percentage points.

On the positive side, feminist and women's group leaders do play an influential role among women who seek office, especially executive office. The fact that women in both parties are more likely to represent a group in their party work confirms the role that the women's movement plays as a corrective to gendered disadvantages women face across party lines.

The findings in this study also provide insights into candidate emergence. Ambition among party men and women emerges here as a complex phenomenon that should be studied in terms of both party and appointive as well as elected public offices and includes multiple behavioral and attitudinal measures. Political party women are ambitious for future public office, and gaps in officeholding based on these data cannot be attributed solely or primarily to a lack of ambition. Consistent with prior political science research outside of women and politics research, ambition can be understood as strategic and learned through multiple stages both within and outside of the parties—rather than simply reflecting gendered individual characteristics.

Overall, persistent gender gaps remain in public office holding despite the high levels of ambition found among party women. However, the gaps found here are less than one might expect in the public at large—if women are among only 15% to 25% of current officeholders, one would expect a similarly sized gender gap among these party elites. This gap was not the case. First, no gender difference could be found in recruitment to party office, but once within the parties, a difference was discovered in gender recruitment to public office. Second, while women do hold fewer public offices and engage in less legislative and executive office seeking behavior compared to party men, the gaps are small and the parties do provide a positive support system to political party women. If, for example, one created a gender officeholding index, instead of a score of 0.08 to a high of 0.40 (among all officeholders using the voting age population as a base), then a comparative party officeholding index using party leaders as the base would be closer to a score of 0.60 or 0.70 (depending on the year considered). Clearly, parties do serve to augment women's ability to achieve leadership statuses not only within party ranks but also in terms of elective public offices.

This particular study did not examine quotas per se. But the finding that recruitment is alive and well in the political parties, and that it has significant impact on office-seeking behavior, suggests that quotas may not provide the same level of party support and influence and skills as is earned through mobilization, party experience, and group, factional, and party ties. In this area, party women are equal to party men—quotas risk women attaining positions without commensurate political experience, creating "politics without power" (Cotter and Hennessy 1964).

These analyses do suggest that each party offers a distinctive culture based in part on different gendered social coalitions that structure how women engage in office seeking. In short, the parties are *differentially* gendered. Republican women, for example, are less ambitious for public office—a systematic factor over time that deserves further exploration in the post–Sarah Palin era. Perhaps the sponsored recruitment of Palin in 2008 has opened the door to the ambitions of more conservative Republican women, but the data presented here would treat any such hypothesis with caution. While more Republican women ran in primaries in 2010, they did not have commensurate success, and the data here support earlier research showing that women in parties are empowered for the long term when they are tied to and represent a group (Baer 2011; Baer and Dolan 1994). Unless the Republican Tea Party faction starts to advance women based on a commitment to women's recruitment beyond short-term strategic electoral concerns, the results here would predict only a temporary blip for increases in conservative women candidates. To the extent that the Republican Party has realigned over opposition to women's rights (Baer 2010; Melich 1996; Wolbrecht 2000), then there is likely a limited pool of conservative potential women candidates. When the facts that Republican women tend to suffer a deficit of individual demographic characteristics (e.g., education and employment) long considered critical to strategic recruitment as well as a deficit of group-based resources beyond family and kinship are considered, one would not expect the partisan gender gap to change markedly despite the singular public prominence of a Sarah Palin or a Michele Bachmann.

In both parties, men who are recruited for a party office are significantly more likely to be recruited for a public office. But overall, the Democratic Party has been more welcoming to party women in the postreform era. This difference means that while ambition is important, group-based institutional and party polarization factors still persist. The Republican Party, for example, typically engages in more recruitment than does the Democratic Party. Yet Republican Party women are systematically disadvantaged in recruitment relative to Republican men, particularly in executive office seeking. In contrast, Democratic women tend to be recruited at a slightly higher rate than Democratic men. And each party has different factional groups who play distinct roles within each party. However, while the parties can and should do more, I found that women are indeed a regular part of the party and public office recruitment processes. While this study can say little about the rise to higher leadership statuses, the parties—if not welcoming women—are not the barriers many have perceived, and working within the party structures will be critical to future advances for women in executive office holding.

Notes

1. Figures are estimated (women's proportion of overall population varies quite a bit from state to state and legislative district to legislative district) using the officeholding percentages for various offices prepared by the Center for the American Woman and Politics. Please see "Current Numbers of Women Office Holders," http://www.cawp.rutgers.edu/fast_facts/levels_of_office/Current_Numbers.php. Accessed June 28, 2012.

2. Political scientist Harvey Mansfeld, for example, posits "manliness" as a key feature of leadership: "Manliness is a quality that causes individuals to stand up for something [and] . . . calls private persons into public life. In the past, such people have been predominantly male, and it is no accident that those who possess this quality have often ended up as political rulers and leaders" (Mansfield 2003, 33).

3. This statement refers to the undisputed fact that mass activism for women's rights has declined and women's movement organizations are smaller and less active today than they were in the 1970s and 1980s. One can argue that women's

movements have simply moved within institutions (e.g., Banaszak 2010; Reger 2005; Whittier 2005) or one can take the position as does the author (Baer 2005; Baer and Bositis 1993) and others (e.g., Freeman 1999) that women's movements are best understood sociologically and that true movements in their active phases have both elite and mass components. This distinction is important for the present analysis in that parties are an institution that reacts primarily to constituent and grassroots pressures and can only be understood at both levels (i.e., as an institution and as a representative, permeable organization).

4. It is interesting that Senator Kay Bailey Hutchison (R-TX), considered by some as "on deck" for presidential consideration in 2008, took the step to author a book on women's history and leadership, entitled *American Heroines: The Spirited Women Who Shaped Our Country* (2004).

5. Where appropriate, additional analysis of the Party Elite data that go beyond the tables presented here will be mentioned in order to provide further insights. These additional analyses are available on request from the author.

6. Since 1980, Democratic conventions require a 50-50 equal gender split among delegates. Inclusion of women among Republican convention delegates is variable and seems to be higher when there is an incumbent Republican president such as was the case in 1992 (Baer 2010).

11

Campaign Finance: A Barrier to Reaching the White House?

Victoria A. Farrar-Myers and Brent D. Boyea

As we gather here today, the 50th woman to leave this Earth is orbiting overhead. If we can blast 50 women into space, we will someday launch a woman into the White House. . . . Although we weren't able to shatter that highest, hardest glass ceiling this time, thanks to you, it's got about 18 million cracks in it. And the light is shining through like never before, filling us all with the hope and the sure knowledge that the path will be a little easier next time.
—Hillary Clinton, concession speech, June 8, 2008

In early 2010, the Minnesota Democratic-Farmer-Labor (DFL) Party gubernatorial primary scheduled for August of that year was shaping up to be a crowded field with at least four prominent candidates running for the nomination. In April, though, Ramsey County attorney Susan Gaertner withdrew from the race. One of the primary reasons for her decision was that

the [DFL's] endorsement of [Minnesota House Speaker Margaret Anderson Kelliher] would pit two women against each other in the primary, and with two self-financed and well-funded male candidates, the resulting struggle would make it extremely difficult to raise sufficient funds for an effective campaign. . . . What is clear is that if I stayed in the race, I could hurt the chances of a woman surviving the primary. (Sundquist 2010)[1]

Gaertner's reasoning strikes at the heart of the challenge facing female candidates for executive offices: although becoming financially viable (as described more fully below) is difficult for any political aspirant, doing so is often seen as a potentially insurmountable barrier for women seeking higher office.

What about the highest executive office that a woman can attain, the US presidency—how substantial a barrier is achieving financial viability for a woman seeking the White House? The idea of having a female president has moved over the years from a "never" to an "if" to perhaps now a "when." Whereas female candidates for president in the past have been rare, over the most recent presidential election cycles, we have seen female candidates knock down barriers and being viewed as having real potential to be elected (Elizabeth Dole in 1999), being viable candidates (Hillary Clinton in 2008), and even being early front-runners for their party's nomination (again, Clinton in 2008). Yet for women to emerge as financially viable presidential candidates, they must first work their way through the pipeline of lower offices and be financially viable candidates along each step of the way, all the while overcoming the barriers impeding women in the electoral arena.

Scholars who have studied the disparity between the percentage of women in the population versus the percentage of female elected officials have found no widespread overt gender discrimination (Woods 2000) but have offered numerous explanations in an attempt to reconcile this fact with the slow rise of women through the political pipeline (Fox and Lawless 2010). The factors identified have been categorized as the following:

- Structural, such as the incumbency advantage (Darcy and Clark 1994);
- Situational, such as female underrepresentation in typical prepolitical careers (Darcy and Clark 1994; Duerst-Lahti 1998);
- Circumstantial, such as gender stereotypes (Fox 1997; Kahn 1996; Koch 2000; Lawless 2004) and geographic differences (Palmer and Simon 2006); and
- Gender role socialization (Lawless and Fox 2005).

Given the challenges facing female candidates, achieving financial viability should also be added to the list of structural barriers impeding the rise of female political aspirants through the pipeline. This perception has been buttressed over the years. For example, when Elizabeth Dole withdrew from seeking the Republican presidential nomination in 1999 prior to the 2000 primaries, she cited a lack of money as her primary reason. Indeed, at the time of her withdrawal, she had raised less than 10% of the amount that George W. Bush had raised to that point. But is the perception correct that achieving financial viability poses a structural barrier to female candidates in a way that men do not encounter? If so, how is that barrier different than the challenges any candidate for executive office faces in achieving financial viability, and how have women been able to overcome this barrier to become financially viable candidates?

This chapter addresses these and other related questions. The chapter begins by considering what it means to be a viable candidate, regardless of gender, particularly as it relates to financial viability. From there, the chapter examines the campaign finance experiences of women in the political pipeline for higher office—governors and members of Congress—to compare their fund-raising profiles with those of their male counterparts. Next, the chapter looks at the financial viability of Hillary Clinton's 2008 campaign for the Democratic presidential nomination, including what she and her campaign did well and where it fell short. Finally, the last portion of the chapter brings together the findings and lessons to assess the challenges facing women when running for executive office, and to consider the fund-raising skills and assets that women have developed to become financially viable candidates as they move through the political pipeline and towards a successful run for the presidency.

Can Women Compete as Fund-Raisers? Comparative Fund-Raising Success of Winning Candidates

Before assessing whether women can compete as fund-raisers, one must first understand what is meant by "overall (or candidate) viability" and "financial viability." Many different factors feed into the seemingly simple concept of overall viability, which is the perception of a candidate's chances of winning (Abramowitz 1989). A number of these factors are tangible in nature and are to some degree within a candidate's control: money, name recognition, network/support, campaign organization, backing of the party, credibility on key issues, and résumé. Others are intangible and require a candidate to be able to turn factors outside of their control to their advantage, such as political timing, political environment and mood, and desire for change.[2]

As one can see, money (i.e., financial viability) is just one factor used for determining a candidate's overall viability, but it "is a core ingredient on which many of the other ingredients of viability hinge" (Farrar-Myers 2007, 122). As Susan Gaertner noted above, money is a necessary component for waging an effective campaign. With money comes, among other things, the ability to build a campaign organization, to mobilize one's network of supporters, and to build name recognition through advertisements. Money is also seen as an early indication of overall viability and is used as a surrogate for such during any preprimary/preelection period because it provides the most objective basis to judge a candidate's level of support.

One way to determine whether and how a female candidate could emerge as a financially viable presidential candidate is to look at the fund-raising experiences of women in the pipeline, in particular governors and members of Congress since either position is often seen as the proving ground for presidential aspirants. How does the campaign finance fund-raising profile of successful female candidates compare to their male counterparts? Have winning female candidates been as successful at fund-raising as men running for the same positions? Are there differences by political party? Are there differences in sources of funds received? Undertaking gender comparisons at both the state executive level and the national legislative level will allow us to determine whether significant differences exist in the campaign finance profiles of successful female and male candidates, as well as what implications these differences or similarities may have for the potential for a woman to be elected president.

In terms of assessing candidate viability, using contributions to candidates is a far more meaningful measure than other potential funding sources. A contribution from an individual is a contribution from a potential voter. The more contributors to a campaign and the higher the amount of contributions a candidate receives enhance a candidate's viability. To a lesser extent, the same can be said about political action committee (PAC) contributions to candidates since they would send a cue to the members of the PAC or its related organization regarding whom the members should support. This latter point is particularly true for ideological or single-issue PACs that are more likely to want to influence elections to achieve an ideological goal rather than achieve access or a partisan goal (Jacobson and Kernell 1981).

Other potential funding sources do not offer candidates such direct or indirect connections to potential supporters at the polls. Public funding, found at some state and local levels, may level the playing field for candidates seeking these offices, but is provided to all candidates who qualify for the funding from a central pool without any connection to just how viable the candidate is otherwise. Further, as candidates move up to the federal congressional level or other positions where public funding is not available, a previous reliance on public funding as a means to establish viability for lower offices could be a fatal flaw in the candidates' rise through the pipeline because they will not have learned how to fund a campaign without public money. As for the top executive office, president of the United States, even though public funding is available, the changing landscape of presidential campaign financing during the first part of the twenty-first century has rendered public funding meaningless for those candidates who wish to be seen as viable.

Other funding sources similarly suffer fatal flaws in terms of enhancing candidates' viability both as they campaign within any given race and as they move through the political pipeline. Party funding is given to the party's candidates and, like public funding, offers no direct tie to voters and sometimes little insight into the overall viability of a candidate. A candidate's self-financing may allow a candidate to kick start the campaign or free the candidate from fund-raising obligations, but it also creates no connection between the candidate and the voters. While independent expenditures may be increasing in the wake of the US Supreme Court's decision in

Citizens United v. Federal Election Commission[3] and may have an impact on the barriers that candidates face to wage viable campaigns (as will be discussed more later), such expenditures are by definition outside the control of a candidate and, thus for the purposes here, have no effect on determining how female candidates can establish pathways of viability to ultimately reach the White House. Only by assessing contributions to a candidate can one determine whether a candidate—male or female—is having success in reaching potential voters and enhancing his or her chances, or at least the perception of his or her chances, of winning an election.

From 1997 through 2008, 14 women were elected as governor on 21 occasions.[4] For the purposes of the following analysis, the female candidates for all 21 elections were paired based on geographic proximity with a winning male gubernatorial candidate.[5] Figure 11.1 shows the average expenditures of the selected female and male governors, including by party.[6] Women ($5.14 million) and men ($5.18 million) averaged about the same level of expenditures over the period under review. Each gender saw a different relationship between their partisans, however. While Democratic women ($5.44 million) outspent Republican women ($4.48 million) on average, Republican men ($6.90 million) outspent their Democratic male ($3.45 million) counterparts by a more significant margin. While the disparity in spending by women and men by party may relate to different state and electoral contexts for individual candidates, spending differences may

Figure 11.1 Average Expenditures for Selected Winning Governors, 1996–2008

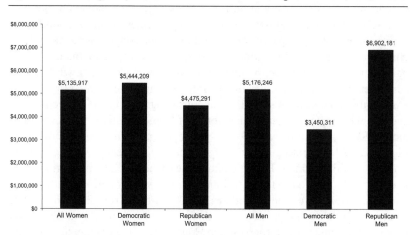

Source: Compiled by the authors from National Institute on Money in State Politics data available at http://www.followthemoney.org.

Note: Democratic women: $N = 14$; Republican women: $N = 7$; Democratic men: $N = 10$; Republican men: $N = 11$.

also demonstrate the different situations for male and female gubernatorial candidates in the two major political parties.

Figures 11.2(a)–(f) reflect the average source of funds for winning male and female gubernatorial candidates by party. One characteristic to note about male candidates, regardless of party, is they generally had similar campaign funding profiles with approximately 55% of their contributions on average raised from individuals. The profiles for female candidates differ significantly by party: female Republican candidates relied heavily on individual contributions to fund their campaigns (78.9% on average), while Democratic women obtained significant funding (34.5%) from their political party and other non-PAC sources. In terms of contributions by PACs (see Figures 11.3[a]–([f]), business PACs were the predominant source of funds for both male and female candidates. Business PACs, however, constituted a higher percentage of PAC contributions to male gubernatorial candidates whereas women drew slightly more from single-issue and ideological sources. This relationship is similar to that found with congressional candidates as discussed more fully below.

The sparse amount of data for successful female candidates for governor (14 winning female candidates in 21 elections over a dozen years) may limit the implications that can be drawn by looking at this level in the political pipeline. Nevertheless, these variations in campaign financing profiles among candidates for governor reflect that there may be different pathways to developing winning campaigns and achieving financial viability. Even though the number of female governors may be small, these women have found ways to build successful and financially viable campaigns, even if they have not relied as much on funds from organized moneyed interests (i.e., PACs generally and business PACs in particular) as male candidates.

Examining the campaigns of successful female congressional candidates eliminates some of the limitations found when looking at gubernatorial campaign financing data since the number of women in Congress, while still a small percentage compared to the overall percentage of women in the general population, has been significant and growing. For the 2008 election, the average winning candidate in the House of Representatives spent approximately $1.37 million during the two-year cycle preceding the election (see Figure 11.4).[7] Separating the winning candidates by gender we see that the average winning female House candidate expended $1.35 million and the average male paid out $1.37 million. This spending relationship between winning male and female candidates in 2008 differs from 2000 and 2004, where comparable analyses showed that successful female candidates had outspent their male counterparts in the House.[8] To some degree, though, this reversal in expenditures can be traced to partisan differences. The 58 Democratic women in 2008 averaged $1.29 million in expenditures and the 17 Republican women on average spent almost $1.55 million, thus maintaining

Figure 11.2 Average Sources of Funds for Female and Male Governors, 1997–2008

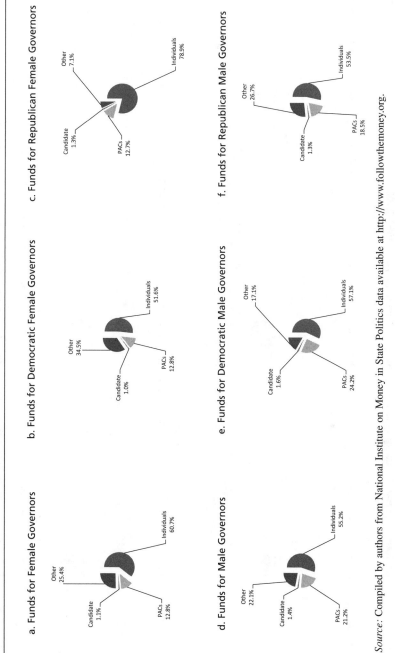

a. Funds for Female Governors

Other
25.4%

Candidate
1.1%

PACs
12.8%

Individuals
60.7%

b. Funds for Democratic Female Governors

Other
34.5%

Candidate
1.0%

PACs
12.8%

Individuals
51.6%

c. Funds for Republican Female Governors

Other
7.1%

Candidate
1.3%

PACs
12.7%

Individuals
78.9%

d. Funds for Male Governors

Other
22.1%

Candidate
1.4%

PACs
21.2%

Individuals
55.2%

e. Funds for Democratic Male Governors

Other
17.1%

Candidate
1.6%

PACs
24.2%

Individuals
57.1%

f. Funds for Republican Male Governors

Other
26.7%

Candidate
1.3%

PACs
18.5%

Individuals
53.5%

Source: Compiled by authors from National Institute on Money in State Politics data available at http://www.followthemoney.org.

Figure 11.3 Average Sources of PAC Funds by Type for Female and Male Governors, 1997–2008

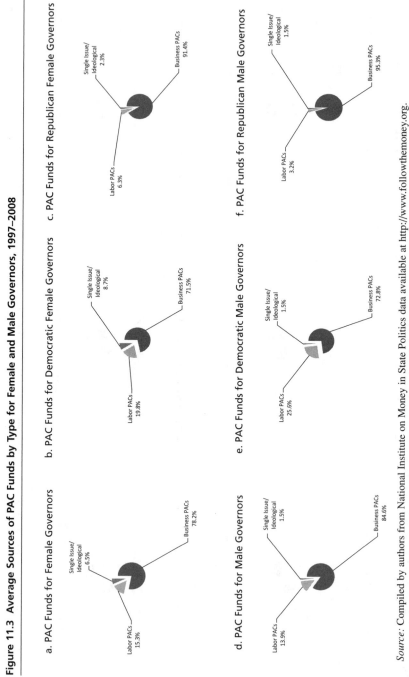

a. PAC Funds for Female Governors

Single Issue/
Ideological
6.5%

Business PACs
78.2%

Labor PACs
15.3%

b. PAC Funds for Democratic Female Governors

Single Issue/
Ideological
8.7%

Business PACs
71.5%

Labor PACs
19.8%

c. PAC Funds for Republican Female Governors

Single Issue/
Ideological
2.3%

Business PACs
91.4%

Labor PACs
6.3%

d. PAC Funds for Male Governors

Single Issue/
Ideological
1.5%

Business PACs
84.6%

Labor PACs
13.9%

e. PAC Funds for Democratic Male Governors

Single Issue/
Ideological
1.5%

Business PACs
72.8%

Labor PACs
25.6%

f. PAC Funds for Republican Male Governors

Single Issue/
Ideological
1.5%

Business PACs
95.3%

Labor PACs
3.2%

Source: Compiled by authors from National Institute on Money in State Politics data available at http://www.followthemoney.org.

Figure 11.4 Average Expenditures for Winning House Candidates, 2008

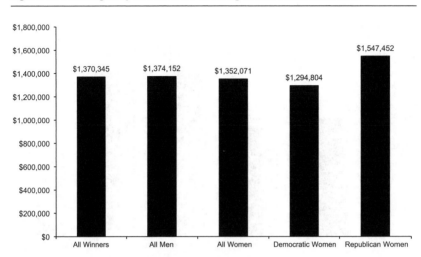

Source: Compiled by authors from Federal Election Commission (FEC) data available at http://www.fec.gov.
Note: Democratic women: *N* = 58. Republican women: *N* = 17.

the traditional money advantage that the GOP enjoys over Democrats. Although the gulf between average female Democratic candidates, male candidates, and female Republican candidates was wider in 2008 compared to prior elections, the order of this relationship is consistent with what was found in 2000 and 2004.[9]

In the Senate, the relationships among expenditures by successful male and female candidates continued to follow those found in prior analyses (see Figure 11.5).[10] The three election cycles between 2004 and 2008 saw all 100 Senate seats contested plus an additional two special elections to fill unexpired terms. In these 102 elections, the average winning candidate spent $7.86 million. Breaking down these candidates by gender, female candidates spent $11.3 million, on average, compared to $7.17 million by male candidates. The relatively small number of women in the analysis (17) means that the expenditures total for winning female candidates is somewhat skewed by the inclusion of Hillary Clinton's 2006 campaign, where she spent in excess of $40 million. Excluding Clinton from this analysis, however, does not substantively change the relationship between winning candidates by gender, as other winning female candidates in the Senate spent an average of $9.47 million, which is still almost one-third above the average for winning male Senate candidates during this period.

When examining women in the Senate, we discover that the 2004–2008 Senate election cycles continued a trend shown in the prior studies in

Figure 11.5 Average Expenditures for Winning Senate Candidates, 2004–2008

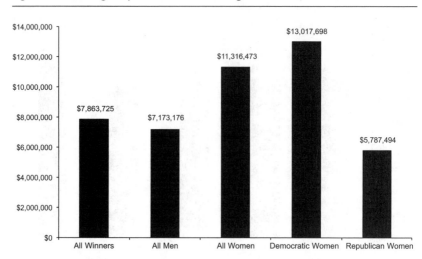

Source: Compiled by authors from data available at http://www.fec.gov.
Notes: N (Democratic Women) = 13. 2004: Boxer (CA), Lincoln (AR), Mikulski (MD), Murray (WA); 2006: Cantwell (WA), Clinton (NY), Feinstein (CA), Klobuchar (MN), McCaskill (MO), Stabenow (MI); 2008: Hagan (NC); Landrieu (LA); Shaheen (NH). N (Republican Women) = 4. 2004: Murkowski (AK); 2006: Hutchison (TX), Snowe (ME); 2008: Collins (ME).

which the traditional Republican fund-raising advantage was reversed. Democrats (including Hillary Clinton) spent on average more than $13.0 million ($10.7 million without Clinton) during this period. Other significant spenders include Maria Cantwell ($16.71 million in 2006), Barbara Boxer ($15.98 million in 2004), and Patty Murray ($12.48 million in 2004). During this period, the four successful female Republican candidates included three from states with small populations (Lisa Murkowski, Alaska, 2004; Olympia Snowe, Maine, 2006; and Susan Collins, Maine, 2008) and a long-term incumbent who faced minimal competition (Kay Bailey Hutchison, Texas, 2006). Of these successful female Republican senators, none spent more than $8 million. Interestingly, former Republican senator Elizabeth Dole spent almost $17.5 million in her failed reelection bid in 2008 when she lost to Democrat Kay Hagan. If Dole's expenditures were added to the four winning female Republican candidates, the average would increase to $8.12 million.

The fund-raising relationships between successful male and female congressional candidates in 2000, 2004, and 2008 show a similar pattern over the years.[11] Successful female congressional candidates on average have spent as much and often more than their male counterparts "and have, indeed, learned to play the campaign finance game quite well" (Farrar-Myers

2007, 117). Whatever campaign financing barriers may have existed for female congressional candidates, these analyses have shown that such barriers can be overcome.

One such barrier for female candidates is the source of campaign funds. Do women obtain their campaign funds from sources different than those utilized by successful male candidates? Fund-raising during the 2000 and 2004 election cycles produced similar results (see Table 11.1).[12] Specifically, successful male and female congressional candidates raised similar percentages of their funds from individuals and PACs, although men tended to receive more of their PAC contributions from business PACs than women did. Perhaps the most interesting finding from the 2000 and 2004 elections was that while Democratic women received a slightly higher percentage of their funds from individual contributions, the reverse was true on the GOP side where Republican men relied more on individual contributions than Republican women.

The 2008 election cycle reflected a slight but substantively different allocation of sources of funds among winning House candidates. Women relied on contributions from individuals more heavily than their male colleagues. This finding includes Republican women, who received 58% of their funds from individuals, as compared to Republican men (51%), thus, reversing the findings from the previous two election studies. A similar result is shown in Table 11.2 with respect to senatorial candidates.[13] In the Senate, successful female candidates have tended to rely more on individual contributions than male candidates with whom they were paired for this analysis based on geographic proximity in terms of the percentage of overall funds raised (65.3% to 56.6% from 1996–2000, and 64.4% to 61.4% from 2000–2004). In the 2004–2008 election cycles, the gap between genders widened as nearly three-fourths (73.8%) of funds raised by successful female candidates came from individual contributions as compared to 59.2% for men.[14]

Breaking down PAC contributions by the nature of the organization, female House candidates continued to receive a smaller percentage of PAC contributions from business PACs than men in the 2007–2008 election cycle, although, in the case of both genders, still at levels comparable to previous cycles. In the Senate, women continued the pattern of receiving a lower percentage of PAC contributions from business PACs, but for both men and women the percentage of business PAC contributions declined throughout the three election cycles. In the Senate, this decline coincides with a rise in the percentage of contributions for both men and women from single-issue, ideological, and other PACs.[15] Female House candidates also have seen a slight increase in the percentage of contributions from single-issue/ideological PACs, although primarily at the relative expense of contributions from labor-related PACs.

Table 11.1 Average Source of Funds of Selected Candidates by Gender, House of Representatives, 2000, 2004, and 2008 (percentage)

	2000			2004			2008		
	Individuals	PACs	Other	Individuals	PACs	Other	Individuals	PACs	Other
House women	49	47	4	55	42	3	53	44	3
Democratic	48	49	3	56	41	3	52	45	3
Republican	48	46	6	53	44	3	58	38	5
House men	51	44	5	55	42	3	49	46	5
Democratic	45	50	5	53	43	3	46	51	4
Republican	57	39	4	56	42	3	51	43	6

	2000			2004			2008		
	Business PACs	Labor PACs	Issue PACs	Business PACs	Labor PACS	Issue PACs	Business PACs	Labor PACs	Issue PACs
House women	56	34	10	56	32	13	57	28	15
Democratic	44	45	11	44	44	13	50	35	15
Republican	85	6	9	76	11	13	81	5	14
House men	71	19	10	65	22	13	73	15	12
Democratic	54	38	8	51	40	10	62	26	13
Republican	86	3	10	78	6	17	83	5	12

Sources: 2000 data: Victoria A. Farrar-Myers. 2003. "A War Chest Full of Susan B. Anthony Dollars: Fund-Raising Issues for Female Presidential Candidates." In *Anticipating Madam President*, edited by Robert P. Watson and Ann Gordon, 81–94. Boulder, CO: Lynne Rienner; 2004 data: Victoria A. Farrar-Myers. 2007. "Money and the Art and Science of Candidate Viability." In *Rethinking Madam President: Are We Ready for a Woman in the White House?* edited by Lori Cox Han and Caroline Heldman, 113–132. Boulder, CO: Lynne Rienner; 2008 data: Compiled by the authors from data from the Federal Election Commission, at http://www.fec.gov.

Table 11.2 Average Source of Funds of Selected Candidates by Gender, Senate, 1996–2008 (percentage)

	1996–2000		2000–2004		2004–2008	
	Women	Men	Women	Men	Women	Men
Source						
Individuals	65.3	56.6	64.4	61.4	73.8	59.2
PACs	18.6	34.6	20.4	32.1	19.2	31.7
Other	16.1	8.8	15.2	6.5	7.0	9.1
Funding from PACs						
Business PACs	71.6	87.9	64.2	75.7	55.7	64.4
Labor PACs	12.8	4.5	17.1	9.4	16.8	16.8
Single-issue/ideological PACs	15.7	7.6	18.7	14.9	27.5	18.8

Sources: 1996–2000 data: Victoria A. Farrar-Myers. 2003. "A War Chest Full of Susan B. Anthony Dollars: Fund-Raising Issues for Female Presidential Candidates." In *Anticipating Madam President*, edited by Robert P. Watson and Ann Gordon, 81–94. Boulder, CO: Lynne Rienner; 2000–2004 data: Victoria A. Farrar-Myers. 2007. "Money and the Art and Science of Candidate Viability." In *Rethinking Madam President: Are We Ready for a Woman in the White House?* edited by Lori Cox Han and Caroline Heldman, 113–132. Boulder, CO: Lynne Rienner; 2004–2008 data: Compiled by the authors from data from the Federal Election Commission, at http://www.fec.gov.

Hillary Clinton: A Case Study in Financial Viability

As alluded to above, Hillary Clinton experienced little trouble raising funds for her two Senate campaigns. She raised and spent more funds than any other Senate candidate in both 2000 and 2006. The funds raised in 2000 for her Senate race rivaled the contribution totals for the leading Democratic presidential contenders that year, Al Gore and Bill Bradley. She brought powerful fund-raising skills to the campaign for the 2008 Democratic presidential nomination, and her case offers insight into how to establish and then utilize financial viability in a presidential campaign.

Hillary Clinton's candidacy in 2008 could easily be seen as not successful, given that she did not win the Democratic nomination for president. So easily dismissing her efforts, however, ignores the many successes of her campaign and the milestones for women reached along the way. The quotation from Clinton's concession speech at the beginning of this chapter captures this distinction quite eloquently. She may not have shattered the glass ceiling of electing a woman as president, but she did leave 18 million cracks in that ceiling—representing the 18 million votes she received during the Democratic primaries. Perhaps just as significantly, Clinton shattered at least one glass ceiling during her presidential bid by becoming the first female candidate to achieve financial and overall viability in running for the presidency.

To put Hillary Clinton's fund-raising successes into historical perspective, Figure 11.6 shows that she raised the third-largest total of individual contributions in presidential campaign history. The $212.7 million received in contributions places Clinton between the two presidential nominees in 2004 (Bush with $236.4 million and Kerry with $209.3 million) and well ahead of the 2008 Republican presidential nominee, John McCain, at $145.6 million. Clinton faced one problem in 2008, though, in running against the most successful fund-raiser in history—Barack Obama. Indeed, Obama's $376.4 million in individual contributions during the primary season was more than Clinton and McCain combined. Nevertheless, the significance of the amount of individual contributions to Clinton's campaign should not be lost in the wake of Obama's incredible fund-raising success.

Financial viability is not measured only in aggregated numbers but can be analyzed in terms of three key ingredients for presidential candidates during the preprimary period: comparatively big money, early money, and small-donor contributions.[16] Clinton's financial viability can be traced to success in each of these ingredients, although her case also reveals the shortcomings of the Clinton campaign vis-à-vis the Obama campaign. The first ingredient, comparatively big money, requires a candidate to raise enough money during the preprimary period to be competitive with other candidates. If one considers the "money primary" to be a "competition for financial resources . . . before the primaries begin" (Adkins and Dowdle 2002, 257), then Clinton could be declared the winner of the 2007 Democratic money

Figure 11.6 Individual Contributions to Presidential Candidates Through July 31 of Election Year, 2000–2008

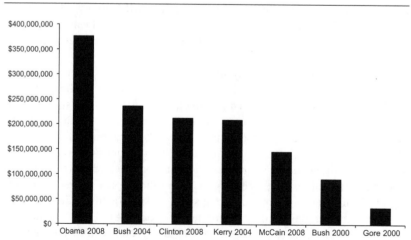

Source: Compiled by authors from data available at http://www.fec.gov.

primary. As of December 31, 2007, Clinton raised $103.7 million in individual contributions and $114.7 million overall. These figures gave her a slight edge over Obama in terms of both individual and total contributions, although the latter was buttressed by $10 million in leftover funds from her 2006 Senate campaign that Clinton transferred to her presidential war chest. Further, she had raised over 75% more in individual contributions than the top Republican fund-raiser to that point (Rudolph Giuliani at $58.1 million) and $26 million more in total funds than Mitt Romney, who led Republican candidates with $88.3 million raised.[17]

The second ingredient, early money, reflects that candidates effectively need to have built up significant funds by no later than the end of the second calendar quarter in the year prior to the presidential election. Recent history has shown that candidates who fail to do so cannot catch up and that candidates who wait until later in the year to start their campaign struggle to establish both their financial and overall viability against the early financial front-runners. By the end of the first quarter of 2007, Clinton and Obama had already separated themselves as fund-raisers from all other candidates, including all Republican candidates, with Clinton and Obama having raised over $25 million in individual contributions. Clinton and Obama also brought in more money during the second calendar quarter of 2007 than the first quarter.[18] In financial terms, as well as in other ways, Clinton was clearly an early front-runner for the Democratic nomination.

The third ingredient of financial viability considers the funds raised from small donors during the preprimary periods. "[S]mall-donor contributions constitute an important indication of financial viability because small donors represent the breadth of support of likely voters come primary or caucus election time" (Farrar-Myers 2011, 52). Clinton certainly had success in raising funds from small donors during the preprimary period. The $9.5 million that the Clinton campaign received in small contributions ($200 or less per contribution) by the end of the third quarter of 2007 outpaced most Democratic candidates and each Republican candidate. Further, the sum of contributions was the fourth largest at comparable points throughout history.[19] Unfortunately for Clinton, Obama had already outpaced her in this key area, raising more than $20.8 million in small contributions at this point.

Even with this deficit, when taking the three ingredients of financial viability together, Clinton demonstrated that she entered the 2008 primary season as a financially viable candidate for the presidency. In doing so, Clinton became the first female candidate to achieve financial viability. As noted above, Elizabeth Dole's withdrawal from the race for the Republican presidential nomination in 1999 was attributed to a lack of money. Yet Dole was seen as a trailblazer for her candidacy, no matter how short lived and despite not achieving financial viability.[20] Similarly, although Clinton did not ultimately obtain the Democratic nomination, she too should be seen as a trailblazer for demonstrating that a woman can, in fact, become a financially viable candidate for president.

One might ask how generalizable the Clinton case is for women seeking the presidency. After all, in many ways, Clinton was unique: the first sitting first lady to be elected to office in her own right, the first former first lady to run for the presidency, a high-profile senator from the nation's second most populous state, and a prolific fund-raiser with contributor lists going back to her husband's presidential campaigns. While Clinton may have had many unique advantages in breaking through the barrier of becoming the first viable female presidential candidate, she did nevertheless break through the barrier as a woman. No longer can people say, "There has never been a viable female candidate for president," because following the Clinton campaign, there has been. Now, when women in 2012 and beyond seek the White House, they can focus on overcoming the challenges that any candidate—male or female—must face in achieving financial and overall viability without the additional burden of being the first woman to do so. To use Clinton's words from her June 2008 concession speech, "the path will be a little easier next time."

The Pathways Toward Financial Viability for Future Female Presidential Candidates: Rising from Lower-Level Offices to Becoming President

The pathway to the White House, the governor's mansion, or any elective office must be paved in gold. That is, for any candidate to be elected to an executive office, regardless of gender, she or he must have sufficient funding first to become a viable candidate and then to be elected. From what the analyses above have shown, a woman's gender does not have to be a barrier to achieving financial viability. Female candidates for governor, the US House of Representatives, the US Senate, and even the presidency have proven to be successful fund-raisers and to have done it as well as, if not better than, men.

These women have also shown that more than one pathway to financial viability exists. This fact is important for female candidates because their collective experience has shown small but important differences between the campaign finance profiles of successful female and male candidates. Perhaps the most significant difference is that women have not had the relative success in raising funds from organized moneyed interests as men.

This difference plays out in two ways. First, female candidates for governor and Congress on average had to rely slightly more on individual contributions than PACs. Second, women lagged behind the percentage of PAC funds from business PACs and instead tended to draw upon a higher percentage of their PAC funds from single-issue/ideological PACs. Recall the percentages for key indicators discussed above for all governors and for the most recent election cycles for Congress, summarized in Table 11.3.

These differences can be interpreted as a perpetuation of some of the structural barriers impeding the movement of women through the political pipeline. Studies have shown that political actors—in a way, gatekeepers—are more likely to seek men to run for office instead of women (Fox and Lawless 2010; Niven 1998; Sanbonmatsu 2006). Further, such differences in recruiting women for political office are "particularly bleak for Republicans" (Fox and Lawless 2010).[21] Along the same lines, the numbers above indicate that the gatekeepers of organized moneyed interests have favored male over female candidates.[22] Republican women are particularly challenged, as female Republican governors and House members had a higher percentage of their funds come from individuals than either men or Democratic women running for the same office (interestingly, though, the four female Republican senators in this study were not similarly affected).[23] This study does not permit one to determine whether this difference is caused directly by some gender-oriented contribution scheme or as a by-product of an alternative factor, such as PACs favoring more senior members of Congress. Regardless, the primary lesson is women may expect a different route to financial viability than the model that works for the typical male candidate.

The extent to which organized moneyed interests have favored male candidates in the past takes on greater importance in the ever-shifting environment of campaign finance regulations. In January 2010, the Supreme Court struck down prohibitions on independent political expenditures by corporations in candidate elections in the *Citizens United* case. Although corporations are still not permitted to contribute funds directly to candidates in federal elections, in the wake of *Citizens United* they are freer to spend funds on electioneering advertisements. Labor unions, whose PAC spending in congressional elections in the past has tended to favor women but at smaller overall contribution levels than business PACS, would have similar flexibility as corporations in campaign spending under the *Citizens*

Table 11.3 Summary of Contribution Sources as a Percentage of All Funds Raised

| | Individual | | Business PACs | | Single-Issue PACs | |
	Women	Men	Women	Men	Women	Men
Governor	60.7	55.2	78.2	84.6	6.5	1.5
House	53.3	48.8	57.1	73.1	14.9	12.1
Senate	73.8	59.2	55.7	64.4	27.5	18.8

United ruling. One simple analysis of 2010 spending by all outside groups indicates that those making independent expenditures in the wake of *Citizens United* may not distinguish based on gender.[24] The full impact of the Supreme Court's decision, however, will take several election cycles to play out and may even eventually be limited legislatively by Congress.[25] But if corporations and labor unions undertake independent expenditures in proportion to the ways in which business and labor PACs have made political contributions to candidates as shown in this study, then the *Citizens United* decision could result in another structural barrier to the advancement of women through the political pipeline. Such results should further emphasize the need for female candidates to blaze their own pathway toward financial viability.

The fact that women can find more than one pathway to financial viability is important in the context of the uniqueness of Hillary Clinton's 2008 campaign for president. As queried above, how generalizable is Clinton's experience for other women considering a run for the presidency? Certainly Clinton followed a pathway that was different than the average female candidate at the lower elective offices analyzed herein. Clinton, particularly early in the preprimary period, took a typical front-runner approach to fund-raising and her campaign, and in particular drew from large donors (i.e., the moneyed interests in a presidential campaign). With multiple pathways to financial viability available, however, a woman wanting to run for president does not have to be Hillary Clinton, or enter the campaign as an immediately viable candidate, in order to effectively run for president.

In fact, the pathway that Barack Obama took to financial viability may be a useful model for female presidential candidates to follow. Obama showed that while having access to big money is important, drawing upon individual small donors can generate large financial returns and a broad base of electoral support. Early indications for Sarah Palin's fund-raising efforts as she considered a potential run for the 2012 Republican presidential nomination were that she had achieved some success in reaching small donors, although she ultimately decided not to seek the Republican nomination.[26] Although small donors constitute only one ingredient of achieving financial viability, they offer a route to the White House whose potential, before Obama, was not fully appreciated.

Herein lies the good news for female candidates aspiring to higher office. The average female candidate in this study has had a slight, but greater, dependence on individual contributions and contributions from single-issue/ideological PACs, which tend to be more grassroots oriented in nature. This experience has already taught women how to achieve financial viability through individuals rather than organized moneyed interests and how to build a broader base of electoral support. In a way, the campaign financing experience of women may be putting the old adage of "what does not kill you makes you stronger" into action. By being forced to overcome structural barriers and to find alternative ways to achieve financial viability, women who succeed initially in building individual donor support may be better situated to find success on their pathway to higher office and eventually the White House.

Notes

1. Kelliher eventually lost in the Democratic primary to former senator Mark Dayton by approximately 8,600 votes.
2. For a full discussion of the factors, or ingredients, of viability, see Farrar-Myers (2007, 120–124).
3. *Citizens United v. Federal Election Commission,* 558 U.S. 50 (2010).
4. Women elected to the office of governor include in 1997, Christine Todd Whitman (R-NJ); in 1998, Jane Dee Hull (R-AZ), Jeanne Shaheen (D-NH); in 2000, Ruth Ann Minner (D-DE), Judy Martz (R-MT), Jeanne Shaheen (D-NH); in 2002, Janet Napolitano (D-AZ), Linda Lingle (R-HI), Kathleen Sebelius (D-KS), Jennifer Granholm (D-MI); in 2003, Kathleen Blanco (D-LA); in 2004, Ruth Ann Minner (D-DE), Christine Gregoire (D-WA); in 2006, Sarah Palin (R-AK), Janet Napolitano (D-AZ), Jodi Rell (R-CT), Linda Lingle (R-HI), Kathleen Sebelius (D-KS), Jennifer Granholm (D-MI); in 2008, Bev Perdue (D-NC), Christine Gregoire (D-WA). Additionally, Jeanne Shaheen was elected as governor in 1996. Contribution data, however, is not available for her 1996 campaign.
5. This pairing of winning female and male candidates was based on their geographic proximity and year elected (similar to the pairing done for senators as described below). Men elected to the office of governor include in 1998, George Pataki (R-NY; paired with Whitman in 1997), Gary Johnson (R-NM), Howard Dean (D-VT); in 2000, Bob Wise (D-WV), John Hoeven (R-ND), Howard Dean (D-VT); in 2002, Bill Richardson (D-NM), Ted Kulongoski (D-OR), Brad Henry (D-OK), Tim Pawlenty (R-MN); in 2003, Haley Barbour (R-MS); in 2004, Joe Manchin (D-WV), John Huntsman (R-UT); in 2006, Butch Otter (R-ID), Bill Richardson (D-NM), Donald Carcieri (R-RI), Ted Kulongoski (D-OR), Brad Henry (D-OK), Tim Pawlenty (R-MN); in 2008, Mitch Daniels (R-IN), John Huntsman (R-UT).
6. Governor-related data was obtained and is available through the National Institute on Money in State Politics, at http://www.followthemoney.org/.
7. Figure 11.5 includes the 75 women who won in 2008, including Hilda Solis (later appointed as secretary of labor) and Kirsten Gillibrand (subsequently named as senator to replace Hillary Clinton).
8. In 2000, winning female candidates on average spent more than $882,000, while male candidates expended approximately $806,000. In 2004, these numbers increased to $1.09 million and $1.02 million, respectively. See Farrar-Myers (2003, 2007).
9. In 2000 and 2004, winning Democratic women in the House spent on average over $780,000 and $1.00 million respectively, compared to $1.10 million and $1.25 million for Republican women, respectively. Male candidates spent on average approximately $800,000 in 2000 and $1.02 million in 2004. See Farrar-Myers (2003, 2007).
10. In the three election cycles between 1996 and 2000, a winning female Senate candidate, on average, outspent an average male candidate by a $7.8 million to

$4.75 million margin; between 2000 and 2004, that margin increased to $10.14 million to $5.85 million, respectively. See Farrar-Myers (2003, 2007).

11. This study builds off of two prior studies (Farrar-Myers 2003, 2007) and, thus, continues their methodology in terms of analyzing women congressional studies. This methodology includes, for example, examining campaign finance data for House races in presidential years (2000, 2004, and 2008) and grouping three election cycles culminating in the last presidential year studied for the House elections (1996–2000, 2000–2004, and 2004–2008) to ensure that all the seats in the Senate had been up for election during each period under consideration.

12. For each election year shown in Table 11.1, a group of winning male candidates, equal to the number of winning female candidates for that year, was randomly selected to compare their fund-raising profiles against the successful female candidates.

13. As with the analysis of House members, an equal number of men were selected to be compared against women. Due to the limited number of female Senators available for analysis (17), men were selected based on their geographic proximity and year elected so as to match up with the women selected. Thus, for example, Mary Landrieu, elected to the Senate in 2008 from Louisiana, was matched with Mark Pryor, elected in 2008 from Arkansas. The men selected for analysis herein were in 2004, Mike Crapo (R-ID), Daniel Inouye (D-HI), Arlen Specter (R-PA), David Vitter (R-LA), and Ron Wyden (D-OR); in 2006, Jeff Bingaman (D-NM), Sherrod Brown (D-OH), Robert Casey Jr. (D-PA), Kent Conrad (D-ND), John Ensign (R-NV), Ben Nelson (D-NE), Bernie Sanders (I-VT), and Jon Tester (D-MT); and in 2008, Lindsey Graham (R-SC), John Kerry (D-MA), Mark Pryor (D-AR), and Jack Reed (D-RI).

14. The groupings of election cycles result in some overlap between groups. The year 2000 is both in the 1996–2000 grouping and the 2000–2004 grouping. Similarly, the year 2004 overlaps both the 2000–2004 and 2004–2008 grouping. On one hand, this overlapping feature may explain, in some part, the continuity of relationships among the groupings. However, it also emphasizes the widened gap in percentage from individual contributions found in the 2004–2008 grouping. This gap can be attributed to the 2006 and 2008 elections, which do not overlap with the 2000–2004 grouping that preceded them. Note, however, that that the 2000 election cycle is found in both studies, making similarities between the two studies not surprising.

15. Table 11.2 also reflects a rise in the percentage of contributions from labor PACs to men, although this increase may be in part due to the switch to Democratic control of the Senate following the 2006 election. Such an explanation, however, is outside the scope of this chapter.

16. For more information regarding the three ingredients of financial viability, see Farrar-Myers (2011). Although these ingredients could also apply to lower offices, the primary periods for congressional offices and governorships are not as lengthy, scrutinized, or publicized as presidential campaigns. Further, the data necessary to analyze these ingredients are more readily available for presidential candidates than for lower offices. Therefore, analyzing financial viability in terms of these three ingredients is limited within this chapter to Hillary Clinton's presidential run.

17. Romney contributed more than $35 million of his own funds to his presidential campaign. This amount is reflected in the $88.3 million reported above.

18. By comparison, the nearest Democratic candidate, John Edwards, raised $14.0 million in the first quarter and $9.0 million in the second. Rudolph Giuliani

was the only other major candidate to earn more from individual contributions during the second quarter of 2007 ($17.4 million) compared to the first quarter ($15.9 million). The corresponding totals for the other top Republican candidates were Romney ($20.6 million and $12.2 million) and McCain ($13.4 million and $11.2 million).

19. Howard Dean raised $13.7 million and George W. Bush brought in $9.52 million through the third quarter of 2003 for the second- and third-highest totals.

20. As Elizabeth Sherman of the University of Massachusetts commented, "On balance, you have to say it's absolutely a net gain. Elizabeth Dole, no matter how you look at it, is a trailblazer" (Barabak 1999, A1).

21. The year 2010 had been dubbed the "Year of the Republican Woman," as a record number of Republican women were running for state and federal office, including 10 candidates for governor and 7 for lieutenant governor. See National Federation of Republican Women (2010, 18).

22. The data used in this analysis also indicate that organized moneyed interests have generally favored incumbents over nonincumbents. Nonincumbent candidates for governor, the Senate, or the House of Representatives have tended to rely more on individual contributions and ideological/single-issue PACs than incumbents regardless of gender. For example, nonincumbent women in this analysis drew 65.7% of their funds on average from individual contributions compared to 61.1% for incumbent women. For men, the respective numbers were 62.3% for nonincumbents and 49.2% for incumbents. In terms of funding from PACs, nonincumbent women received 23.1% on average from ideological/single-issue PACs compared to 11.4% for incumbent women. For men these numbers were 22.3% for nonincumbents and 6.7% for incumbents. Thus, by analyzing incumbency as the only factor, a female nonincumbent does not face significant additional campaign financing challenges than a male nonincumbent faces.

23. Of all the female Senators elected between 2004 and 2008, the three from small populous states (Snowe and Collins in Maine and Murkowski in Alaska) had the three smallest totals for percentage of funds from individuals. The fourth female Republican senator, Kay Bailey Hutchison, also came in below the average percentage of funds from individual contributions.

24. Specifically, the top 25 House candidates for which outside groups spent "For Democrats" and the top 25 "For Republicans" were identified using data compiled by the authors at www.opensecrets.org. Over the "For Democrats" group, 5 of the 25 were women; for the "For Republican" group, three were women. This overall proportion (8/50 = 16.0%) is roughly equal to the overall number of women in the House of Representatives following the 2010 elections (71/435 = 16.3%).

25. In 2010, Congress attempted to pass legislation regarding disclosure in the wake of the *Citizens United* decision; however, the bill failed in the Senate after winning approval in the House.

26. In an analysis by an Internet political blogger, Palin's political action committee, SarahPAC, raised 60% of its contributions in the first half of 2009 from individual donations of less than $200 per contribution. Compared to the 2008 presidential candidates, this percentage trailed only Ron Paul (62%) in terms of percentage of funds from small donors and exceeded Obama's 38%. See Silver (2009).

12

Turning the Tables: Behind Every Successful Woman

Kelly Dittmar

EXECUTIVE OFFICES IN THE UNITED STATES ARE GENDERED IN multiple ways that benefit men while posing additional challenges to women who run and serve. In this chapter, I argue that the masculinity of executive political institutions is also maintained by a more direct transcendence of private role expectations into the public sphere of politics. Traditional spousal expectations that characterize husbands as dominant and wives as deferent shape perceptions of who is suited to lead, as the inability to view male spouses in a "helpmate" role—and viewing female spouses as little else—denies women's capacity to be seen as autonomous executives. Moreover, female candidates are often burdened with proving their independence from male spouses and disproving the presumptions that behind every successful woman lays a dominant male spouse who not only provides her access to the office but influences her decisionmaking and validates her exercise of executive power.

Nowhere is this barrier greater than in the executive institution of the presidency, where male occupants are framed as lone heroes and great men whose masculinity is affirmed by the presence of an appropriately feminine "helpmate" spouse, charged with reflecting the strength and dominance of her male partner. This gendered framing of political spouses perpetuates norms regarding who is suited to be president, leaving female candidates without the benefit of spousal reflection and with the potential barrier of spousal interference. Using the 2008 presidential election, I ask in what ways a male spouse challenges a female candidate's image as a capable and independent executive. Moreover, in demonstrating the media's framing of both male and female spouses on the campaign trail, I analyze the extent to which coverage reflects a transgendering, or equal gender valuing, of candidate

231

spouses' roles. I find a combination of spousal role evolution and constraint in media frames, simultaneously empowering presidential spouses while attributing greater gender power to the masculine partner—whether candidate or spouse.

Executive Spouses and the Masculine Executive

Based in theories of masculinism and institutions, Duerst-Lahti (1997) describes the presidency as a gendered space in which masculine norms and images are reified as the ideal. Beyond the implicit assumption of strength and power—not traditionally attributed to women—executives are imagined as singular masculine leaders, or heroes, presumed to act alone. Yet Campbell contends that the US presidency is a two-person career, where an "appropriately feminine first lady is needed to compliment her chief executive husband and serve as a testament to his masculinity" (1996, 188). The first lady acts primarily as a reflection of her husband's sexuality and, in turn, dominance. Duerst-Lahti cites the double standard in presidential partnerships: "The problem for women . . . is that men are assumed to be entitled to a helpmate wife who seldom threatens his stature, whereas a woman can have a helpmate only under unusual circumstances and in most cases will not be seen as uninfluenced by him" (1997, 23). Thus, women candidates for presidential office are disadvantaged by the incompatibility of their gendered image to the traditional expectations of male "heroes" in the Oval Office. Moreover, they lack the benefit of having a partner that reflects their suitability for executive office, instead of highlighting the disjuncture between their gender role and political ambition. Duerst-Lahti writes, "Women struggle to be known as independent actors, whereas men are known as little else—even when they themselves acknowledge the supportive connections that make their performance possible" (1997, 23). More clearly, "the lone woman at the top has not yet become a transgendered image" (23).

What does it mean to transgender the executive? Duerst-Lahti and Kelly explain the process by which leadership and governance actions are transgendered: "By this we mean moving toward a world in which traits and behaviors exhibited by leaders, and actors at all levels and positions, can be seen as suitable for the socially situated context in which they occur regardless of the biological sex or sexual orientation of the person who happens to be the leader or actor at the moment and place" (1995, 262–263). A transgendered executive, then, would not assign sex-specific gender roles, nor maintain an imbalance of gender power, in the president's professional life or personal relationships. Until this ideal becomes reality, spousal expectations will differ for male and female executive candidates.

To disrupt the male-masculine normativity entrenched in the executive image, women candidates must be seen as singular, independent leaders. The media plays a significant role in shaping this image via framing (Entman 1993; Gitlin 1980; Norris 1997). For women candidates across levels of office, coverage overemphasizes personality traits and relationships, evaluates appearance over substance, and doubts women's electoral viability (Bystrom et al. 2004; Devitt 1999; Duerst-Lahti 2006; Kahn 1994, 1996; Lawrence and Rose 2010). Norris (1997) describes the novelty frames that hurt female candidates for head of state worldwide. Heldman, Carroll, and Olson (2005, 323) find similar frames in coverage of Elizabeth Dole in 2000 and add that the media's emphases on her marital relationship further cast her as a wife and dependent. They conclude that the repeated references to Bob Dole—in over 40% of news stories about her—undermined Dole's independent stature and presidential image. Demonstrating the tie between media frames and public interpretation, Duerst-Lahti agrees, arguing, "It is hard to be perceived as the 'single great leader alone at the top' if one is always mentioned in connection with a husband" (2006, 37).

The treatment of male spouses like Bob Dole is inconsistent with an extensive literature on presidential spouses, both as candidates' wives and first ladies. This literature elaborates on the gendered expectations for presidential spouses (Caroli 1995; Troy 1997; Winfield and Friedman 2003). Troy explains, "We use the first lady not only as a role model but also as a metaphor for what the modern American woman is all about" (quoted in Copeland 2002, C1). For most of history, this reduction to symbolism has meant that first ladies are largely expected to "smile in public and act discreetly behind the scenes" (Stooksbury and Edgemon 2003, 105). Similarly, Parry-Giles and Parry-Giles (1996) argue that the masculinization of the presidency casts women in the role of supporter rather than active participant. When women try to take a more active role, failing to simply reflect the masculine power of their partner, as Hillary Clinton did in the early 1990s, they often experience a backlash against themselves and their husband (Mayo 1995).

Stooksbury and Edgemon (2003), however, demonstrate first ladies' shift from playing more traditional protocol, or ceremonial, roles to winning greater respect as policy advisers to their husbands (Rosebush 1987; Watson 2000; Winfield and Friedman 2003). Spouses are also playing a more significant role on the campaign trail, acting as surrogates and even influencing vote choice (Mughan and Burden 1995; Tien, Checchio, and Miller 1999). In 2004, these women were charged with the common spousal task of "providing a window to the candidate's character" (Grimes 1990, 16), or humanizing him, and attracting women voters (Watson 2000). Together, the literatures on first ladies and spousal roles on the campaign trail point to a difficult balance for female partners, a role that is both plagued with traditional gender constraints and charged with greater substantive responsibilities and expectations over time. While the evolution, however stunted, of the spousal role is evident, the continued constraint on female spouses and overall inability to imagine a male "helpmate" spouse for a female presidential candidate maintain the unequal gender valuing of the executive institution so inhibiting for the women who have dared to run.

What happens when women *do* run for presidency? More specifically, what is expected of male spouses and how do these expectations impact the gendered imagery of executive office and, most significantly, their wives' bids for office? While a handful of women have run for the presidency in major party contests, thorough examination of spousal roles has been difficult due to their early departures from the race and, often, perceptions that their candidacies were novel instead of viable.[1] In this chapter, I examine the extent to which the candidacy of the most viable woman presidential candidate to date—Hillary Clinton—and the particularly strong presence of presidential candidates' spouses were able to transgender executive imagery. More specifically, I analyze media coverage of candidates' spouses to determine the degree to which ideals of male dominance and female deference are reinforced, to the detriment of female candidates' executive images.

In 2008, presidential candidates' spouses—wives and husband—garnered unprecedented amounts of media and, increasingly, scholarly attention (see MacManus and Quecan 2008). Each Democratic candidate's spouse had influential identities beyond their spousal role, as a former president (Bill Clinton), stage IV breast cancer patient (Elizabeth Edwards), or potential first African American woman to serve in the East Wing (Michelle Obama). Bill Clinton's uniqueness was not only due to his political legacy, but also to his political brand—one strongly linked to Hillary Clinton. The establishment of the Clintons' political brand and their fragile relationship with the media assuredly preceded and impacted the election, as did Elizabeth Edwards's role in the 2004 presidential race. Any analysis of the race must situate itself within this history and context, cautioning generalization to future presidential elections. Despite its uniqueness, the 2008 election also presents a valuable opportunity to illustrate how traditional spousal roles and expectations in private spheres might translate into hurdles in establishing women's public images as potential executives. I take advantage of this opportunity below with hopes that this glimpse into the masculinized ideals of presidential partnerships establishes foundations for future research on women in executive offices—both as candidates and spouses.

Method

In the 2008 presidential election, were the norms and assumptions surrounding a masculine executive upheld? More specific to spousal influence, to what degree was Hillary Clinton covered independently of her male spouse? Finally, did the media frame Bill Clinton *differently* than Michelle Obama and Elizabeth Edwards, demonstrating prevailing gender expectations within the presidential institution and a potential barrier for women running for executive offices?

In order to answer these questions, I performed a content analysis of newspaper coverage of the three major Democratic candidates of 2008 (Hillary Clinton, Barack Obama, and John Edwards) from February 11, 2007, to June 3, 2008.[2] I limited my sample to Democratic candidates due to complications of comparability, including the stunted timeline of the Republican race, the media's more limited coverage of the Republican candidate selection, and the unique presence of a serious female contender in the Democratic presidential nomination contest. Additionally, concentrating on the Democratic nomination controls for contextual factors exclusive to the Democratic race, including policy issue focus, competitiveness of contests, primary and caucus schedule, and constituency appeal. If media coverage is influenced by candidate presentation, the historical precedence of Republicans' "family values" appeal to a more conservative constituency presents an additional challenge to comparing spousal coverage across party primaries (Freeman 1993). Better comparisons can be made in general election contexts or in future Republican races with male and female candidates.

To develop my sample, I completed name-based searches through LexisNexis for the Democratic candidates and their spouses from February 2007 to June 2008, excluding pieces where the candidate is not a significant focus (mentioned less than four times).[3] I used the first search, including 10 national and regional newspapers, to count the number of spousal mentions in coverage of each candidate in the country's most circulated newspapers.[4] I focused on the newspapers most circulated nationwide due to the national scope of the presidential contest and because these papers have the most expansive influence on public perceptions of a masculine executive. I limited the second search to four of these newspapers in an effort to designate a manageable sample for more detailed content analysis.[5] The final sample includes 301 articles, including editorials and commentary.[6]

In performing a content analysis on this sample, I coded articles for *spousal frame, spousal influence,* and *spousal role. Spousal frame* measures the primary responsibility of the candidates' spouses. Depending upon the titles attributed and tasks assigned to each spouse, I coded each article's framing of the spouse as a traditional supporter, an advocate, a defender/ attacker, an adviser, or a cocandidate. The traditional supporter role is derived from historical expectations of first ladies, indicating media frames that emphasize a spouse's ceremonial role and presence, sacrifice of personal career or ambitions, and no indication of a professional or influential role in campaigning. The advocate frame mirrors that of a traditional supporter but differs in its attribution of professional experience or credentials to the supportive spouse, providing them greater credibility. Unlike an advocate frame, the adviser frame allows for spousal influence on campaign strategy. The cocandidate frame indicates that the candidate's spouse is *more than* a political adviser and that electing the candidate will mean bringing the spouse into the political fold. Finally, spousal frames were coded as defender or attacker when articles described spouses as challenging accusations against the candidate, attacking pundits or opponents, or making claims that the candidate was being treated unfairly. I then coded the articles for *spousal influence,* a variable measuring whether the article described the spouse as having a positive or negative influence on the candidate's campaign. Finally, I included a variable to describe *spousal role,* coding for whether candidates' spouses were referred to as spouses, professionals, or both; this aspect is particularly useful to consider for Bill Clinton, whose role as a former president would make media coverage more likely.[7]

Due to the complexity and often-veiled nature of gendered media coverage, I take a more in-depth look at how the media deployed these spousal frames for each Democratic candidate's spouse. I elaborate on the gendered assumptions underlying these frames—and their execution—in the remainder of the chapter. I also compare frames, roles, and themes of coverage among spouses, testing my hypothesis that Bill Clinton would not only be covered more, but *differently,* than his female peers. In combining the quantitative data with detailed textual examples and trends, I analyze spousal coverage and its impact not only on the Democratic candidates, but also on the gendered imagery of the presidential office and the challenges it presents to female candidates. I conclude this chapter by discussing the implications of gendered spousal expectations for lower-level executive offices and offering questions for future research on gender and executive spouses.

Spousal Presence

Consistent with my expectation that Bill Clinton would be mentioned more often than the other candidates' spouses in coverage of the Democratic nomination contest, he was mentioned in 50.3% of articles on Hillary Clinton (see Table 12.1). This pronounced presence is in contrast to Michelle Obama, mentioned in 8.1% of articles about Barack Obama, and Elizabeth Edwards's inclusion into 14.5% of articles that discuss John Edwards. In the months of coverage after John Edwards left the race (February 11–June 3, 2008), Bill Clinton was mentioned in 45.1% of articles about Hillary Clinton and, despite Barack Obama's electoral successes, Michelle Obama maintained a minimal presence in articles referring to her husband.

These findings alone do not demonstrate gender bias, as Bill Clinton's celebrity as a former president would predict greater coverage. However,

Table 12.1 Spousal Mentions in Candidate Coverage (percentage of total coverage)

	10-Paper Sample	4-Paper Sample
Feb. 11, 2007–Feb. 11, 2008		
Bill Clinton	50.3	53.9
Elizabeth Edwards	14.5	15.9
Michelle Obama	8.1	7.4
Feb. 12, 2008–June 3, 2008		
Bill Clinton	45.1	45.7
Michelle Obama	7.8	6.0

they are inconsistent with the presence of each candidate's spouse on the campaign trail. For example, in the year leading up to the first Democratic contest, the Iowa caucus, news media tracking of candidate and spousal appearances shows Elizabeth Edwards with 109 appearances and Michelle Obama with 79 appearances, while Bill Clinton is only reported to have attended 36 campaign events in the same time period. Though he stayed off of the campaign trail, Bill Clinton is mentioned in 49% of articles about Hillary Clinton while his more present female counterparts are mentioned in less than 15% of articles about their husbands during this period.[8] Despite the difficulty in isolating gender in these findings, the evidence does indicate that Bill Clinton's campaign presence was amplified by media portrayals. This amplification of spousal presence is particularly problematic for female candidates, as it paints women in relation to, instead of independently of, their male spouses; moreover, it challenges claims that a candidate can serve autonomously as "the lone woman at the top."

Spousal Profiles

Candidates' spouses were not only covered to different numerical degrees, but also covered *differently* (see Table 12.2). Media output is influenced by campaign strategy and behavior by candidates and their spouses, like Bill Clinton's repeated references to his presidential legacy, Michelle Obama's focus on family, and the Edwardses' decision to bring their children on the campaign trail. However, coverage themes ultimately reflect choices journalists make over what to cover and how to communicate it to the public. These choices, in news reports and editorials, have implications for the gendered imagery of the executive office.

Narrowing my sample to four newspapers ($N = 301$), I compare the type of coverage given to each candidate's spouse.[9] Unlike the wives of the 2008 Democratic race, Bill Clinton was framed more often as an adviser or cocandidate, was viewed as being much more of a negative influence than other spouses, and was never covered as a spouse alone. Embedding these

Table 12.2 Types of Spousal Coverage (percentage of all spouse-included articles in four-paper sample)

Spousal Frame	Bill Clinton[a,b]	Elizabeth Edwards[a,c]	Michelle Obama[b,c]
Traditional supporter	0.5	5.4	6.5
Defender/attacker	14.1	12.5	0.0
Advocate	20.5	28.6	64.5
Adviser	23.9	32.1	6.5
Cocandidate	14.6	0.0	0.0

Spousal Influence	Bill Clinton[a,b]	Elizabeth Edwards[c]	Michelle Obama[c]
Positive	55.1	94.0	85.7
Negative	44.9	6.0	14.3

Spousal Role	Bill Clinton[a,b]	Elizabeth Edwards[a,c]	Michelle Obama[b,c]
Professional	27.3	0.0	0.0
Spouse	12.7	85.7	66.7
Professional-spouse	60.0	14.3	33.3

Notes: Numbers do not add to 100% for spousal frame because an additional category of "not applicable" was included in coding. This category included articles that mentioned the spouse out of the electoral context.

Analyses based on chi-square measurements between paired spouses for each variable.

a. Coverage in this area significantly different from Michelle Obama ($p < .01$).

b. Coverage in this area significantly different from Elizabeth Edwards ($p < .01$).

c. Coverage in this area significantly different from Bill Clinton ($p < .01$).

frames—along with role attribution and tone of coverage—into broader themes allows for a more nuanced and particularized review of how gendered expectations influenced media coverage of the candidates and their spouses.

Bill Clinton: No Ordinary Political Spouse

In reflecting on the first 13 months of Hillary Clinton's presidential campaign, the *Washington Post* writes, "The campaign had long ago discovered its limitations in dealing with the former president. He was, after all, no ordinary candidate's spouse" (Baker and Kornblut 2008, A1). I argue here that not only is Bill Clinton not an ordinary husband, but also nor was he covered by the media in an ordinary, or traditional, way as a presidential candidate's spouse. The print media framed Bill Clinton as an advocate or adviser in nearly half of the articles mentioning both him and his wife, with similar percentages of pieces framing him as either a defender/attacker or a cocandidate. While Elizabeth Edwards was also covered in diverse roles, she was never framed as a cocandidate and was more likely to be portrayed in a traditionally supportive role than Bill Clinton, who almost never fit that role. These findings demonstrate that Bill Clinton was unlikely to be framed in a traditionally feminine spousal role of "helpmate" and, instead, was more likely to be partnered with Hillary Clinton as a cocandidate by whom she was inevitably influenced, one who negated her autonomy for executive office.

Beyond being an adviser and advocate, Bill Clinton was also described as a celebrity, a "free agent," a cocandidate, and Hillary's "chief validator." While it may seem easy to attribute this coverage to Bill Clinton's political fame or even behavior on the trail instead of gendered expectations, similar themes of dominance and intervention were evident in the coverage of an otherwise unknown and apolitical husband: Todd Palin. Early campaign profiles of the former "first dude" of Alaska, Todd Palin, characterized him as a "shadow governor," "de facto chief of staff," and a "central figure in his wife's policy agenda" as governor of Alaska. Despite his image on the campaign trail—silently standing by vice presidential candidate Sarah Palin and frequently taking the caretaker role to the couple's youngest children— profiles of Todd Palin often referenced his Alaskan reputation as a guberna- torial spouse with unprecedented involvement.[10] These themes—for gover- nor, vice presidential, and presidential candidates alike—present hurdles to female candidates striving to appear as strong and independent leaders.

Dominant player and partner. In a major theme of Hillary Clinton's media coverage, print sources emphasized Bill Clinton's persistent influ- ence in the campaign. Particularly early on in the campaign, journalists pro- filed Bill Clinton as a powerful force both behind the scenes and on the campaign trail. Framed as both a top campaign adviser (23.9% of coverage) and a cocandidate (14.6% of coverage), he was seen largely as the domi- nant Clinton, only ceding the spotlight to his wife by his own doing.

Bill Clinton, especially early on, was described as both a "master strategist" and operative head of the campaign.

> Bill Clinton's connections and his endless supply of chits, only begin to capture his singular role in his wife's presidential candidacy, advisers and friends of the couple say. He is the master strategist behind the scenes; the consigliere to the head of "the family," as some Clinton aides refer to her operation; and a fundraising machine who is steadily pulling in $100,000 or more at receptions. (Healy 2007d, 1)

In the same article, Patrick Healy (2007d) of the *New York Times* called the former president a "field general" and pointed to a time in the campaign when Bill Clinton would have his own campaign plane, press corps, and schedule of events. This theme persisted into the campaign for the Demo- cratic nomination, as Healy again called Bill Clinton "the most powerful force in [Hillary Clinton's] political operation besides the candidate herself" in the weeks before the Iowa caucuses (Healy 2007b, A1). More blatant references described Bill Clinton as a near puppeteer of the Clinton campaign, pulling the strings from behind the scenes with a patronizing bend: "Mr. Clinton gently coached his wife on some of her line readings and facial expressions between takes. . . . And he has dispensed advice, praise and neck-and-shoulder massages in their three-day trip here" (Healy 2007a, A1). Richard Cohen, of the *Washington Post,* was most direct in describing Bill Clinton's control: "Hillary Clinton is a creature of her husband. This is reality, not a put-down" (2008, A19).

From his first weekends on the stump for Hillary to the end of the primary and caucus season, journalists described Bill Clinton as the dominant spouse who had the capacity to outshine his candidate wife for better or for worse. He was described as a "rock star" and an "Oscar-worthy supporting actor" capable of upstaging or outshining Hillary Clinton "simply by breathing" (Healy 2007a; Kornblut 2007b; Leibovich 2008). Unlike the traditional surrogate-spouse, Bill Clinton did not reflect his wife's image as a strong executive but was instead viewed as an independent force of publicity and substance.

The difficulty in viewing Bill Clinton anywhere but in the center was evident as the media profiled Bill Clinton's evolution from candidate to spouse as being fraught with problems. Journalists described Clinton's "new and delicate strategy" once on the campaign trail—one that included ceding the stage at some rallies "so that [Hillary Clinton] could speak unadorned" (Healy 2007a, A1; Healy and Nagourney 2007, A14). They emphasized his supposed discomfort in a supporting role—common to the perceived notion that a man would be out of place in the role of first spouse, unable to adopt the sex-specific traits and behaviors of the role. "Mr. Clinton seemed to struggle with the proper posture for him at his wife's side, alternately sitting up straight on his stool or slouching slightly, crossing his legs or crossing his ankles, keeping his hands in his pocket or putting a hand on his chin" (Luo 2007). Many journalists argued Bill Clinton's self-centered focus on the stump demonstrated his discomfort: "At times, his pitch for his wife is focused so much on his own accomplishments as president that it almost sounds as if he himself is running for reelection" (Kornblut and MacGillis 2007, A01). In choosing to emphasize his legacy over simply reflecting Hillary Clinton's strengths, Bill Clinton violated spousal expectations and was often viewed as a negative influence on his wife's presidential campaign.[11] Bob Dole was viewed as similarly uncomfortable in a supporting role in 2000, evident when he called Bush's lead insurmountable and hinted that he might donate to McCain even before Elizabeth Dole left the race for the Republican nomination (Berke 1999). In this way, reluctant male spouses may present challenges to female candidates independently of media portrayals of them.

Framing Bill Clinton as a rogue spouse reinforces the perception that a male spouse would be unable (or unwilling) to cede center stage to his wife or limit himself to the spousal reflection provided by his female counterparts. Without doing so, the male spouse leaves the female candidate unable to separate herself from her spouse in a way that mimics the traditional "lone man" imagery of the executive. Moreover, she is viewed as unable to control her spouse, unlike the control and power elicited by the masculine leader. Anne Kornblut kindled this fear most succinctly in her characterization of Bill Clinton as a "free agent" who attended strategy meetings and oversaw the campaign without any defined campaign role (2007b, A01). In the few instances where Hillary Clinton was described as being the dominant spouse, the coverage accused her of emasculation. "Bill Clinton is dutifully traveling from state to state and small town to small town on behalf of his wife's presidential candidacy. But the growling and snapping Bill Clinton . . . has been muzzled and leashed" (Broder 2008, A20). In this instance, among others, Hillary Clinton was cast as the worst type of woman—one who not only emasculates her male partner but attempts to appear "manly" herself. While female spouses are capable of reflecting the masculinity of their husbands by contrasting it to their femininity, Bill Clinton was only capable of supporting his wife by taming his own masculinity and staying out of the spotlight—evidence that the "helpmate" spouse is not a gender-neutral, or even transgendered, conceptualization in the executive partnership.

Cocandidate. Despite Hillary Clinton's attempts to individuate herself from her husband, in both her experience and policies, the 1990s theme of "two for the price of one"—originating from Bill Clinton himself—plagued her and her campaign.[12] Bill Clinton was framed as a cocandidate in 14.5% of articles mentioning him. The textual examples are vast, but can be generally defined as evoking fears of a copresidency in which Bill Clinton, again, could not be controlled by his president-wife. *USA Today* was most blunt in its perception of Clinton's dominant role in the supposed partnership when the newspaper commented, "What does his role suggest about who's in charge?" ("Campaigner in Chief" 2008, A10) Other commentaries were similarly skeptical about Hillary Clinton's capacity to keep Bill "in check." One, from the *Washington Post,* said, "Does anyone think that William Jefferson Clinton would confine himself to the bland, inoffensive pronouncements we've come to expect from presidential spouses? I'd give him two weeks of ribbon-cuttings and ceremonial visits before he felt compelled—and perhaps entitled—to jump into policy" (Robinson 2007b, A35). Another, from the same newspaper, suggested, "If they make it there—a big if—the only unanswered question is where Bill will choose to hang his hat. Will it be in her old space in the East Wing, or will he set up shop in the

West Wing? Smart money is on Billary settling in the Oval Office with 'his' and 'hers' desks." (King 2008, A17). Viewed as only one part of an overly ambitious political team, Hillary Clinton was judged *with* her husband and, often, *by* his actions. Consistent with Duerst-Lahti's (1997) finding that female candidates are often viewed in connection with others, the pervasive image of "Billary" undermined Clinton's capacity to present herself as an independent candidate for an office so dependent on singularity.

Finally, the media was not alone in discounting Hillary Clinton's capacity to run, win, or serve autonomously. Her fellow candidates were quick to associate Hillary with her husband, arguing that they were cocandidates. At a debate in South Carolina, Barack Obama said, "I can't tell who I'm running against sometimes" (Harper 2008, AA01). He made a similar comment on *Good Morning America* soon after the debate: "You know, we've got a formidable opponent—actually two formidable opponents at this point, between Senator Clinton and President Clinton" (January 22, 2008). Mitt Romney joined in the charge at a Republican debate in January 2008, when asked by Tim Russert, "How would you run against Hillary and Bill Clinton in November?" Taking the lead in framing from the question itself, Romney responded, "I just think that we want to have a president, not a whole—a team of husband and wife thinking that they're going to run the country. . . . Bill Clinton's been there [DC] too long. The last thing America needs is sending the Clintons back to Washington" (Dowd 2008b, 16). Between media fascination with "the Clintons," profiles of Bill Clinton as uncontrollable and power hungry, and candidates' embrace of the "two for the price of one" ideology, Hillary Clinton was largely unable to shake the image of a presidential partnership with Bill Clinton at the helm.

Chief validator. Hillary Clinton's ability to transgender the image of the executive was also stunted by media coverage and commentary that profiled Clinton as being validated by her husband throughout the country. While more analyses of his actual comments place him in the advocate role so shared by the other candidates' spouses, the media's frame for Bill Clinton was different. I argue that this characterization, whether knowingly or not, is gendered, wherein the male spouse validates, and the female spouse supports. These two frames diverge in the power dynamics: "On the campaign trail, as one staff member put it, Bill Clinton is Sen. Hillary Rodham Clinton's chief validator. He zips around the country . . . reassuring Democrats, above all, that she is ready but he has her back" (Slevin 2008). Again, the media was not alone in using this frame. An audience member in Iowa was quick to note that Hillary Clinton would not stand alone: "She's the better man, so to speak, even though she's the woman . . . [and] I believe she's got a good backbone. She's got Bill to back her up" (Balz 2007a, A5). Barack Obama challenged the validity of Clinton's claim of experience by arguing it was dependent on her husband's résumé. In July 2007, he said at a Chicago fund-raiser, "The only person who would be prepared to be president on Day One would be Bill Clinton—not Hillary Clinton" (Kornblut 2007a, A4). Later, he argued that being first lady did not give Hillary Clinton executive credentials: "I don't think Michelle would claim she is the best qualified person to be a U.S. Senator by virtue of me talking to her on occasion about the work I've done" (Kornblut 2007c, A1). These comments both discounted first ladies' substantive roles and gendered the 2008 presidential debate by reminding voters of Clinton's secondary role as a wife instead of her image as a political leader. Likewise, Maureen Dowd described Hillary Clinton as "the feminist icon who is totally dependent on her husband to do the heavy lifting" (2008b, 16).

This paradox in which Hillary Clinton was both the most competitive female candidate for president to date and a candidate perpetually profiled in the shadow of her husband may not be a paradox at all. Instead, as analysis of Bill Clinton's coverage shows, the discomfort with such an "unordinary" traverse of gender roles and behaviors—by both female candidate Clinton and her male spouse—makes evident the barriers faced by women seeking an office so associated with a male face. Whether this inability to transgender both the executive and spousal roles, thus maintaining power in the masculine partner, is unique to the "Clintons" will be important to study in future research on women candidates for executive offices—from the presidency to lower-level executive offices like governor or mayor.

Michelle Obama: The Evolution of a Political Wife

Coverage of Michelle Obama exemplifies some progress made in challenging political spouses' confinement to expectedly feminine traits and behaviors. She was framed most frequently as an advocate (64.5% of mentions) for her husband who brought her own professional experience and credibility, instead of being framed as a traditional supporter-spouse (6.5% of her coverage). However, Michelle Obama's coverage throughout the campaign for the Democratic nomination also illustrates the persistent constraints placed on political wives, accentuated further by the Obamas' challenge of reconciling race-based expectations with popular conceptions of a "first family." Michelle Obama's early sarcasm and reluctance to embrace a political life was amended in popular media as the frame shifted to one of dedicated wife and mother. In casting Michelle Obama as an updated version of the supporter wife, the media simultaneously cast her in contrast to Bill and Hillary Clinton—the domineering cocandidates. A comparison of Obama's coverage to that of Bill Clinton demonstrates that the ability to place candidates' wives in their semitraditional roles both appeases the media (yielding more positive coverage) and maintains the gendered imagery of the executive office wherein the female body—candidate or spouse—is tied to stereotypically feminine traits and tasks.

From cynic to supportive spouse. In her first weeks on the campaign trail, Michelle Obama embraced an unusual, but arguably progressive, strategy to both humanize her husband and maintain her own identity. She cited his weaknesses and faults, talking about dirty socks strewn about the house and her difficulty reconciling the images of "Barack Obama the phenomenon" and "the Barack Obama that lives with me in my house," who she claimed was "a little less impressive" (Dowd 2007, A27). While the feedback was mixed, some journalists were uncomfortable with her challenge to the traditional role of building up the male hero. *New York Times* columnist Maureen Dowd harshly criticized Obama: "Many people I talked to afterward found Michelle wondrous. But others worried that her chiding was emasculating, casting her husband—under fire for lacking experience—as undisciplined" (2007, A27). This criticism may well have had racial nuances as well, drawing upon stereotypical tropes of black women as the "matriarch" who controls the home and, in doing so, emasculates the men therein (White 1985; Woodard and Mastin 2005). While Obama rebuked the criticism of her untraditional tactics, the media soon noted changes in her stump speeches and bluntness on the trail. In early profiles of the potential first lady, she was described as averse to political life, especially reluctant to support her husband's campaigns for both the Senate and, then, the presidency. As the campaign progressed, however, this imagery changed: "Two years and one presidential announcement later, the sarcasm is gone, and a woman who has said she dislikes politics is assuming a starring role in her husband's campaign for the White House" (Kantor and Zeleny 2007, A1). Not only was Michelle Obama viewed as adapting to life on the campaign trail, but she was also taming the more direct tone that violated behavioral norms of a proper political wife.

This shift away from a more sarcastic rhetoric—or at least the media's declining attention to it—allowed journalists to frame Michelle Obama as an evolving political wife and mother—not traditional by history's standards, but revolutionary neither. In this sense, she was at the same time progressive and constrained. She was a lawyer and a wife, an academic and a mother, a woman embodying the contradictions that are difficult to overcome without a true transgendering of political imagery. While Michelle Obama held on to her autonomy as her evolution as a political wife came to pass, the media continually challenged the image of her as an independent partner.[13] Particularly, Obama was often characterized as a wife and mother who had sacrificed her ambition for that of her husband and for the well-being of her family—the most traditional of all women's roles: "The Obamas begin their careers as equals. . . . But now she is ceding her career to his"

(Kantor and Zeleny 2007, A1). Another journalist commented, "Michelle learned early that being married to Barack Obama often means that when he is gone chasing his dreams, she must cut back on her own—in her work and especially in building a two-parent world for their two daughters, Malia, 9, and Sasha, 6" (Slevin 2007, C1). Unlike their treatment of her early candor, the media valorized Obama's sacrifice, emblematic of women's struggles to balance personal ambition with popular expectations of gender roles and responsibilities. Peter Slevin (2007), of the *Washington Post,* described Obama's balancing act in a November profile: "Michelle's willingness to accept anew the harried life of a political spouse made possible the race that launched his national career" (C1). He cited the selflessness in her own comments: "The selfish part of me says, 'Run Away! Just say no!' because my life would be easier. But that's the problem we face as a society, we have to stop making the me decision and we have to make the we and us decision" (C1). Slevin concluded, "Mostly, she juggles, backing her husband and the political vision that they have come to share" (C1).

The Everywoman. Michelle Obama's "juggling" persona became a media symbol of both the progress of political spouses and a twenty-first-century model of "the everywoman." A May 2007 *New York Times* article was titled, "Mrs. Obama is trying a fresh approach: running as everywoman, a wife, professional, mother, volunteer" (Kantor and Zeleny 2007, A1). From then on, journalists framed Obama as a mother and wife balancing professional and personal life. In embodying the everywoman, Obama could appeal to voters, especially women who may have otherwise leaned toward Hillary Clinton (Keen 2007). The *New York Times* commented, "Mrs. Obama is his more down-to-earth counterpart, drawing parallels between the voters' daily balancing acts and her own . . . and yet confines it safely to the domestic sphere" (Kantor and Zeleny 2007, A1). In framing Michelle Obama's speaking style as a more down-to-earth appeal to voters reminiscent of sitting around the "kitchen table," the media bolstered her everywoman image: "Mrs. Obama takes voters into daily life in her Chicago kitchen" (Kantor and Zeleny 2007, A1). Comparing her to Bill Clinton, Peter Slevin said, "She, too, talked of her spouse's readiness, but in different terms and tones, less a policy seminar than a plea delivered around a kitchen table" (2008, C1). This frame placed Obama in a domestic setting traditionally allocated to women, one that perpetuated gendered expectations—and even appropriate locatedness—of female spouses.

Michelle Obama made inroads in creating a new image of the political wife—one who balances work and family and is not relegated to the silent sidelines. And while Obama challenged traditional expectations, the media's coverage of her role perpetuated many ideals of political wives—casting her in a role as an "everywoman" bringing voters to her kitchen table, as a wife sacrificing her own ambitions to act as her husband's strongest advocate, and, finally, as a mother dedicated first and foremost to her children's well-being.

The intersection of Michelle Obama's race and gender complicates any conclusions about how these frames did or will affect the public psyche, particularly in the public's different expectations of black and white mothers. Patricia Hill Collins (1996) has described the unique experiences of women of color, where work and family have rarely functioned as dichotomous spheres. As a result, "motherwork" has been an alternative framework to motherhood, and gender roles in the family are less clearly delineated between private and public (Collins 1990, 1996). Moreover, while liberal feminism of the past may have encouraged women's liberation *into* the workplace, historically marginalized and exploited black women have often sought liberation *from* it (Williams 2009). Therefore, while modern conceptions of the "everywoman" reflect white women's shift into the labor force, stereotypical tropes of black women as "the mammy," "the matriarch," "the sex siren," or "the welfare mother/queen" blur the similar experiences of black women professionals today (Woodard and Mastin 2005).

While framing Michelle Obama as an "everywoman" maintains the domesticity of the spousal role in presidential imagery, this frame simultaneously challenges public perceptions of black mothers and families that have too easily deferred to race-based archetypes.[14] Additionally, framing the Obamas as an idealized middle-class (and stereotypically white) family—by both the campaign and the media—deterred fears and criticism among those in the public unsure about putting a black man and his family into the White House. These complexities of race and gender for Michelle Obama continue to play out in her role as the nation's first African American first lady.

Anti-Hillary. While Michelle Obama took to the advocate role for her candidate husband on the campaign trail, she was increasingly wary of moving beyond this role to that of adviser or even cocandidate. The quantitative findings demonstrate her success, as the media never characterized her as a cocandidate and only rarely profiled her as Barack Obama's adviser (6.5% of coverage). Though she made comments early in the campaign to indicate her influence over her husband—characterizing their marriage as an equal partnership—the media did not translate this into a cocandidacy, as they did with the Clintons. In a *USA Today* interview in May 2007, Michelle Obama was asked what happens when her husband wants her input on policy issues. Keen writes, "Her reply isn't surprising: 'Do you think I would ever hold my tongue?'" (2007, A1). The piece continues, however, by distinguishing Michelle Obama from the vilified image of an imperious first lady—Hillary Clinton: "Michelle Obama has a resume packed with accomplishments. But her campaign appearances are not meant to signal that Obama and Obama offer voters 'two for the price of one,' which is what Bill Clinton told voters they would get in 1992 if he and Hillary Rodham Clinton moved into the White House" (Keen 2007, A1). Other pieces were quick to place Michelle Obama in more of a supporting role, casting her as the "anti-Hillary." In contrast to hopes that Hillary Clinton had regendered the role of first lady or political spouse, the media continued to isolate Michelle Obama from this more progressive—and growingly negative—image of partner-wife, or co-candidate. With a tone of relief, for example, Susan Saulny wrote, "There is no confusing Michelle Obama for her husband on the campaign trail" (2008, A1). Unlike Bill Clinton, she reflected her spouse's suitability for office, instead of invoking doubts that he could govern alone.

The media coverage of Michelle Obama stands in sharp contrast to Bill Clinton's coverage. Michelle Obama was covered as a woman capable of adapting to the accepted role of political wife, albeit with professional credentials and personal autonomy in tow. On the trail, Michelle Obama's sarcasm was criticized as emasculating while Bill Clinton's discussions of Hillary Clinton's daily life were seen as humanizing. On the other hand, Michelle Obama's strong opinions and influence were viewed as secondary to her personal sacrifice, whereas Bill Clinton's professional experience was assumed to dominate his wife's candidacy and possibly presidency. While Michelle Obama could be framed as her husband's primary supporter and advocate, the media framed Bill Clinton as a cocandidate and the dominant partner on the campaign trail. Even in the couple's missteps and misstatements on the trail, Clinton's behavior was scrutinized as if he were running for president while Michelle Obama's gaffes sparked far less extensive and derisive reactions from the media, political opponents, or the public.[15] Michelle Obama was overwhelmingly profiled as an asset, but only a passive player in her husband's campaign. As first lady, Michelle Obama is described similarly—a strong force supporting her husband but framed in comfortably feminine roles including "mom-in-chief," fashion icon, and "wifely helpmate" (Westfall 2009).

Elizabeth Edwards: It Takes a Partnership

Recognized as the more politically inclined of the couple, Elizabeth Edwards was less constrained than most political wives before her—accepted as a professional woman engaged in the campaign without being vilified for breaking gender norms. Even in her attacks on candidates and pundits—viewed as the most masculine of behaviors—Edwards was cast as a "rock" for her husband, his ultimate source of strength and his fiercest defender. She was also a courageous crusader battling stage IV breast cancer, whose story captivated voters and journalists alike. With overwhelmingly positive coverage, Elizabeth Edwards did not face media backlash to her influential role. However, the persistent reminders of Edwards's maternal role in media coverage make evident remaining constraints for female spouses. The media presented dual images of Elizabeth Edwards, first, as a progressive political partner and dedicated wife and mother and, second, as both master campaigner and supportive spouse. While Edwards evidences spousal role evolution *and* constraint, a contrast of her coverage to Bill Clinton's demonstrates how we have yet to consider the role of a male spouse supporter, and more importantly, accept a lone woman who can have a strong "helpmate" spouse without being undermined or overshadowed by him.

Master strategist and campaigner. Coverage of Elizabeth Edwards is indeed unique for a political spouse, as she was most often positively framed as a strong adviser and political partner to her husband (32.1% of coverage). In many instances, she was described, like Bill Clinton, as a "master strategist" and campaigner who played an important role both behind the scenes and on the campaign trail. Most importantly, instead of simply providing spousal reflection as a way to masculinize her candidate husband, journalists framed her as someone on whom John Edwards was dependent. Lynne Duke and Lois Romano described her as the "center of her husband's world," adding, "During the 2004 presidential race, Elizabeth Edwards almost always traveled with her husband and aides knew she was the ultimate gatekeeper and her husband's closest adviser. She sat in on every debate practice and 'not as a cheerleader,' said one person involved in that campaign" (2007, C1). Elizabeth Edwards was described as the "more skillful political thinker of the pair," said to improve John Edwards's campaigning when she was at his side (Bai 2007) and known for interrupting him on the stump or during interviews, wanting to clarify a particular policy point or add her own perception of the situation or issue (Nagourney 2007). Elizabeth Edwards, then, was framed as an active participant in her husband's political life, not the passive observer or soft-toned surrogate of first ladies past.

While the media described Elizabeth Edwards's strong influence on her husband, she was reluctant to admit to such a powerful role in the campaign. Interestingly, her denial of a strategic or advisory role may have demonstrated her political aptitude, recognizing both the public and the media's discomfort with political wives embracing atypical gender traits and behaviors. This approach may also demonstrate an "anti-Hillary" effect, wherein modern political wives seek to avoid the demonization associated with the active role Hillary Clinton played in her husband's administration. In an interview with ABC's *Nightline* in April 2007, Edwards assured the public that she did not overstep the boundaries of her role in saying, "What I am is a sounding board for John. . . . I'm a true believer in the chain of command" (April 2, 2007). She was similarly self-effacing in July of the same year in combating claims that she was a driving force in John Edwards's campaign: "I get a lot more credit for, you know, being the puppeteer than I am. I express my opinion. Honestly, I'm not the decision maker" (Balz 2007b, A1).

Her insistence seemed to ease fears of a Clinton-like cocandidacy. Eugene Robinson of the *Washington Post,* who so overtly warned of a Clinton copresidency (see the earlier discussion), was uncharacteristically permissive, and even laudatory, in his profile of Elizabeth Edwards. Of the Edwards couple, he wrote, "It takes a partnership to win the White House," and added, "Run, John and Elizabeth, run. Enjoy the campaign, every thrilling minute. Enjoy it together" (Robinson 2007a, A17). The media's acceptance of the Edwardses' political partnership, I argue, was partly due to Elizabeth Edwards's blended image as a political adviser *and* a supportive wife, mother, and cancer patient. In challenging traditional spousal expectations, Edwards was given, and was herself aware of, her own limitations to transgendering the spousal role.

Feminine role reminders. Those limitations were evident in media reminders of Elizabeth Edwards's feminine role as wife and mother. Many articles that described Elizabeth Edwards as a political partner and behind-the-scenes adviser returned to discussion of her family, especially her role as mother and as a survivor of both personal illness and tragedy.[16] Reporters often tied this role to the sacrifice Elizabeth Edwards made to cede time with her family to support her husband's ambitions. While Michelle Obama's sacrifice was viewed as largely professional and ideological, Elizabeth Edwards selflessly insisted that her husband keep campaigning in light of her terminal diagnosis. "'Yes, it's another hurdle,' she said. But she said the country needs her husband as president and she wouldn't stop him 'just because I want to sit home, feeling perfectly well, but wanting his company'" (Robinson 2007a, A17). Elizabeth Edwards said she could not live with denying John Edwards the chance to be president. She told Katie Couric of *CBS News,* "That I'd taken out this fine man from—from the possibility of—of giving a great service. I mean, I don't want that to be my legacy" (March 26, 2007).

Media framing of Elizabeth Edwards provides stunted optimism about the perceived role of a political wife. Edwards was portrayed as a vital partner in her husband's campaign—a great political mind—without the vilification usually accompanying the violation of traditional gender roles. However, the persistent focus on her personal roles as wife and mother serves as a reminder of spousal constraint and the expectations of spousal reflection—especially in her sacrifice and support—for a masculine executive office holder. Below, I compare media frames of Elizabeth Edwards and Bill

Clinton, demonstrating how similarities in their campaign roles and behaviors are covered differently. This different understanding of similar behaviors by men and women makes evident the gendering of spousal roles and frames and demonstrates the "propensity to reassert gender where none need exist" (Duerst-Lahti and Kelly 1995, 28).

Defending her husband, attacking his critics. Elizabeth Edwards was not shy in attacking her husband's fellow candidates, reflected in the media framing of her as a defender/attacker in 12.5% of coverage. Winfield and Friedman (2003, 552) include the role of defender in their categorization of political wives' coverage on the campaign trail, noting that it is perceived as part of their surrogate role that demonstrates their passion for their husband's success, not a sign of aggression. Interestingly, however, the media was unable or unwilling to translate the same acceptance to Bill Clinton's comments—demonstrating the incapacity of a male spouse to adopt a feminized, or even transgendered, role of political spouse. While Bill Clinton was framed as a defender/attacker in a similar proportion of articles (14.1%), his coverage was far more negative. For example, in accusing the media and Hillary Clinton's fellow candidates of bias against a female candidate, Bill Clinton said, "I can't make her younger, taller or change her gender" (Dowd 2008a, 19). This evoked a quick response from media pundits like Maureen Dowd, who wrote, "Bill played 'the poor-little-woman card" (2008a, 19). There was very little reaction, and definitely not nearly as negative, from a comment made by Elizabeth Edwards on her husband's race and gender. She said, "We can't make John black. We can't make him a woman. Those things get you a lot of press, worth a certain amount of fund-raising dollars" (Seelye 2007, 1).

In a second example, Bill Clinton was lambasted in the popular media for calling Barack Obama's claim to be consistently against the Iraq War as "a fairytale." Print media first released a series of pieces accusing Bill Clinton of calling the Obama campaign itself a fairytale, neglecting the context in which the comments were made. Once corrected, the story continued as supposed evidence of racism and unfair attacks on Obama by the former president. This event and its subsequent media attention are attributed with hurting Hillary Clinton's relationship among black voters and, specifically, expanding Barack Obama's electoral margin of victory in the South Carolina primary.[17] Interestingly, and unbeknownst to most of the public due to a lack of media coverage, Elizabeth Edwards made a similar comment in the summer before the primaries and caucuses began. She told a progressive magazine that Obama was behaving in a "holier than thou" way on the war, arguing that his 2002 speech was "likely to be extraordinarily popular in his home district" (Bacon 2007, A1). Again, neither the media nor the public latched onto this comment. Though the racialized context of the

South Carolina primary likely fueled the media's hypersensitivity there and the Clintons' contentious relationship to the press did not help induce positive coverage overall, reactions to Bill Clinton's comments throughout the campaign demonstrated the intense scrutiny placed on Bill Clinton as both a former president and "dominant," male spouse.

Of Heroes and Helpmates:
Gender and Presidential Spouses

Existing scholarship has asked what impact female spouses have on their candidate husbands—what roles they play, what influence they have, and how much they disrupt gender expectations. This chapter asks what happens when we turn the tables to also consider the impact male spouses have on female executive candidates. How does the executive relationship function if the most traditional gender roles and expectations of wife and husband are disrupted? Media coverage of candidates and their spouses in the 2008 contest for the Democratic nomination provides one illustration of how the masculine norms and expectations steeped in the executive office persist. Analyzing the media's coverage of presidential candidates and their spouses demonstrates one dimension of this inherent masculinity, as tied to the president's image as a "lone male hero" with a less visible "helpmate" wife. While female spouses serve as a boon to male candidates—reflecting their masculinity—male spouses may do little more than reinforce women's feminine roles—roles that are in near opposition to executive ideals of singularity, heroism, and masculine power. Beyond demonstrating that the "hair, hemlines, and husbands" trifecta of gender-based challenges persists in media coverage of female candidates, this chapter posits that the gendering of the presidential partnership constrains female partners—candidates and spouses alike—and maintains a masculinized executive institution.

Both my qualitative and quantitative findings—though constrained to one race and a set of unique candidates and spouses—point to this trend. Bill Clinton's persistent presence in coverage of Hillary Clinton undermined her image as an independent candidate uninfluenced by her spouse and, instead, reaffirmed the dominance of masculinity—as embodied by Bill Clinton—in the image of an executive. Fears of his dominance were further affirmed by media frames that defined him as a cocandidate guided by his own ambition and left uncontrolled by his candidate spouse. Unlike his female counterparts who were valorized for their sacrifice and selflessness, Bill Clinton's image as a reluctant spouse demonstrated the media's—and possibly Clinton's own—discomfort with a man in the spousal role. As his partner, Hillary Clinton was viewed as either dependent or emasculating, unable to adopt the "manly presence" so desired in the nation's top executive role.

Male candidates traverse the gendered terrain of executive politics aided by these expectations of masculinity. Not only do they tout "manly" traits of strength and leadership, but their female spouses reflect their masculine identities. While both Michelle Obama and Elizabeth Edwards challenged traditional conceptions of political wives in the 2008 Democratic contest, they were unable to break completely free of gender role expectations that benefited their candidate husbands. Michelle Obama's shifting narrative, as characterized by the media, from a reluctant political spouse to an "everywoman" and supportive political wife is demonstrative of the media's expectation for women to adapt to the gendered expectations of the spousal role. Similarly, while Elizabeth Edwards—in contrast to political wives of the past—was recognized as an astute political mind and professional woman, the media tempered her challenge to traditional gendered imagery by reminding the public of her domestic role as wife and mother. This balance remains one to be struck by female partners, while male partners are presumed to hold public and primary roles. These spousal expectations translate into executive institutions like the presidency, challenging female candidates to balance "wifely" expectations with a masculine role and leaving male spouses little room to be perceived as anything but dominant (Pogrebin 2008).

Behind *Every* Woman?
Spousal Expectations in Lower-Level Executive Offices

Does the challenge of gendered spousal expectations persist in executive offices other than the presidency? Moreover, do expectations of gender-office congruency advantage men over women in lower-level executive offices? Answering this question requires consideration of the degree of masculinity in gubernatorial and mayoral institutions, for example, and the attention paid to spouses of these candidates and officeholders. Unlike the presidency, women have been successful in winning subnational executive posts. The precedence of women executives in states and localities may deter skepticism that a woman is capable of serving at this level, in addition to the compatibility of responsibilities and issue environments facing officeholders at these levels with women's perceived areas of expertise—education and social welfare, for example. Additionally, the scrutiny placed upon the presidential partnership is far greater than the attention paid to subnational executive candidates or officeholders and their spouses. Private and public roles are more easily blurred for US presidents, as it is often said that the nation not only elects a president but elects a "first family."

However, spousal expectations are not without effect in state and local executive offices. Female executives face a historical precedent of women entering office as substitutes for their deceased or term-limited husbands; the first three women governors in US history, for example, took office as their husbands' successors, confirming perceptions that women would only win executive office on the shoulders of men. Even in executive roles, then, these women reflected the power and agendas of their husbands. As women win executive posts in their own right, questions have emerged over how their husbands will respond to their gender-role disjuncture. At the mayoral level, for example, former DC mayor Sharon Pratt cites that people continually assumed that her husband played a larger role in decisionmaking than he did (Copeland 2007). At the gubernatorial level, few first gentlemen have taken as active of roles in their wives' administrations as have their female counterparts, arguably working to prevent similar assumptions and to preserve their wives' images as autonomous executives. Some male spouses of female governors have played on the gender ambiguity of their roles, trying on titles like "first dude," "first hunk," or "first lad" without spending much time challenging gendered expectations of their spousal roles.

Former first gentleman of Michigan, Dan Mulhern, took a more direct approach to investigating, and potentially disrupting, gender norms in state executive office. In explaining his self-designated title soon after Governor Jennifer Granholm took office, he wrote, "I am proud and humbled to serve my wife. As 'first lady' connotes a respect for her husband and her governor, it seems like 'first gentleman' is an appropriate mirror image that conveys respect to the leader of the state" (Mulhern 2002). He quickly held a number of "first man forums" on sex roles and continued a dialogue on gender and leadership through his weekly newsletter, radio show, and speeches around the state. In reflecting on his transition into a supportive role, he described what he hopes is a "second, quiet revolution" to women's advancement: "Women have won a new opportunity not only for themselves but for men. Men now have the chance to be great supporters of powerful women, to relate to them in whole new ways, to nurture and empathize with our children, and central to it all, to develop our own full humanity" (Mulhern 2009, 319). This revolution—and more accepted traverse of gender roles and gender power—reflects a transgendering of public and private institutions so defined by masculinity and femininity. For women running for executive offices, this shift would remove a barrier they currently face in proving that they are neither subordinate to nor dependent on their male spouse.

Future research should investigate how this "revolution" might occur within executive institutions at the local, state, and national levels. First, greater evidence is needed to explore the role of spousal expectations and dynamics at the local and state levels of executive office. Second, more research is needed on the dynamics and influence of spousal expectations for executive candidates and officeholders who are unmarried, who are unpartnered, or who have diverse sexual orientations.[18] In the absence of a traditional masculine-feminine dyad, how do these candidates fare? Future research should also pay greater attention to racial differences in spousal expectations and influence. Finally, scholars should continue to push the boundaries of research on executive spouses and first ladies to consider how traditional spousal roles and expectations gender executive institutions to the detriment of female partners. Previous work has been content to discuss women's "helpmate" roles and successes in spousal reflection. As women turn the tables to be candidates themselves, researchers must grapple with men's influence in executive partnerships and its implications for transgendering executive office imagery and expectations. Recognizing spousal role expectations as an indicator of gendered executive institutions and, more specifically, as a potential barrier to female executive candidates prescribes a new line of research on gender and executive office at the local, state, and national levels.

Notes

1. Falk (2008) describes how the media has traditionally framed women candidates as unviable, whether questioning their "readiness" or citing their poor poll standings. She notes 2000 as the first year where the media cited bias and prejudice as a challenge to women's electoral viability. Falk concludes that perceptions of viability are one potential predictor for the amount of news coverage of and, more generally, attention to a particular candidate.

2. This time period begins soon after Barack Obama's announcement of candidacy and ends with the final Democratic presidential primary in the nomination contest.

3. To determine the general counts of spousal mentions, I first searched for a total number of articles on each candidate for each time period: "Candidate Name" and atl 4([Candidate first name] and [Candidate last name]) and date aft 2/10/2007 and date bef 2/12/2008. I then performed the same search, including the spouses' names: "[Candidate Name]" and atl 4([Candidate first name] and [Candidate last name]) and "[Spouse Name]" and date aft 2/10/2007 and date bef 2/12/2008. To create a sample for detailed coding, I used the same search terms with a smaller selection of newspapers (see endnote 5). In an effort to avoid articles mentioning Bill Clinton only as a former president, I adapted the search to ensure there were at least four mentions of him within the sample articles: "Hillary (Rodham) Clinton" and atl 4(Hillary and Clinton) and "Bill Clinton" and atl 4(Bill and Clinton) and date aft 2/10/2007 and date bef 2/12/2008. Finally, the second time sample for Obama and Clinton includes the same searches from February 11, 2008, to June 3, 2008.

4. The 10 newspaper outlets include *USA Today,* the *Wall Street Journal,* the *New York Times,* the *Los Angeles Times,* the *Washington Post,* the *New York Daily News,* the *New York Post,* the *Denver Post,* the *Dallas Morning News* (including McClatchy-Tribune News Service pieces), and the *Houston Chronicle.* These represent the top 10 most circulated papers available on LexisNexis. The *Chicago Tribune* and the *Philadelphia Enquirer* are excluded (although they are in the top 10) because they are unavailable on LexisNexis.

5. This sample includes articles from *USA Today,* the *Wall Street Journal,* the *New York Times,* and the *Washington Post.*

6. While some studies exclude these forms of coverage to avoid potential bias, the purpose of this study is to understand the lens through which candidates' spouses were viewed in 2008. Point-of-view pieces like newspaper editorials provide some of the best sites through which to see these lenses and frames of coverage and commentary.

7. For each category—spousal frame, spousal influence, and spousal role—pieces were given one code that was derived from the author's coding of each spousal reference in the piece and count of the most common type of reference. In other words, the dominant frame, influence, or role used within each article is reflected in its coding.

8. Appearance data is from ABC News' *The Note "Sneak Peek,"* which listed daily candidates' and spouses' appearances throughout the 2008 election. The website's data from the Democratic nomination contest season are less consistent and, therefore, not included. Available at http://abcnews.go.com/Politics/TheNote/story?id=2767484.

9. Findings on spousal coverage from this sample are consistent with those from the 10-paper sample.

10. See Kaye (2008). Alex MacGillis and Karl Vick wrote, "But since his wife became governor 20 months ago, [Todd Palin's] portfolio has broadened: househusband, babysitter, senior adviser, legislative liaison, and—when the occasion warrants—enforcer and protector" (2008, A01). A 2008 Ethics Report to the Legislative Council in Alaska cited that Todd Palin was given access to state resources and subordinates in order to push for the firing of his former brother-in-law, Mike Wooten (Branchflower 2008).

11. While Michelle Obama and Elizabeth Edwards were overwhelmingly painted as assets to their husbands' campaigns, Bill Clinton was covered as a positive influence only 55.1% of the time.

12. On the campaign trail in 1992, Bill Clinton said, "Elect me, and you get two for the price of one," referring to his partnership with wife Hillary Clinton.

13. In an interview on the *Today Show* on May 1, 2008, Michelle Obama expressed support for her husband's campaign, but was quick to add, "I don't want to sound like the cheering wife."

14. For contemporary discussions of Michelle Obama's influence on perceptions of black motherhood, see Harris-Lacewell (2009), Givhan (2009), and Williams (2009).

15. In February 2008, Michelle Obama said, "For the first time in my adult lifetime, I am really proud of my country—and not just because Barack has done well, but because I think people are hungry for change" (Cooper A19, February 20, 2008). While the comment garnered a lot of media attention as allegedly emblematic of her lack of patriotism, very little commentary appeared on its effect on the Obama campaign more generally and the issue soon faded away. This reaction contrasts with the explosive nature of coverage resulting from some of Bill Clinton's comments on the trail.

16. Profiles of Edwards often refer to the death of her eldest son, killed in a car accident at 16.

17. See last-minute voter breakdown in "South Carolina Democratic Primary Poll," *Rasmussen Reports* (January 26, 2008). Accessed April 2010. http://www.rasmussen reports.com/public_content/politics/elections/election_2008/2008_presidential_election/south_carolina/election_2008_south_carolina_democratic_primary.

18. Doan and Haider-Markel's (2010) exploration of intersectional stereotyping of gay and lesbian candidates points to the potential advantages for lesbian candidates, who might benefit both from shared gender identity among women and perceptions that they hold masculine traits and issue expertise. While they do not explore the role of these candidates' partners or families, their findings imply that traditional gender role expectations may be less influential in voter evaluations of lesbian, gay, bisexual, or transgender candidates.

Part 4

Conclusion

13

Defining the Executive Women Research Agenda

Melody Rose

AS WE HEAD INTO THE 2012 ELECTIONS, THE LESSONS FROM THIS volume should inform our thinking about executive candidate advancement, both in terms of the opportunities that lie ahead for women as well as some of the barriers uncovered here. As scholars and students of executive women in US politics, we will find new opportunities for research on the role of executive women in the twenty-first century. Our efforts here have uncovered a number of lessons that contribute to understanding and point to gaps that we hope will be filled by future research.

One of the critical and perhaps implicit benefits of the volume we have produced is the demonstration that new, diverse, and rigorous methods are available to scholars in this field. For a generation, scholars of women in legislatures have had the advantage of large numbers, making large-scale (and therefore generalizable) studies de rigueur. Those interested in women in executive roles have contributed to the dialogue through case study and biography; to these methods we now can add a variety of large-scale qualitative and quantitative methods as demonstrated by this volume. And while these methods also reveal limitations and sometimes prove challenging to those who employ them, at least the toolbox for our work has expanded in meaningful ways.

Beyond methodological innovation, this volume has contributed a number of explicit, empirical insights. In an effort to understand the pathways and performance of women in twenty-first-century executive politics, we have been challenged here simply to define the term. In offering our definition of executive positions at the outset, we realize room can be found for refinement and for wider inclusion; though we have not studied every variation of executive female leadership here, we have certainly defined

259

executive office as a discrete subfield of study and invite other scholars to join in this dialogue.

Through this critical analysis of executive roles, we have advanced a collective observation that the theory of pipeline is more limited than popular language would allow. The notion that women will advance in all levels of elected service (or in this case, executive service) by flooding that pipe at the local level has proved problematic in these pages. We discovered that the pipeline has breaches, and that progress is not inevitable. Filling the pipe at one end does not, it turns out, guarantee a robust result at the other end. In part, the reason lies in the fact that different groups of women may enter and exit the pipe at different places, and for diverse reasons. Pipeline thinking can be useful in election settings as a tool for motivating more women to pursue office, but as an analytical tool, it has limits.

Related to this observation is the more pointed one that pathways are multiple because ambition does not enjoy a homogenous definition. Earlier work on women's political ambition was connected to pipeline theory: if we can inspire women's initial ambition for service, and then bolster their progressive ambition, we might see women assume roles that progress from community through state and, ultimately, to national service.

But the pages here have challenged the underpinnings of this argument: maybe women are driven by ambitions distinct from their male counterparts. The significant number of African American women serving as mayors of smaller cities is testimony to the argument that sometimes, the ultimate ambition is service to local community. As we move this research agenda further along, I hope this volume can inspire a refreshed look at female political ambition and pipeline that takes into account the ways in which female political behavior is distinct from men's, and variant also across communities of women.

Finally, this book has reconsidered some of the known obstacles to women's advancement (parties, media, and finance) while also introducing a new one: marital status and the role of the "spouse." Our authors here produce some new results around old barriers, discovering that parties, media, and finance are somewhat diminished obstacles, and that women do find multiple pathways to success through them. While these three elements were once thought to be the three major hurdles for any female candidate, our scholars here produce more nuanced results from the twenty-first century, revealing that while these barriers remain in certain venues, women have gained ground and have developed some innovative ways of mediating their effects. At the same time, more than one author in this text revealed the implicit (and sometimes explicit) challenges that women's family choices have on their campaigns. Dealing with the spouse, and the stereotypes that exist about family roles, remains a challenge and requires additional examination.

Charting a Course: Filling the Gaps in the Literature

Although we accomplished much in this collection, more remains to be learned and to be shared. If this subfield of executive women research continues, a number of areas are ripe for additional examination. Chief among these is the ongoing challenge of considering gender as one of many significant variables affecting women's advancement. Multivariate analyses will become more possible through ever-growing numbers of women in executive offices. Understanding, for instance, the interactivity of office, party, gender, and ethnicity will continue to be the frontier in our research. It may be that the barriers of money, parties, and media depend greatly upon party affiliation, office sought, or race (Fowler and Lawless 2009). In some areas of executive life these analyses are possible: chiefly, the numbers of female mayors have become large enough to do such work. At the level of governor, this analysis may not yet be possible.

Furthermore, one implicit conclusion we can draw from the work here on spousal effects is that gender analysis needs to take a step forward. While we often affiliate femininity (gender) with women candidates (sex), one particular contemporary challenge may exist for lesbian candidates: What can the lessons for spouses herein predict for lesbian candidates for executive office? And are there lesbian executive candidates whose experiences can shed new understanding on our gender analysis going forward for all women?

Furthermore, the traditional executive offices (mayor, governor, and vice/president) may have similarities but their dissimilarities are significant as well. Some of these offices may be more challenging for women based upon the content of the role and the incongruous relationship between office and gender expectations: Should we expect women to have an easier time with media, money, and parties when they seek gubernatorial roles, where the policy arena dovetails with female gender norms, than, say, when they seek the presidency? And it should not be overlooked that many additional executive statewide posts are not included in our study: attorney general, lieutenant governor, and secretary of state/education/labor are all executive roles that could provide additional knowledge about women as executive candidates and leaders.

More consideration is also needed for the thesis that power shifts away from executive offices as women assume them. Dee Dee Myers (2008), for instance, reports in her book that as the first woman press secretary, she found the role marginalized vis-à-vis others in the president's circle. Scholarship from the twentieth century predicted this result, but our work here did not test it against twenty-first-century data. Examining this hypothesis and testing it will also make the executive women literature richer.

And when we get beyond the traditional executive offices, and continue to consider the appointed roles we include here (executive appointee/

bureaucrat, speaker), have we exhausted our understanding? Much of the extant media literature has focused on the media-saturated campaign environments such as the presidency, and our own work here extends that literature to mayoral and gubernatorial candidates. We know little of the media coverage of cabinet members, judges, or even the House Speaker. Do these executive women face similar or distinct media challenges as their colleagues in the traditional roles?

More than 15 years ago Duerst-Lahti and Kelly (1995) challenged scholars to consider the gendered nature of political office. Since then, advances have taken place in understanding women in the bureaucracy in particular, and also a growing body of work has been devoted to capturing the impact of media scrutiny on presidential candidates. In offering this collection we hope to inspire a discourse around gender in a broader set of executive roles and a discussion on how twenty-first-century women can and will fare in them. We look forward to a lively and expanded discussion as future scholars critique and expand upon our contributions here.

Bibliography

Abramowitz, Alan I. 1989. "Visibility, Electability, and Candidate Choice in a Presidential Primary Election: A Test of Competing Models." *Journal of Politics* 51:977–992.

Acker, Joan. 1992. "Gendered Institutions: From Sex Roles to Gendered Institutions." *Contemporary Society* 21 (4): 565–569.

Aday, Sean, and James Devitt. 2001. "Style over Substance: Newspaper Coverage of Elizabeth Dole's Presidential Bid." *Harvard International Journal of Press and Politics* 6 (2): 52–73.

Adkins, Randall E., and Andrew J. Dowdle. 2002. "The Money Primary: What Influences the Outcome of Pre-primary Presidential Nomination Fundraising?" *Presidential Studies Quarterly* 32: 256–275.

Adkison, Danny M. 1982. "The Electoral Significance of the Vice Presidency." *Presidential Studies Quarterly* 12:330–336.

Allen, Mike. 2008. "Ad: Palin More Qualified than Obama." *Politico.com,* September 3. Accessed June 21, 2012. http://www.politico.com/news/stories/0908/13111 .html.

Alozie, Nicholas O., and Lynne L. Manganaro. 1993. "Women's Council Representation: Measurement Implications for Public Policy." *Political Research Quarterly* 46 (2): 383–398.

Arnold, R. Douglas. 1990. *The Logic of Congressional Action.* New Haven, CT: Yale University Press.

Atkeson, Lonna Rae, and Timothy B. Krebs. 2008. "Press Coverage of Mayoral Candidates: The Role of Gender in News Reporting and Campaign Issue Speech." *Political Research Quarterly* 61 (2): 239–252.

Bacon, Perry, Jr. 2007. "War Critics Question Obama's Fervor—Some Say Actions Don't Match Talk." *Washington Post,* September 15, A01.

Baer, Denise L. 1993a. "Political Parties: The Missing Variable in Women and Politics Research." *Political Research Quarterly* 46:547–576.

———. 1993b. "Who Has the Body? Party Institutionalization and Theories of Party Organization." *American Review of Politics* 14:1–32.

———. 2005. "What Kind of Women's Movement? Community, Representation and Resurgence." In *Women in Politics: Outsiders or Insiders,* 4th ed., edited by Lois Duke Whittier. Upper Saddle River, NJ: Prentice Hall.

————. 2011. "The New Gendered Partisan Divide and Representation of Women and Women's Organizations." In *Women in Politics: Outsiders or Insiders,* 5th ed., edited by Lois Duke Whittier, 89–112. Boston: Longman.

Baer, Denise L., and David A. Bositis. 1988. *Elite Cadres and Party Coalitions: Representing the Public in Party Politics.* New York: Greenwood Press.

————. 1993. *Politics and Linkage in a Democratic Society.* Englewood Cliffs, NJ: Prentice Hall.

Baer, Denise L., and Julie Dolan. 1994. "Intimate Connections: Political Interests and Group Activity in State and Local Parties." *American Review of Politics* 15:257–289.

Baer, Denise L., and John S. Jackson III. 2009. "American Political Development and the Advent of Genuine Intermediary Factions Within Contemporary Democratic and Republican Parties." Presented at the 2009 Midwest Political Science Association Annual meeting, Chicago, April 22–25.

Bai, Matt. 2007. "The Poverty Platform." *New York Times Magazine,* June 10.

Baird, Karen L. 1999. "The New NIH and FDA Medical Research Policies: Targeting Gender, Promoting Justice." *Journal of Health Politics, Policy and Law* 24 (3): 531–565.

Baker, Peter, and Anne E. Kornblut. 2008. "Even in Victory, Clinton Team Is Battling Itself." *Washington Post,* March 6.

Balz, Dan. 2007a. "Hillary Clinton, Stumping with Burgers and Bill." *Washington Post,* September 4, Section A, Final Edition.

————. 2007b. "A True Political Partner." *Washington Post,* July 30.

Banaszak, Lee Ann. 2010. *The Women's Movement Inside and Outside the State.* Cambridge: Cambridge University Press.

Barabak, Mark Z. 1999. "Dole Drops Bid for Presidency, Leaves a Legacy." *Los Angeles Times,* October 21, A1.

Barnello, Michele A., and Kathleen A. Bratton. 2007. "Bridging the Gender Gap in Bill Sponsorship." *Legislative Studies Quarterly* 32(3): 449–474.

Barone, Michael, and Richard E. Cohen. 2007. *The Almanac of American Politics 2008.* Washington, DC: National Journal Group and Atlantic Media.

Barth, Jay, and Margaret R. Ferguson. 2002. "Gender and Gubernatorial Personality." *Women and Politics* 24:63–82.

Beck, Susan Abrams. 2001. "Acting as Women: The Effects and Limitations of Gender in Local Governance." In *The Impact of Women in Public Office,* edited by Susan J. Carroll, 49–67. Bloomington: Indiana University Press.

Berke, Richard L. 1999. "As Political Spouse, Bob Dole Strays from Campaign Script." *New York Times,* May 17.

Borrelli, MaryAnne. 2002. *The President's Cabinet: Gender, Power and Representation.* Boulder, CO: Lynne Rienner.

Borrelli, MaryAnne, and Janet M. Martin. 1997. *The Other Elites: Women, Politics and Power in the Executive Branch.* Boulder, CO: Lynne Rienner.

Boyles, Denny. 2008. "Mayoral Foes' Paths Have Been Different—Swearengin, Perea Play Up What Sets them Apart." *Fresno Bee,* September 14, A1.

Branchflower, Steve. 2008. "Report to the Legislative Council." State of Alaska, October 10.

Bratton, Kathleen A., and Kerry L. Haynie. 1999. "Agenda Setting and Legislative Success in State Legislatures: The Effects of Gender and Race." *Journal of Politics* 61:658–679.

Broder, John M. 2008. "Now on the Campaign Trail, a Reined-In Bill Clinton." *New York Times,* February 27, National Desk Section, Late Edition-Final.

Bullock, Charles S., III, and Susan A. MacManus. 1990. "Municipal Electoral Structure and the Election of Councilwomen," *Journal of Politics* 53 (1): 75–89.

Bureau of Labor Statistics. 2011. *Labor Force Statistics from the Current Population Survey.* Accessed June 21, 2012. http://data.bls.gov/pdq/SurveyOutput Servlet.

Burns, Nancy, Kay Lehman Schlozman, and Sidney Verba. 2001. *The Private Roots of Public Action: Gender, Equality, and Political Participation.* Cambridge, MA: Harvard University Press.

Burrell, Barbara. 1992. "Women Candidates in Open Seat Primaries for the U.S. House of Representatives, 1968–1990." *Legislative Studies Quarterly* 17: 493–508.

————. 1994. *A Woman's Place Is in the House: Campaigning for Congress in the Feminist Era.* Ann Arbor: Michigan University Press.

Burt-Way, Barbara J., and Rita Mae Kelly. 1992. "Gender and Sustaining Political Ambition: A Study of Arizona Elected Officials." *Western Political Quarterly* 45 (1): 11–25.

Bystrom, Dianne. 2003. "On the Way to the White House: Communication Strategies for Women Candidates." In *Anticipating Madam President,* edited by Robert P. Watson and Ann Gordon, 95–106. Boulder, CO: Lynne Rienner.

————. 2006. "Media Content and Candidate Viability: The Case of Elizabeth Dole." In *Communicating Politics: Engaging in Public in Democratic Life,* edited by Mitchell S. McKinney, Dianne G. Bystrom, Lynda Lee Kaid, and Diana B. Carlin, 123–134. New York: Peter Lang.

————. 2008. "Gender and U.S. Presidential Politics: Early Newspaper Coverage of Hillary Clinton's Bid for the White House." Paper presented at the annual meeting of the American Political Science Association, Boston, August 29.

Bystrom, Dianne G., Mary Banwart, Lynda Lee Kaid, and Terry Robertson. 2004. *Gender and Candidate Communication: Videostyle, Webstyle, and Newsstyle.* London: Routledge.

Bystrom, Dianne G., Terry Robertson, and Mary Banwart. 2001. "Framing the Fight: An Analysis of Media Coverage of Female and Male Candidates in Primary Races for Governor and U.S. Senate in 2000." *American Behavioral Scientist* 44:1999–2013.

"Campaigner in Chief." 2008. *USA Today,* January 25, News Section, Final Edition.

Campbell, Karlyn Kohrs. 1996. "The Rhetorical Presidency: A Two-Person Career." In *Beyond the Rhetorical Presidency,* edited by Martin J. Medhurst, 179–195. College Station: Texas A&M Press.

Carlin, Diana B., and Kelly L. Winfrey. 2009. "Have You Come a Long Way, Baby? Hillary Clinton, Sarah Palin, and Sexism in 2008 Campaign Coverage." *Communication Studies* 60 (4): 326–343.

Caroli, Betty Boyd. 1995. *First Ladies.* New York: Oxford University Press.

Carroll, Susan J. 1985a. "Political Elites and Sex Differences in Political Ambition: A Reconsideration." *Journal of Politics* 47:1231–1243.

————. 1985b. *Women as Candidates in American Politics.* Bloomington: University of Indiana Press.

————. 1987. "Women in State Cabinets: Status and Prospects." *Journal of State Government* 60:204–208.

————. 1989. "The Personal Is Political: The Intersection of Private Lives and Public Roles Among Women and Men in Elective and Appointive Office." *Women and Politics* 9 (1): 51–67.

————. 1994. *Women as Candidates in American Politics.* 2nd ed. Bloomington: Indiana University Press.

————. 2001. "Representing Women: Women State Legislators as Agents of Policy-Related Change." In *The Impact of Women in Public Office,* edited by Susan J. Carroll, 3–21. Bloomington: Indiana University Press.

———. 2003. *Have Women State Legislators in the United States Become More Conservative? A Comparison of State Legislators in 2001 and 1988.* New Brunswick, NJ: Center for American Women and Politics.

———. 2009. "Reflections on Gender and Hillary Clinton's Presidential Campaign: The Good, the Bad, and the Misogynic." *Politics & Gender* 5:1–20.

Carroll, Susan J., and Barbara Geiger-Parker. 1983. *Women Appointed to State Government: A Comparison with All State Appointees.* New Brunswick, NJ: Center for American Women and Politics.

Carroll, Susan J., and Kira Sanbonmatsu. 2009. "Gender and the Decision to Run for the State Legislature." Paper presented at the Midwest Political Science Association Annual Meeting, Chicago, April 2–5.

Carroll, Susan J., and Wendy S. Strimling. 1983. *Women's Routes to Elective Office: A Comparison with Men's.* New Brunswick, NJ: Center for American Women and Politics, Eagleton Institute of Politics, Rutgers University.

Center for American Women and Politics (CAWP). 2000. *Women in Elective Office 2000.* Fact sheet. National Information Bank on Women in Public Office, Eagleton Institute of Politics. New Brunswick, NJ: Rutgers University.

———. 2010a. *History of Women Governors Fact Sheet.* New Brunswick, NJ: Center for American Women and Politics.

———. 2010b. *Summary of Women Candidates 2010.* New Brunswick, NJ: Center for American Women and Politics.

———. 2010c. *Women Appointed to Presidential Cabinets.* New Brunswick, NJ: Center for American Women and Politics, Eagleton Institute of Politics, Rutgers University.

———. 2011a. *Statewide Elective Executive Women.* New Brunswick, NJ: Center for American Women and Politics.

———. 2011b. *Women in Elective Office 2011.* Fact sheet. National Information Bank on Women in Public Office, Eagleton Institute of Politics. New Brunswick, NJ: Rutgers University.

Chambliss, Teresa. 1992. "The Growth and Significance of African American Elected Officials." In *From Exclusion to Inclusion: The Long Struggle for African American Political Power,* edited by Ralph C. Gomes and Linda Faye Williams, 53–70. Westport, CT: Greenwood.

Chu, Judy. 1989. "Asian Pacific American Women in Mainstream Politics." In *Making Waves: An Anthology of Writings By and About Asian American Women,* edited by Asian Women United of California, 405–421. Boston: Beacon.

Clift, Eleanor, and Tom Brazaitis. 2003. *Madam President: Women Blazing the Leadership Trail.* New York: Routledge.

CNN/Opinion Research Corporation Poll. 2008, August/September. iPOLL Databank, Roper Center for Public Opinion Research, University of Connecticut. Accessed May 14, 2011. http://www.ropercenter.uconn.edu/data_access/ipoll/ipoll.html.

Coffey, Daniel. 2005. "Measuring Gubernatorial Ideology: A Content Analysis of State of the State Speeches." *State Politics and Policy Quarterly* 5:88–103.

Cohen, Jeffrey E., ed. 2006. *Public Opinion in State Politics.* Stanford, CA: Stanford University Press.

Cohen, Marty, David Karol, Hans Noel, and John Zaller. *The Party Decides: Presidential Nominations Before and After Reform.* Chicago: University of Chicago Press, 2008.

Cohen, Richard. 2008. "Hail to the Chief of Staff." *Washington Post,* February 5, Editorial.

Collins, Patricia Hill. 1990. *Black Feminist Thought: Knowledge, Consciousness, and the Politics of Empowerment.* New York: Routledge.

———. 1996. "Shifting the Center: Race, Class, and Feminist Theorizing About Motherhood." In *Representations of Motherhood*, edited by Donna Bassin, Margaret Honey, and Meryle Mahrer Kaplan, 56–74. New Haven, CT: Yale University Press.

Cooper, Joseph, and David W. Brady. 1981. "Institutional Context and Leadership Style: The House from Cannon to Rayburn." *American Political Science Review* 75 (2): 411–425.

Cooper, Michael. 2008. "Comments Bring Wives into Fray inWisconsin." *New York Times*, February 20.

Copeland, Libby. 2002. "Metamorphosis: The 'Big Boss' in the Maryland Governor's Office is Now a Silent First Lady." *Washington Post*, March 8.

———. 2007. "The Rules for a Fair Fight." *Washington Post*, November 7.

Corsaro, Ryan. 2008. "Palin's Parents Told to Listen to Radio." *CBS News*. Accessed April 16, 2010. http://www.cbsnews.com/8301-502163_162-4395877 -502163.html.

Cotter, Cornelius P., and Bernard Hennessy. 1964. *Politics Without Power*. New York: Atherton.

Cottle, Michelle. 2009. "The Third Obama: What Does Valerie Jarrett Do?" *The New Republic*, July 15.

Cox, Gary W., and Jonathan Katz. 2002. *Elbridge Gerry's Salamander: The Electoral Consequences of the Reapportionment Revolution*. Cambridge: Cambridge University Press.

Cox, Gary, and Mathew D. McCubbins. 1993. *Legislative Leviathan*. Berkeley: University of California Press.

Crenshaw, Kimberle Williams. 1989. "Demarginalizing the Intersection of Race and Sex." *University of Chicago Legal Forum* 39:139–167.

———. 1991. "Mapping the Margins: Intersectionality, Identity Politics, and Violence Against Women of Color." *Stanford Law Review* 43 (6): 1241–1299.

Cronin, Thomas, and Michael Genovese. 1998. *The Paradoxes of the American Presidency*. New York: Oxford University Press.

Darcy, R., Susan Welch, and Janet Clark. 1994. *Women, Elections, and Representation*. 2nd ed. Lincoln: University of Nebraska.

Deckman, Melissa. 2006. "School Board Candidates and Gender: Ideology, Party, and Policy Concerns." *Women, Politics & Policy* 28 (1): 87–117.

———. 2007. "Gender Differences in the Decision to Run for School Board." *American Politics Research* 35 (4): 541–563.

DeHart-Davis, Leisha, Justin Marlowe, and Sanjay K. Pandey. 2006. "Gender Dimensions of Public Service Motivations." *Public Administration Review* 66: 873–887.

Department of Homeland Security. 2010. "Secretary Janet Napolitano." Accessed June 28, 2012. http://www.dhs.gov/xabout/structure/gc_1232568253959.shtm.

Department of the Treasury. 2010. "Treasury Officials: Timothy Geithner." Accessed June 28, 2012. http://www.treasury.gov/organization/bios/geithner-p .shtml.

DeSantis, Victor, and Tari Rennar. 1992. "Minority and Gender Representation in American County Legislatures: The Effect of Election Systems." In *United States Electoral Systems: Their Impact on Women and Minorities*, edited by Wilma Rule and Joseph F. Zimmerman, 143–152. New York: Greenwood.

Devitt, James. 1999. *Framing Gender on the Campaign Trail: Women's Executive Leadership and the Press*. Washington, DC: The Women's Leadership Fund.

DiLeo, Daniel. 1997. "Dynamic Representation in the United States: Effects of the Public Mood on Governor's Agendas." *State and Local Government Review* 29:98–109.

Dill, Bonnie Thornton, and Ruth Enid Zambrana. 2009. *Emerging Intersections: Race, Class, and Gender in Theory, Policy, and Practice.* New Brunswick, NJ: Rutgers University Press.

Dimitrova, Daniela V., and Elizabeth Geske. 2009. "To Cry or Not to Cry: Media Framing of Hillary Clinton in the Wake of the New Hampshire Primary." Paper presented at the annual meeting of the International Communication Association, Chicago, August 29.

Doan, Alesha E., and Donald P. Haider-Markel. 2010. "The Role of Intersectional Stereotypes on Evaluations of Political Candidates." *Politics and Gender* 6 (1): 63–91.

Dodson, Debra L. 2006. *The Impact of Women in Congress.* New York: Oxford University Press.

Dodson, Debra L., and Susan J. Carroll. 1991. *Reshaping the Agenda: Women in State Legislatures.* New Brunswick, NJ: Eagleton Institute of Politics.

Dolan, Julie. 2000. "The Senior Executive Service: Gender, Attitudes, and Representative Bureaucracy." *Journal of Public Administration Research and Theory* 10 (3): 513–529.

———. 2001a. "Political Appointees in the United States: Does Gender Make a Difference?" *PS: Political Science & Politics* 34 (2): 213–216.

———. 2001b. "Women in the Executive Branch: A Review Essay of Their Political Impact and Career Opportunities." *Women & Politics* 22 (4): 89–104.

———. 2002. "Representative Bureaucracy in the Federal Executive: Gender and Spending Priorities." *Journal of Public Administrative Research and Theory* 12 (3): 353–375.

———. 2004. "Gender Equity: Illusion or Reality for Women in the Federal Executive Service?" *Public Administration Review* 64 (3): 299–308.

Dolan, Julie, Melissa Deckman, and Michele L. Swers. 2007. *Women and Politics: Paths to Power and Political Influence.* Upper Saddle River, NJ: Pearson Prentice Hall.

Dolan, Julie, and David H. Rosenbloom. 2003. *Representative Bureaucracy: Classic Readings and Continuing Controversies.* Armonk, NY: ME Sharpe.

Dolan, Kathleen A. 1998. "Voting for Women in the 'Year of the Woman.'" *American Journal of Political Science* 42 (1): 272–293.

———. 2004. *Voting for Women: How the Public Evaluates Women Candidates.* Boulder, CO: Westview.

———. 2005. "Do Women Candidates Play to Gender Stereotypes? Do Men Candidates Play to Women? Candidate Sex and Issues Priorities on Campaign Websites." *Political Research Quarterly* 58:31–44.

Dowd, Maureen. 1987. "Schroeder: At Ease with Femininity and Issues." *New York Times.* August 23. Accessed March 20, 2009. http://www.nytimes.com/1987/08/23/us/schroeder-at-ease-with-femininity-and-issues.html?sec=&spon=&pagewanted=all.

———. 2007. "She's Not Buttering Him Up." *New York Times,* April 25, Editorial Section, Late Edition-Final.

———. 2008a. "Can Hillary Cry Her Way Back to the White House?" *New York Times,* January 9, Editorial Section, Late Edition-Final.

———. 2008b. "It's Not Guiliani Time in Florida." *New York Times,* January 27, Editorial Section, Late Edition-Final. Accessed April 2010. http://www.nytimes.com.

Downs, Anthony. 1967. *Inside Bureaucracy.* Boston: Little, Brown.

Dudley, Robert L., and Ronald B. Rapoport. 1989. "Vice-Presidential Candidates and the Home State Advantage: Playing Second Banana at Home and on the Road." *American Journal of Political Science* 3 (2): 537–540.

Duerst-Lahti, Georgia. 1997. "Reconceiving Theories of Power: Consequences of Masculinism in the Executive Branch." In *The Other Elites: Women, Politics, and Power in the Executive Branch,* edited by MaryAnne Borrelli and Janet M. Martin, 11–32. Boulder, CO: Lynne Rienner.

———. 1998. "The Bottleneck, Women as Candidates." In *Women and Elective Office,* edited by S. Thomas and C. Wilcox, 15–25. New York: Oxford University Press.

———. 2006. "Presidential Elections: Gendered Space and the Case of 2004." In *Gender and Elections: Shaping the Future of American Politics,* edited by Susan J. Carroll and Richard L. Fox, 12–42. New York: Cambridge Press.

———. 2007. "Masculinity on the Campaign Trail." In *Rethinking Madam President: Are We Ready for a Woman in the White House?* edited by Lori Cox Han and Caroline Heldman, 87–112. Boulder, CO: Lynne Rienner.

Duerst-Lahti, Georgia, and Rita Mae Kelly, eds. 1995. *Gender Power, Leadership and Governance.* Ann Arbor: University of Michigan Press.

Duke, Lynne, and Lois Romano. 2007. "Ready for Another Tough Campaign—Her Cancer Back, Elizabeth Edwards Remains Open and Honest." *Washington Post,* March 23, Style Section, Final Edition.

Durning, Dan. 1987. "Change Masters for States." *State Government* 60:145–149.

Entman, Robert M. 1993. "Framing: Toward Clarification of a Fractured Paradigm." *Journal of Communication* 43 (4): 51–58.

Environmental Protection Agency. 2009. "Administrator Lisa Jackson: Biography." Accessed June 28, 2012. http://www.epa.gov/Administrator/biography.htm.

Falk, Erika, 2008. *Women for President: Media Bias in Eight Campaigns.* Urbana: University of Illinois Press.

———. 2010. *Women for President: Media Bias in Eight Campaigns.* 2nd ed. Urbana: University of Illinois Press.

Falk, Erika, and Kate Kenski. 2006. "Sexism Versus Partisanship: A New Look at the Question of Whether America Is Ready for a Woman President." *Sex Roles* 54:413–428.

Farrar-Myers, Victoria A. 2003. "A War Chest Full of Susan B. Anthony Dollars: Fundraising Issues for Female Presidential Candidates." In *Anticipating Madam President,* edited by Robert P. Watson and Ann Gordon, 81–93. Boulder, CO: Lynne Rienner.

———. 2007. "Money and the Art and Science of Candidate Viability." In *Rethinking Madam President: Are We Ready for a Woman in the White House?* edited by Lori Cox Han and Caroline Heldman, 113–132. Boulder, CO: Lynne Rienner.

———. 2011. "Donors, Dollars, and Momentum: Lessons for Presidential Candidates in Waging a Viable Campaign for the Nomination." In *From Votes to Victory: Winning and Governing the White House in the Twenty-First Century,* edited by Meena Bose, 36–71. College Station: Texas A&M University Press.

Fehr, Stephen C. 2010. "Recession Could Reshape State Governments in a Lasting Way." The Pew Center for the States. Accessed May 26, 2011. http://www.stateline.org/live/details/story?contentId=454018.

Fenno, Richard. 1973. *Congressmen in Committees.* Boston: Little Brown.

———. 1996. *Senators on the Campaign Trail.* Norman: University of Oklahoma.

Ferguson, Kathy E. 1985. *The Feminist Case Against Bureaucracy.* Philadelphia: Temple University Press.

Ferguson, Margaret R. 2003. "Chief Executive Success in the Legislative Arena." *State Politics and Policy Quarterly* 3:158–192.

Ferguson, Michaele L., and Lori Jo Marso, eds. 2007. *W Stands for Women: How the George W. Bush Presidency Shaped a New Politics of Gender.* Durham, NC: Duke University Press.

Ferguson, Miriam, and May Nelson Paulissen. 1995. *Miriam: The Southern Belle Who Became the First Woman Governor of Texas.* Waco, TX: Eakin Press.

Fisher, Louis. 2007. *Constitutional Conflicts Between Congress and the President.* 5th ed. Lawrence: University of Kansas Press.

Flammang, Janet A. 1985. "Female Officials in the Feminist Capital: The Case of Santa Clara County." *Western Political Quarterly* 38 (1): 94–118.

———. 1997. *Women's Political Voice: How Women are Transforming the Practice and Study of Politics.* Philadephia, PA: Temple University Press.

Fleischmann, Arnold, and Lana Stein. 1987. "Minority and Female Success in Municipal Runoff Elections." *Social Science Quarterly* 68 (2): 378–385.

Fletcher, Michael A. 2009. "High-Powered and Low-Key; Washington Observes the Influence of Obama Adviser Valerie Jarrett." *Washington Post,* March 15, A1.

Flowers, Julianne F., Audrey Haynes, and Michael Crespin. 2003. "The Media, the Campaign and the Message." *American Journal of Political Science* 47 (2): 259–273.

Follett, Mary Parker. 1904. *The Speaker of the House of Representatives.* New York: Longman, Green.

———. 1924. *Creative Experience.* New York: Longmans, Green.

Fowler, Linda L., and Jennifer L. Lawless. 2009. "Looking for Sex in All the Wrong Places: Press Coverage and the Electoral Fortunes of Gubernatorial Candidates." *Perspectives on Politics* 7:519–536.

Fowlkes, Diane. 1984. "Ambitious Political Women: Counter Socialization and Political Party Context." *Women & Politics* 4:5–32.

Fox, Richard L. 1997. *Gender Dynamics in Congressional Elections.* Thousand Oaks, CA: Sage.

Fox, Richard L., and Courtney Feeley. 2001. "Gender and the Decision to Run for Office." *Legislative Studies Quarterly* 26:411–435.

Fox, Richard L., and Jennifer L. Lawless. 2003. "Family Structure, Sex-Role Socialization and the Decision to Run for Office." *Women & Politics* 24:19–48.

———. 2004. "Entering the Arena? Gender and the Decision to Run for Office." *American Journal of Political Science* 48:264–280.

———. 2005. "To Run or Not to Run for Office: Explaining Nascent Political Ambition." *American Journal of Political Science* 49:642–659.

———. 2010. "If Only They'd Ask: Gender, Recruitment, and Political Ambition." *Journal of Politics* 72:310–326.

Fox, Richard L., and Zoe M. Oxley. 2003. "Gender Stereotyping in State Executive Elections: Candidate Selection and Success." *Journal of Politics* 65:833–850.

Fox, Richard A., and Robert A. Schuhmann. 1999. "Gender and Local Government: A Comparison of Men and Women City Managers." *Public Administration Review* 59:231–242.

Freeman, Jo. 1986. "The Political Culture of the Democratic and Republican Parties." *Political Science Quarterly* 101:327–356.

———. 1993. "Feminism vs. Family Values: Women at the 1992 Democratic and Republican Conventions." *PS: Political Science & Politics* 26 (1): 21–28.

———. 1999. "On the Origins of Social Movements." In *Waves of Protest: Social Movements Since the Sixties,* edited by Jo Freeman and Victoria Johnson, 7–24. Lanham, MD: Rowman and Littlefield.

———. 2000. *A Room at a Time: How Women Entered Party Politics.* New York: Rowman & Littlefield.

Fridkin, Kim, and Patrick Kenney. 2009. "The Role of Gender Stereotypes in U.S. Senate Campaigns." *Politics & Gender* 5:301–324.

Fulton, Sarah A. 2011. "When Gender Matters: Partisanship, Ideological Proximity and Valence." Paper presented at the annual meeting of the Western Political Science Association, San Antonio, TX, April 22.

Funk, Carolyn L. 1996. "The Impact of Scandal on Candidate Evaluations: An Experimental Test of the Role of Candidate Traits." *Political Behavior* 18 (1): 1–24.

Gallup, 2010. LexisNexis Academic. Retrieved May 20, 2010.

Garcia, Rogelio. 1997. *Women Appointed by President Clinton to Full-Time Positions Requiring Senate Confirmation, 1993–1996*. Washington, DC: Congressional Research Service.

Garcia, Sonia R., and Marisela Marquez. 2001. "Motivational and Attitudinal Factors Amongst Latinas in U.S. Electoral Politics." *NWSA Journal* 13 (2): 112–144.

Garcia, Sonia R., Marisela Marquez, Irasema Coronado, Valerie Martinez-Ebers, Sharon A. Navarro, and Patricia Jaramillo. 2008. *Politicas: Latina Trailblazers in the Texas Political Arena*. Austin: University of Texas Press.

Gay, Claudine, and Katherine Tate. 1998. "Doubly Bound: The Impact of Gender and Race on the Politics of Black Women." *Political Psychology* 19 (1): 169–184.

Gitlin, Todd. 1980. *The Whole World Is Watching*. Berkeley: University of California Press.

Givhan, Robin. 2009. "Echoes of TV's First Lady." *Washington Post,* June 19.

Glazer, Sarah. 1994. "Women's Health Issues: Will Women Benefit from Increased Research Funding?" *CQ Researcher* 4 (18): 409–432.

Goetz, Anne Marie. 2005. "Political Cleaners: How Women Are the New Anti-corruption Force: Does the Evidence Wash?" A paper originally presented at the Institute of Development Studies (IDS), University of Sussex, July 2–4, 2003, revised 2005.

———. 2007. "Political Cleaners: Are Women the New Agents of Anti-corruption?" *Development and Change* 38 (1): 87–105.

Golden, Marissa Martino. 2000. *What Motivates Bureaucrats? Politics and Administration During the Reagan Years*. New York: Columbia University Press.

Graber, Doris A. 1976. "Press and TV as Opinion Sources in Presidential Campaigns." *Public Opinion Quarterly* 40 (3): 285–303.

———. 2001. *Mass Media and American Politics*. Washington, DC: Congressional Quarterly Press.

Graham, Pauline, ed. 1996. *Mary Parker Follett: Prophet of Management*. Cambridge, MA: Harvard Business School Press.

Green, Matthew N. 2010. *The Speaker of the House: A Study of Leadership*. New Haven, CT: Yale University Press.

Greenhouse, Steven. 2009. "As Labor Secretary, Finding Influence in Her Past." *New York Times,* July 6, A11.

Grimes, Ann. 1990. *Running Mates: The Making of a First Lady*. New York: William Morrow.

Grofman, Bernard, and Lisa Handley. 1989. "Black Representation: Making Sense of Electoral Geography at Different Levels of Government." *Legislative Studies Quarterly* 14:265–279.

Gross, D. A. 1989. "Governors and Policymaking: Theoretical Concerns and Analytic Approaches." *Policy Studies Journal* 17:764–787.

Hall, Thad E. 2002. "Changes in Legislative Support for the Governor's Program over Time." *Legislative Studies Quarterly* 27:107–122.

Halloran, Liz. 2008. "McCain Wages Negative TV Ad Campaign Against Obama." *U.S. News and World Report,* October 8. Accessed June 28, 2012. http://www.us

news.com/articles/news/campaign-2008/2008/10/08/mccain-wages-negative-tv
-ad-campaign-against-obama.html.

Han, Lori Cox, and Caroline Heldman, eds. 2007. *Rethinking Madam President: Are We Ready for a Woman in the White House?* Boulder, CO: Lynne Rienner.

Hancock, Ange-Marie. 2007. "Intersectionality as a Normative and Empirical Paradigm." *Politics & Gender* 3:248–254.

Harari, Oren. 2002. *The Leadership Secrets of Colin Powell.* New York: McGraw-Hill.

Hardy-Fanta, Carol. 1993. *Latina Politics, Latino Politics: Gender, Culture, and Political Participation in Boston.* Philadelphia: Temple University Press.

———. 1997a. *Latino Electoral Campaigns in Massachusetts: The Impact of Gender.* Boston: Center for Women in Politics and Public Policy and the Mauricio Gaston Institute, University of Massachusetts Boston.

———. 1997b. "Latina Women and Political Consciousness: La Chispe Que Prende." In *Women Transforming Politics: An Alternative Reader,* edited by Cathy J. Cohen, Kathleen B. Jones, and Joan C. Tronto, 223–237. New York: New York University Press.

Hardy-Fanta, Carol, Pei-te Lien, Dianne Pinderhughes, and Christine Sierra. 2006. "Gender, Race, and Descriptive Representation in the United States: Findings from the Gender and Multicultural Leadership Project." *Journal of Women, Politics and Policy* 28 (3/4): 7–40.

Hardy-Fanta, Carol, Pei-te Lien, Christine M. Sierra, and Dianne M. Pindershughes. 2007. "A New Look at Paths to Political Office and Political Ambition: Moving Women of Color from the Margins to the Center." Paper presented at the annual meeting of the American Political Science Association, Chicago, August 30–September 2.

Harper, Timothy. 2008. "Obama, Clinton Throw Off the Gloves in TV Debate." *Toronto Star,* January 22.

Harris, John, and Beth Frerking. 2008. "Clinton Aides: Palin Treatment Sexist." *Politico,* September 11. Accessed May 9, 2010. http://www.politico.com/news/stories/0908/13129.html.

Harris-Lacewell, Melissa. 2009. "Michelle Obama, Mom-in-Chief." *The Nation,* May 5.

Hart/McInturff. 2008. NBC News/Wall Street Journal Survey. Study #6080. March 12. Accessed June 28, 2012. http://msnbcmedia.msn.com/i/msnbc/sections/news/080312_NBC-WSJ_Poll_Full.pdf.

Hatfield, Mark O. 1997. Essays adapted from Mark O. Hatfield, with the Senate Historical Office, Vice Presidents of the United States, 1789–1993. Washington, DC: U.S. Govt. Printing Office. Accessed April 7, 2010. http://www.senate.gov/artandhistory/history/common/briefing/Vice_President.htm.

Healy, Patrick. 2007a. "Clintons Adjust to Her Star Turn in His Old Role." *New York Times,* July 5, National Desk Section, Late Edition-Final.

———. 2007b. "In '08 Race, the Other Clinton Steps Up, for Better or Worse." *New York Times,* December 17, National Desk Section, Late Edition-Final.

———. 2007c. "In Elderly Women, Clinton Sees an Electoral Edge." *New York Times,* November 27. Accessed June 28, 2012. http://www.nytimes.com/2007/11/27/us/politics/27ladies.html.

———. 2007d. "In New Role, Senator Clinton's Strategist in Chief." *New York Times,* May 13, National Desk Section, Late Edition-Final.

———. "The Real '08 Fight: Clinton v. Palin?" *New York Times,* September 5. Accessed April 14, 2009. http://www.nytimes.com/2008/09/06/us/politics/06web-healy.html.

Healy, Patrick, and Adam Nagourney. 2007. "Husband at Her Side, Clinton Seeks to Revive Iowa Bid." *New York Times,* July 3.

Healy, Patrick, and Michael Luo. 2008. "$150,000 Wardrobe for Palin May Alter Tailor-Made Image." *New York Times,* October 23. Accessed June 28, 2012. http://www.nytimes.com/2008/10/23/us/politics/23palin.html.

Heflick, Nathan A., and Jamie L. Goldenberg. 2009. "Objectifying Sarah Palin: Evidence That Objectification Causes Women to Be Perceived as Less Competent and Less Fully Human." *Journal of Experimental Psychology* 45 (3): 599–601.

Heilman, Madeline. 2001. "Description and Prescription: How Gender Stereotypes Prevent Women's Ascent up the Organizational Ladder." *Journal of Social Issues* 57 (4): 657–674.

Heith, Diane J. 2001. "Footwear, Lipstick and an Orthodox Sabbath: Media Coverage of Non-traditional Candidates." *White House Studies* 1 (3): 35–49.

———. 2003. "The Lipstick Watch: Media Coverage, Gender, and Presidential Campaigns." In *Anticipating Madam President,* edited by Robert P. Watson and Ann Gordon, 123–130. Boulder, CO: Lynne Rienner.

Heldman, Caroline. 2007. "Cultural Barriers to a Female Presidency in the US." In *Rethinking Madam President: Are We Ready for a Woman in the White House?* edited by Lori Cox Han and Caroline Heldman, 17–42. Boulder, CO: Lynne Rienner.

Heldman, Caroline, Susan Carroll, and Stephanie Olson. 2005. "'She Brought Only a Skirt': Print Media Coverage of Elizabeth Dole's Bid for the Republican Presidential Nomination." *Political Communication* 22 (3): 315–335.

Heldman, Caroline, Sarah Oliver, and Meredith Conroy. 2009. "From Ferraro to Palin: Sexism in Media Coverage of Vice Presidential Candidates." Paper presented at the annual meeting of the American Political Science Association, Toronto, Canada, September 3–6.

Helgesen, Sally. 1990. *The Female Advantage.* New York: Doubleday.

Herrera, Richard, and Karen Shafer. 2008. "Ideological Representation in the Governor's Mansion: Constituency Influence on Governors' Policy Agendas." Paper presented at the annual meeting of the Southern Political Science Association, New Orleans, January 10.

Herrnson, Paul S., J. Celeste Lay, and Atiya Kai Stokes. 2003. "Women Running 'as Women': Candidate Gender, Campaign Issues, and Voter-Targeting Strategies." *Journal of Politics* 65 (1): 244–255.

Herzik, Eric B. 1991. "Policy Agendas and Gubernatorial Leadership." In *Gubernatorial Leadership and State Policy,* edited by Eric B. Herzik and Brent W. Brown, 1–24. New York: Greenwood.

Herzik, Eric B., and Brent W. Brown, eds. 1991. *Gubernatorial Leadership and State Policy.* New York: Greenwood.

Herzik, Erik B., and Charles W. Wiggins. 1989. "Governors vs. Legislatures: Vetoes, Overrides, and Policymaking in the American States." *Policy Studies Journal* 17:841–848.

Hiller, Mark, and Douglas Kriner. 2008. "Institutional Change and the Dynamics of Vice Presidential Selection." *Presidential Studies Quarterly* 38 (3): 401–421.

Hoffman, Jan. 2008. "The Upshot on Palin and Her Updo." *New York Times,* September 12. Accessed April 26, 2011. http://www.nytimes.com/2008/09/14/fashion/14hair.html?scp=20&sq=sarah+palin&st=nyt.

Huddy, Leonie, and Nayda Terkildsen. 1993. "Gender Stereotypes and Perceptions of Male and Female Candidates." *American Journal of Political Science* 37: 119–147.

Hughes, Karen. 2004. *Ten Minutes from Normal.* New York: Penguin.

Hutchison, Kay Bailey. 2004. *American Heroines: The Spirited Women Who Shaped Our Country.* New York: Harper Collins.

Jacobson, Gary C., and Samuel Kernell. 1981. *Strategy and Choice in Congressional Elections.* New Haven, CT: Yale University Press.

Jacoby, William G., and Saundra K. Schneider. 2001. "Variability in State Policy Priorities: An Empirical Analysis." *Journal of Politics* 63:544–568.

Jamieson, Kathleen Hall. 1995. *Beyond the Double Bind: Women and Leadership.* New York: Oxford University Press.

Jennings, Jeannette. 1991. "Black Women Mayors: Reflections on Race and Gender." In *Gender and Policymaking,* edited by Deborah Dodson, 73–79. New Brunswick, NJ: Rutgers University Press.

Jewell, Malcolm E., and Sarah M. Morehouse. 2001. *Political Parties and Elections in American States.* 4th ed. Washington, DC: Congressional Quarterly.

Jewell, Malcolm E., and Marcia Lynn Whicker. 1993. "The Feminization of Leadership in State Legislatures." *PS: Political Science & Politics* 26:705–712.

———. 1994. *Legislative Leadership in American States.* Ann Arbor: University of Michigan Press.

Johnson, Marilyn, and Susan Carroll. 1978. "Profile of Women Holding Office II." In *Women in Public Office: A Biographical Directory and Statistical Analysis,* 2nd ed., 1a–71a. Metuchen, NJ: Scarecrow Press.

Junn, Jane, and Nadia Brown. 2008. "What Revolution? Incorporating Intersectionality in Women and Politics." In *Political Women and American Democracy,* edited by Christina Wolbrecht, Karen Beckwith, and Lisa Baldez, 64–78. New York: Cambridge University Press.

Jurkowitz, Mark. 2008. "PEJ Campaign Coverage Index, August 25–31, 2008." *Project for Excellence in Journalism.* Accessed April 21, 2010. http://www.journalism.org/node/12612.

Kahn, Kim Fridkin. 1994. "The Distorted Mirror: Press Coverage of Women Candidates for Statewide Office." *Journal of Politics* 56:154–173.

———. 1996. *The Political Consequences of Being a Woman: How Stereotypes Influence the Conduct and Consequences of Political Campaigns.* New York: Columbia University Press.

Kahn, Kim Fridkin, and Edie N. Goldenberg. 1991. "Women Candidates in the News: An Examination of Gender Differences in U.S. Senate Campaign Coverage." *Public Opinion Quarterly* 55:180–199.

Kaiser Family Foundation. 2010. "Medicaid and the Uninsured." Kaiser Commission on Medicaid Facts. Accessed May 26, 2011. http://www.kff.org/medicaid/upload/7580-07.pdf.

Kamen, Al. 2009. "Mixed Doubles, Anyone?" *Washington Post,* December 4.

Kantor, Jodi, and Jeff Zeleny. 2007. "Michelle Obama Adds New Role to Balancing Act." *New York Times,* May 18, National Desk Section, Late Edition-Final.

Karnig, Albert K., and B. Oliver Walter. 1976. "Election of Women to City Councils." *Social Science Quarterly* 56:605–613.

Karnig, Albert K., and Susan Welch. 1979. "Sex and Ethnic Differences in Municipal Representation." *Social Science Quarterly* 60 (3): 465–481.

Kaye, Randi. 2008. "Todd Palin: 'First Dude' or 'Shadow Governor'?" CNN, September 19. Accessed April 2010. http://articles.cnn.com/2008-09-19/politics/todd.palin_1_todd-palin-complete-partisanship-walt-monegan?_s=PM:POLITICS.

Kedrowski, Karen, and Rachel E. Gower. 2009. "Gender and the Public Speakership: News Media Coverage of Speaker Nancy Pelosi." Paper prepared for the Southern Political Science Association Annual Meeting, New Orleans, January 7–10.

Keen, Judy. 2007. "Candid and Unscripted, Campaigning Her Way—Initially Wary of Politics, She's on the Trail—and Telling Voters That Her Husband's No 'Messiah.'" *USA Today,* May 11, News Section, Final Edition.

Kemp, Roger L. 2007. *Forms of Local Government: A Handbook on City, County, and Regional Options.* Jefferson, NC: McFarland.

Kenney, Sally J. 1996. "New Research on Gendered Political Institutions." *Political Research Quarterly* 49:445–466.

Kincaid, Diane D. 1978. "Over His Dead Body: A Positive Perspective on Widows in the U.S. Congress." *Western Political Quarterly* 31:96–104.

King, Colbert I. 2008. "Billary's Adventures in Primaryland." *Washington Post,* January 26, Editorial Section, Final Edition.

Kirkpatrick, David. 2008. "Abortion Issue Again Dividing Catholic Votes." *New York Times,* September 6. Accessed June 28, 2012. http://www.nytimes.com/2008/09/17/us/politics/17catholics.html.

Kirkpatrick, Jeane. 1974. *Political Woman.* New York: Basic.

Klamer, Carl E., and Andrew Karch. 2008. "Why Do Governors Issue Vetoes? The Impact of Individual and Institutional Influence." *Political Research Quarterly* 61:574–584.

Knowles, Mary S. 2008. "Why Women Run: Motivations for Entry into Local Politics." MA thesis, Rutgers University.

Koch, Jeffrey W. 2000. "Do Citizens Apply Gender Stereotypes to Infer Candidates' Ideological Orientations?" *Journal of Politics* 62:414–429.

———. 2002. "Gender Stereotypes and Citizens' Impressions of House Candidates' Ideological Orientations." *American Journal of Political Science* 46:453–462.

Kornblut, Anne E. 2007a. "In Iowa, Clinton Camp Scripts Bill's Role to Keep Focus on Hillary." *Washington Post,* July 1, Section A, Final Edition.

———. 2007b. "In His Wife's Campaign, Bill Clinton Is a Free Agent." *Washington Post,* October 30, Section A, Final Edition.

———. 2007c. "Oprah Winfrey, Bill Clinton Bring Star Power to Iowa—Talk Show Host, Former President Back Democratic Rivals." *Washington Post,* November 27, Section A, Final Edition.

Kornblut, Anne, and Alec MacGillis. 2007. "Hillary Clinton Embraces Her Husband's Legacy." *Washington Post,* December 22, Section A, Final Edition.

Krehbiel, Keith. 1991. *Information and Legislative Organization* (Ann Arbor: University of Michigan Press).

Kunin, Madeleine. 2008. *Pearls, Politics and Power: How Women Can Win and Lead.* White River Junction, VT: Chelsea Green.

Lai, James S., Wendy K. Tam Cho, Thomas P. Kim, and Okiyoshi Takeda. 2001. "Asian Pacific American Campaigns, Elections, and Elected Officials." *PS: Political Science & Politics* 34 (3): 611–617.

Lawless, Jennifer L. 2004. "Women, War, and Winning Elections: Gender Stereotyping in the Post–September 11th Era." *Political Research Quarterly* 57:479–490.

———. 2012. *Becoming a Candidate: Political Ambition and the Decision to Run for Office.* New York: Cambridge University Press.

Lawless, Jennifer L., and Richard L. Fox. 2005. *It Takes a Candidate: Why Women Don't Run for Office.* New York: Cambridge University Press.

———. 2010a. "If Only They'd Ask: Gender, Recruitment, and Political Ambition." *Journal of Politics* 72 (2): 310–326.

———. 2010b. *It Still Takes a Candidate: Why Women Don't Run for Office.* Cambridge: Cambridge University Press.

Lawrence, Regina, and Melody Rose. 2010. *Hillary Clinton's Race for the White House: Gender Politics and the Media on the Campaign Trail.* Boulder, CO: Lynne Rienner.

Leeper, Mark Stephen. 1991. "The Impact of Prejudice on Female Candidates: An Experimental Look at Voter Inference." *American Politics Quarterly* 19:248–261.

Leighley, Jan E. 2004. *Mass Media and Politics: A Social Science Perspective.* New York: Houghton Mifflin.

Liebovich, Mark. 2008. "In New Hampshire, Less Spark for Bill Clinton." *New York Times,* January 7, National Desk Section, Late Edition-Final.

Lien, Pei-te. 2002. "The Participation of Asian Americans in U.S. Elections: Comparing Elite and Mass Patterns in Hawaii and Mainland States." *UCLA Asian Pacific American Law Journal* 8 (1): 55–99.

Long, Norton E. 1952. "Bureaucracy and Constitutionalism." *American Political Science Review* 46 (3): 808–818.

Lowe, Will. 2011. "JFreq: Count Words, Quickly." Java software version 0.5.4. http://www.williamlowe.net/software/jfreq.

Lublin, David, and Sarah E. Brewer. 2003. "The Continuing Dominance of Traditional Gender Roles in Southern Elections." *Social Science Quarterly* 84: 379–396.

Luo, Michael. 2007. "'Comeback Kid' of '92, Now Half a Combo, Returns to New Hampshire." *New York Times,* July 14, National Desk Section, Late Edition-Final.

MacGillis, Alex, and Karl Vick. 2008. "'First Dude' Todd Palin Illustrates Alaska's Blend of Private and Public." *Washington Post,* September 22.

MacManus, Susan A. 1981. "A City's First Female Officeholder: 'Coattails for Future Female Officeseekers'?" *Western Political Quarterly* 34 (1): 88–99.

———. 1992. "How to Get More Women in Office: The Perspectives of Local Elected Officials." *Urban Affairs Quarterly* 28 (1): 159–170.

———. 1996. "County Boards, Partisanship and Elections." In *The American Counties: Frontiers of Knowledge,* edited by Donald C. Menzel, 53–78. Tuscaloosa: University of Alabama Press.

MacManus, Susan A., and Charles S. Bullock III. 1993. "Women and Racial/Ethnic Minorities in Mayoral and Council Positions." In *The Municipal Year Book 1993,* 70–84. Washington, DC: International City/County Management Association.

MacManus, Susan A., and Charles S. Bullock III. 1995. "Electing Women to Local Office." In *Gender in Urban Research,* edited by Judith A. Graber and Robyne S. Turner, 155–177. Urban Affairs Review 42. Thousand Oaks, CA: Sage Publications.

———. 1999. "Diversity of Representation and Election Systems." In *Local Government Election Practices,* edited by Roger L. Kemp, 172–216. Jefferson, NC: McFarland.

MacManus, Susan A., Charles S. Bullock III, Karen Padgett, and Brittany Penberthy. 2005. "Women Winning at the Local Level: Are County and School Board Positions Becoming More Desirable and Plugging the Pipeline to Higher Office?" In *Women in Politics: Insiders or Outsiders,* 4th ed., edited by Lois Duke Whitaker, 117–136. Upper Saddle River, NJ: Prentice Hall.

MacManus, Susan A., and Andrew F. Quecan. 2008. "Spouses as Campaign Surrogates: Strategic Appearances by Presidential and Vice Presidential Candidates' Wives in the 2004 Election." *PS: Political Science & Politics* 41 (2): 337–347.

Madsen, Susan R. 2009. *Developing Leadership: Learning from the Experiences of Women Governors.* Lanham, MD: University Press of America.

Major, Lesa Hatley, and Renita Coleman. 2008. "The Intersection of Race and Gender in Election Coverage: What Happens When the Candidates Don't Fit the Stereotypes?" *The Howard Journal of Communication* 19:315–333.

Malveaux, Suzanne. 2009. "Valerie Jarrett Balances Role of Friend, Official Adviser to Obama." CNN, November 5. http://articles.cnn.com/2009-11-05/politics/ jarrett.malveaux_1_valerie-jarrett-white-house-team-body-language/3?_s=PM: POLITICS.

Mansbridge, Jane. 1999. "Should Blacks Represent Blacks and Women Represent Women? A Contingent Yes." *Journal of Politics* 6:628–657.

Mansfield, Harvey. 2003. "The Manliness of Men." *American Enterprise* 14:32–39.

Markus, Gregory B. 1982. "Political Attitudes During an Election Year: A Report on the 1980 NES Panel Study." *American Political Science Review* 76 (3): 538–560.

Marschall, Melissa J., and Anirudh V. S. Ruhil. 2006. "The Pomp of Power: Black Mayoralties in Urban America." *Social Science Quarterly* 87:828–850.

Marshall, Brenda DeVore, and Molly A. Mayhead. 2000. *Navigating Boundaries: The Rhetoric of Women Governors.* Westport, CT: Praeger.

Martin, Janet M. 1989. "The Recruitment of Women to Cabinet and Subcabinet Posts." *Western Political Quarterly* 42 (1): 161–172.

———. 1991. "An Examination of Executive Branch Appointments in the Reagan Administration by Background and Gender." *Western Political Quarterly* 44 (1): 173–184.

———. 2003. *The Presidency and Women: Promise, Performance & Illusion.* College Station: Texas A & M Press.

Mayo, Edith P. 1995. *First Ladies: Political Role and Public Image.* Washington, DC: National Museum of American History.

McDermott, Monika L. 1997. "Voting Cues in Low-Information Elections: Candidate Gender as a Social Information Variable in Contemporary United States Elections." *American Journal of Political Science* 41:270–283.

Meier, Kenneth J. 1993. *Politics and the Bureaucracy: Policy Making in the Fourth Branch of Government.* Pacific Grove, CA: Brooks/Cole.

Melich, Tanya. 1996. *The Republican War Against Women: An Insider's Report from Behind the Lines.* New York: Bantam Books.

Merritt, Sharyne. 1977. "Winners and Losers: Sex Differences in Municipal Elections." *American Journal of Political Science* 21 (4): 731–743.

Moncrief, Gary, Peverill F. Squire, and Malcolm E. Jewell. 2001. *Who Runs for the Legislature?* Upper Saddle River, NJ: Prentice Hall.

Montoya, Lisa, Carol Hardy-Fanta, and Sonia Garcia. 2000. "Latina Politics: Gender, Participation, and Leadership." *PS: Political Science & Politics* 33:555–561.

Moore, Robert G. 2005. "Religion, Race, and Gender Differences in Political Ambition." *Politics & Gender* 1 (4): 577–596.

Morehouse, Sarah McCally. 1998. *The Governor as Party Leader: Campaigning and Governing.* Ann Arbor: University of Michigan Press.

Morgan, David R., Robert E. England, and John Pelissero. 2007. *Managing Urban America.* 6th ed. Washington, DC: CQ Press.

Moriarty, Sandra, and Mark Popovich. 1989. "Newsmagazine Visuals and the 1988 Election." Paper presented at the annual meeting of the Association for Education in Journalism and Mass Communication, Washington, DC, August 10–13. ERIC (ED309488).

Mosher, Frederick C. 1968. *Democracy and the Public Service.* New York: Oxford University Press.

Mughan, Anthony, and Barry C. Burden. 1995. "The Candidates' Wives." In *Democracy's Feast,* edited by Herbert Weisberg, 136–152. Chatham, NY: Chatham House Publishers.

Mulhern, Daniel G. 2002. "What's in a Name?" Accessed July 16, 2010. http:// www.michigan.gov/granholm/0,4587,7-168—58601—,00.html.

————. 2009. "A Second, Quiet Revolution." In *The Shriver Report: A Woman's Nation Changes Everything,* edited by Heather Boushey and Ann O'Leary, 318–319. Washington, DC: Center for American Progress.

Myers, Dee Dee. 2008. *Why Women Should Rule the World.* New York: Harper-Collins.

Nagourney, Adam. 2007. "On the Campaign Trail with Elizabeth Edwards," *New York Times,* June 18, National Desk Section.

National Association of Latino Elected and Appointed Officials (NALEO). 2009. *National Directory of Latino Officials.* Los Angeles: NALEO Education Fund.

National Federation of Republican Women. 2010. "Year of the Republican Woman." *Republican Woman* (Summer): 18–21.

National Institutes of Health (NIH). 2001. "NIH Policy and Guidelines on the Inclusion of Women and Minorities as Subjects of Clinical Research." Accessed July 15, 2010.http://grants.nih.gov/grants/funding/women_min/guidelines _amended_10_2001.htm.

————. 2010. "About the National Institutes of Health: NIH Mission." Accessed July 15, 2010. http://www.nih.gov/about/mission.htm.

Nelson, Kimberly L. 2002. *Elected Municipal Councils,* Special Data Issue (3). Washington, DC: International City/County Management Association.

Nelson, Michael. 1988. "Choosing the Vice President." *PS: Political Science & Politics* 21 (4): 858–868.

Niven, David. 1998. *The Missing Majority: The Recruitment of Women as State Legislative Candidates.* Westport, CT: Praeger.

————. 2006. "Throwing Your Hat Out of the Ring: Negative Recruitment and the Gender Imbalance in State Legislative Candidacy." *Politics & Gender* 2 (4): 473–489.

Norris, Pippa. 1997. "Women Leaders Worldwide: A Splash of Color in the Photo Op." In *Women, Media, and Politics,* edited by Pippa Norris, 149–165. New York: Oxford University Press.

O'Connor, Karen L. 2001. *Women and Congress: Running, Winning, and Ruling.* New York: Haworth.

Office of History and Preservation, Office of the Clerk, U.S. House of Representatives. 2006. *Women in Congress 1917–2006.* Washington, DC: US Government Printing Office.

Office of Personnel Management (OPM). 2010. "Gender Distribution by Senior Executive Service for Cabinet Agencies." Unpublished data made available to author.

Ong, Elena. 2003. "Transcending the Bamboo and Glass Ceilings: Defining the Trajectory to Empower Asian Pacific American Women in Politics." In *Asian American Politics: Law, Participation, and Policy,* edited by Don Nakanishi and James Lai, 331–354. Lanham, MD: Rowman & Littlefield.

Ornstein, Norman J., Thomas E. Mann, and Michael Malbin. 2008. *Vital Statistics on Congress 2008.* Washington, DC: Brookings Institution.

Ostrander, Katie E., and Pei-te Lien. 2010. "Structural and Contextual Factors in the Election of Women and Minorities to Sub-national Offices: A Review of Literature." Paper presented at the annual meeting of the Western Political Science Association, San Francisco, April 1–3.

Oxley, Zoe M., and Richard L. Fox. 2004. "Women in Executive Office: Variation Across American States." *Political Research Quarterly* 57:113–120.

Palmer, Barbara, and Dennis Simon. 2006. *Breaking the Political Glass Ceiling: Women and Congressional Elections.* New York: Routledge.

Parry-Giles, Shawn J., and Trevor Parry-Giles. 1996. "Gendered Politics and Presidential Image Construction: A Reassessment of the 'Feminine Style.'" *Communication Monographs* 63 (4): 337–353.

Parsons, Christi. 2008. "Valerie Jarrett Is Named a Senior Aide to Obama." *Los Angeles Times,* November 15, A19.

Patterson, Thomas E., and Richard Dani. 1985. "The Media Campaign: Struggle for the Agenda." In *The Elections of 1984,* edited by Michael Nelson, 111–127. Washington, DC: Congressional Quarterly.

Paul, David, and Jessi L. Smith. 2008. "Subtle Sexism? Examining Vote Preferences When Women Run Against Men for the Presidency." *Journal of Women, Politics & Policy* 29 (4): 451–476.

PBS. 2007. "Representative Nancy Pelosi (D-Calif.)." *The Lehrer News Hour.* Accessed March 13, 2009. http://www.pbs.org/newshour/108th/bio_pelosi .html.

Pelosi, Nancy. 2008. *Know Your Power: A Message to America's Daughters.* New York: Doubleday.

Perkins, Perry. 1986. "Political Ambition Among Black and White Women: An Intragender Test of Socialization Mode." *Women & Politics* 6 (1): 27–40.

Persons, Georgia. 2007. "From Insurgency to Deracialization: The Evolution of Black Mayoralties." In *Perspectives in Black Politics and Black Leadership,* edited by John Davis, 73–98. Lanham, MD: University Press of America.

Peters, Ronald M., Jr., and Cindy Simon Rosenthal. 2010. *Speaker Nancy Pelosi and the New American Politics.* New York: Oxford University Press.

Pew Research Center. 2008. "Issues and the 2008 Election." August 21. Accessed May 28, 2010. http://pewforum.org/docs/?DocID=339.

Pfiffner, James P. 1996. *The Strategic Presidency: Hitting the Ground Running.* 2nd ed. Lawrence: University Press of Kansas.

Pinderhughes, Dianne M., Pei-te Lien, Christine M. Sierra, and Carol Hardy-Fanta. 2009. "How *Do* We Get Along? Linked Fate, Political Allies, and Issue Coalitions." Paper presented at the annual meeting of the American Political Science Association, Toronto, Canada, September 2–6.

Policy Agendas Project. 2006. "Datasets & Codebooks." Accessed May 28, 2011. http://www.policyagendas.org/page/topic-codebook.

Polsby, Nelson W. 1968. "The Institutionalization of the U.S. House of Representatives." *American Political Science Review* 62 (1): 144–168.

Prewitt, Kenneth. 1970. *The Recruitment of Political Leaders:* A Study of Citizen-Politicians. Indianapolis: Bobbs-Merrill.

Prior, Markus. 2007. *Post-broadcast Democracy: How Media Choice Increases Inequality in Political Involvement and Polarizes Elections.* Cambridge: Cambridge University Press.

Pogrebin, Letty C. 2008. "The Wife, the Candidate, the Senator, and Her Husband." In *Thirty Ways of Looking at Hillary: Reflections by Women Writers,* edited by Susan Morrison. New York: Harper Collins.

Pulliam, Russ. 2008. "Daniels Isn't Always All Business." *Indianapolis Star,* October 11, A10.

Rasmussen, Scott. 2008. "South Carolina Democratic Primary Poll." *Rasmussen Reports,* January 26. Accessed April 2010. http://www.rasmussenreports.com/ public_content/politics/elections/election_2008/2008_presidential_election/south _carolina/election_2008_south_carolina_democratic_primary.

Reger, Jo, ed. 2005. *Different Wavelengths: Studies of the Contemporary Women's Movement.* New York: Routledge.

Reingold, Beth. 2000. *Representing Women: Sex, Gender, and Legislative Behavior in Arizona and California.* Chapel Hill: The University of North Carolina Press.
———, ed. 2008a. *Legislative Women: Getting Elected, Getting Ahead.* Boulder, CO: Lynne Rienner.
———. 2008b. "Women as Officeholders: Linking Descriptive and Substantive Representation." In *Political Women and American Democracy,* edited by Christina Wolbrecht, Karen Beckwith, and Lisa Baldez, 128–174. Cambridge: Cambridge University Press.
Riccucci, Norma M., and Judith R. Saidel. 2001. "The Demographic of Gubernatorial Appointees: Toward an Explanation of Variation." *Policy Studies Journal* 29:11–22.
Rigby, Elizabeth. 2006. "Governors as Policy Entrepreneurs: State Preschool Investment 1990–2005." Paper presented at the annual meeting of the Midwest Political Science Association, Chicago, April 18.
Ripley, Randall B., and Grace A. Franklin. 1991. *Congress, the Bureaucracy, and Public Policy.* 5th ed. Belmont, CA: Wadsworth.
Roberts, Barbara. 2011. *Up the Capitol Steps: A Woman's March to the Governorship.* Corvallis: Oregon State University Press.
Robinson, Eugene. 2007a. "Choosing to Live." *Washington Post,* March 23, Editorial Section, Final Edition.
———. 2007b. "A Problem Like Bill." *Washington Post,* December 21, Editorial Section, Final Edition.
Rohde, David. 1991. *Parties and Leaders in the Post-reform House.* Chicago: University of Chicago Press.
Romano, Andrew. 2008. "Palin Favorability Ratings Begin to Falter." *Newsweek,* September 16. Accessed April 14, 2009. http://blog.newsweek.com/blogs/stumper/archive/2008/09/16/palin-s-favorability-ratings-begin-to-falter.aspx.
Rosebush, James S. 1987. *First Lady, Public Wife.* Lanham, MD: Madison.
Rosenthal, Alan. 1990. *Governors and Legislatures: Contending Powers.* Washington, DC: CQ Press.
Rosenthal, Cindy Simon. 1998. *When Women Lead: Integrative Leadership in State Legislatures.* New York: Oxford University Press.
———, ed. 2002. *Women Transforming Congress.* Norman: Oklahoma University Press.
Rosenthal, Cindy Simon, and Ronald M. Peters Jr. 2010. *Speaker Pelosi and the New American Politics.* New York: Oxford University Press.
Rosenwasser, Shirley, and Norma Dean. 1989. "Gender Roles and Political Office." *Psychology of Women Quarterly* 13:77–85.
Rosenwasser, Shirley, and Jana Seale. 1988. "Attitudes Toward a Hypothetical Male or Female Presidential Candidate: A Research Note." *Political Psychology* 9 (4): 591–598.
Rosser-Mims, Dionne M. 2005. "An Exploration of Black Women's Political Leadership Development." Unpublished doctoral dissertation, University of Georgia Athens.
Rourke, Francis E. 1984. *Bureaucracy, Politics and Public Policy.* Boston: Little, Brown.
Ruthhart, Bill. 2008. "Despite Quiet Demeanor, Candidate Shows She Is Willing to Put Up a Tough Fight." *Indianapolis Star,* October 26. http://www.indystar.com.
Saad, Lydia. 2008. "Economy Reigns Supreme for Voters." Gallup Poll, October 29. Accessed July 15, 2010. http://www.gallup.com/poll/111586/economy-reigns-supreme-voters.aspx.
Salisbury, Robert H., and Kenneth A. Shepsle. 1981. "U.S. Congressman as Enterprise." *Legislative Studies Quarterly* 6 (4): 559–576.

Saltzstein, Grace Hall. 1986. "Female Mayors and Women in Municipal Jobs." *American Journal of Political Science* 30 (1): 140–164.

Sanbonmatsu, Kira. 2002a. *Democrats, Republicans and the Politics of Women's Place.* Ann Arbor: University of Michigan Press.

———. 2002b. "Gender Stereotypes and Vote Choice." *American Journal of Political Science* 46:20–34.

———. 2006. *Where Women Run: Gender and Party in the American States.* Ann Arbor: University of Michigan Press.

Sanbonmatsu, Kira, Susan J. Carroll, and Debbie Walsh. 2009. *Poised to Run: Women's Pathways to the State Legislatures.* New Brunswick, NJ: Center for American Women and Politics, Eagleton Institute of Politics, Rutgers University.

Sanbonmatsu, Kira, and Kathleen Dolan. 2009. "Do Gender Stereotypes Transcend Party?" *Political Research Quarterly* 62:485–494.

Sapiro, Virginia. 1981/1982. "If U.S. Senator Baker Were a Woman: An Experimental Study of Candidate Images." *Political Psychology* 3:61–83.

Saulny, Susan. 2008. "Michelle Obama Thrives in Campaign Trenches." *New York Times,* February 14, National Desk Section, Late Edition-Final.

Scheer, Teva J. 2005. *Governor Lady: The Life and Times of Nellie Tayloe Ross.* Columbia: University of Missouri Press.

Schlesinger, Joseph. 1966. *Ambition and Politics: Political Careers in the United States.* Chicago: Rand McNally.

———. 1991. *Political Parties and the Winning of Office.* Ann Arbor: University of Michigan.

Schreiber, Ronnee. 2002. "Injecting a Woman's Voice: Conservative Women's Organizations, Gender Consciousness, and the Expression of Women's Policy Preferences." *Sex Roles* 47 (7/8): 331–342.

———. 2008. *Righting Feminism: Conservative Women & American Politics.* Oxford: Oxford University Press.

Seelye, Katharine Q. 2007. "They Stand by Their Men, Loudly." *New York Times,* August 26, Week in Review, Late Edition-Final.

———. 2008. "Palin and the Women's Vote." *New York Times,* August 29. Accessed April 16, 2010. http://thecaucus.blogs.nytimes.com/2008/08/29/palin-and-the-womens-vote/.

Serafini, Marilyn Werber. 2009. "Obama's Health Team." *National Journal,* March 3, 18.

Shafer, Karen, and Richard Herrera. 2009. "Testing the Validity and Robustness of Wordscore to Derive the Ideological Positions of Governors: Are Female Governors More Liberal Than Their Male Counterparts?" Paper presented at the annual meeting of the American Political Science Association, Toronto, Canada, September 4.

———. 2010. "Who's in the Governor's Mansion? Gender Differences in the Policy Priorities of Governors." Paper presented at the annual meeting of the American Political Science Association, Washington, DC, September 5.

Sierra, Christine Marie. 2010. "Latinas and Electoral Politics Movin' on Up." In *Gender and Elections: Shaping the Future of American Politics,* 2nd ed., edited by Susan J. Carroll and Richard L. Fox, 144–186. New York: Cambridge University Press.

Sigelman, Lee, and Paul J. Wahlbeck. 1997. "The 'Veepstakes' Strategic Choice in Presidential Running Mate Selection." *American Political Science Review* 91 (4): 855–864.

Silver, Nate. 2009. "Palin: All Tail, No Head." *FiveThirtyEight,* July 15. Accessed May 2, 2010. http://www.fivethirtyeight.com/2009/07/palin-all-tail-no-head.html.

Simien, Evelyn, and Rosalee Clawson. 2004. "The Intersection of Race and Gender: An Examination of Black Feminist Consciousness, Race Consciousness, and Policy Attitudes." *Social Science Quarterly* 85 (3): 793–810.

Sinclair, Barbara. 1995. *Legislators, Leaders, and Lawmaking.* Baltimore: Johns Hopkins University Press.

Slevin, Peter. 2007. "Her Heart's in the Race—Michelle Obama on the Campaign Trail and Her Life's Path." *Washington Post,* November 28, Style Section, Final Edition

———. 2008. "The Accompanists—Bill Clinton and Michelle Obama Warm Up to Their Parts in Orchestrating Victory." *Washington Post,* February 2, Style Section, Final Edition.

Smith, Adrienne, Beth Reingold, and Michael Leo Owens. 2009. "Women and Politics in Cities: Determinants of the Descriptive Representation of Women in City Halls and Councils." Presented at the annual meeting of the American Political Science Association, Toronto, Canada, September 3–6.

———. 2012. "The Political Determinants of Women's Descriptive Representation in Cities." *Political Research Quarterly* 65:330–345.

Smith, Jessi L., David Paul, and Rachel Paul. 2007. "No Place for a Woman: Evidence for Gender Bias in Evaluations of Presidential Candidates." *Basic and Applied Social Psychology* 29 (3): 225–233.

Smith, Kevin B. 1997. "When's All Fair: Signs of Parity in Media Coverage of Female Candidates." *Political Communication* 14:71–81.

Stewart, Debra W., ed. 1980. *Women in Local Politics.* Metuchen, NJ: Scarecrow.

Stivers, Camilla. 1993. *Gender Images in Public Administration: Legitimacy in the Administrative State.* Newbury Park, CA: Sage Publications.

Stone, Clarence, and Robert Whelan. 2009. "Through a Glass Darkly: The Once and Future Study of Urban Politics." In *The City in American Political Development,* edited by Richardson Dilworth, 98–118. New York: Routledge.

Stooksbury, Kary E., and L. Maxwell Edgemon. 2003. "The First Lady Scholarship Reconsidered: A Review Essay." *Women and Politics* 25 (3): 97–111.

Strahan, Randall. 2007. *Leading Representatives: The Agency of Leaders in the Politics of the U.S. House.* Baltimore: Johns Hopkins University Press.

Sundquist, Betsy. 2010. "Gaertner Drops Out of Governor's Race." *Politics in Minnesota,* April 26. Accessed April 30, 2010. http://politicsinminnesota.com/blog/2010/04/gaertner-drops-out-of-governors-race/.

Swers, Michele L. 2002. *The Difference Women Make: The Policy Impact of Women in Congress.* Chicago: University of Chicago Press.

Takash, Paule Cruz. 1993. "Breaking Barriers to Representation: Chicana/Latina Elected Officials in California." *Urban Anthropology* 22 (3/4): 325–359.

Takeda, Okiyoshi. 2001. "The Representation of Asian Americans in the U.S. Political System." In *Representation of Minority Groups in the U.S.: Implications for the Twenty-First Century,* edited by Charles Menifield, 77–109. Lanham, MD: Austin & Winfield.

Tasker, Yvonne, and Diane Negra, eds. 2007. *Interrogating Post-feminism: Gender and the Politics of Popular Culture.* Durham, NC: Duke University Press.

Tenpas, Kathryn Dunn. 1997. "Women on the White House Staff: A Longitudinal Analysis, 1939–1994." In *The Other Elites: Women, Politics and Power in the Executive Branch,* edited by MaryAnne Borelli and Janet Martin, 91–106. Boulder, CO: Lynne Rienner.

Thomas, Sue. 1991. "The Impact of Women on State Legislative Policies." *Journal of Politics* 53:958–976.

————. 1994. *How Women Legislate.* New York: Oxford University Press.

————. 1997. "Why Gender Matters: The Perceptions of Women Officeholders." *Women & Politics* 17:27–53.

Thomas, Sue, and Susan Welch. 1991. "The Impact of Gender on Activists and Priorities of State Legislators." *Western Political Quarterly* 44:445–456.

Tien, Charles, Regan Checchio, and Arthur H. Miller. 1999. "The Impact of First Wives on Presidential Campaigns and Elections." In *Women in Politics: Outsiders or Insiders,* edited by Lois Duke Whitaker, 149–168. New York: Prentice Hall.

Tolleson-Rinehart, Sue. 2001. "Do Women Leaders Make a Difference? Substance, Styles, and Perceptions." In *The Impact of Women in Public Office,* edited by Susan J. Carroll, 149–165. Bloomington: Indiana University Press.

Tonn, Joan C. 2003. *Mary P. Follett: Creating Democracy, Transforming Management.* New Haven, CT: Yale University Press.

Trounstine, Jessica. 2009. "All Politics Is Local: The Reemergence of the Study of City Politics." *Perspectives on Politics* 7:611–618.

Trounstine, Jessica, and Melody E. Valdini. 2008. "The Context Matters: The Effects of Single-Member Versus At-Large Districts on City Council Diversity." *American Journal of Political Science* 52 (3): 554–569.

Troy, Gil. 1997. *Affairs of State: The Rise and Rejection of the Presidential Couple Since World War II.* New York: Free Press.

US Census Bureau. 2002. "2002 Census of Governments, Volume 1, Number 1, Government Organization, GC02(1)-1." Washington, DC: US Government Printing Office.

Van Assendelft, Laura A. 1997. *Governors, Agenda Setting, and Divided Government.* Lanham, MD: University Press of America.

Vinovskis, Maris A. 2008. "Gubernatorial Leadership and American K–12 Educational Reform." In *A Legacy of Innovation: Governors and Public Policy,* edited by Ethan G. Sribnick, 185–203. Philadelphia: University of Pennsylvania Press.

Walsh, Kenneth T. 2001. "A Prime Seat at the Table." *US News and World Report,* April 30, 25.

Watson, Robert P. 2000. *The Presidents' Wives: Reassessing the Office of First Lady.* Boulder, CO: Lynne Rienner.

Watson, Robert P., and Ann Gordon, eds. 2003. *Anticipating Madam President.* Boulder, CO: Lynne Rienner.

Weikart, Lynne, Greg Chen, Daniel W. Williams, and Haris Hromic. 2006. "The Democratic Sex: Gender Differences and the Exercise of Power." *Journal of Women, Politics & Policy* 28 (1): 119–140.

Weir, Sara J. 1996. "Women as Governors: State Executive Leadership with a Feminist Face?" In *Women in Politics: Outsiders or Insiders? A Collection of Readings,* 2nd ed., edited by Lois Lovelace Duke, 187–196. Upper Saddle River, NJ: Prentice Hall.

Welch, Susan, and Albert K. Karnig. 1979. "Correlates of Female Office Holding in City Politics." *Journal of Politics* 41 (2): 478–491.

Welter, Barbara. 1966. "The Cult of True Womanhood: 1820–1860." *American Quarterly* 18 (2): 151–174.

Westfall, Sandra Sobieraj. 2009. "Michelle Obama 'We're Home.'" *People Magazine,* March 9.

White House Database. 2010. "Nominations & Appointments." Accessed May 28, 2010. http://www.whitehouse.gov/briefing-room/nominations-and-appointments.

White, Deborah Gray. 1985. *Ar'n't I a Woman? Female Slaves in the Plantation South.* New York: W. W. Norton.

Whittier, Nancy. 2005. "From the Second to the Third Wave: Continuity and Change in Grassroots Feminism." In *The U.S. Women's Movement in a Global Perspective*, edited by Lee Ann Banaszak, 45–68. Lanham, MD: Rowman & Littlefield.

Williams, Linda F. 2001. "The Civil Rights–Black Power Legacy: Black Women Elected Officials at the Local, State, and National Levels." In *Sisters in the Struggle: African American Women in the Civil Rights–Black Power Movement,* edited by Bettye Collier-Thomas and V. P. Franklin, 306–331. New York: New York University Press.

Williams, Patricia J. 2009. "Mrs. Obama Meets Mrs. Windsor." *The Nation*, April 8.

Wilson, Woodrow. 1885. *Congressional Government: A Study in American Politics.* PhD diss., Johns Hopkins University.

Winfield, Betty Houchin, and Barbara Friedman. 2003. "Gender Politics: News Coverage of the Candidates' Wives in Campaign 2000." *Journalism & Mass Communication* 80 (3): 548–566.

Winter, David G. 1987. "Leader Appeal, Leader Performance, and the Motive Profile of Leaders and Followers: A Study of American Presidents and Elections." *Journal of Personality and Social Psychology* 52:196–202.

Witt, Linda, Karen M. Paget, and Glenna Matthews. 1994. *Running as a Woman: Gender and Power in American Politics.* New York: The Free Press.

Wolbrecht, Christina. 2000. *The Politics of Women's Rights: Parties, Positions, and Change.* Princeton, NJ: Princeton University Press.

"Women in Politics: Does Gender Bias Hurt Female Candidates." 2008. *CQ Researcher* 18 (12): 265–288.

Woodall, Gina Serignese, and Kim L. Fridkin. 2007. "Shaping Women's Chances: Stereotypes and the Media." In *Rethinking Madam President: Are We Ready for a Woman in the White House?* edited by Lori Cox Han and Caroline Heldman, 69–86. Boulder, CO: Lynne Rienner.

Woodard, Jennifer Bailey, and Teresa Mastin. 2005. "Black Womanhood: 'Essence' and Its Treatment of Stereotypical Images of Black Women." *Journal of Black Studies* 36 (2): 264–281.

Woods, Harriet. 2000. *Stepping Up to Power.* Boulder, CO: Westview.

The Contributors

Denise L. Baer is director of the Boston University Washington Academic Center and a member of the Graduate Faculty of Political Science at Boston University. Her academic areas of specialization include governance, political parties and campaigns, Congress, democratization and political development, women and politics, and research methods. She is the author of three books on political parties and a forthcoming book on performance measurement for SAGE Press. Her research has appeared in a variety of peer-reviewed journals including *Political Research Quarterly, American Review of Politics,* and *Women and Politics.*

Brent D. Boyea is associate professor of political science at the University of Texas at Arlington. His primary research and teaching interests include US political institutions, state politics, judicial politics, and elections. He has published articles in several journals, including the *American Journal of Political Science, Social Science Quarterly,* and *American Politics Research.*

Narren Brown is a doctoral candidate in educational leadership and policy studies at Iowa State University. He serves as the assistant director of analytic support and institutional research at Grinnell College. He has conducted research on youth voters and is the coauthor of a book chapter on the strategies used by female and male gubernatorial, US Senate, and presidential candidates in their television commercials in 2008.

Dianne Bystrom is director of the Carrie Chapman Catt Center for Women and Politics at Iowa State University. A frequent commentator about women's and political issues for national and international media, she has contributed to fifteen books on gender, politics, and communication. Her research focuses on the styles and strategies used by female and male political candidates in their campaign communication and their coverage by the media.

Jill Carle is a PhD candidate in American politics at Arizona State University's School of Politics and Global Studies. Her primary interests are in campaigns and elections, along with women and media in politics.

Susan J. Carroll is professor of political science and women's and gender studies at Rutgers University and senior scholar at the Center for American Women and Politics (CAWP) of the Eagleton Institute of Politics. Her publications include *Women as Candidates in American Politics,* 2nd ed.; *The Impact of Women in Public Office; Women and American Politics: New Questions, New Directions;* and *Gender and Elections: Shaping the Future of American Politics,* 2nd ed. (with Richard L. Fox).

Kelly Dittmar is assistant research professor at the Center for American Women and Politics of the Eagleton Institute of Politics. She was an American Political Science Association (APSA) congressional fellow from 2011 to 2012. Her research focuses on the role of gender within political institutions and the gender dynamics of US campaigns and elections.

Julie Dolan is associate professor of political science at Macalester College in St. Paul, Minnesota. She has authored or coauthored six books, including *Representative Bureaucracy: Classic Readings and Continuing Controversies* (with David H. Rosenbloom) and *Women and Politics: Paths to Power and Political Influence* (with Melissa Deckman and Michele L. Swers). Her journal articles have appeared in *PS: Political Science & Politics, Public Administration Review, Journal of Public Administration Research and Theory, Women & Politics,* and *Harvard International Journal of Press/Politics.* She is currently working on a project that investigates how the Veterans Health Administration is adapting to meet the needs of its increasingly female clientele.

Victoria A. Farrar-Myers is professor and Distinguished Teaching Professor of Political Science at the University of Texas at Arlington. She specializes in the US presidency, presidential-congressional relations, separation of powers, and campaign finance reform. Recent publications include *Scripted for Change: The Institutionalization of the American Presidency, Legislative Labyrinth: Congress and Campaign Finance Reform* (with Diana Dwyre), *Limits and Loopholes: The Quest for Money, Free Speech and Fair Elections* (with Diana Dwyre), and *Corruption and American Politics* (with Michael Genovese).

Megan Fiddelke is a doctoral student in political science at Colorado State University. She is the recipient of a fellowship funded by the National Science Foundation that supports interdisciplinary approaches to bioenergy research. She has conducted research on gender and racial representations of key political figures in nonmainstream media.

Kim L. Fridkin has contributed articles to the *American Political Science Review, American Journal of Politics,* and *Journal of Politics.* Her publications include *No-Holds Barred: Negative Campaigning in U.S. Senate Campaigns* and *The Spectacle of U.S. Senate Campaigns* (both with Patrick J. Kenney), and *The Political Consequences of Being a Woman.* Her current research interests are negative campaigning, women and politics, and campaigns and elections.

Richard Herrera is associate professor of political science at Arizona State University. He has contributed articles to the *American Political Science Review, Journal of Politics, Legislative Studies Quarterly,* and *State Politics and Policy Quarterly.* His current research interests are focused on US governors and their ideology, policy agendas, and representative functions.

Regina G. Lawrence holds the Jesse H. Jones Centennial Chair in School of Journalism at the University of Texas at Austin. She is the author of *The Politics of Force: Media and the Construction of Police Brutality* and *When the Press Fails: Political Power and the News Media from Iraq to Katrina* (with W. Lance Bennett and Steven Livingston). Her most recent book, *Hillary Clinton's Run for the White House: Media, Gender Strategy, and Campaign Politics* (coauthored with Melody Rose) won an honorable mention Carrie Chapman Catt Prize for Research on Women and Politics from the Catt Center for Women and Politics at Iowa State University. Lawrence has written numerous articles analyzing media coverage of high-profile news events and policy issues, including the Abu Ghraib prison scandal, shootings in public schools, the obesity epidemic, welfare reform, and television coverage of the September 11 terrorist attack.

Pei-te Lien is professor of political science at the University of California, Santa Barbara. Her primary research interest is the political participation and representation of Asian and other nonwhite Americans. Most of her recent work examines the intersection of race, ethnicity, gender, and nativity in political behavior, both of the elites and the masses. Her most recent book is *The Transnational Politics of Asian Americans* (coedited with Chris Collet). She is a coprincipal investigator of the Gender and Multicultural Leadership project (http://www.gmcl.org).

Ronald M. Peters Jr. is Regents' Professor of Political Science at the University of Oklahoma. The founding director of the Carl Albert Congressional Research and Studies Center at the University of Oklahoma, he is the author of *The American Speakership: The Office in Historical Perspective.* In his research, he has interviewed every speaker to hold the office over the past 40 years.

Melody Rose is vice-provost for academic programs and instruction at Portland State University. She is also the founder of the Center for Women, Politics, and Policy at Portland State University and has served as professor and chair of the Division of Political Science. Her research is focused on the descriptive and substantive representation of women in US government, and she has authored a number of award-winning books, articles, and chapters on the presidency, social policy, women and politics, and elections. Her recent publications include *Hillary Clinton's Race for the White House: Gender Politics and the Media on the Campaign Trail* (with Regina Lawrence).

Cindy Simon Rosenthal is the Carlisle Mabrey and Lurleen Mabrey Presidential Professor of Political Science at the University of Oklahoma and director and curator of the Carl Albert Congressional Research and Studies Center. The author of *When Women Lead* and editor of *Women Transforming Congress,* she currently serves as mayor of Norman, Oklahoma.

Kira Sanbonmatsu is professor of political science at Rutgers University and senior scholar at the Center for American Women and Politics (CAWP) of the Eagleton Institute of Politics. Her research focuses on gender, race, parties and elections, public opinion, and state politics. She is the author of *Where Women Run: Gender and Party in the American States* and *Democrats, Republicans, and the Politics of Women's Place.* Her articles have appeared in such journals as *Journal of Politics* and *Politics & Gender.* She coauthored (with Susan J. Carroll and Debbie Walsh) the CAWP report *Poised to Run: Women's Pathways to the State Legislatures.*

Karen Shafer is faculty at the School of Public Policy and Administration, Walden University. She has contributed to an article in the *Journal of Politics.* Her current research interests include the policy agenda of US governors, gender differences among governors, and media coverage of governors.

Katie E. O. Swain is a PhD candidate in the Department of Political Science at the University of California, Santa Barbara. Her dissertation explores the possibility of substantive citizenship for racial minorities in the era of race neutrality in local governance.

Gina Serignese Woodall is a lecturer in the School of Politics and Global Studies at Arizona State University. She enjoys research on women and campaigns, including media coverage of them. Previous work with colleagues has been in the *Journal of Politics* and *International Press/Politics*, as well as various book chapters.

Index

291

About the Book

WHAT UNIQUE CHALLENGES DO WOMEN FACE AS THEY SEEK AND attain high-ranking positions in the executive branches of government? How can these challenges be overcome? Is there an established "pipeline" to office, or must women find their own ways to achieve power? Is there any relationship between gender and job performance? Addressing these questions, the authors of *Women and Executive Office* take stock of the strides that women are making in their paths to and tenure in high-level executive service.

Melody Rose is vice chancellor for academic strategies for the Oregon University System. Her recent publications include (with Regina G. Lawrence) *Hillary Clinton's Race for the White House: Gender Politics and the Media on the Campaign Trail.*